The Rise and Fall of The Pahlavi Dynasty

Memoirs of Former General Hussein Fardust

The
Rise and Fall of
The Pahlavi Dynasty

Memoirs of Former General Hussein Fardust

Translated and Annotated by

ALI AKBAR DAREINI

MOTILAL BANARSIDASS PUBLISHERS
PRIVATE LIMITED • DELHI

First Edition: Delhi, 1999

ISBN: 81-208-1642-0

Also available at:
MOTILAL BANARSIDASS
41 U.A. Bungalow Road, Jawahar Nagar, Delhi 110 007
8 Mahalaxmi Chamber, Warden Road, Mumbai 400 026
120 Royapettah High Road, Mylapore, Chennai 600 004
Sanas Plaza, 1302, Baji Rao Road, Pune 411 002
16 St. Mark's Road, Bangalore 560 001
8 Camac Street, Calcutta 700 017
Ashok Rajpath, Patna 800 004
Chowk, Varanasi 221 001

PRINTED IN INDIA
BY JAINENDRA PRAKASH JAIN AT SHRI JAINENDRA PRESS,
A-45 NARAINA, PHASE I, NEW DELHI 110 028
AND PUBLISHED BY NARENDRA PRAKASH JAIN FOR
MOTILAL BANARSIDASS PUBLISHERS PRIVATE LIMITED,
BUNGALOW ROAD, DELHI 110 007

Dedicated to my wife, Akram,
and my daughter, Homa,
for everything

Acknowledgments

Any book of this size, covering more than six decades of Iran's political history, necessarily owes debts of gratitude that can be acknowledged in a few paragraphs even if it is a translation like this one.

I gratefully record my obligations to the writers, translators and journalists whom I have quoted not only because of their expertise in the field of understanding Iran, but also because they said what I wanted to add to my translation, to make this book a complete account of an extraordinary period in the history of Iran.

I extend my gratitude to the librarians at the Kayhan Group of Newspapers and Tehran University Library who provided me with the books and documents I needed, and Iran's National Library which provided me with the pictures I requested.

The wide range of regions and languages covered in this book made consistent transliteration a problem. My solution has been to adopt a simplified version of the systems of transliteration employed in the well-known books. The words that have entered English have been spelled according to the dictionary, and well-known names have been written in their habitual form, and I left to the editors when they expressed a strong preference for one of two legitimate transliterations of a foreign term.

Literally many of my friends and scholars, here and abroad, have directly or indirectly contributed to the preparation of this volume. It was upon the strong recommendations of Mr. Abbas Salimi Namin which I undertook this great task. I should mention that Mr. Valiollah Ramezani was among those who commented on particular parts of the manuscript.

For assistance in the typesetting of the manuscript, I am happy to recognize that Mr. Naser Ghabchi was instrumental, without whose assistance the publication of the book would have been delayed for several months.

Preface

Since 1979, there has been a flood of books and articles on pre-revolutionary Iran, many of them lacking complete and accurate information from within the Shah's regime.

This book contains accurate inside information from the Shah's government and the events which other books have failed to disclose because it is the memoirs of a man who was Shah's "eyes and ears".

General Hussein Fardust, a classmate of Mohammad Reza Pahlavi, grew up with him and was finally able to drive into the Palace unchallenged. A letter from Fardust to the Shah was enough to get every official sacked from a minister down to a clerk.

Hardly a day went by without Fardust and the Shah spending an hour or more alone in audience. They lunched or dined together even when the Shah had Soraia as his wife. No one else enjoyed such access to him as Fardust did.

The Shah rarely referred to his aides as his "friends" but Fardust was among the "circle of selected friends" whom the Shah referred to as his "special friend" and "good companion" (see *Mission for My Country: His Imperial Majesty Mohammad Reza Shah Pahlavi*).

Fardust's greatest advantage was that the Shah had full "trust" in him and the monarch had, through 52 years of friendship, come to believe in Fardust's loyalty to his dynasty. Even when rumours reached Shah's ears during his exile in Egypt that Fardust had betrayed him, he did not believe them. Fardust was a trusted man of the regime and a confidant of the Shah who created the regime's "Special Information Bureau" (SIB) and reorganized and modernized Shah's secret service, SAVAK, to cope with the modern challenges.

The book covers the remarkable changes and developments that have occurred in Iran since the coup d'etat of 21 February 1921 which marked the beginning of the end of the Qajar dynasty, though it was not until April 1926 that Reza Khan crowned himself Shahanshah, King of Kings, in the Gulestan Palace, and thus, contrary to his early attempts for introduction of a republic on the model of neighbouring Turkey, founded the Pahlavi dynasty.

Fardust found his way into Reza Shah's family when he was chosen to study in Tehran's military school together with the Crown Prince Mohammad Reza Pahlavi at the age of 8. Fardust's great talent and his good knowledge won him favour from Reza Shah and he was sent to Switzerland, together with the Crown Prince, to study when the Shah decided to familiarize his son with the Western culture. This was when Reza Shah, with the backing of the British government, had established a strong central government and had crushed rebellions in different corners of Iran. When Reza Shah established cordial relations with Germany's Hitler during World War II, the British could not tolerate this degree of independence and decided that he should abdicate in favour of his son.

Fardust enumerates behind-the-curtain events which forced the ailing Reza Shah to abdicate and explains how the British who had brought the man to the throne, prepared the ground for the succession of his son on September 16, 1941, and how the Allied forces occupied Iran as an easy way to ship weapons to Russia to fight Hitler.

At the time of Reza Shah's abdication, Fardust was Mohammad Reza Pahlavi's only intimate friend. He was the messenger who took the final message of British support for Mohammad Reza's succession to him. Fardust uncovers the decisions which led to the withdrawal of Russian troops and dismantling of the Moscow-backed Pishevari autonomous government in Iran's Azerbaijan when Russia failed to pull out of Iran in accordance with the Tripartite Treaty.

Fardust discloses the details of how the U.S. Central Intelligence Agency (CIA), in close collaboration with Britain's MI-6, toppled the popular Mossaddiq government in 1953 after the nationalization of oil crisis and brought the Shah back to power after he had fled to Italy.

This is a book which reveals how the Shah and his family treated the country's assets and belongings as their private possessions, and how corruption had reached into almost all governmental departments. Fardust tells how Shah's "White Revolution" destroyed Iran's system of life and how his "land reforms" destroyed Iran's agricultural structure and made Iran a huge importer of foodstuff.

Fardust, who underwent special intelligence training in Britain, established the SIB, on the model of the Britain's Joint Intelligence Committee (JIC), reorganized SAVAK, that played the role of America's FBI and CIA, and set up the Imperial Investigations Organization. He discloses the untold stories about the performance of the Shah's government, and offers evidence showing that it were the U.S. and British embassies in Tehran which were making decisions for Iran and not the Sa'dabad Palace.

The General explains how and why the Shah underestimated the power of the mullahs in challenging his regime and how he cut himself out of the situation in his society. The Shah learned no lesson from the 1963 uprising and it was one of the reasons why he miserably failed to cope with the same popular movement that kicked him out of power one and a half decades later.

After the oil boom in the 70s, the Shah grew prouder and wealthier, thus further distancing himself from his people. He had become a dictator who did not even listen to his aides. He had little knowledge of the state of affairs in the country and his SAVAK did not dare to tell him the truth.

Fardust elaborates that the upheaval which drove the Shah from his throne was the materialization of a long historical process which had its origins and roots in the Iranian society and the people's religious beliefs, which burst out abortively during the crisis over the nationalization of the oil industry but succeeded the next time.

He spells out in detail how the Shah's regime and Washington became paralyzed in dealing with the revolution and how the "island of stability" (to quote U.S. President Carter) drowned in the ocean of opposition to Shah's rule, and how a regime which was considered to be America's "pillar of diplomacy" in the Persian Gulf region was destroyed before the helpless eyes of Washington.

Whatever judgement history may reserve for Iran's unique Islamic Revolution, Fardust offers the chronicle of the uprising under the leadership of Ayatollah Khomeini which irrevocably changed Iran. In the words of the then principal White House aide for Iran, Gary Sick, not since the fall of Saigon had a series of foreign policy events so shaken the United States.

Unlike many of Shah's aides, Fardust did not leave Iran after the 1979 revolution. He survived prosecution under the blessings of the Provisional Government led by the late Mehdi Bazargan but he went into a fearful hiding, thus saving his life from the wave of post-revolution executions. A mentally distressing life in hiding and the fear of his relatives who had given refuge to Fardust facilitated his arrest, five years after the revolution, by intelligence authorities who found in him a man of valuable asset who could tell many untold stories about the Shah's government.

His stay in Iran, however, prompted rumours spread by opponents of the newly-established Islamic government that Fardust was collaborating with post-revolution intelligence bodies in reorganizing SAVAK with a new name called SAVAMA (the Persian acronym for the Iranian National Security and Information Organization). However, the authorities swiftly denied the opposition accusations and described them as efforts to undermine the purity and sincerity of the newly-established intelligence organs.

Fardust died of a heart attack on May 17, 1987 before being able to put all his memoirs on paper.

This book includes Fardust's handwritings during years of his association with the Shah as well as his confessions during detention which was compiled by the *Institute for Political Studies and Research*.

For the purpose of this English edition, it has been thought best to delete or radically reduce and add the following classes of entry:

- Issues that were considered to be redundant or had been repeated in different parts of the book have been deleted.
- Part of the memoirs which cite events of different periods have been brought in this edition in a chronological order to avoid confusion.
- Historical information has been added from published works where necessary information was required.
- Title of personalities has been mentioned according to their official status e.g. Reza Pahlavi was known as "Reza Khan" before his 1921 coup but he was referred to as "Reza Shah" after his accession in 1926.
- Vital information and historical facts that were either considered to be missing or were required to make the book comprehensive and complete have been brought in with references at the end of the book.
- The political history of and the major changes that have occurred in the countries covered in this book have been

updated with the latest developments to make it more relevant and meet all the historical requirements of the readers.

Tehran,
December 1996

ALI AKBAR DAREINI

List of Illustrations

Table of Contents

IRAN AND NEIGHBOURING STATES (LATE 1980s)

SOUTH-WEST ASIA

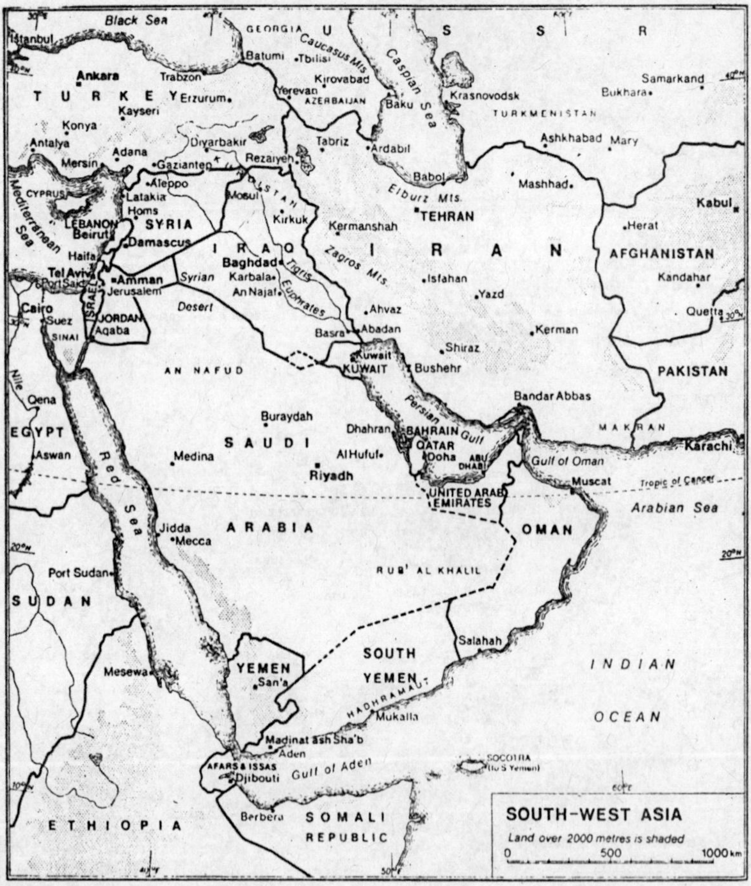

Chapter 1

From My Entry into Court to Fall of Reza Shah

HOW DID I GET INTO COURT?

I was born in 1917 in Tehran. My father, Seifollah, was a gendarmerie officer. He was promoted to the rank of captain before retirement and in the last days of service guarded ammunition depots in Abbass Abad, north Tehran.

My father's service in the army encouraged me to follow in his footsteps from childhood. In 1925, I began studying at a military school in the capital.

My family was poor and my father undertook postings in remote cities with harsh climates for the extra benefits he got. In this way he was able to feed his wife, five children and dependent mother.

Prior to 1931, with extra benefits, his salary amounted to 47 tumans. He sent 30 tumans to us and lived on the rest himself. We later managed to buy a house but, students still made fun of my poor clothes.

Later, when I entered the Crown Prince's special class, the poorest student—in terms of social status—was the son of a Brigadier-General at a time when the number of generals in Iran was not more than fingers on a hand. My father at the time was a third lieutenant. Other students were sons of ministers.

We had to eat lunch at school. My mother would cook rice and put it in a bowl, to make it look more. I took the bowl with me to school by foot while others came by coaches.

At noon, servants took our bowls to the dining-room. Non-commissioned officers always mocked me by saying, "look at this boy; what he has brought with him". They humiliated me deliberately to provoke me into bringing more food as any surplus was given to them. Although my food was hardly sufficient to feed me, I always left a few spoonful for them.

Financial difficulties and humiliation by others made me humble and perhaps my behaviour attracted the attention of Reza Shah Pahlavi, the King of Iran, and his eldest son, Crown Prince Mohammad Reza.

One afternoon less than three months after I started school, Major-General Amir Mowassaq Nakhjavan who was then in charge of military academies, visited our school. The motive behind his visit was unknown to me or the others at the time, but later I realized that Reza Shah had ordered a special class for the Crown Prince, and an additional 20 students were to enrol.

Nakhjavan was to pick three suitable pupils from our school. Two boys from aristocratic families were immediately chosen, one from a Bakhteyari tribal leader's family and the other the son of a high ranking military officer. With his walking stick, Nakhjavan gave a flick of his hand, asking them to step forward. The principal of our school, a tall, handsome Captain then whispered in Nakhjavan's ear and the latter put his stick on my shoulder and asked me to join the two. Nakhjavan ordered the school principal to accompany us to Crown Prince's special class the folloing morning, which he did.

MY FIRST MEETING WITH THE PRINCE

The class was located in a separate building in the Officer's College. At the time, only a few small buildings existed, one of which was given exclusively for the class. Further buildings were added later.

We were a few minutes late in arriving and were introduced to the new instructor, Colonel Mohammad Baqerkhan. The bell rang for break and the Crown Prince was the first to leave, which he did somehow proudly, so that we understood he was the Crown Prince. We, the three newcomers, were standing in a corner when the Crown Prince approached us. Our ages ranged from six to eight years. The Crown Prince was two years younger than I. He looked at the other two but did not appear to like them. He showed his interest in me by smiling. We spent a few minutes exchanging pleasantries and then started a friendly chat. Other pupils were looking at me with jealousy because of our closeness.

After the break, we re-entered the class. The instructor started teaching but the Crown Prince repeatedly turned back and looked at me.

"Would you like to become my friend?" he asked with a smile.

"Of course, I'd be very pleased to", I answered seriously.

No fundamental change took place in our relationship. We were friendly but not so intimate as to be invited to his residence.

In the final exams I achieved the highest grade. The Crown Prince was not included in the grading. The following year, the school was transferred to a building called "dormitory" in Golestan Palace. The building dated back to the Qajar period and a wall divided the building from the Palace.

In the basement, governmental jewels were being kept in big safes. It became clear to me that it was Shah's decision to transfer the class to the Palace to keep it close to Prince's residence.

One day, Reza Shah dropped into the class as the instructor was teaching. Baqerkhan who seemed to have read the Shah's mind pointed me out to him. My heart was racing as the Shah came closer and stood beside me.

I waited for him to leave but he turned to me and said, "When class is finished each day, and including holidays, you should come to the Prince's residence and assist him with his homework until he retires for the night". I guessed he chose me to help the Crown Prince as my grades were the highest. Anyhow, after class I went along with the Crown Prince to his residence and from that day, we sat together in class.

MME ARFA

A French nurse called Mme Arfa who had been married to the son of Arfa-ol-Dowleh, an official of the Qajar family, was looking after the Crown Prince. At the time, it was said that her husband had died and that was why she was carrying the surname of her husband.

Arfa looked after the Prince since Reza Shah's coronation in 1926 until Crown Prince's departure to Switzerland. Upon seizing power, Reza Shah ordered the Crown Prince to stay with me and live separately from his family. No one was permitted to interfere in his affairs except his supervisor Mme Arfa. Reza Shah had given Arfa a well-calculated schedule which determined when the Crown Prince should eat, prepare his assignments, play, sleep etc., and

Mme Arfa was responsible for seeing that the schedule was carefully adhered to.

Mohammad Reza's mother was living in a building nearby. The Crown Prince used to visit her twice a day and I always accompanied him.

Reza Shah officially received Arfa twice a week and asked her some questions about Mohammad Reza and advised her how to solve problems, if any. However, she was permitted to meet Reza Shah whenever she wished and Reza Shah respected her views and always replied positively to her demands. Mme Arfa taught the Crown Prince French everyday and I joined them when I had the spare time to remain in Crown Prince's room.

At the time of our departure to Switzerland, the Crown Prince had a better command over French. Anyhow, Arfa supervised all the affairs of the Crown Prince for six years until we went to Switzerland in 1931.

After Crown Prince's departure, Arfa went to France and purchased a luxurious house and two hotels in Paris, each with 100 rooms with the money Reza Shah had given to her. Her daughter, Firuzeh, was in charge of the hotels. Later, whenever I travelled to Paris I called on them and they treated me kindly.

I have to acknowledge here that Arfa-al-Dowleh was a wealthy man and all his family were pro-British. He was living in a luxurious house in southern France in the last days of his life.[1]

AMIR AKRAM AND I

Cheraqalikhan Amir Akram, Reza Shah's cousin, after whose name was also a street in Tehran, was a servant of the Prince.[2] He was the second strong man in the Imperial Court after Teimourtash, the powerful Court Minister.

Then, all the people at the Court had uniforms. Teimourtash had four bands on his arm and Amir Akram three. Ordinary employees had no bands. Despite his strong position in the court, Amir Akram was not allowed to intervene in the affairs of the Crown Prince because Reza Shah believed that Mme Arfa who had no relatives to manipulate the Crown Prince was the best choice while Amir Akram had many people around him and wanted to impose them on the Crown Prince.

Amir Akram had a nephew called Naser whose surname was

"Pahlavi" which he was ordered to change to "Pahlavani" in order to avoid similarity with the Shah's surname. Amir Akram was insisting to bring Naser to Crown Prince's building and make them friends. Naser was very lazy and did not study adequately and for this very reason, Arfa hated him. Once Amir Akram took Naser to Crown Prince's building. Arfa informed Reza Shah of the issue. The Shah rushed there and threatened Naser who was about seven years old to avoid approaching the Crown Prince or face severe punishment. Naser who had been frightened ran away.

Since then, Amir Akram became very hostile to me and tried to keep me away from the Prince. However, upon Reza Shah's order, the Crown Prince and I came together from the school, played for a while and then started doing our assignments. Reza Shah visited us frequently without any notice in advance and appreciated us for studying our lessons. He used to call me by first name and usually said, "Hussein, well done, continue".

The Crown Prince usually spent his summer holidays in Farahabad, a pleasant region in the suburbs of Tehran and I had to remain with him. The long way from Farahabad to our house in southern Tehran made me to visit my family only once a week. One day, as I was walking by myself in Farahabad's garden, suddenly Amir Akram approached me and angrily said, "go home otherwise you will be in trouble". He warned that he would take tough measures against me if I mentioned anything about his threat. I returned home on foot and stayed indoors for a few days. Again, a man came and took me to Farahabad. I informed Reza Shah that I had been under threat. Reza Shah temporarily discharged Amir Akram from work for punishment.

Since then, I found a strong influence within the court and everybody was convinced that I had the backing of the Shah. Sometime later, the Shah bought a motorcycle for the Crown Prince. Naturally, I became interested to have it but the Crown Prince refused to give me a ride. Once, I rode his motorcycle home without permission and did not return to the court. Again I was called to Shah's summer residence in Sa'adabad Palace. When I entered the yard, I saw Reza Shah leaning on a tree branch.

"Where have you been?", he asked with a strong voice.

"Home, Sir", I answered.

"So, you were staying with your mummy", he asked again.

"Yes", I replied.

He changed his mood and friendly said, "It is better for you to stay here. Do not worry about the motorcycle. Perhaps, I may purchase a new motorcycle for the Crown Prince and give the old one to you".

Anyhow, it was the first, and as far as I remember the last chastisement, but did not hurt my credibility in the court.

CROWN PRINCE'S TALENT

The Crown Prince was very weak in mathematics and was reluctant to spend enough time thinking on vital issues since childhood. He became tired very soon and was willing to accept proposals even without a careful study. His lack of interest to ponder on vital issues made him a weak leader in his future life. He was good at history and literature and whatever did not require a deep thinking. During his school time both in Iran and in Switzerland he used to copy the assignments I had done for myself. When I wanted to explain for him how to answer the questions he refused to listen and said, "no, give your copy to me ".

It was very surprising for me and hard to swallow why he unconditionally accepted proposals and preferred to cheat. He did not even care if the instructor asked him to write answers on the blackboard. In Tehran our instructor did not annoy him since he was the Prince but in Switzerland he was treated equally like other students. It repeatedly happened that our mathematics instructor wanted him to the blackboard but Mohammad Reza was unable to answer. Then the instructor asked who had done it for him. He remained silent. I raised my hand and said, "I".

In 1931, the Crown Prince and I headed for Switzerland through sea and land. At the time of the trip, I was about 14. I had already learned that we would go to Switzerland but I was not aware of the motive behind studying abroad. Even the Crown Prince had made no mention of the trip. Perhaps he did not know himself or he did not want to disclose it me.

One day, as we were playing football Reza Shah came to me and said, "It has been decided that you and the Prince will go to Switzerland to study". It was a bad news for me since I did not want to leave my parents.

As soon as the Shah went, I told the Crown Prince I was not willing to study in Switzerland. Mohammad Reza made no comments. Later, I learned that he had passed my words to his father. Again Reza Shah came to me and slowly said, "Why don't you like to study abroad?".

"It is very difficult for me to stay away from my family", I replied.

The Shah asked me slowly again, "Don't worry. You'd better count on me. I'll allow your family to travel to Switzerland once every six months. Any objections now?"

"I'll be very glad", I replied.

My father was living in a remote town. I requested the Prince to help transfer my father to Tehran. Within 48 hours, my father arrived in Tehran and became commander of a Company based near "Edam Square" in southern Tehran. So my father joined the family and that pacified my mind.

VOYAGE THROUGH USSR

Shah's family, a number of ministers and high-ranking government officials and the guard of honour had arrived in Bandar Anzali, a port city in the Caspian Sea, to see off our delegation. I had also taken my parents there in a car and had rented the only mansion in the city for them. I stayed with them until we started our voyage.[3]

Our delegation comprised Crown Prince Mohammad Reza and his brother Prince Ali Reza, Teimourtash and his son Mehrpour, Dr. Moadab-al-Dowleh Nafisi, Prince's guardian and personal physician, Mostashar-al-Mamalek, Prince's Farsi instructor and I. In European dress, we bade goodbye to all and got on a Russian ship heading north.

Two Russian Generals and about 100 other military figures in special uniform accompanied us during our voyage. The sea was calm in the pleasant afternoon. The ship was sailing without much shake. The Russians were, as usual, drinking vodka, making love with women and chatting in groups but we felt odd there. They spent the fortune on gambling. Cloud of cigarette smoke billowed around their faces as they were quarrelling over cards. After an hour, we went to the ship's restaurant and had our dinner. The Russians went back to drinking, gambling and womanizing until late in the morning. Teimourtash who had fallen to the way of the Russians also joined them.

We arrived in Baku in southern Russia, where the Iranian consulate was based, in the morning. A few Iranian businessmen were waiting for our entourage. We had a short stop there. Then, Russian military officials still with us, we continued our trip by train. It was strange to me that living in a Communist country, they all were expensively and elegantly dressed including their wives and other women on the ship who were heavily made up with a lot of jewellery around their necks and hands.

They were eager to talk to us but only Teimourtash was fluent in Russian and he picked up only pretty women for talking. While Reza Shah spoke only a little Russian, learned during his days with the Persian Cossak Brigade, Teimourtash spoke Russian as a result of being educated in Russia; he could also speak French and understood English. He kept talking and drinking with women until late in the evening. Upon our request the Russians, through Teimourtash, said that the clothes and jewels were not theirs but the government's and they had orders to use them occasionally. One of the two generals, Stalin's bodyguard, who had two houses, one for winter and the other for his summer residence said that the communist government had provided him with many facilities. He was allowed to invite up to 20 guests twice a week and serve them with the expensive caviar and other delicious foods. He had two cars, one for his wife and the other for himself.

We stopped over in Russia only at one station for refueling; however, it took us three days to get to Poland by train. The aura of poverty overwhelmed me as I witnessed hundreds of bare-footed people begging for food in the streets. On the Russian-Poland border, we changed our train since the railroad in Russia was bigger in size than other parts of the world. In Warsaw, Poland's capital, we stopped over. The Iranian ambassador, Assad Bahador along with his wife and his two children welcomed us at the railway station.[4]

In Poland, the situation looked better. I could see many elegantly dressed people in the streets and there was less poverty in sight. After a brief stay in Poland, we headed for Germany and then to the city of Lausanne in Switzerland, our final destination.

MANSION IN LE ROSEY

We were expected to study at Le Rosey boarding school, one of the most famous Swiss private schools. Since the registration arrangements had not been completed yet, we were taken to an ordinary private school temporarily in Lausanne. Mehrpour and I stayed in the school round-the-clock but Crown Princes Mohammad Reza and Ali Reza rented a mansion house for themselves. The house belonged to a Swiss university professor named Mr. Mercier who took the Crown Princes to the school in his private car.

Mercier had quite a family, including three sons, and two daughters. A sports teacher had been employed for the Crown Prince who was a boyfriend of one of Mercier's two daughters.

One day, I paid a courtesy call to Mercier. As we entered the guest room, I saw his younger daughter and a boy kissing and necking. Mercier immediately closed the door and said, "excuse me". For me as an Iranian, it was hard to swallow that a man allowed his daughter to sleep with a man before marriage.

We studied at the school for a year. The students were mostly Swiss nationals and many of them from low-income families. Mohammad Reza was always quarrelling with the students especially those who were physically weak. He had become strong physically and wanted to test his muscles. An Egyptian student who was famous for his strong fists was looking for a rival in the class. When girls were still in the class, the Prince, to attract their attention, invited the Egyptian for a fight. Both were equal and the fighting usually led to the injury to both. Sometimes, they were hospitalized for treatment.

Anyhow, sporadic disputes with the students repeatedly humiliated Mohammad Reza but gradually he conformed himself with the class.

AT LE ROSEY SCHOOL

At the beginning of the second year of our study in Switzerland, we were transferred to Le Rosey.[5] There were only a few Swiss students there because of the high tuition fee. A student had to pay 2400 Swiss Francs a year for the tuition in addition to about 1200 Francs for his personal expenses. Dr. Nafisi and Mostashr were living in Role who called on Mohammad Reza every day.

At the new school, the Prince changed his behaviour and had therefore little dispute with other students but at the same time, he was trying to proudly identify himself as the Prince to all other students.

His behaviour caused other students to mock him and some sporadic quarrels erupted again. The new atmosphere persuaded him to adopt a new policy and make friendly gestures with those interested to talk to him. The majority of his friends were older than him and friendship with other students later caused a great weakness to the extent that he easily forgot his friend's offenses. Later during his rule over Iran, he pardoned many offenders upon recommendation from "older" friends.

At College Le Rosey, I helped Mohammad Reza to do his assignments and sometimes I spent three to four hours on mathematics but the Prince did not listen and was not willing to do his homework. I got the first grade in the final exams and won an award. Later, I took my award with me to Iran.

Unlike me, the Prince was good at sports and always got the best grade. Since he could not impose his bullying on others, he deliberately began to practise sports in order to make himself distinguished. These two characteristics became more visible during his monarchy later.

He did not care for the consequences of his actions. Though his behaviour was sometimes humiliating, he proudly used to expose himself before the students and vaunt.

In the third year of our stay in Switzerland, Reza Shah allowed his wife and two daughters to meet the Prince in summer when only make-up classes were running. Later, the Shah sent his other son to the Le Rosey school who studied only for two years.

EARNEST PROUN

Earnest Proun, a soft-spoken man in his 50s, was responsible for cleaning the halls and classrooms. He used to do his cleaning before the Prince arrived in the class. Proun, a native of Switzerland, had been employed a few months before we arrived in Switzerland.

He shortly became very friendly with the Prince. Despite being a servant, Proun turned out to be well-informed in literature and philosophy. It was difficult for me to swallow why a well-educated man was cleaning the classrooms and was willing to spend his leisure time with the Prince.

They had struck up a good friendship and Proun used to read novels for him every night before going to bed. Although Proun had a magnetic personality, I was in no way interested to listen to the fiction stories he was reading for the Prince. I was living in a single room next to the Prince. Proun appeared to be a poet too.

When we finished high school in 1936, the Prince promised Proun before returning home to recommend his father to invite him to Iran. Their friendship remained a mystery to me. I gave a lot of thought about Proun's paradox but I could not learn why Proun spent a lot of time with the Prince. I mulled why the principal allowed an educated man to clean the classrooms and provide him with the necessary opportunities to become so friendly with the Prince. Later, I learned that the principal was a native of Belguim and had an American wife. He was a politician and had connections with the British intelligence. However, it was disclosed that Proun had been assigned, with the blessing of the principal, by the British intelligence service to try to read the thoughts of Mohammad Reza and put him under observation throughout the period.

PRINCE'S GIRLFRIEND

During our stay in Switzerland, Mohammad Reza was keeping an eye for any girls he might be able to lure into his bed. He could not tolerate to see Nafisi, an old man in his 60s, having love with young women but he remaining without a girlfriend. Nafisi who had been assigned by the Shah to look after the Prince, had two mistresses. One of them regularly travelled by train back and forth between Geneva and our residence almost every two days and the other came once a week on Sundays, I don't know wherefrom. Nafisi was living in an expensively decorated flat separately from us. He had a maid servant who was living with her daughter. The daughter, in her early 20s, was very attractive and had won Mohammad Reza's heart. The Prince was looking for an opportunity to lure her into his bed and often told me, "I love her. I like to hug and kiss her."

Referring to Nafisi he said "look at this old man. He is keeping this pretty girl in his house while having two other mistresses..."

However, he could not meet his passion with the girl. He was afraid his wrongdoings may reach the ears of the Shah; sell he could not continue without a girl. The Prince always complained to Proun about Nafisi and did not know that he was Nafisi's pimp.

Finally the trouble came when Mohammad Reza had an affair with one of the 40 girls who were working at Le Rosey. She was a

22-year old attractive, tall brunette girl whom Mohammad Reza had fallen in love with the first time he met her. He ordered the Proun to take the girl to his room and Proun did what he was told. They had love for quite a few days.

A week later, the Prince came to me with weeping eyes. He took me to his room. I saw the half-naked girl pretending to be weeping too.

"Hussein, please help me. I slept with her and now she says she is pregnant", the embarrassed Mohammad Reza requested.

The Prince paced up and down the room thinking how to get rid of his troublesome girlfriend. He feared the story may reach the ears of his father. He did not have to emphasize his concern to me.

I urged him to exercise restraint.

I mulled a few options and finally suggested to pay the girl. The Prince welcomed the idea and clapped his hands together in applause. Of course, I doubted the girl's honesty since she did not care to sleep with others. Moreover, they could have used contraceptives to avoid pregnancy.

The girl said, "If the principal learns he will fire me and moreover, I have to abort".

She asked for 5000 Francs while her monthly salary did not exceed 150 Francs. The Prince was not able to pay that much since Nafisi was keeping all the money.

To help the Prince solve the matter, I proposed to him to ask Nafisi to write to the Shah that Hussein, I, had a family problem and needed that much money. Nafisi promised to see to the request but Mohammad Reza insisted it was urgent. Nafisi did not refuse and requested the money from Tehran. The Prince got the cash within days. I counted the money. Exactly 5000 Francs. Not one less, not one more. I gave it to the girl and the Prince's worries ended. Now the burden was off his shoulders and he had a feeling of relief. After the incident, the girl was not dismissed but she requested to be transferred to another school. I do not know the reason; perhaps, she could; have a pleasant life with that money in another school.

TEIMOURTASH AND THE SOVIETS

Mirza Abdul Hussein Khan Teimourtash, the powerful Court

Minister, was dismissed and tossed into jail in 1933 on charges of spying for the Soviets. It was in the early months of our stay in Switzerland that the astonishing report reached us. Teimourtash's son, Mehrpour, was immediately recalled and was sent back to Iran within 24 hours. The post of Court Minister was abolished. Adib-ol-Saltaneh Samei was commissioned as the chief of the court's protocol office. In the last years of Reza Shah's reign, the post was renewed and it went to Mahmoud Jam who was famous for his connections with the British.

Reza Shah initially intended to allow only me to study in Switzerland with the Prince but Teimourtash with his flattering language persuaded the Shah to include his son in the list. He was also allowed to head our delegation and was expected to stay in Switzerland for a few weeks.[6]

The events of our journey flashed through my mind. His fluency in Russian, his close connections with the Russian generals. My instinct had told me that there was something wrong with Teimourtash. His connections with the Soviets were already known but it had not been proved that he had turned his back to the Shah.

During his stay in Switzerland, Teimourtash was living in a nicely decorated hotel with stylish leather furniture in Lausanne. Everyday afternoon, we paid a courtesy call on him. Next to him were Diba, the financial manager of the Imperial Court, and his wife. Teimourtash had given Diba the post to keep his mouth shut when it came to his illegal relations with the man's wife. Teimourtash made no secret of his love to the woman even before Diba.

When one day we went to Teimourtash's hotel, the woman, lightly dressed and heavily made up, had made herself comfortable at Teimourtash's arms having love with him. She had worn a tight skirt and a short-sleeved shirt. It was obvious she was not wearing a bra. The woman, in her 30s, was a Soviet native from Caucasus region. They usually communicated in Russian.

The woman was not attractive at all and I wondered why Teimourtash who was handsome and had many girlfriends had fallen in love with a married woman.

One day, the woman, Teimourtash and our group went for a walk in a Lausanne street. As we were passing a jewellery store, Teimourtash offered her to take whatever she wanted. She asked different kinds of jewels exceeding hundreds of thousands of

Francs. Teimourtash drew a cheque. The man accepted it without any argument since he had confidence in Teimourtash and had become quite friendly with him.

Later, it was revealed that Teimourtash had espionage links with the woman. Newspapers reported that Teimourtash had been arrested on charges of committing treason against the Shah and spying for the Soviets. The Prince also told me that Teimourtash had planned to assassinate the Shah and take over the leadership himself.

Later, it was disclosed that on his way back home from Switzerland, Teimourtash had a short stop in Moscow and had handed over a number of documents to the Soviets. British agents had spilled the beans and the Shah ordered his arrest. Immediately after the arrest, a Soviet delegation headed by the Soviet deputy foreign minister arrived in Tehran to mediate and secure the release of Teimourtash but in vain. Teimourtash was executed. About 20 days after Teimourtash's execution, his family were exiled to Kashmar in Khorasan province, their native city. They remained in exile until after the fall of Reza Shah but when Mohammad Reza came to power, he forgave them and allowed them jobs in high places.

BACK TO IRAN

The Crown Prince returned home earlier than the rest of us after we finished the high school at Le Rosey. We travelled back a few days later through the earlier route but the Prince went by land through Greece and Turkey since Iran-Soviet relations had been strained over the Teimourtash affair.

Major-General Naqdi, an experienced instructor had taught both the Prince and me Russian for about three years before the crisis erupted in Tehran-Moscow ties.

I spent the summer at Sa'adabad Palace with the Prince. We used to play tennis and enjoy ourselves. Whenever the Shah walked by us, he paused for a moment to learn who was ahead of the other. We were equal but I usually preferred to declare the Prince the winner since I did not want him to feel uncomfortable.

The Shah used to make his decisions while walking in the garden. He was fond of walking. A minister or a high ranking official was always hovering around to take his orders. He walked about four hours a day through pine trees. Later, I realized that the pine tree had a calming substance widely used in medicine.

In Switzerland, I had decided to study medicine in France. The Prince did not have any objections but I needed Shah's approval too. The Shah in one of his regular weekly letters to the Prince wrote that he agreed in principle to allow me to study in France but emphasized that I had to return home first.

The day after we arrived in Iran, Reza Shah called me into his office. The office was expensively decorated with the Persian carpet, foreign-made chandeliers, the green, white and red flag of Iran and a few coffee tables at which he entertained his guests. Dressed in his military uniform, he was looking out of the window when I bade him good morning.

"The best job for a man is to be a soldier and serve his country. I want you to register in the Officer's College and study with Mohammad Reza," he said seriously.

He gave me a smile when I confirmed his order by saying "Yes, Sir". The same day, I was drafted into the army and an officer came to the palace and took me to the Officer's College. It was summer and the academic year had not started yet.

OFFICER'S COLLEGE

All students stood in attention when the special ceremonies started to mark the official inauguration of the new academic year. Many newcomers were delighted with the ceremonies and a few feared the strong discipline and hard physical training awaiting them. The Shah laughed and clapped his hands in mock applause when he saw me in my loose military uniform.

A special Company and within that a special platoon was formed and the best students were picked up to study with the Prince. The classes started almost immediately. Many newcomers could hardly endure the hard physical training. Sweat poured from all over their body when the commander ordered them to jump up and down the nets around them. Of course, our platoon was treated more kindly and studying in Prince's class gave us a sense of relief.

Our commander was Captain Mahmoud Amini, brother of Dr. Ali Amini.[7] A serious man in his 30s, he was a well-experienced officer with a very good knowledge of military training affairs. The training period was two years and students were graduated with the rank of Second Lieutenant. Amini remained our commander for the whole period. After graduation, all of us including the Prince were granted the Second Lieutenant rank. Mohammad Reza was quickly promoted to the rank of Captain while normally it took four years for a First Lieutenant to become a Captain. He remained Captain until 1941 when he became the Shah.

During our study in the college, chief of the army's inspection department went to the Prince. He regularly inspected military units and gave orders sometimes at random, to make himself felt. Reza Shah assigned Sani'i to protect the Prince. Sani'i, a Major, was a staunch backer of Bahaism. He was later promoted to the rank of Brigadier-General. Sani'i was War Minister for a time and served in another portfolio in the last years of his life. He remained Prince's special guard until Mohammad Reza's coronation. The Shah was sympathetic towards Bahais. This will prove correct when you read the role of the four-starred General Ayadi in the next chapter.

PROUN AT COURT

Reza Shah initially opposed Crown Prince's request to invite Proun to Iran on the grounds that he was a gay but finally gave in to Prince's persistent demand. Proun's close friendship with the Prince had already paved the way for him to gain popularity in the court and Reza Shah's opposition was no big hurdle. Reza Shah did not hide his hatred towards Proun. Once the Prince asked his father why he hated Proun. Reza Shah argued that Proun was a British spy and he did not want to see a spy in his palace.[8]

After about a year, Proun's influence had increased and he had formed a team of gays in the court. Reza Shah could no longer tolerate Proun and this time decided to expel him from Iran. Mohammad Reza again insisted and the Shah who usually gave in to Prince's demands, accepted to allow him to stay in Iran but ordered to send him to Ramsar, a resort city on the Caspian, to look after a garden. Proun stayed in Ramsar until 1941 but secretly came to Tehran every other week to meet the Prince. Of course, Reza Shah was informed of Proun's visits but he turned a blind eye to him.

MOHAMMAD REZA MARRIES FAWZIA

In 1938, Mohammad Reza was offered to marry Princess Fawzia, sister of King Farouq of Egypt. The marriage, initially planned by the British, was aimed at bringing the two regimes of Iran and Egypt closer.[9] The British colonialistic plan followed certain long term objectives as the children born after the marriage would be half-blooded.

Fawzia's father, King Foad, was a well known British puppet in the Middle East. He seized power with the blessings of London when Egypt was a British colony. King Foad died about five years before her eldest daughter, Fawzia, was married to Mohammad Reza. After Foad's death, his son Farouq came to power. Farouq had only a son named Foad the Second. He had four sisters, Fawzia being the eldest.

The family was believed to be of European origin. There were no similarities between the family and the local Egyptian citizens. All members of the family were pale-skinned, green-eyed with fair hair.

The proposal for marriage was made abruptly and the decision was finalized within a week or two. The British involvement was almost obvious. I was informed of the imminent marriage by Mohammad Reza himself.

"My father has decided to get me King Farouq's sister as my bride", the Prince told me after the proposal had been made. He lay his hands clasped beneath his head and stared at the ceiling. There was approval in his glance. A delegation headed by Court Minister Mahmoud Jam was dispatched to Cairo for a courtesy call on Farouq and make preparations for the marriage. After two weeks, the delegation returned to Tehran carrying King Farouq's "welcome" message. Farouq had already been informed of the proposal in advance by the British and the delegation's visit was just a formality since the decision had already been made.

Soon, Fawzia arrived in Iran for a permanent stay. She was accompanied by her mother, and her three sisters. King Farouq did not come. They travelled by sea to Khoramshahr, a port city in southwestern Iran, and then by train to Tehran. Reza Shah gave them a red-carpet treatment at the railway station and he personally accompanied them to the Palace.

A glorious wedding ceremony was held at Golestan Palace. The

Arabic formula for entering into a contract of marriage had already been read in Egypt. Fawzia's family returned to Cairo after a few days of celebrations and she was left with Mohammad Reza. She was extremely pretty but languidly shy. She was, in no way, willing to attend official banquets. Whenever she talked to people, her beautiful face turned red. Fawzia talked to Mohammad Reza in French, the only language they could communicate. The Prince did not know Arabic and Fawzia had not yet learned Persian.

Fawzia's only confident after the Crown Prince was her Egyptian servant who had accompanied her to Iran. She was reluctant to be friendly with Mohammad Reza's sisters for reasons not clearly known to me. Fawzia never tried to make Iranian friends and preferred to spend her leisure time with her Egyptian servant, a young woman, and the Egyptian ambassador to Iran and his family. The ambassador's family were her guests two or three times a week at the Palace in order that she did not feel homesick

SHAMS AND ASHRAF MARRY

In 1938, the Shah decided to have her two daughters Princesses Shams and Ashraf married. Among the many candidates, the Shah accepted the proposals of Fereidyun Jam, son of the Court Minister Mahmoud Jam who later became a field marshal, and Ali Qavam, son of Ebrahim Qavam. Both families were famous for their connections with the British.

The elder sister Shams had chosen the tall and handsome Jam and the younger Ashraf received the compact, hard faced Qavam. The same day the families of the bridegrooms paid a courtesy call on the Shah to fix the wedding day. Princess Ashraf privately told me her fiance was not the man she has been looking for. She was dressed in the royal purple sheet of finest silk and wearing just too much of expensive perfume but her face was as hard as a stone. I could easily read in her face that she would not live for a long time with Qavam.

Qavam-al-Molk Shirazi was a British favourite and Governor of the southern Fars Province. He had no academic studies but was very clever and was able to read and write. He used to live in the way his ancestors did. He spent his days in meetings with guests in his century-old house in the middle of an incredibly large garden. About ten servants were at work serving the guests with local fruits, tea and hubble-bubble pipe, one or two of them always hovering to make sure table requirements were met. Always dressed in his traditional shirt and big trousers, he sat in the corner of the guest room enjoying a hubble-bubble pipe and chatting on for hours with his guests. Shirazi possessed 350 plots of land and was the wealthiest in Fars Province. The staff of the British Embassy dropped in his house with their families to spend their weekends. Usually they came without invitation because of their friendship with the family and Shirazi treated them like members of his family.

Qavam's emissaries always shuttled back and forth between Shiraz and Tehran to carry messages from or to Qavam but he spoke to the British himself if a sensitive political issue came up. For instance, when the political situation got aggravated in August 1941, Qavam met the British Plenipotentiary Minister Sir Reader Bulard and exchanged views with him about Reza Shah's fate. The decision had already been made which also received the support of Shirazi: Reza Shah would abdicate and leave the country and his son would take over.

Shirazi had two sons and two daughters. His elder daughter was married to Dr. Nafisi, a children physician, and his younger daughter was married to Amir Assadollah Alam who later became Prime Minister. Shirazi was committed to serving the policies of London and the British did their share of commitment by giving him political support.

Mahmoud Jam was a Freemason and happened to be a British agent. As the Court Minister, it was easy for him to remain in touch with the British Embassy without any difficulty.

He had a garden in Hashmat-ol-Dowleh district in Tehran which he left by inheritance to his only boy and girl who were living in Britain and Italy respectively after his death. They sold the garden to Major-General Nazem, Jam's closest friend, about four years before the 1979 Islamic Revolution and purchased houses abroad. Jam had family relations with Qashqai tribe leaders.

At the time of marriage, Fereidyun was a student at the Officer's College in France and Ali was studying in Cambridge, Britain. Within a week, both were recalled home and they started studying at the Tehran's Officer's College. Fereidyun was enrolled in the second class since he had studied for a year in France but Qavam was enrolled in our class. Qavam was not intelligent.

As long as Reza Shah was alive, Princesses Shams and Ashraf

were compelled to live with their husbands but after Shah's death they were immediately divorced.

Shams was married to Mehrdad Pahlbod, a violinist. The couple took residence in Egypt for the rest of their life. Fereidyun married Firuzeh, a girl friend of Mohammad Reza. Fereidyun, a highly conservative man, was aware of Firuzeh's relations with the Crown Prince and for the same reason Mohammad Reza always met Fereidyun's requests to keep his mouth shut.

Princess Ashraf also left Qavam for her boy friends and Qavam married another woman who had connections with the British. Of course, the information she passed to the Embassy was no news since they were not classified but the British kept her as one of their contacts. Qavam had a brother who like himself was studying in Britain. I did not know him but it was said he was close to the intelligence circles in Britain. He was the Governor of the Hamadan Province and then Kurdestan for some time.

Princess Ashraf's marriage with Qavam left disastrous consequences for the rest of her life. Unlike Shams, Ashraf, Mohammad Reza's twin, was hungry for sex and betrayed her husband's trust by sleeping around whenever possible. Shah's death opened the way for her to manoeuvre in the Court and strike up friendship with the men she liked.

GOWHARSHAD UPRISING AND ASSASSINATION ATTEMPT AGAINST SHAH

One of the policies adopted by Reza Shah during his reign was banning clerics from wearing their special dress as well as women from wearing Islamic hijab. A cleric in the holy city of Mashhad, the capital of the northeastern Province of Khorasan, known as Bohlul categorically opposed Shah's secular policies. Bohlul encouraged the people to uprise against Shah's government in his popular speeches delivered in the famous Gowharshad Mosque.

Only a few government-appointed clerics were allowed to preach in the mosques and those critical of the government were defrocked. Any violations were met with strong police measures. Violators were arrested and were pulled in the streets with their turbans tight around their necks as punishment. The punishments were aimed at humiliating the clerics in the public and discourage people from supporting them.

One day, a large group of people, upon a call by Bohlul, staged a sit-in protest at the premises of Imam Reza's holy shrine, the Eighth Shi'ite Imam, and warned that they would continue the protest and would go on strike if the government did not lift the ban on hijab.

Commander of Mashhad military division Brigadier-General Iraj Matbouie reported to the Shah on the unrest. The Shah ordered the riot police to use tear gas and even open fire if the crowd refused to disperse. Matbouie, in a private conversation with me after retirement, said he urged the Shah to take the political atmosphere into consideration and adopt a more moderate stance but the Shah rejected the argument and called for tough measures to be adopted to suppress the uprising. The Shah commissioned Brigadier-General Alborz to join Matbouie and curb the riots. The military intervened. The protestors scuffled with the military and as a result scores of people were killed in the clash.

People's opposition to Shah's secular reforms also led to the intervention of the military in Qom after angry people denied Mohammad Reza's mother Taj-ol-Moluk, his sisters Princesses Shams and Ashraf to pay homage to the holy shrine of Masoumeh (A.S.) without hijab.

Public discontent led to an abortive assassination attempt against the Shah. As far as I can remember, the attempt was engineered by Colonel Ahmad Khan Puladin. Puladin who was the commander of Shah's special security guard had formed a secret group and planned to assassinate the Shah during an appointment with him. The attempt was foiled since the group had been spied by the country's intelligence services. Security forces who had already been put on full alert grabbed him before he could act and tossed him into jail.

REZA SHAH'S SENTIMENTS

One of Reza Shah's attractive characteristics was his discipline due to his Cossack training. Everything went according to schedules anticipated for his daily life. A servant was always hovering to carry out his orders. Flicks of his hand had meanings known only to his servants.

No matter what time he went to bed, the Shah got up early in the morning to look after his daily affairs. He had his lunch at sharp noon, his supper at 6 p.m. and his dinner at 8. A glass of wine was always on a desk next to his bed during the night since he was used to midnight drink.

His family members were obliged to attend the lunch and dinner on time otherwise they were denied a meal. He forgave Mohammad Reza and Shams if they were not too late.[10]

Reza Shah was reluctant to attend official banquets given in his honour. Sometimes he took Mohammad Reza and I to Golestan Palace where banquets were usually held but he left soon. He made fun of European women guests who wore skimpy dressed and showed up heavily made-up. History was Reza Shah's favourite. He used to devote part of his leisure time especially in the night to study history books. Mohammad Reza once told me that his father was a pro-Zorestorian and praised the religion. He was addicted to opium. He smoked a certain piece everyday since and believed that an opium smoker would remain sound and healthy if he observed moderation.

Iran's political tides in 1941 were clearly running against him. He lost the backing of the allied governments due to his support of Hitler. He had no longer the feeling of self-confidence. His orders were subject to constant change. He made contradictory statements and even consulted low-level officials in every tiny matter. Within days, his physical health deteriorated. Despite illness, he was taken to the southern port city of Bandar Abbass and got on the board of a British liner and sent to South Africa. The Shah weakened steadily. In less than two years, he lost much of his weight and finally died in exile in 1944.

REZA SHAH'S WIVES

Sofieh was Reza Shah's first wife. She was not from a wealthy family nor famous to the public. Reza Khan, as he was called at the time, married her when he was on a long duty in Hamedan, Western Iran. The fruit of their marriage was a girl, Hamdamol-Saltaneh but they got divorced a year later.

His next wife was Tajol-Moluk who happened to become Mohammad Reza's mother. Moluk was a Russian Azeri immigrant who had immigrated with her family to Iran after the 1917 Bolshevik Revolution. Moluk's father was a Brigadier-General and Reza Shah was proud of marrying a military official's daughter. Moluk, a big woman but of average height with yellow hairs streaked with gray and a fat face, became the mother of four children; Shams, Mohammad Reza and Ashraf (twins), and Ali Reza.

In 1927, Reza Shah fell in love with Maleke Turan, a girl from the Qajars. Gholam Reza was the fruit of their marriage. Unlike Moluk, Turan was an attractive tall woman with enormous firm breasts and an incredibly small waist. Moluk did not want to see the Qajar woman on the earth and was always locked in disputes with her. Although she was not very attractive, her father's position bought her influence over Reza Shah. She filled Reza Shah's ears with rumours about Turan and finally convinced him to divorce her.

About two years later, Reza Shah married another girl from the Qajars called Esmat. She was attractive and of average height. Her face was a scimitar of arrogant beauty, the mouth wide and the eyes like emeralds. She looked no more than 25 at the time but all stories about her claimed that she was around 30 and had remained young by her creams and lotions and her way of life.

According to his schedule, Reza Shah was in the bathroom on Thursdays at noon to take a hot both. Esmat was already waiting to give him a relaxing massage. In between, they had loving sports together and all pregnancies happened there.

Reza Shah's relations with Esmat provoked Moluk's jealousy. This time her efforts failed to get Esmat out of the Palace like she did with Turan. Moluk had employed trusted intimates to keep her informed of the secrets at the Court and help get rid of the troublesome women who could win Reza Shah's heart.

Reza Shah, after Ali Reza's birth, had no sex with Moluk perhaps because of her arrogant behaviour. Mohammad Reza told me that his father had been indifferent with women since the age of 35. At the time of his coup, he was about 40 and nobody heard of him to have picked up a mistress. Moluk who was very jealous and curious about these matters also did not complain about him.

When I got into the Court, Moluk's relations with Esmat had reached their climax. Separate buildings had been constructed for each Pahlavi family member. Moluk ordered her intimates to storm Esmat's house at any opportune time. Esmat, as soon as she learned of the imminent attack, closed the doors and cried for help. Reza Shah slowly walked in and the intimates escaped. The arrogant Moluk reprimanded them for fearing Reza but they did not dare to go ahead with their plans when Reza Shah intervened.

Reza Shah was not critical of his wives for their clashes and even was happy to see two women quarrelling for his sake. He loved Esmat very much and did not hide his love toward her even before Moluk. Esmat, despite Reza's love in her, turned down his request in the last days of his life to stay with him to the end after he was exiled to Mauritius Island in the Indian Ocean.[11]

BASTION OF REZA SHAH'S GOVERNMENT

At the beginning of the Pahlavi monarchy, Court Minister Teimourtash who was an educated and influential figure at the Royal Court proposed establishment of "Iran New Party". The Shah agreed and the political party was immediately established. Despite all that Reza Shah was not satisfied with Teimourtash.

All members of the party, led by Teimourtash, were influential government officials. After some time, Reza Shah dissolved the party after he learned that it was not protecting his throne but was a bastion of Teimourtash.

Reza Shah did not believe in any party or ideological formation and relied only on the army. He was only counting on Tehran army divided into two equally powerful divisions. Reza Shah always provoked rivalries between the two divisions so that they turned into two hostile rivals competing for greater powers.

Reza Shah equally armed the two divisions with modern and highly expensive and that day's sophisticated weapons purchased from abroad so that the rest of the Iranian army were not able to challenge any of them. At the time, Iran's army did not exceed 100,000 troops and the two divisions alone held 50,000 of the total army. The two divisions, committed to protect Reza Shah's throne, refused to grant aid to any outside units throughout the country. Until September 1941, Reza Shah's position seemed stabilized.

Reza Shah allowed promotion of only a few officers during his era. Brigadier General Fazlollah Zahedi[12] who was a mediator between Reza Shah and Sheikh Khazal to settle their differences through political dialogue upon the recommendation of the British, was among his top aides.

Amir Ahmadi, commander of an army division in the western Province of Kurdestan successfully crushed the long lasting Kurdish rebellion in the province and was promoted to the rank of a General, the only General during Reza Shah period. Shortly, he was stripped of his powers since he was emerging to challenge the Shah.

Ahmadi had taken many jewels with him as war reparations from Kurdestan and purchased about 500 houses in Tehran's Hassanabad district. His image improved following Reza Shah's collapse. During Mohammad Reza's reign, he was elected a Senator and later died.

Reza Shah allowed any officers to get as many properties as they could and plunder the wealth of the people. Governors had to obey army commanders otherwise they would be sacked.

Reza Shah did not reshuffle his cabinet and usually reinstated his ministers and other high ranking officials in their posts unless they became a threat to him. No complaints were accepted from the army officials since Reza Shah believed that they would not make any mistakes.

He hated jandarms because of bitter rivalries between Cossacks, supervised by the Soviets, and jandarms influenced by the British but ironically he had chummed up with Major General Zarqami, a jandarmeri officer. Zarqami held the post of chief of staff of the army for about eight years and defused several plots aimed at overthrowing or undermining Reza Shah's rule.

Bluffs, gestures and military showup had taken the place of real power in the army and the low spirit of commanders caused the army to break down on September 11, 1941.

The two divisions used to exercise six months of the year to prepare for February 22 celebrations marking the commemoration of the anniversary of Reza Shah's coup d'etat.

Maneuvres were carried out annually by the two divisions. In the remaining six months of the year, we were used to prepare ourselves in the deserts for the manoeuvres.

REZA SHAH'S INTELLIGENCE SERVICES

After seizing power, most probably upon London's recommendations, Reza Shah ordered the police (Shahrbani) to investigate the political activities of the opposition groups. Police seriously pursued the affair, and during Brigadier General Mokhtari's tenure, they even infiltrated into all the families required.

This way, the statesmen of the time learned how the police had been turned into an "appalling" secret intelligence service.

Reza Shah always asked the police to explain and brief him on all the developments happening at home and abroad in detail. At the same time, the police apparatus was not a well-organized secret service and, therefore, had to get the required information from the Iranian diplomatic missions abroad through the Ministry of Foreign Affairs.

The second branch of the army was also acting as an intelligence and counter-intelligence section. Four main branches were operating in the army: personnel, intelligence, operations and logistics respectively. The second branch of the army received military information from Iranian military attaches in the target countries.

At the time, a big French contingent were teaching Iranian officers both at the Officer's College and the War University on how to improve their intelligence operations. They were from the French elite army officers. To make it possible for the Iranian officers to understand the lessons, their books were translated into Persian and interpreters were also available in the classes for quick interpretation. The contingent left Iran before the outbreak of the World War II and left some lessons unfinished. In short, the French should be named as the founders of Iran's army intelligence service.

Later, the British intelligence contributed a greater share of service to the newly-established Iranian intelligence apparatus. Despite adoption of an iron fist policy by the government to defuse the domestic opposition and suppress the opponents, the British intelligence was playing the main role in providing the secret information and helping the government to curb the opposition. It was the British intelligence which helped discover Teimourtash's secret illegal contacts with the Soviets, which led to his execution.

REZA SHAH AND THE BRITISH

Reza Shah was a definite British agent. According to existing evidence and documents, the February 1921 coup attempt was hatched in British army General Sir Edmund Ironside's meeting with Reza Khan in which journalist Seyed Ziyauddin Tabatabai was also in attendance.[13]

The British had admitted that to remove Qajars some military force was required. They saw the re-organized Persian Cossack Brigade stationed in Qazvin under Reza Khan able to finish the job. On 18 February 1921, the Qazvin Cossack began their advance; on 20 Reza and Ziya met outside Tehran and made their plans in coordination with the British and on 21 Reza entered Tehran and seized power in an almost bloodless coup.[14]

Six weeks after the coup d'etat he was appointed Minister of War, and this was the only post he held until 1923, when he became Prime Minister as well. Since the coup was carried out, it took Reza Khan about five years to be crowned the first Shah of the Pahlavi dynasty.[15]

One day Shahpour J. showed me a book. The book was not available to the general public. In a paragraph it read that the Indian ruler (when India was a British colony) was pondering to select an appropriate agent to administer Iran. Upon his order, his father, Ardeshir Reporter, introduced Reza Khan to him which could be interpreted that the Pahlavi dynasty was founded by Ardeshir Reporter who was also a staunch British puppet.

Reza Khan and the British authorities had hired some contacts. Two of them were Khan Akbar and father of Shahpour J. Military commander As'ad Bakhteyari, once war minister, was the third contact.

Reza Shah was very cautious not to approach Britons publicly. If an important meeting or affair occurred such as oil talks and purchase of weapons, he empowered the Prime Minister to handle the negotiations with the British officials and sign the agreements.

A key element who was well aware of Reza Shah's secrets was Suleiman Behbudi. At first, Behbudi was a non-commissioned officer who was appointed by Reza Shah to look after his residence. Gradually, Behbudi won Reza Shah's confidence and was allowed to carry out the private affairs of members of the royal family. He did their shoppings and everything the family required. Behbudi reported all his shoppings to the Shah on a regular basis. Reza Shah was very accurate and carefully calculated the items Behbudi had purchased and occasionally chastised him for over consumption of the foodstuff.

Behbudi remained Reza Shah's confident until Shah's death in exile in South Africa. He handed over 1,200,000 tumans remained out of 2,000,000 to Mohammad Reza after he returned to Iran. The Crown Prince had given him the money to meet the daily requirements of Reza Shah during his exile. Behbudi, during Mohammad Reza's era, was promoted to the post of deputy court minister. His son, with his blessings, was elected parliamentary deputy for a term.

Behbudi was still alive up to a few years before the revolution and sometimes came to meet me in my house. Major General Mohajer was acting as the chief of the tribes section under his command.

Dr. Meimandinejad, a journalist, who was in charge of Rangin Kaman newspaper and a former dean of veterinary faculty, wrote Reza Shah's public life in series in his newspaper after consultations with Behbudi.

Another mediator and important figure was Mohammad Ali Forughi who played a distinguished role in helping Reza Shah and his son seize power. I will write in detail about his character and role in the next chapter.

REZA SHAH AND THE SOVIETS

> Reza Shah was born about 1873, coming from a small family from Alasht in the Savad Kuh region in Mazandaran. His mother's parents were Caucasians who had left their home in one of the districts ceded to Russia under the Treaty of Turkomanchai. His father and grandfather were army officers but his father died shortly after his birth and the young Reza joined the Persian Cossack Brigade as an ordinary recruit. He rose rapidly through the ranks and by the beginning of the First World War held the rank of Colonel."[16]

Since the Cossacks were under the command of the Soviet officers, Reza Khan, as he was called at the time, naturally was in touch and familiar with the high ranking Soviet military officials. I have personally seen Reza Shah's personal album showing him with the Soviets in military uniform.

Although Britons had deep influence in the upper echelons of the Iranian government long before Reza Shah's rule, the Soviets enjoyed credibility only in some aristocrat families. They lost their influence in Iran after the 1917 Bolshevik Revolution but later they launched a new political campaign to regain their influence in Iran. The Soviets, prior to the Bolshevik Revolution exerted their influence through Cossacks and after their Communist revolution they used to practise secret penetration. They encouraged their contacts to help establish political parties and invite people to join them in order to maintain their influence in Iran.

Reza Shah, despite being elevated to the highest military rank with the blessings of the Cossacks, showed no sympathy toward Communists and launched a massive campaign to crush all Communist groups in Iran.

Dr. Mohammad Taqi Erani[17] was the leader of the famous "53-member group" who was executed in jail. In August 1941, all Communists were released from prison. Among them was Jafar Pishevari. The weakness of Reza Shah's intelligence services failed to discover all Communist networks in the country.

REZA SHAH AND THE GERMANS

At the climax of German superiority in the world, Reza Shah ordered formation of a cabinet led by the pro-German Matin Daftari aimed at approaching Berlin. This caused expansion of political and economic relations between Iran and Germany.

After Britain, Germany had the largest number of experts in Iran during World War II. The Crown Prince came out in sympathy with Germans after their troops captured Eastern Europe and approached the Caucasus region. Even Reza Shah sometimes criticized the British for fighting Germans.

> The German presence in Iran—the dispersal of Germans in key positions in the railways and wireless stations, the presence of German boats in the Persian Gulf, watched over by the Iranians but not disarmed - appeared to the British to constitute a fifth column of the most dangerous potential. If, on the other hand, they were removed, the possibility opened up of a highly advantageous link being established by which Britain could send supplies to Russia instead of incurring the catastrophic losses of the arctic convoys.[18]

The British government was showing increasing concern about the number of Germans in Iran and were unconvinced by Iran's explanation that they were needed to assist with equipment ordered from Germany and were kept under proper surveillance.

The majority of the people at the Court were British elements and all these developments were not hidden to London.

The Germans' defeat in the last years of the World War II embarrassed Reza Shah. When the British and Russian troops entered Iran on 25 August 1941, at last Shah's government agreed to the expulsion of more than 600 German experts from Iran within 24 hours. The Germans were taken to Turkey by road.

Reza Shah was hopeful that the expulsion of German experts would help save him but it was too late. At four o'clock in the morning on September 11, 1941 the Allied troops including British, Russian and American entered Iran from the west, the north and the south respectively. Reza Shah abdicated in order to preserve the dynasty on 16 September 1941 and despite illness was taken on exile to South Africa where he died on 26 July 1944.[19]

"The British Government had since mid-1940 become increasingly apprehensive about such Nazi activities in Iran. They had gone so far as to give the Persian Government several friendly warnings, suggesting a reduction in the number of German technicians and other nationals. My father, however, pointed out the difficulty of replacing the technicians and the certainty that the Germans would interpret such a move as a violation of Iran's neutrality... on 26 June 1941, only four days after Hitler invaded Russia, the Russians added their protests to those of the British. Russia claimed among other things to have evidence that the Germans were planning a coup d'etat. On 19 July, the British and Russians sent a joint note of protest, followed on 16 August by a stronger one. They received what they regarded as a half-hearted response to these notes. Unfortunately, my father's Cabinet, with whose members the Allied authorities had been in frequent consultation, lacked the courage to tell my father that the Allies were prepared to back their warnings with force.

On 25 August, the British and Russians, in new notes to our Government, said that they were now obliged to take more direct action; and Persia was simultaneously invaded by the Russians from the north and by the British from the south. Later in the same day, my father told the British and Russian diplomatic representatives in Tehran that he would comply with their

Government's wishes, but the Allies replied that their troops would continue to advance."[20]

REZA SHAH'S DESPERATE ATTEMPTS FOR SURVIVAL AND OCCUPATION OF IRAN

As I said earlier, Reza Shah dramatically improved relations with Germany after Hitler's troops continued their advance to the Caucasus region. The Allied forces were aware of Reza Shah's sympathy toward the Germans. They feared that if German troops reached the Iranian border, Reza Shah would surrender and, therefore, Germans could capture Britain's colonies including India and spread their hegemony all over the Middle East.

To me, Reza Shah's sympathy with Hitler was not an empty rhetoric of politicians but a reality which derived from the two leader's ambitious desires. Reza Shah had established stable relations with Germany and was hopeful of Hitler's victory in the World War II. The Crown Prince also shared a similar view and in his conversations with me he predicted German's victory in the war. He closely followed the developments. I marked for him all the cities occupied by Germans one after the other on his big world map attached to the wall of his study room. Reza Shah, although had received Cossack-style military training, had no classic military information nor a good understanding of the world politics and therefore was somehow influenced by the Prince.

Reza Shah's dreams soon turned into despair. Following German's defeat, he reshuffled the cabinet, removed Matin Daftari from office and asked the pro-British Mansur to form a new cabinet in June 1940.

Mansur held intensive talks with the British, American and Russian ambassadors aimed at seeking ways to keep Reza Shah in power. He held private talks with the British Plenipotentiary Minister, Sir Reader Bulard and American Embassy officials. I never heard that he had privately met the Soviet ambassador. Mansur told Reza Shah that the Allied countries no longer trusted him. The embarrassed Reza Shah assured the Allied governments he would seek good ties and would be ready to sign security pacts with them but his verbal assurances did not satisfy the British who had in-depth information about his government and possessed documents showing his contacts with the Germans. British officials told Mansur that as a sign of good will, Reza Shah, as the first step, has to expel all German experts together with their families from Iran within 48 hours and then they would decide what to do next. Reza Shah immediately ordered the expulsion of all German experts and even invited the British embassy officials to supervise the execution of the decision. The British pretended to be willing to trust Reza and that made the Shah happy presuming he would remain in power.

In a next meeting, Mansur was told that the Allied countries wanted Iran to provide facilities for them to send weapons to the Soviet Union to fight off German advances. Reza Shah not only agreed to their condition but also promised to provide security to their convoys. Mansur conveyed Shah's message to them but they said they wanted to control the roads themselves. The Crown Prince informed me of all the talks between Mansur and the British in detail. Reza Shah summoned Bulard and the Soviet Ambassador to Sa'adabad for further briefings. Their stance remained unchanged. The Shah protested and said he was able to provide security to them. The decision had already been made and there was nothing the Shah could do about.

The Allied troops entered Iran and the now weakened Reza Shah ordered the army to "resist" the Allied "invasion" of the country. Of course, he was convinced that the army officers who were mostly pro-British would not resist the three powerful Allied armies but his motivation to call for resistance, Mohammad Reza said, was a face-saving gesture in order to pretend that he made every effort to fight the alien forces.

To me, Shah's decision to "resist" the Allied troops was a wise political manoeuvre which helped keep his dynasty in power and create a favourable ground for the public to recognize his son as his legal successor. Perhaps that was a recommendation put forward by the British themselves in the last minute.

Allied troops entered Iran; Americans invaded the southern cities in Khuzestan Province; Britons whose troops were based in Iraq entered Iran from the western borders of Kermanshah and the Soviets from the north.

> "The need to pass munitions and supplies of all kinds to the Soviet Government, and the extreme difficulties of the Arctic route, together with future strategic possibilities, made it

eminently desirable to open the fullest communication with Russia through Persia. I was not without some anxiety about embarking on yet another new campaign in the Middle East, but the arguments were compulsive.

The Persian oilfields were a prime war factor, and if Russia were defeated we would have to be ready to occupy them ourselves. And then there was the threat to India. The suppression of the revolt in Iraq and the Anglo-French occupation of Syria, achieved as they were by narrow margins, had blotted out Hitler's Oreintal Plan, but if the Russians foundered he might try again. An active and numerous German mission had installed itself in Tehran, and German prestige stood high. On the eve of my voyage to Placentia (Placentia Bay, in Newfoundland, where on 9 August, 1941, Churchill had first meeting with Roosevelt) I had set up a special committee to coordinate the planning of an operation against Persia, and during my absence at sea they reported to me by telegram the results of their work, which had meanwhile been approved by the War Cabinet. It was clear that the Persians would not expel the German agents and residents from their country, and that we should have to resort to force. On August 13 Mr. Eden received M. Maisky at the Foreign Office, and the terms of our respective Notes to Tehran were agreed. A joint Anglo-Soviet Note of August 17 met with an unsatisfactory reply, and the date for the entry of British and Russian forces into Persia was fixed for the 25th."[21]

AT PRINCE'S PRIVATE HEADQUARTERS

A few hours after the Allied troops entered Iran from three directions on the morning of August 25, 1941, Reza Shah delegated all his military powers to the Crown Prince. Mohammad Reza ordered Brigadier General Mahmoud Amini who previously was our Company commander in the Officer's College to set up an emergency private headquarters. About 15 top military officials were summoned the same day to Sa'adabad. I was among them. We were ushered to the "operations room" and immediately went into session. Two expert teams were assigned to inspect troops who had already taken positions in eastern and western suburbs of Tehran to counter any possible attacks on the capital. The inspection was aimed at improving the morale of the troops and assess the situation.

Military units were stationed in the desert near the capital with no defensive positions while they could better defend themselves in Karaj where a main road was passing the heights. A unit was stationed in Mehrabad where troops had no bunkers or embankments to protect themselves against attacks.

"What embankments. Even we have no guns to fight with" the unit commander told me after I asked him to explain his failure to prepare his troops to defend the capital. I examined his gun. It was a target gun used exclusively in military exercises. Our visit was not helpful to the demoralized soldiers who were afraid of attacks from the well-equipped Allied forces.

Reza Shah had been left in no doubt that he would be toppled sooner or later and his decision to delegate his powers to the Crown Prince was aimed at paving the way for Mohammad Reza to succeed him. Shah's motive was twofold. Not only he wanted to save his monarchy but also he wanted to hide his professional weaknesses from the public. He was convinced that the Crown Prince was superior to him in terms of military expertise since Mohammad Reza had learned military tactics in the Officer's College. The Crown Prince was young and his shortcomings could be ignored. Of course, members of his private headquarters, who all were seasoned military experts helped him make sound decisions on military issues if not political problems.

Reza Shah's servant told me the Shah did not go to bed on schedule. He just paced up and down his sleeping room pondering how to save his monarchy.

Resistance against the Allied invasion required a strong decision-making body with committed officers while the Crown Prince was obviously convinced that the officers at his private headquarters were British puppets. Although soldiers were demoralized, the problem was with the top officers who were the brains and not the soldiers who were the legs.

ALLIED TROOP DEPLOYMENT AND RESISTANCE SHOW UP

I spent much of my time with Mohammad Reza in his private headquarters seeing to his orders. I remained with him even when he discussed the situation with his father. As they were accustomed to, they walked in the garden and I walked behind them hovering to carry out their orders.

In the south, commander of the naval forces, Brigadier General Bayandor bravely resisted the American fleet. A heavy fighting broke out in the coastal waters. Bayandor's troops halted the Americans after they launched a counter-offensive against them. Exchange of gun fire shots and cannon rounds partly damaged a fleet but the well-armed Americans barraged Bayandor's boat. The boat exploded into pieces killing Bayandor and his companions. This was the only serious resistance against the intruders.

In the north in Azerbaijan, the army put down its arms and fled to mountains after a short gunfire exchange with the Soviets. It was the same in Mashhad, the capital of the northeastern Province of Khorasan. There was also little resistance against the British on the western borders.

REZA SHAH, FOROUGHI AND FREEMASONARY

In the last days of his rule, Reza Shah appealed to Mohammad Ali Foroughi, an influential politician who was famous for his connections with the British to help save his monarchy.

Foroughi was an influential British contact and a top member of the Freemasonry. He played a significant role in helping Reza Shah to seize power. He was an educated person and was highly respected in the Iranian cultural and scientific circles. He was very curious not to let others learn of his membership in the higher echelons of Freemasonry. He was superior to almost all Iranian Freemasons. Even British Plenipotentiary Minister, Bulard paid courtesy calls to him.

Reza Shah saw in Foroughi a last hope who could save his throne. The Crown Prince told me that on 26th of August, his father had gone to Foroughi's house, a rare event during Shah's rule, to seek his support for his dynasty. In the meeting, Reza Shah entreated him to help save his throne. Foroughi had replied that there was no way for him to stay in power but that his pro-British efforts could prevent further aggravation of the situation. First, he was told, he should declare an immediate ceasefire in order to avoid the fall of the capital. The northern cities had fallen to the Soviets and they were continuing their advance toward Tehran. Foroughi made it clear that he could not guarantee his safety. Second, the only choice left to him was to abdicate and leave the country.

Reza Shah accepted the offer but begged Foroughi to guarantee that the Pahlavi dynasty will remain in power. Foroughi promised to do his best but again made it clear that he could not guarantee the survival of the Pahlavi dynasty.

REZA SHAH SURRENDERS

On 27th of August 1941, the Shah ordered the military to stop resistance against the Allied troops. The Shah was steadily weakening. With his back bent, he was assisted by a walking stick and sat on a rocking-chair in his garden. It was not difficult for me to read despair on his face. His weakned body had dwarfed in the large rocking-chair. His face was like a stone, cold and grey. If you had struck him with a knife, he would not have bled. He was not able to make decisions and his orders were contradictory.

In the evening of August 27, Acting War Minister Major General Ahmad Nakhjavan and chief of the army's engineering department, Brigadier General Reyazi requested an appointment with the Shah. Their request was immediately met. They were ushered to the garden and started talking to the Shah after a brief exchange of pleasantries. I was about fifty meters away and unable to hear them. Suddenly, Reza Shah stood up and shouted at his guests. He ordered his security men to arrest them and toss them into jail.

Later, the Crown Prince told me that they carried a message from Britons calling on the Shah to order the two Tehran Divisions to stop resistance and return to their barracks. The message upset Reza Shah who presumed they were betraying him.

The two were jailed in Sa'adabad and lost their ranks. As I was passing their room, they entreated me to request the Shah to show mercy and forgive them. They said they just conveyed the message of the Allied governments to the Shah and were innocent.

On 28th of August, Mansur conveyed a message from the British government to the Shah.

"The Soviets have threatened that they would capture Tehran if the two Tehran Divisions did not immediately lay down their arms", the message read.

The message was clearly aimed at putting more pressure on the Shah and frighten him. It also became clear that Nakhjavan and

Reyazi were innocent. After the message was read, Reza Shah went to the army barracks and ordered the commanders to send all soldiers on leave. His order aggravated the already spreading chaos in the country. The hungry soldiers who had not reached their barracks deserted their arms and started looting shops and wherever they could meet their requirements to get them home.

While a slight damage on a gun bought a soldier 30 days in jail, only some 20,000 guns were left on the ground on the outskirts of Tehran. I was in the Imperial Investigations and aware of all of the developments. A few experts were assigned (I was one) to look to the deserted guns and report to the superiors. Too much water and dust had rotted many of the guns. I kicked one of the many guns deserted in small streams on the outskirts of Tehran after I had examined a first one. Flakes of dust fell away. On our way back to the Investigations Department, many soldiers were still roaming in the capital looking for enough food to get them home.

A few days later, Bulard in a message through Foroughi, who had just become Prime Minister, recommended to call back all the military forces to their units. Upon Reza Shah's order, all soldiers were returned to their barracks but just 30% of the officers and ranking officials carried the order and the rest refused.

TROOP PULLOUT AND MOHAMMAD REZA'S MONARCHY

In the last two weeks of Reza's rule, I was engaged in intensive diplomatic efforts which determined the fate of the Pahlavi dynasty.

Strong relations and close friendship between the Crown Prince and I had turned me into an influential player in the events in those fateful days. I shuttled back and forth between the Palace and the British Embassy to carry messages for the Crown Prince and the British intelligentsia.

During these days, I was the only confident of Mohammad Reza in solitude. Earnest Proun had left Iran about two months before the fall of Reza Shah on the pretext of being homesick and wishing to see his family (He returned to Iran about six months later). Mohammad Reza sent his wife, Fawzia and his little daughter, Shahnaz, to Egypt to keep them away from the developments. So, I was his only confident in the Court.

In a September afternoon, the Crown Prince ordered me to rush to the British Embassy and meet a man called Trout who was London's intelligence representative in Iran and the second powerful man in the embassy and consult with him about the dynasty's fate. I do not know who had introduced Trout to Mohammad Reza, perhaps Foroughi or someone else.

I telephoned the embassy and talked to Trout. We made an appointment at eight in the evening of the same day. He gave his particulars to me and I was expected to wait for him in front of the embassy. The embassy had moved to its summer office in Golhak, a district in northern Tehran with a pleasant climate. I arrived a few minutes early. I was watching around. Although we were into summer, a chilly wind was sweeping across the street. Tall trees had surrounded the main embassy building. It was sharp eight. The embassy's main door opened and a tall and rather thin man in his 40s walked to me. The particulars were accurate.

"Are you Fardust?", he asked in fluent Persian.

"The Crown Prince wants to know what will happen to him if his father abdicates", I said after confirming that I was Fardust.

We briefly talked about the deepening crisis in the country. He regretted that the Crown Prince had shown sympathy toward Germans and said, "We have accurate information proving that the Crown Prince was listening to foreign radios and had a map in which you were marking the cities the Germans occupied one after the other!" I made it clear that I was only carrying Mohammad Reza's message. Then, Trout said he was prepared to discuss any urgent matter with me even if it was in the midnight. I said I would get back to him if the Crown Prince wanted me to.

I returned to Sa'adabad and informed Mohammad Reza of what I had been told. The Crown Prince got embarrassed when he learned that Trout was aware of even tiny affairs in the Court.

"Servants might be spying for the British ", he suspected.

He ordered me to talk to Trout again and tell him that he no longer listened to foreign radio broadcasts unless approval was obtained from them in advance and that the map was destroyed.

The next evening, we had a brief meeting. Trout said Mohammad Reza has to fulfil his promise and prove his honesty. He did not speak too much, a rule observed by intelligence agents. His face was tough and uncompromising but he was very kind to me.

Mohammad Reza abandoned listening to foreign radio broadcasts and ordered to remove the map from his room. The

Crown Prince was afraid that the British may choose his brother, Ali Reza, as Reza's successor. I remained in constant touch with Trout. He had nothing to tell for a few days.

After three days since our last meeting, we met again. As usual Trout arrived on time. He said how good it was to see me once again.

"The Crown Prince has fulfilled his promise and now we are satisfied with him. The Soviets have rejected a monarchical system of government outright and favour a Republican regime in Iran. The Americans are indifferent but somehow support the Soviets since they are familiar with a Republican system. And we, the British government, support a monarchical rule here. The Americans are not aware of the problems a Republican system may cause for them but the Soviets are well aware of our aims. We are now trying hard to persuade the Americans to support a monarchical system in Iran. Should we win America's support, we will discuss the matter with the Soviets", Trout explained.

A few days later, we had another meeting. Trout said the British meant whatever they say. He said Americans were now convinced that a monarchical regime could better serve their interests.

"The Americans have given us assurances that they would support us against our joint rival, the Soviet Union," he added. Trout believed that Moscow would surrender to London's views since they needed U.S. military assistance.

In the next meeting, he said he had failed to persuade the Soviets to support Mohammad Reza's succession to the throne. He said U.S. envoy had threatened that Washington would reconsider its relations with Moscow (of course it was a bluff) if they continued their opposition to a monarchical system in Iran. I doubted his honesty. Perhaps he was deliberately trying to teach Mohammad Reza lessons for the future. The anxieties of the past few weeks had left him exhausted. Ali Qavam, Princess Ashraf's husband, also provoked Mohammad Reza's fear and anxiety. He used every opportunity to frighten Mohammad Reza. Whenever a plane appeared in the sky, he cried and said, "Look, Soviet fighters are attacking us". He deliberately spoke loud so that his voice could reach the ears of the Crown Prince.

Finally on 15th September, Trout happily told me to inform Mohammad Reza to show up in the Parliament in order to be officially sworn in as his father's successor. I rushed to the Palace.

Mohammad Reza got delighted with the news. In the midnight, he happily informed me that final preparations have been made for his official succession to the throne.

The next day on 16th September, Reza Shah resigned and his son replaced him and the day after Mohammad Reza was sworn in the Parliament and formally acquired the title of the Shahanshah, king of kings.

THE BRITISH AND ALI REZA

Reza Shah and Mohammad Reza's tendencies toward Germans caused the British to doubt Crown Prince's honesty and feared he, once powerful, may join the Germans again and turn his back to London. Therefore, to make him obedient, they brought Prince Ali Reza, Crown Prince's younger brother, as a challenger to him. Ali Reza was 19 at the time. He was despot and ruthless. Of course, the British preferred Mohammad Reza's personality and their verbal support to Ali Reza was just to make Mohammad Reza more faithful to the British.

Trout implicitly but persistently emphasized that Mohammad Reza was not the only choice in the family to succeed Reza Shah. He was, indeed, trying to let Mohammad Reza understand that his support of Germans had not been forgotten by London. Even after Mohammad Reza's position was stabilized, the British kept their relations with Ali Reza almost until his murder.

The Americans needed the co-operation of Britain since London had a long experience in Middle East affairs. I am certain that the British wanted Mohammad Reza well understand that it was the British who brought him to power and he had to consider London's expectations.

REZA SHAH ESCAPES

Reza Shah signed a resignation letter already provided by Foroughi and headed toward Isfahan in the morning of September 16th, 1941.

The night before, Mohammad Reza informed me that his father would show up for a farewell ceremony at Marmar Palace. The Court's Protocol Department immediately called on ranking officials to rush to the palace. I also attended the short ceremony which did not last more than a few minutes. Reza Shah arrived in the Palace and made a brief speech. I did not join other officers and stood where I could hear him.

Reza Shah addressing the audience said, "I am old enough to resign. The country requires an energetic and young leader and I am introducing the Crown Prince as my successor. I expect all of you to support him".

The audience bowed before him as a sign of agreement. He raised his walking stick and bade goodbye to all. The car was waiting for him outside the building. He ordered his escort to remain in the capital since nothing was threatening him. As he was walking to his car, he paused for a moment and after studying my face gave me a false smile and said, "goodbye Hussein".

His family had earlier travelled to Isfahan and he was in a hurry to leave the capital to escape the Soviet troops who at any moment could reach Tehran.

Despite Reza Shah's order, Naser Khan Amirpour, Reza's escort commander who was a close friend of mine said he did not want to leave Reza Shah alone and decided to personally follow him. Amirpour said he had tried not to be seen by Reza Shah on the way to Isfahan since he sometimes looked back to see if anybody was following him. On the road to Qom, he said, the main junction was closed. The British army was heading toward Tehran with the capacity of a brigade. After a few minutes, a British ranking officer who immediately recognized Reza ordered his soldiers to open the road and let Reza's car to move on. The Brigade commander saluted Reza and his car passed.

> "Mohammad Reza once described to me the last meeting he had with his father. He said it was the first time in his life he had seen him behave like a father, and not, as always before, like a king or a commander-in-chief. There were tears in the old man's eyes when they met, and the young man felt too moved to speak. The father's first remark was a question, "Can you keep the throne?" The son said nothing. "I didn't fail to keep the throne", the father went on, "but forces stronger than me defeated me. I kept the throne for you. Will you be able to keep it?" The son could only nod. Reza Shah continued, "Pay attention, my son. Don't resist. We and the whole world are facing a storm that is bigger than any of us. Bow your head till the storm passes." And then he added, "Get a son!" He repeated this "Get a son!"

And then he went out of the room and into exile in South Africa, where he died."[22]

QAVAM SHIRAZI AND PAHLAVI PROPERTIES

Reza Shah arrived in Isfahan in the afternoon of the same day and spent the night in the house of an aristocrat called Kazeruni. The same night, Ebrahim Qavam Shirazi and Dr. Sajadi, a Freemason and a British puppet, arrived in Isfahan to discuss the royal properties.

Head of a notary public officer was called and Reza Shah left all of his movable and immovable properties to Mohammad Reza. Reza then headed to Kerman and Qavam returned to the capital. He gave the testament to Prime Minister Foroughi who read it out in a Parliament open session a few days later.

Reza Shah, during his era, forced owners of fertile lands in northern Iran to sell their properties to him. The Prince was determined by the Shah and the owners had no right to object. After his fall, newspapers for some time were disclosing Reza's usurpation of people's lands in series. Major General Karim Aqakhan Buzarjmehri was administering Shah's properties in northern Iran. The revenues from the same of rice and other products cultivated in the lands annually topped 62 million tumans.

When the ailing Reza was in exile in South Africa, his children complained that they had been deprived of any bequeathment. Reza in a letter to Mohammad Reza urged him to share the Palaces with his sisters and brothers and pay them one million tumans each. Mohammad Reza immediately carried out the will of his father.

If Reza Shah wrote his memoirs, it would have been very interesting to learn his motivation behind seizing the lands of the people.[23]

During the Allied occupation of Iran, The British Broadcasting Corporation (BBC) radio broadcasted some programmes on the properties of Reza Shah for three consecutive days and said Reza's greatest service to his people was occupying their lands.

Mohammad Reza showed understanding toward the criticism of his father. It seemed that he had been advised to keep calm so to avoid any crisis. Of course in his heart, Mohammad Reza was jealous. He was superior to his father in terms of military expertise and liked the people to praise him against his father.

END OF A DICTATOR

Reza Shah, accompanied by his family, except the twins (Crown Prince Mohammad Reza and Princess Ashraf), and Mahmoud Jam left Isfahan for Kerman and settled in the house of a merchant. Reza's health deteriorated but he continued his trip. His next destination was the southern port city of Bandar Abbass where a British liner was waiting to take him to Bombay (now Mumbai), India. Near Bombay, a British diplomat got on the board and told Reza that he had to go to Mauritius Island in the Indian Ocean. Reza got disappointed but there was no other option left to him. He was provided a house together with a garden in the island.

The moist weather deteriorated Reza's health and upon his insistence, he was taken to the port city of Durban in South Africa and from there he was transferred to Johannesburg.

Reza Shah died of a heart attack in Johannesburg on 25th of July 1944. At the time, Iran's political tides were clearly running against Reza Shah and, therefore, his body was transferred to Egypt and was entombed for six years in Al Rifaie Mosque. After the political atmosphere in Iran was eased, preparations were made to take Reza's body to Iran. In 1949, the Parliament described Reza Shah as "His Majesty" and Razmara, the then chief of the joint staff of the army, was assigned to take the body to Tehran.

Special ceremonies were held in Egypt and the body was taken to the southwestern port city of Khoramshahr by sea and from there it was transferred to Tehran by train. I also attended the overwhelming ceremonies marking the burial of Reza Shah's body in a cemetry in Tehran.

Fig. 1: Mohammad Reza (left) and Hussein Fardust when they entered the Military School

Fig. 2: Reza Shah, in the early years of his rule

Fig. 3: Taj-ol-Moluk, mother of twin Mohammad Reza and Ashraf

Fig. 4: Hussein Fardust, Shah's "eyes and ears"

Fig. 5: Fardust speaking on national television after his arrest

Fig. 6: Mohammad Reza, aged 6, with Princess Shams (left) Princess Ashraf (right) and Prince Gholamreza

Fig. 7: Reza Shah and (left to right) Crown Prince Mohammad Reza Princesses Shams and Ashraf

Fig. 8: The coronation of Reza Shah at the Golestan Palace

Fig. 9: Court Minister, Teimourtash

Chapter 2

Early Years of Mohammad Reza's Reign

A GLANCE AT MOHAMMAD REZA'S MONARCHICAL RULE

Mohammad Reza's reign could be categorized into three periods:

1. From his coronation to the withdrawal of Allied troops from Iran.
2. From the Allied pullout to the August 19, 1953 coup.
3. From then to his departure from Iran in 1979.

When the throne was passed to him, Mohammad Reza turned to British and American forces deployed in Iran for support. The Iranian army, including two rival divisions set up during his father's reign, were stationed in the same garrison but they were demoralized and depleted soldiers without any plan of action. The armed forces personnel numbered around 80,000.

Mohammad Reza had grown up in an atmosphere of educated sophistication unknown to his father. In the first years of his reign he was an inexperienced young man who tried to work within the limits specified by the Constitution. Of course, he considered himself the commander-in-chief and owner of the armed forces and his observance of the Constitution excluding the army, brought him the total consensus of his government among the people.

That Cabinet ministers were consulting him on the important state problems which seemed to be mere formalities. He mixed with his people, especially sportsmen, and talked to them. His initiatives helped tighten his grip on power. Later, he changed his mood and favoured an obedient Prime Minister.

After the Allied pullout Mohammad Reza considered the successful resistance against Russian invaders and the return of Azerbaijan a great victory for himself. From then a fundamental change was witnessed in his public life and he adopted an authoritarian attitude. He had become thoroughly dissatisfied and impatient with the obstacles in his taking decisive action.

That he should exert more active leadership and exercise greater authority in government became a familiar theme in conversations between him and the British and American representatives. He no longer held a ceremonial post and did not wish to be inferior to the Prime Minister in accordance with the Constitution. He consulted the British about a line to be taken on constitutional reforms in Iran. The real overall objective was to give more power to the Shah.

Although Mohammad Reza lacked the intimidating physique and presence of his father, he understood very well the importance of the military in bringing the Pahlavi family to power and keeping it there.

The Shah's instinct for accumulating all real power in his own hands and operating through compliant ministers and political representatives was evident after the downfall of Mossaddiq.

In June 1950, the Shah appointed General Ali Razmara Prime Minister. He seemed to be listening to the Shah. He was a prominent military figure but with less political knowledge. He had secret links with both the pro-Soviet Tudeh Party and American as well as British agents. He was at the same time thirsty for power. The February 1949 assassination attempt against the Shah, who escaped with minor injuries, is attributed to him and does not seem unlikely.

Rivalry and hostility reached a climax when Mohammad Mossaddiq became Prime Minister. The Shah could not tolerate Mossaddiq because of political differences with him. The determination of Mossaddiq and his National Front to nationalize the oil industry had added to their rivalry.

> "The two great crises of the Shah's life to that time - the trauma of foreign military occupation during and after the Second World War and the near-loss of political control to Mossaddiq in the early 1950s - had taught the Shah two lessons which shaped his attitudes and behaviour in the decades to follow. The first was the vital importance of a strong, well-equipped military force to deter foreign intervention. The other was the political danger of

permitting an independent or charismatic rival close to the seat of real power."[1]

The third and last period was the period of Shah's absolute dictatorship. Government bodies were stooges in his hand. He firmly believed that the Prime Minister, the Majlis (Parliament) and other powerful bodies in the country had to obey his orders.

To that end, he changed Articles 48 and 49 of the Constitution giving himself the power to dissolve the Majlis and the right to veto the laws passed by the Majlis.

Amir Abbass Hoveida was the best choice for the post of Prime Minister to help accomplish Shah's aims. Land reforms, labour and profession were things he always stressed in order to portray that he was trying to propagate his plans both at home and abroad. He claimed Iran would become the world's fifth power should his plans be accomplished. The outcome of his plans were already clear. He founded an ailing economy which was based neither on agriculture nor on industry. His policies prompted mass immigration of villagers to cities and inflation began to rise dramatically.

Mohammad Reza was the centre of power. He differed from his father in behaviour and understanding of power. To me, Mohammad Reza was more despot than his father. Reza Shah perpetrated many injustices on the people, such as usurping their lands but compared to his son he deserved gratitude.

After he was crowned Reza Shah in April 1926, the monarch encouraged domestic investment in industries and the rate of inflation was much less than that in the reign of his son. During Reza Shah's reign, Tehran's population was about 300,000. He devoted oil revenues to strengthen the army and nobody was entitled to spend a single rial without his permission. Non-oil revenues were spent for economic development projects. He controlled everything and did not allow embezzlement. He did not undertake big projects except road building. Compared to his son, Reza Shah made less mistakes. He lived very economically but his son did not bother himself about the expenses, sometimes spending millions of tumans in a day for his family.

Reza Shah had little deposits in foreign banks and was very keen to avoid extra government spending but Mohammad Reza did otherwise. Reza Shah scarcely left Iran except for a state visit to Turkey in 1934 with the least formalities, while Mohammad Reza made expensive trips to several countries in a year and invited guests from all corners of the globe for the annual festivals to commemorate the 2500 years of Iranian monarchical rule. At the spectacular ruins of the Palace of Cyrus the Great near Persepolis, he constructed an elegant tent city for several days and entertained his guests. Hours of parades by soldiers in uniforms of the past celebrated the centuries of Iran's military triumphs.

Reza Shah did not leave any memories behind him. There were many controversial and secret things in his time of great interest for the new generation to study had he written them but Mohammad Reza wrote a few books about himself and paid reporters to write in his favour.

Mohammad Reza's dictatorship facilitated huge financial embezzlements by influential figures at the Court, by those close to him as well as cabinet ministers. His many weaknesses finally left the Iranian people no choice but to remove him from power.

ALLIES IN TEHRAN

The first period of Mohammad Reza's rule coincided with the trilateral Allied occupation of Iran during the Second World War. The Tripartite Treaty, signed by Iran, Britain and the Soviet Union on 29 January 1942 set out the terms and conditions by which Britain and Russia remained in Iran during the course of the war. Their forces had already entered Iran in early 1941 and the Americans joined them later.

> "By its terms Iran conceded to the Allies rights for the transit of war material through the country to the Soviet Union. With this went Allied control, as far reaching as necessary, of all communications in Iran, and they also undertook to assist in procuring materials and labour... In return, Britain and Russia assured Iran that their presence did not constitute an 'occupation'... So far as possible, they would help to alleviate the economic hardships which would inevitably accompany war-time conditions. By article I the Allied pleaded to respect Iran's 'territorial integrity, sovereignty, and political independence'. According to article V, which took on a special significance towards the end of the war, Allied forces should leave Iran not later than six months after the cessation of

hostilities 'between the Allied Powers and Germany and her Associates."[2]

The United States had withdrawn its troops from Iran by December 31, 1945 and the British followed on March 2, 1946; both were within the six-month time fixed by treaty obligations but the Soviets let the deadline pass and deployed six of their total eight Divisions in northern Iran. Russian troops did not show up in Tehran's streets except once when they marched in Naderi street where Armenian immigrants welcomed them with flowers. A reliable source had told me that the commander of the Soviet forces had ordered his soldiers to remain in their barracks in western Tehran and that they would be severely punished and even executed if they failed to obey the order.

The same, but to a less extent, applied to the British forces but it was totally otherwise in case of the Americans. They had a club in Amirabad, northern Tehran which was quickly turned into a prostitution house. American lorries were roaming in the capital's streets taking girls to their club. They lured the girls to their club just by offering them a portion of their food ration. They were given food enough for six to each of them. One of the prostitutes was maternal aunt of the Shah.

> "Russia and Britain had concluded an agreement with Iran in 1942 which allowed Russian and British troops to be stationed on Iranian soil for a period ending six months after the termination of hostilities. At the London Conference of Foreign Ministers in September 1945, Bevin and Molotove had agreed that this meant that all foreign troops would be withdrawn from Iran not later than March 2, 1946.
>
> However, during the month of November the State Department received reliable reports that instead of preparing for withdrawal the Russians were adding to their forces. It was also reported that the Russians were interfering with efforts by the government in Tehran to suppress rebellious elements in the northern part of the country, and especially in the province of Azerbaijan.
>
> On November 23, I had Secretary Byrnes bring up the matter before the Cabinet. Byrnes suggested at that time that we speed up the departure of American troops in Iran. We had used Iran

as a supply route to Russia by arrangement with the British, the Russians, and the Tehran government. This meant that we maintained a few thousand service troops in the country. While this involved only a relatively small force, we intended to set the example of withdrawal and then ask the Russians to agree that all foreign troops would be out of that country by January 1.

The approach to Russia was made on this basis, but on December 3 the Russians rejected the proposal. A few days later the Moscow radio informed the world that a revolutionary government had been set up in Azerbaijan. The Iranian government at once charged that this rebel government owed its existence to the Russians and was supported by Russian military forces...

On January 19, Iran formally charged Russia before the Security Council of the United Nations with interference in her internal affairs. But the Security Council was unable to act because Russia contended that the dispute was not a matter which that body was competent to handle. The Russians simply announced that they would ignore any questions they might be asked about Iran. The Security Council then agreed to let Russia and Iran settle the matter by direct negotiation. It was, of course, unlikely that Iran would be able to resist Russian demands while Soviet troops were still occupying her territory. Under such conditions there could hardly be any equality at the bargaining table.

March 2, the day on which the Russians had agreed with Britain and Iran that they would withdraw their troops, came and passed, but the Russians did not leave Iran. On the contrary, Moscow announced that "some troops" would remain in Iran for an unspecified time.

This was a gross violation of the agreements made. It also meant that Iran would be required to negotiate with Russia while a gun was at her head. I decided that the Russian government ought to be informed on how we felt about this kind of conduct in international relations. I asked Secretary Byrnes to bring with him, to his weekly conference with me, all available documents on the Iranian situation... Byrnes sent a note to Moscow that would, while still being diplomatically polite, make it very plain that we did not like the way Russia was behaving in Iran... There was no official reply to this note. Russian press reports, however, said that the State Department was "mistaken" that there were no Russian troop movements in Iran. Then the Kremlin shifted tactics... our intelligence continued to report the presence of Russian troops in Iran. The Iranians, moving into areas from which the Russians had said they had pulled out, found the roads blocked by Russian troop units... The signs were plain that Russia was determined to have her way and that she intended to ignore the U.S. and the U.N. alike.

As I saw it, three things were involved. One was the security of Turkey. Russia had been pressing Turkey for special privileges and for territorial concessions for several months. The Turks had resisted all these demands, but their position would be infinitely more difficult if Russia, or a Russian puppet state, were able to outflank her in the east. The second problem was the control of Iran's oil reserves. That Russia had an eye on these vast deposits seemed beyond question. If the Russians were to control Iran's oil, either directly or indirectly, the raw-material balance of the world would undergo a serious change, and it would be a serious loss for the economy of the Western world...

I talked over all these points with Secretary Byrnes and Admiral Leahy. Then I told Byrnes to send a blunt message to Premier Stalin. On March 24 Moscow announced that all Russian troops would be withdrawn from Iran at once..."[3]

FIRST DAYS OF MOHAMMAD REZA'S REIGN

After consultations with Trout, the twenty-two-year-old Mohammad Reza, who now had been installed on the Peacock Throne, was sworn into office in the Majlis in September 1941.

On his way to the Majlis, many high-ranking military officials approached the new Shah flattering and expressing loyalty to him. There was no public opposition to the new Shah. The people did not know what the young Shah would do and were not aware of his policies. Mohammad Ali Foroughi, an elder politician, was elected Prime Minister.

Foroughi personally was not interested in assuming the post and preferred to remain indoors and study but the British found him the best choice to get Iran out of the crisis. Foroughi was, however, a scapegoat for the new inexperienced Shah to escape criticism.

"Hussein, since I have no organized establishments, I'd like you to act as my special aid-e-camp and help me restore order", the Shah told me after the ceremony.

Shah's Palace called "Special Palace" was located just opposite the Marmar Palace in central Tehran. Everything moved smoothly and satisfactorily. Ministers, MPs and other influential figures paid courtesy calls on the new Shah who received them with open arms. The Shah was happy to see influential figures expressing loyalty to him.

> "When Reza Shah was succeeded by his son, tribes reasserted themselves and government's opponents strove to regain lost ground. Newspapers and political parties emerged in profusion. Of particular significance was the reappearance of the Communist party, outlawed by Reza Shah, under the name of Tudeh (masses) party...
>
> Throughout 1942, the numbers of Americans in Iran increased as did their influence. Americans became responsible for operating the southern section of the railway and later extended their participation to road transport though the British remained responsible for security of communications throughout the war. Given the history of Anglo-Russian diplomacy in Iran, the legacy of distrust this had engendered, the American presence seemed the most promising avenue for improved management and efficiency".[4]

There were three Iranian governments in 1942 alone. Foroughi fell in March. He was succeeded by Ali Soheili who lasted only until July. Qavam al-Saltaneh then became Prime Minister who was an elder statesman and a strong man.

BULARD AND MOHAMMAD REZA

What called my attention in the early years of Mohammad Reza's monarchical rule was his relations with the British Plenipotentiary Minister in Tehran Sir Reader Bulard.[5]

The Shah was not in good terms with Bulard and for that he asked the British authorities to recall him to London. Britain turned down the request and Bulard remained in Tehran until the end of his mission.

The British wanted the young Shah understand that it were the British who installed him on the Peacock Throne. Personally, I was acting as a mediator between the British intelligence representative in Iran, Allen Charles Trout and the Shah in stabilizing the latter's rule.

To me, Mohammad Reza's cold relations with Bulard had nothing to do with Britain's policy to crown him as the head of state.

Later, head of the MI-6 at the British Embassy told me that his reports were directly dispatched to his London headquarters and the ambassador was not necessarily informed of the reports.

MEETING WITH STALIN

On December 1, 1943, the three heads of the then superpowers, Winston Churchill of Britain, Franklin D. Roosevelt of U.S. and Josef Stalin of the Soviet Union arrived in Tehran for a summit meeting in the Iranian capital.

During their meeting which took place at the Soviet Embassy, they signed the Tehran Declaration in which they pledged to respect Iran's territorial integrity, sovereignty and political independence.[6]

It was in this summit that Iran was described as the "Bridge of Victory" during the Second World War but that was not aimed at appeasing Iran but to let the world understand that the Soviets would not be able to defeat the Germans without U.S. help through Iran. During their stay in Tehran, Churchill and Roosevelt failed to meet Mohammad Reza but Stalin personally called on him.

Ahmad Ali Sepehr had coordinated for this meeting. He was among those who played a distinguished role in the early years of Mohammad Reza's rule. One morning on the eve of the conference Sepehr telephoned me and asked for an urgent meeting. I drove to his old but large house without any hesitation. He said he had remained in touch with the Soviet Embassy through all the night and that he had met the ambassador several times.

"I requested the ambassador to invite Stalin for a meeting with the Shah. Since Churchill and Roosevelt had not anticipated a meeting with the Shah in their scheduled visit to Iran, Stalin's initiative to meet the Shah would make His Majesty very happy", he said vigorously.

He said that after consultations with Stalin, the ambassador had informed him of his will to meet the Iranian monarch. Sepehr was told to make preparations for the meeting but on the condition that only Soviet security guards should be in the Palace during the meeting.

I passed Sepehr's message to Mohammad Reza. The Shah, delighted with the news, ordered his security chief to withdraw all his subordinates from the Palace.

Everything went like a clock. Stalin was given a red-carpet welcome by the Shah in his Palace and both expressed satisfaction with the historical meeting. The meeting lasted about half an hour and at the end, they posed to cameramen for memorial photographs. Although Mohammad Reza always remembered Stalin's friendly move, the meeting did not bring an early withdrawal of Soviet troops from Iran.

Sepehr gradually became friendly to me. One day, he explicitly told me, "I am entitled to have links with the Soviets but since long time ago I have been in touch with the British. I have some friends in the Soviet Embassy and Britons are happy with that. In fact I am a contact between the two embassies".

Sepehr had a friend called Sheikh Hussein Lankarani. He usually preached for the people. Once, Sepehr took me to Lankarani's house for a courtesy meeting. Lankarani welcomed me and said it was good to meet him at convenient moments. His brother who was a Tudehi was living with him but he did not want him to show up before me.

Gradually, Sepehr and Lankarani came to meet Mohammad Reza to discuss political issues and also improve their personal image. Lankarani later in a bid to weaken Qavam urged Mohammad Reza to recommend that Sepehr be included in Qavam's cabinet. He anticipated that Sepehr would be able to remove Qavam from power for once and all. Mohammad Reza accepted the proposal and Sepehr was introduced as minister but failed to replace Qavam because the latter in a pre-emptive gesture fired Sepehr and sent him into exile to Kashan in central Iran.

ESTABLISHMENT OF KAYHAN NEWSPAPER

Mostafa Mesbahzadeh, a celver but dishonest and pro-British, had a Ph.D. in law from Paris University. His father was a servant of Ebrahim Qavam Shirazi. Qavam possessed about 400 pieces of land in Fars province and distributed them among his five servants and Mesbahzadeh was inherited a share. He had enough wealth to send his son to Paris to study there in addition to his family expenses. Around 1941, Mesbahzadeh several times approached me and solicited me to help him set up a newspaper.

"Masoudi, director-in-charge of Ettela'at newspaper, is a businessman and not a journalist. He advertises for whoever pays him and his newspaper is more or less similar to an advertisement publication. Now, there is a vacuum for a newspaper to fill the gap and meet the social and political requirements of the people. A number of my friends who no longer wish to write for Ettela'at and I are willing to set up a newspaper. I will be grateful if you help in accomplishment of our aims," he requested politely but vigorously.

I informed the Shah of Mesbahzadeh's request. Mohammad Reza was not satisfied with Ettela'at's Masoudi. Masoudi had enjoyed the support of Reza Shah but was disliked by Mohammad Reza because of his criticism of the Shah. The Shah agreed and ordered to take him to his palace for a meeting. Soon, we held a trilateral meeting and Mesbahzadeh repeated his reasons for setting up a newspaper. Then, he requested 200,000 tumans. The Shah drew a cheque and asked for a receipt. Mesbahzadeh said he could not give a receipt but agreed to register the newspaper and give the shares to the Shah. He set up the "Kayhan" newspaper and later gave the registered shares to me to be passed on to the Shah. I handed it over to the Shah but he returned it to me and said, "this is yours". I kept it in my house in Shahnaz alley.

About nine months later, the first issue of Kayhan newspaper came out on 24 May 1942. Mesbahzadeh gradually imported modern printing machines and surpassed Ettela'at. Rivalries between the two newspapers were in the shape of open hostilities.

Later, Mesbahzadeh who was not satisfied with only being in charge of a newspaper again requested me to help him be elected to the Majlis. I informed the Shah of his new request who favoured Mesbahzadeh's candidacy and told me to order the city's military commander to propagate for him but the British had already nominated Abdullah Galehdari as their favourite and therefore Mesbahzadeh failed to find his way to the Majlis. With Shah's recommendations, he was elected in the next parliamentary elections.

Mesbahzadeh soon became a powerful and wealthy man and did not pay anything for share interests. He married the daughter of the wealthy Jafar Ettehadieh who owned "Iran Javan" club. Since then, he directly called on the Shah and from time to time paid courtesy calls on me.

SETTING UP 'JAVIDAN GUARD'

Since he had himself crowned as Reza Shah Pahlavi in April 1926 until his abdication on September 16, 1941, Reza Shah had employed an army infantry Company to protect his family. At the time, a Company included three platoons and each platoon comprised 30 soldiers.

The responsibility to guard governmental offices in Tehran was with the two rival Divisions based in the capital. Since within the army regular replacements used to take place, the Company protecting Shah's family was changed every month with another one from the rival Division.

After the throne passed to the twenty-two-year-old Mohammad Reza, Captain Jafar Shafaqat and Captain Bayandur, commanders of the rival companies tried to win the new Shah's support to have their own Company stationed permanently in the Royal Palace. The Shah agreed to a rotating responsibility. Bayandur's Company remained in the palace for a time and later was replaced by that of Shafaqat. Then, a Second-Colonel called Mahvi was appointed in charge of the guards who, after consultations with the Shah, delegated the responsibility of protecting Shah's family to three Companies on a rotating basis. The brigade no longer received orders from its Division but was run directly by the Shah.

Later, Mahvi expanded the brigade into a regiment which included three brigades plus a tank Company. A huge budget was spent to meet the regiment's requirements.

I was a major when after a few months the Shah ordered me to form a new "special guard" to protect his personal palace. He insisted to employ physically strong and extremely tall soldiers for that purpose. The elite troops had to undergo special training courses including explosive sabotage and karate. I devoted all my energy to carefully selected members of the elite guard. I appointed Abbass Qarabaqi whom I had known for years my deputy. We picked up two distinguished officers after carefully studying their past records. We decided to employ 300 personnel on a voluntary basis. All of them had to undertake security clearance procedures. We intentionally selected soldiers with a degree of less than B Level or secondary school from remote villages so that they did not pose any threat to the Shah. Qarabai travelled to every corner of the country to select the eligible soldiers. They undertook adequate intensive trainings and were given special uniforms of ancient Persia to make them distinguished from the rest of the guards. They were retired after 30 years.

Within nine months, the elite guard was ready to be reviewed by the Shah. The Shah reviewed the honour guard which was named "Javidan Guard". He paused for a moment as he passed every soldier. He was very happy and appreciated Qarabaqi for his excellent selection of physically strong people. Javidan Guard was used to welcome foreign head of states during their visits to Iran.

The Shah appointed Qarabaqi to run the guard and told me to remain his close advisor.

"You are my confident. It is not appropriate for you to remain the guard's commander", he said.

Gradually, both the Javidan Guard and other units protecting Shah's family expanded reaching over 700 people each which needed a heavy budget from the army.

I was only the founder of the guard but I had no role in expanding it. Commanders of the guard were my friends and I was well informed of the affairs within the guard.

Despite all these precautionary measures, the Shah was targeted several times but escaped death. When the military wing of the Tudeh Party was discovered it was revealed that two top officers had penetrated into the guard. Of course I was not to be blamed since the army's counter-intelligence had confirmed their eligibility. Anyhow, everything vanished and the Shah succumbed to people's will and was forced to leave the country after about three decades of rule. This is an aspect of the Iranian revolution and a manifestation of people's power which I should admit.

DEPENDENT PARTIES TO THE COURT

Another attempt by Mohammad Reza to strengthen his position and monopolize power was setting up parties and paramilitary groups which later formed the basis of his government.

One of the parties was "SOMKA", a Persian acronym of the national socialist workers of Iran, set up by Davood Monshizadeh[7] and financed by Mohammad Reza himself. Daryush Homayun was also a member of the party.

Encountering the opponents of Mohammad Reza was the strategy of the party. Its members were honoured to be described as the "Shah's worshippers".

Monshizadeh was very interested in Hitler and was trying to make his appearance like him. The party's descipline, uniform, salute were like Nazis, even the emblem of the party. Of course, the similarity was just in shape and there was no political link between the party and the Nazis. The majority of the party members were under 20 who showed up in the capital's streets in their military uniforms attacking Shah's critics. The party gradually lost ground after the defeat of Nazis in Germany.

Another party created by Brigadier General Hassan Arfa was "Arya" party which absorbed some members of the defunct "SOMKA". The party had a military wing with Brigadier General Deyhami being in charge and Hassan Akhavi being the brain of the wing. Colonel Hussein Manuchehri who later changed his name into Bahram Aryana with pro-Nazi tendencies, Aminzadeh, Yahyai and Mahmoud Eram were among its distinguished members. Though members of the party were numbered, all of them held high posts. The aim of the party was to assume key posts. Arfa, a rival of Razmara, successfully became chief of the joint staff of the army three times.

Controlling the party was very easy since those who joined the party were just trying to keep their jobs or promote their positions. One of the most important principles of the party was staunch opposition to Communism and all members of the party were pro-British. Later, some of them adopted pro-U.S. tendencies.

Among the party members were some who had already been arrested and jailed by British forces when they were in Iran. They had been jailed on charges of supporting Hitler's Germany but later after the withdrawal of foreign troops from Iran it became clear that many of them were pro-British.

"In 1958 the Milliyun (Nationalist) Party, led by Dr. Manuchehr Eqbal and the Mardom (People's) Party, led by Assadollah Alam had been formed of people and groups trusted by the regime... In December 1963, the rising young politician Hassan Ali Mansur supported by the Shah also formed the Iran Novin Party. Appointed Prime Minister in March 1964, he was fatally shot in January 1965 by a religious fanatic. The attempted assassination of the Shah in April of the same year showed how fragile were the foundations of internal stability. The Shah appointed Amir Abbass Hoveida to succeed as Prime Minister. A founder member of the Iran Novin Party, he was elected as its Secretary-General in 1974. For a decade the Iran Novin dominated party politics. At no time has the Mardum party been able to function as a viable alternate party. In the 1967 Majlis it held only 29 seats as against 180 for Iran Novin. In March 1975, the Shah announced that parties would merge into the Iran Resurgence Party (Rashtakhiz) for the purpose of mobilizing the country's human resources with Prime Minister as Secretary General."[8]

TUDEH PARTY AND THE ARMY

Lots of stories have been cited about the activities of the Tudeh Party in the army after 1941. Here, I suffice to explain the measures taken by the government to curb the activities of the party:

1. The Communist Party which had been suppressed by Reza Shah resumed political activities under the name of Tudeh Party after Reza Shah's abdication on 16 September 1941. So long as the Red Army remained in Iran, the Tudeh Party flourished but neither the army's counter-intelligence nor the police attempted to discover its underground networks. Of course, unofficial military organs under Major General Arfa tried to identify Tudeh Party members and obstruct their way to assume key military posts as recommended by the British embassy.
2. After the withdrawal of Soviet troops from northern Iran and the subsequent collapse of the Pishevai autonomous government, not only efforts were not intensified to uproot the party but also the military counter-intelligence stopped campaign against Tudehis.
3. After a suspected Tudeh member attempted to assassinate the Shah on 4 February 1949, the army's intelligence started

an all-out campaign against Tudehis both within the army and the police. Many observers believed the attempt on the Shah's life had been only part of a more widespread left-wing plan to take over the government.

4. After Mossaddiq became Prime Minister, members of the party dramatically increased causing fears in Washington and London that Iran could slip under Communist control. The Shah determined to rule as well as reign with a thoroughly restructured national army as his base. In the course of rooting out pockets of opposition the scale of Tudeh infiltration was discovered. Over 500 members had penetrated the army officer corps.
5. After the 16 August 1953 coup sentences of death or imprisonment were passed on numerous Tudeh members. 26 of them were executed and the rest imprisoned but gradually were pardoned or their sentences were commuted.
6. Americans, to ensure that Communists had no chance to gain power in Iran, created the counter-intelligence department in the army. Attempts to fight anti-Shah forces in the army were stepped up. All those with anti-Shah records were retired and suspicious elements were denied top posts. The counter-intelligence, however, was not able to effectively deal with the opposition.
7. SAVAK (the Farsi-language acronym for National Security and Information organization) was established in 1956 and was given wide latitude to identify and intimidate political enemies of the Shah especially the Tudeh members. Ever since, the army's counter-intelligence was just covering the army personnel and SAVAK was responsible for the civilians.

AZERBAIJAN EVENTS

The Allies had promised that foreign troops would be withdrawn after the war. The Tripartite Treaty specified the date as six months after the close of the war. The U.S. withdrew its troops from Iran by December 1945 and the British followed on March 1946; both were within the time fixed by treaty obligations but Russia tightened her hold in her zone and maintained six to eight of her Divisions in Iran's East Azerbaijan Province.

In the immediate post-war years, Mohammad Reza turned decisively to the United States and Britain for assistance in seeking the withdrawal of Soviet troops from northern Iran. Neither the requests by the Iranian government nor the diplomatic pressure applied by the United States and Britain to their wartime ally had been effective but Shah's words indicated that he had the full support of both Washington and London in his political campaign against Moscow.

With unequivocal American and British support, Iran took her grievances concerning the state of affairs in Azerbaijan Province and the alarming increase and disposition of Russian military forces to the newly created United Nations Security Council in 1946. It was the first complaint ever submitted to the council. The Shah assigned Hussein Ala to raise the issue at the United Nations. Ala who had already served as Court Minister and Prime Minister was fluent in French and excellent in speaking.

Newspaper reports suggested that Ala was successful in his mission but it were the Americans who in secret worked against the accomplishment of Soviet aims. This went on to the extent that the U.S. envoy to the United Nations issued an ultimatum to the Soviet leaders and warned that if they refused to withdraw their troops from Iran within the designated period, they should expect a Third World War and cautioned that the U.S. would be the victor since it remained safe during the Second World War. The U.S. stance was crucial in securing the withdrawal of Soviet troops which was completed by May of that year.

America's active support of Iran and the collapse of the Soviet puppet government persuaded the Shah to turn to the United States. Britain's weakness, culminating in her departure from India in 1947, made a profound impression and that was too effective in leaning towards Washington. Later during his visit to America, he thanked American leaders for their support to Iran in its fight against the Soviet Union. Though it were the British who put him on the throne, he considered the Americans as savior of Azerbaijan.

"These Americans are so powerful. Our reliance on them really helped us take our territory back from the Soviets", once the Shah told me in a private talk.

He also admitted this in his meeting with President Roosevelt when he said, "I owe my throne to God, my people, my army and to you!"

Azerbaijan events were a beginning for Mohammad Reza to incline towards a superior power, the United States. Of course, the Shah, at the same time, kept his cordial relations with Britain.

In the early 1946, Soviet troops pulled out of Iran but kept their puppet government in the province. In 1945, Jafar Pishevari who had spent many years in the Soviet Union had formed the Firqah-i-Dimukrat. He and his party appealed in proclaiming the Azerbaijan separatist movement in the autumn of 1945. Pishevari, with the blessings of Moscow, established his autonomous republic with the capital Tabriz on December 12, 1945. Gholam Yahya Danesheian was in charge of its army.

In January, Qavam al-Saltana had become Prime Minister. Qavam adopted a reconciliatory stance towards the Firqah-i-Dimukrat. To him, there was nothing wrong with granting autonomy to the opponents. He appointed Salam-ol-llah Javid as Governor General. Javid was a sympathizer of the Firqah-i-Dimukrat but at least in appearance showed to be loyal to the central government in Tehran.

> "During a visit to Moscow, Qavamal-Saltana, by a series of concessions (interpreted by many observers as having gone too far) in direct negotiations with Russia, had agreed to the formation of a Soviet-Iranian oil company with exclusive rights in northern Iran. The Soviets to have 51 per cent of the stock, and to the withdrawal by the Iranian delegate of the complaint against Russia at the United Nations. Qavam also understood the importance the Russian Government attached to having the Persian Government so reconstituted that it would take a more sympathetic and flexible attitude towards Russian interests including the autonomous Republic of Azerbaijan but he bided his time... Elections for the 15th Majlis should have been held in March. The acute instability and preoccupation with Azerbaijan separatism and Russian demands meant that no elections were held until December. Becuase of the atmosphere which had prevailed throughout the year - with Tudeh-inspired demonstrations in Tehran followed by Tudeh-fomented riots and strikes at Abadan in addition to a Soviet-oriented government in Azerbaijan - predictions were rife that a left-wing government would be returned. This did not happen. Iranian troops were sent to various parts of the country to preserve order during the

elections. They were welcomed in Azerbaijan with minimal resistance to find the rebel government discredited and its leadership gone. The American ambassador to Moscow wrote:

'Collapse of Azerbaijan house of cards was a major victory for UN - and for a firm policy toward USSR. It must not be thought, however, that Kremlin will resign itself to this humiliating reverse. It will continue to manoeuvre not only for oil concessions but also for political and strategic ascendancy in Iran.'

Disorder continued in Tehran and was widespread throughout much of the country. One general cause of discontent was the oil agreement with Russia. The Shah disliked both it and Qavam. The Soviet Government having, as they thought, traded troop withdrawal for oil, pressed strenuously for the development of their concession. Simultaneously, opposition to it grew in Iran. Qavam had signed an oil agreement which was supposed to come before the Majlis on or before October 24, 1946. That he had signed it at all provoked criticism since such power belonged to the Majlis but he may have thought the Majlis could not consider the agreement within the time limit because of delays in holding elections. The temper of the Majlis was violently hostile to the oil agreement. On October 22, 1947, by a nearly unanimous vote (only two exceptions), the Majlis rejected the proposed Irano-Soviet venture."[9]

Qavam was the brother of Vothoq-ol-Dowleh who signed the 1919 Convention on the basis of which Iran was divided into northern and southern domination zones between Russia and Britain with the central zone remaining neutral. Now is it imaginable that Qavam signed the agreement without consultations with the British?

Mohammad Reza whose control over the country was spreading, went into quarrel with Qavam over Azerbaijan policy. Once I was in Shah's private room when he engaged in a telephone dispute with Qavam. First I picked up the receiver when the telephone rang. Qavam wanted to talk to the Shah. "No, I'll never agree to this", the Shah repeated several times. After their conversation, the Shah said Qavam wanted him to approve promotion of those officers who had been fighting along with Pishevari against the state.

With unequivocal American and British support, Iranian armed forces with the capacity of two Divisions were sent to Azerbaijan to restore order in the northwestern province. Brigadier-General Pourhashemi and Brigadier-General Zarabi were commanders of the two Divisions. Pourhashemi was a native of Tabriz who enjoyed popularity there and Zarabi was a native of Kashan. When the army started moving towards Tabriz, the Shah, Razmara who at the time was chief of staff of the army and I reviewed them by helicopter and Razmara explained his plan with a map.

Supporters of Pishevari had destroyed a main bridge which was the only supply route for the army to pass through the Qaflan range of mountains near Mianeh city but that did not spoil the operation.

On December 13, 1946, Mohammad Reza ordered me to fly to Tabriz and study the situation. I was carrying some five million tumans requested by Brigadier-General Pourhashemi. Upon landing at the Tabriz airport, I saw some buildings burning. A truck took me to the city. Iranian troops had seized the province with minimal resistance and had found the rebel government discredited and its leadership gone. People of all walks of life had poured into the streets almost all of them with a gun in their hand. They chanted slogans in support of the Iranian army. I saw some 3,000 bodies littered in the streets killed by the people. Of course, I was told that some of the killings had been personally-motivated.

I directly went to the municipality's building which was the army's headquarters. I handed over the money to Pourhashemi. He ordered his guard commander to accompany a local officer to show me the city. He was a native of Tabriz and claimed that he knew a majority of the member factions operating in Tabriz. He took me to prisons and ammunition depots, most of which had been seized by government troops. Upon return to Tehran, I briefed the Shah on the outcome of my trip.

The following year, Mohammad Reza declared December 12 as "Azerbaijan's Liberation Day" and ordered the army and governmental departments to celebrate the occasion.

Later, the Shah triumphantly visited the northern province and then Kurdestan. Unlike his Azerbaijan tour, the Shah was not welcomed in Kurdestan because of execution of Qazi Mohammad.

MOHAMMAD REZA'S SECRET MEETINGS

One of my notable memories which I have always kept in mind was Shah's secret meetings with influential and political figures. I was playing the role of intermediary.

The first time I came to know about it when the Shah ordered me to invite Dr. Sanjabi to the Court so that nobody learns of his presence. I called on Sanjabi and accompanied him to the Royal Court in the darkness of the night. They talked for about two hours privately. Then I was told to take Sanjabi back home.

As far as I can remember, I accompanied five or six other notables to their secret meetings with the Shah. Among them was Fereidyun Keshavarz, a top member of the Tudeh Party. I was not allowed to attend the meetings but it seemed the meetings were held in an atmosphere of trust and friendship. The second time he met the Shah, two others accompanied him. I spotted one of them to be Dr. Morteza Yazdi, another prominent member of the Tudeh Party. They met several times.

Once, Keshavarz praised the Shah as an educated and cultivated man. He said Shah's interests laid in his cooperation with the Tudeh Party and emphasized that he would reap the benefit of his cooperation later.

All the meetings took place in the Special Palace and usually lasted two hours. All the meetings were held in camera. I took, as first ordered, the guests back to their home without letting others learn of their presence in the Court. Although he had become very close to me, Keshavarz refused to comment on his meetings with the Shah. I am sure he perceived that the Shah would inform me of what he wanted me to know. The Shah also did not tell anything about his meetings with the notables to me.

Within a few months, Keshavarz, Yazdi and one of their fellow Tudeh members named Eskandari joined Qavam's cabinet and the meetings ceased. Yazdi, a physician, was arrested and convicted after August 19, 1953 coup but was pardoned by the Shah after a short period of detention and resumed his political activities.

HAJIR ASSASSINATION AND FADAEYAN-E-ESLAM

Hajir was one of the reliable agents of the British. His father lacked any political record but he was engaged in political activities since his younghood. He became Prime Minister for several times after 1941 and following the collapse of the Qavam cabinet in 1948, he again was accorded premiership. People's opposition to his government forced him to leave the cabinet. He was appointed Court Minister and was assassinated at this post by Fadaeyan-e-Eslam group.

When the news of Hajir's assassination reached the Shah, he and a number of notables were on picnic in Farahabad. It was a Friday. I was also there. In the afternoon, Hajir's assassination was announced and it loomed the political circles. We rushed to the army's hospital No. 2 where Hajir had already been taken for treatment. Shah entered the room and I followed him. Hajir looked in a relatively good condition. His doctor, Colonel Latifi, a liar and an unreliable person, said Hajir was in good health and would be discharged within a few days. Five or six hours later, we were informed that Hajir had succumbed to his wounds. Rumours immediately spread in the capital pointing to Razmara as the man behind the assassination.

At the time, Razmara was seriously engaged in political activities striving to gain a top post. As I said before, he was fond of power and was very intelligent.

Dismayed with the charges and stressing he was innocent, Razmara requested the Shah to appoint a reliable person to investigate the assassination. The Shah ordered me to scrutinize the case. The assassin Seyed Hussein Imami had already been arrested and tossed into jail. First, I got to the prison and asked the warden to directly take me to the assassin's cell.

A physically strong man, he was bidding the beads of a rosary and praying. He stood towards kiblah, prayer direction, and started saying a lengthy prayer. I could not understand why he prolonged his prayer. I sat on a chair in the corner of his cell waiting for him to finish his prayers. He seemed to be ignoring me. When he finished his prayer, he sat on a wooden bed and took his rosary again and started bidding. Suddenly he stopped and wanted to know what I wanted. I asked him to tell who had ordered the assassination. I promised him freedom if he told me the truth. He said he had done his religious obligation and was ready to welcome any judgement or punishment, though he was sure that he would be executed.

I persistently asked him if Razmara was behind the assassination.

He rebuffed and said that it was quite nonsense for him to carry out the order of Razmara. The next day, he repeated what he had told me the day before. My investigations proved that Razmara was innocent.

When I was on my way to report my findings to the Shah, Razmara approached me, anxious to know what the assassin had confessed. I declared that the assassin had denied any link with him. As ordered, I informed the Shah of my findings. The assassin was put on trial and then hanged.

TRIP TO BRITAIN AND U.S.

One of my interesting memories of this period was the trip to Britain, France, Switzerland and Italy of the Shah in July 1948. I was accompanying the Shah as his aid-de-camp and so was Court Minister Jam.

Shah's trip to Britain, the fifth time that a ruler of Iran had done so, was at the invitation of the then George VI, father of the present Queen Elizabeth. We were accommodated with separate rooms at the Bukingham Palace but Shah's entourage were not allowed to leave residence without prior permission from the British authorities.

The trip to London was just a formality and quite different from Shah's next trip to the U.S. where he received a red carpet welcome by the then President Truman. Again I accompanied the Shah in his 1950 visit to the U.S. Richard Nixon was holding the post of vice-president. The Iranian government had continued to be strongly oriented to the U.S. and Shah's cordial reception and favourable press pointed to close relations. Many banquets were given in his honour, one of them an evening banquet arranged by the U.S. Chief of Joint Staff of the armed forces, General Bradly.[10] Many high-ranking American military officials as well as Iranians attended the banquet, all in military uniforms.

During the banquet, General Bradly approached me and after some hesitation said he wanted me to pass a message to the Shah. He said the U.S. administration was very interested in the Shah and did not like to get him offended. The Shah, he said, has asked the U.S. to intervene and come to Iran's aid should the Soviets invade Iran from the north. He said the Soviets could occupy Iran in a short period of time because of their geographical proximity with Iran and the U.S. could not deploy any forces in less than fifteen days in Iran's southern ports. He begged me to inform the Shah of the U.S. government's negative response in a way he is not offended. The day after, a joint commission was scheduled to be held at the Pentagon and if the Shah was aware of the U.S. stance, the outcome of the talks would be very fruitful.

I passed the message to the Shah and he accepted the American view but insisted on American military assistance to Iran in order to deter any possible foreign aggression.

Nixon found the Shah prepared to cooperate with U.S. in opposing Soviet ambitions in the region and he was intrigued at the prospect of a close strategic relationship between the two countries.

Military assistance to the tune of $ 829 million were provided between 1950 and 1963. Iran had appeared militarily vulnerable which might easily slip into the Communist orbit. To prevent this happening was the consideration to which all else was subordinate.

RAZMARA AND THE SHAH

General Ali Razmara succeeded Ali Mansur as Prime Minister on June 26, 1950 when efforts had already reached its climax to nationalize the oil industry. Immediately after taking office, Razmara, an opponent to nationalization of oil, adopted a policy of detente with Moscow. This was when the Russians were still continuing to broadcast their provocative anti-Iran radio programmes. The Tudeh Party was active, but was underground.

Razmara was known as an educated officer in the army. He was the author of 12 books called "Iran's Military Geography". A man thirsty for power, there was nothing impossible for him and he relied on his intelligence and bravery in accomplishing his ends. Although he enjoyed a sharp memory, he lacked a good political understanding of Iran and the world. He did not stick to logic and mostly preferred to do whatever was impossible for others. He, however, was arrogant and his leniency towards the Shah was just to get him promotion and quickly achieve his objectives. Any position less than head of state was not acceptable to him.

The political upheavals created after the Allied occupation of Iran provided an excellent opportunity for Razmara to launch his manoeuvres and strive for his long-awaited post. At the beginning,

Chief of the Joint Staff of the armed forces General Arfa was his staunch rival. The political developments gradually further stabilized his position. He was in constant touch with foreign diplomatic missions in Tehran. His links with foreign ambassadors especially the British and American representatives was not something secret and he publicly invited ambassadors to his home.

"Razmara, 49, was a graduate of St. Cyr Military Academy, and had played a leading role in the forcible suppression of the Pishevari regime in Azerbaijan. He had made little secret of wanting the top job, though it was understood that 'the Shah intends, if he can, to keep him on the leash.' Razmara faced a situation of extreme difficulty. In 1948 negotiations had begun between the Government and the AIOC for a Supplemental Agreement to raise the terms arranged between the Company and Reza Shah in 1933, by which the company paid the Iranian government a flat rate of 4 million pounds a year, raising it with the rise in production to 16 million pounds in 1950. The new Supplemental Agreement, which would have substantially increased the benefits accruing to the Government, was signed in July 1949 and immediately went to the Majlis for approval. But the Majlis was dissolved before the agreement could be approved, or even debated, and in June 1950 it was passed for examination to a parliamentary sub-committee of eighteen members, whose chairman was Mossaddiq.

Razmara wanted to see the agreement implemented, but the mounting fevour of nationalism and religion, which was concentrating its energies on the demand for the nationalization of oil and had found in Mossaddiq a charismatic spokesman, was too strong for him. He had tried to mollify the opposition by asking the Shah to describe him, in the decree announcing his appointment as Prime Minister, not as General Razmara but as Haji Ali Razmara. He was not in fact a haji in the usual sense of the term - someone who has made the pilgrimage to mecca - but in Iran anyone born on the first day of the islamic year (as Razmara was) can be called Haji as a sort of courtesy title. So it was as Haji Ali, and in a civilian suit, not in uniform, that Razmara presented himself to the Majlis. He was met with a storm of abuse from Mossaddiq:' You're not a haji! Why try to hookwink us? You're a General - a fox dressed up as a cat! Go back to the person who sent you!' There was a terrific row, but in the end the Majlis approved Razmara's appointment."[11]

Although he did not support Communism, he had friendly relations with the top members of the Tudeh Party. Before being appointed Prime Minister he had made every effort to grab the post but there was an obstacle in his way, Hajir, an intelligent politician and an obvious agent of the British. That is why the assassination of Hajir was attributed to Razmara. I was assigned to investigate the abortive coup. All-out investigations proved that Razmara had no hand in the assassination attempt. The February 1949 assassination attempt against the Shah who escaped with minor injuries was also attributed to him. At the time of the assassination attempt, he was the Chief of the Joint Staff of the armed forces. There were some rough evidences indicating his involvement in the assassination attempt.

I was in the Shah's Palace with Proun on February 4, 1949 when the news of the assassination reached me that day. The Shah had gone to the Law Faculty of the Tehran University to attend a ceremony. Javidan Guard security officers were escorting the Shah. That day, Major-General Daftari, a confident of Razmara, was the Shah's guard chief. As the Shah attempted to go up the steps leading to the Law Faculty, an armed assailant some twenty meters away from the Shah fired five shots at the Shah. Mohammad Reza made acrobatic movements to escape the bullets but all the five hit him. Shah's men had taken refuge behind the trees. The assassin went out of shots. Then the gaurds, on Daftari's order, instead of arresting him barraged him with bullets. Daftari himself also fired a shot at the assassin's head.

Proun and I immediately rushed to the army's hospital No. 1 where the Shah had been taken for treatment of his wounds. Numerous officials, mostly military figures, were in the hospital to express sympathy with their leader and pray for his survival. The Shah's doctor, Brigadier-General Najafabadi, was dressing his wounds when we entered the room. Najafabadi said there was no need for surgery. Within a few hours, the Shah was discharged from the hospital. Proun and I were astonished with the attempt on Mohammd Reza's life. We did not leave him alone and even slept beside his bed in the Palace. Najafabadi visited his patient every two hours.

The assassination was blamed on Ayatollah Kashani and the Tudeh Party but fingers of suspicion were also pointed to Razmara. The Shah asked Razmara why he did not accompany him during the ceremony in the Tehran University.

"When Your Majesty embark on a visit, I am committed to take care of security matters and issue adequate orders to my subordinates", he replied.

"This time they did not carry out your orders!", was the Shah's last words to him.

However, there were rumours about the likelihood of Razmara's involvement in the assassination attempt and his connections with the Tudeh Party. Chief of the army's intelligence Mobser found a collection of Razmara's memoirs in his house after the latter's assassination. Mobser did not give me the notebook nor disclosed the contents of the memoirs. He said he had handed over the notebook to the Shah. I didn't ask the Shah about the memoirs but later he told me "what a dangerous man Razmara was". That convinced persuaded me that Razmara in a way had been connected with the attempt on Shah's life.[12]

Undoubtedly, Razmara would have become the undisputable head of state if the assassination had succeeded. On March 1951 on their way to a mosque to attend a funeral service, Razmara and Assadollah Alam were shot by a member of Fadaeyan-e-Islam.

NATIONALIZATION OF OIL

I heard of the first attempts aimed at nationalizing the oil industry by Zanganeh in 1947. Zanganeh was a Majlis deputy from Kermanshah and belonged to a wealthy and influential family. He was married to a very attractive woman. His family were advocates of the British policies and Zanganeh had close connections with the top authorities at the Court. He was selected Majlis deputy for several terms and I was one of his recommenders.

My good opinion of Zanganeh cemented our relations. He also enjoyed good links with the British diplomats in Tehran and was considered a reliable British agent. The British were gathering information about western provinces, especially Kermanshah through Zanganeh.

One day, Zanganeh in a private talk with me said that Americans were backing nationalization of Iran's oil industry and were hatching some conspiracies in that respect.

Throughout 1949 and 1950, Mossaddiq and his National Front had fostered anti-foreign feelings which they turned against the oil agreement. By the end of 1950, Mossaddiq felt his position strong enough to denounce the oil concession. He and the National Front began to talk openly of nationalizing the oil industry.

> "Mossaddiq represented the political wing of the nationalist movement. The religious wing was led by Ayatollah Abdul Qasm Kashani, who had been exiled to Lebanon by Reza Shah but was allowed back after the war."[13]

Mass demonstrations, organized mainly by Ayatollah Kashani and the National Front, became commonplace. The front, to further this objective, once staged a sit-in protest in front of Marmar Palace. There were many parliamentarians and a large group of about 1,000 front supporters led by Mossaddiq. For me and those who were aware of demonstrator's characters was quite clear that no such gathering was possible if Americans were not behind the issue. Mossaddiq was living next to Marmar Palace. He used to come in front of the Palace every day by walking. The mob took him over their hands cheering and crying out 'hurrah' in appraisal.

One day, the demonstrators remained in the street up to the evening. Mohammad Reza asked me to see what the demonstrators were demanding and talk to their leader. I talked to Mossaddiq to see what he and his supporters were protesting for. He requested to allow demonstrators to stage their sit-in inside the Palace and warned that they would sleep at the junction in the street if they were denied entry. I informed the Shah of Mossaddiq's request and the Shah agreed. He ordered his Court Minister Hajir to allow them in. Teaman of the Palace was assigned to entertain them. Mossaddiq remained there during the night. The next day he announced his Front's determination to nationalize the oil industry during a meeting with the Shah.

> "By March 1950, Mossaddiq had made it absolutely clear that it would be the policy of the National Front to nationalize the oil industry. Mossaddiq had achieved a position of considerable influence in oil affairs as Chairman of the Majlis special committee on the Supplemental Agreement.

By the end of 1950 Mossaddiq felt his position strong enough to denounce the Supplemental Agreement openly in one of Tehran's leading newspapers. The Government answered promptly, but the National Front began to talk openly of nationalizing the oil industry. On 25 November the oil committee passed a resolution stating that the bill did not adequately safeguard the nation's interests. This resolution was referred to the Majlis for debate. Before the debate Kashani, who was specifically and ferociously anti-British as well as anti-foreign, issued a manifesto advocating nationalization. He organized public demonstrations to further this objective. As Professor Lambton has observed: 'it was not until the movement was interpreted by the religious classes in terms of Islam that it received wide support...'

On March 8, the oil committee, spurred on by Mossaddiq, adopted a resolution which affirmed nationalization of oil industry in principle and extended for two months the time for the committee to determine how to execute it.

Large demonstrations were taking place in Tehran. They were organized by several groups which were offshoots of both Kashani's organization and the National Front. They included the Muslim Fellowship, the Iran Party, the Society of Campaigners for the Nationalization of the Oil Industry, the Committee of Youth, the Merchants and Bazaar Workers Guild, and the Organization of Student and Militant Youth...

On December 2 Mossaddiq put forward a bill with 'triple urgency' which provided that:

In respect of oil concessions no Prime Minister, Acting Ministers or Under Secretaries have the right to enter into conversations having official or legal effect with any official or unofficial representative of neighbouring Governments, or other Governments, or with representatives of oil companies or other persons; nor have they the right to sign any agreement connected with oil.

Offenders would be severely punished. This was passed by the Majlis with great speed."[14]

Razmara who became Prime Minister in June 1950 and attempted to reach a detente with Russia decided to withdraw the oil bill already presented to the Majlis for debate. This was done on 26 December by his Finance Minister, Abolqasem Foruhar who delivered a speech in the Majlis stressing against nationalization. "How a country which is not able to produce a shovel can it administer a nationalized oil?" was part of his speech against nationalization.

> "The Majlis, in an emotional state, applied a unanimous vote of censure to Foruhar's speech by a motion of 'triple urgency' on January 4. He resigned shortly thereafter."[15]

After Razmara's assassination, the Shah appointed Hussein Ala to the post of Prime Minister. He was succeeded by Mossaddiq, who was better known as the leader of 'oil nationalization movement', on March 29, 1951.

On April 26, 1951, the oil committee had agreed upon a resolution for submission to the Majlis. This came to be known as the nine point law which was passed by the Majlis on the 28th, the Senate on the 29th and received royal assent on May 1.

Mossaddiq's premiership brought a period of difficulty for Mohammad Reza. Mossaddiq was assuming more and more power to himself at the expense of the Shah and this ran against Mohammad Reza's desires who saw Mossaddiq as the main obstacle in the way of his taking decisive action.

> "When, in the summer, Mossaddiq asked for wider powers he encountered stiff opposition in the Majlis. He resigned when the Shah refused to make him Minister of War. Qavam al-Saltana succeeded him, but only for five bloody and chaotic days from July 17 to 21. Then the Majlis gave Mossaddiq the powers he had requested earlier, and subsequently passed bills for the prosecution of Qavam and for the release from prison of Razmara's assassin... Throughout 1953 Iran continued without oil revenues and in a state of political turbulence. Differences between the Shah and Mossaddiq in February foreshadowed the separation which would come in August. In the Majlis there was, on occasion, fighting. In the course of debates over curbing the Shah's powers, Kashani broke with Mossaddiq and he was succeeded as President of the Majlis by Dr. Abdullah Muazzami, a Mossaddiq supporter. Mossaddiq's position became ever more precarious. He had promised the millennium when

nationalization was complete and the British driven out. The millennium had not come and the world had survived without Iranian oil. He had threatened the United States with a Communist Iran unless her policies received wholehearted support and substantial financial backing. Eisenhower's cold response which became known in July shattered that illusion."[16]

Once more, Mossaddiq met the Shah to be sworn in as Prime Minister. To meet the formalities, he met the Shah a few times at the first month but later stopped meeting him on the ground that he was sick. Ever since, Court Minister Hussein Ala met Mossaddiq who usually carried an attache case full of letters and documents. Any matter, even issues related to the army, had to first meet Mossaddiq's approval and then was handed over to the Shah for signature just to meet the formalities.

The process of governmental affairs annoyed the Shah to the extent that he was openly complaining even in front of his servants that such a way of rule was nonsense. Mossaddiq, in international circles, was known as Iran's most powerful man and this was totally unacceptable to the Shah. To the best of my knowledge, he held many meetings with U.S. ambassador to Tehran. Indeed, he had deprived the Shah of all his powers and controlled the armed forces. Shah's only role was just to sign letters after approval by Mossaddiq.

In 1952 with Shah's permission, I together with Fakhr Moddarress decided to fly to Paris to study law at the doctorate level. Mossaddiq had also agreed to my trip. As I reached the Tehran airport I understood I had been banned by Mossaddiq to leave the country. I informed the Shah of the matter at once. Shah ordered Court Minister Ala to inquire about Mossaddiq's decision to see why, despite his own earlier approval, he was refusing to allow the two to travel to France for study. Mossaddiq made no comments. Therefore, I rushed to see Defence Minister Reyahi. He got embarrassed and immediately called on Mossaddiq to inquire the matter. After some fifteen minutes, he returned from the meeting and told me I could leave for Paris immediately. He also said that Mossaddiq was pertinacious and was trying to let the Shah understand he could even nullify orders already met with his own approval. The next day, I flew to Paris. After a period of residing in the French capital, I was informed that Mohammad Reza's family including his mother, his two sisters, Shams and

Ashraf and her daughter Shahnaz had arrived in Paris for a long stay.

They said that Mossaddiq had sent them into exile and that they were not allowed to return to Iran without his permission.[17] Iranian ambassador to France, Baqer Kazemiwho was a firm supporter of Mossaddiq did not show up at the Paris airport to receive Shah's family. Kazemi chastised the Embassy's First Secretary Jazayeri when he learned he had welcomed them at the airport. Jazayeri had conversations with Shah's family every day. I was aware of his meetings with the family because I visited them every day. It seemed to me that Jazayeri had ill-intentions and looked suspicious because he was at the family's residence even during his working hours. I can understand that he was appointed by the ambassador himself to get information and then hand it over to him.

During this period, Princess Ashraf made several trips to Tehran and met the Shah. Once she privately told me that airport officials in Tehran tried to prevent her from leaving the airport during one of her trips to Tehran but she ignored the warning and walked away. She had organized teams to launch pro-Shah activities for troubled days as a precautionary measure to protect his brother's throne. One of the well known figures who helped Princess Ashraf carry out the team's activities was Assaddollah Rashidian. I knew Rashidian since a long time. His family were among the local staffers of the British Embassy in Tehran. Therefore, even during Mossaddiq's peak of power, Ashraf was able to travel to Tehran. Now a question comes to the mind was Mossaddiq aware of Princess Ashraf's activities and her meetings with Rashidian? I have to say with certainty that Mossaddiq was fully aware of all the activities but what has still remained ambiguous is why Mossaddiq did not take any measures to curb Rashidian's influence?

Of particular importance during Mossaddiq's tenure was Hussein Ala's taking up of the post of Court Minister. Ala was one of the outstanding political figures of his time. He was the son of Alaoddolleh, a prominent statesman of the Qajar period. Ala had studied in France. He was an opponent of Reza Shah's government and opposed a proposal to get Reza Khan crowned Reza Shah when it was first discussed in the Majlis. Mohammad Reza had repeatedly told me of Ala's opposition to his father's monarchy. In short, both Ala and Mossaddiq shared identical views on the Pahlavi monarchy. For the same reason, during Reza Shah's rule, the two were denied any key posts. Ala was a staunch supporter of Britain. Since Mossaddiq and Ala were both Majlis deputies, they were close to the Shah. I have no doubt that Ala was acting as an intermediary between Mohammad Reza and the American-British representatives and Mossaddiq.

As I said I was in Iran during the first year of Mossaddiq's premiership but I was studying in Paris during remaining two years of Mossaddiq's rule. Later, I was told that the Shah preferred to spend his time in solitude and used to have his dinner with his Empress Thoraia only. There were no Friday parties of the past any longer.

Mohammad Reza's patience was running out. He was not permitted even to withdraw money more than Mossaddiq had allowed. He even could not object if his trusted people were removed by Mossaddiq. It was not so difficult to read desperation in his words. He was so disappointed that he was preparing to leave the country.

19TH AUGUST COUP

The collapse of Mossaddiq government which happened after the successful August 19, 1953 coup had originally been planned and financed jointly by the British and the Americans and brought about the 25 years of Mohammad Reza's dictatorship.[18] CIA's Roosevelt had arrived in Iran prior to the coup to closely watch the affairs.

To me, the British played the key role during the coup. General Fadhlollah Zahedi was a British puppet. Major-General Hassan Akhavi, who engineered the coup was the mastermind of Britain and a top member of Arfa team. I have already explained Rashidian's close relationship with the British officials. Therefore, the British succeeded in getting Ala's consent to carry out the coup and remove Mossaddiq from power.

> "The British government had acquired a controlling interest in the company (AIOC) which had assured British influence in economic and political affairs in Iran for more than forty years.
>
> Negotiations with the British soon broke out and the British initiated a world-wide boycott of Iranian oil. Although Iran was experiencing economic disruption because of the boycott,

Mossaddiq's uncompromising campaign against a foreign power was immensely popular in Iran.

The outgoing Truman administration was deeply concerned that the failure to resolve the dispute with the British would force Iran to move closer to Moscow. These fears were given substance by anti-American riots in Tehran. Washington made a last concerted effort to devise an acceptable compromise in late 1952, but AIOC and the British Government rejected it. At the same time, Mossaddiq's internal support was eroding. He had never had the full support of the army in his efforts to undermine the power of the Shah, but now the clergy and significant elements of the commercial and financial community of the bazaar deserted him.... Mossaddiq was becoming increasingly dependent on the Tudeh party, leading to fears in Washington that Moscow was laying the ground work for a pro-Communist coup. Simultaneously popular support for the Shah was growing. Under these circumstances the newly installed Eisenhower administration approved U.S. participation in a plan to oust Mossaddiq in favour of the Shah. This plan, originally proposed by the British and code-named Ajax, was coordinated by Kermit Roosevelt of the CIA, who described his activities in a slim volume written a quarter century after the event."[19]

"After the Shah fled to Rome on August 16, 1953, the U.S., with the aid of its strong propaganda tactics, fed to the public by its media, distributed copies of the royal decree throughout Iran. On August 19, Roosevelt's Iranian agents staged a "parade" through Tehran.

Operation Ajax, bankrolled by a one million dollar CIA fund at the U.S. Embassy, was to oust Mossaddiq. During this parade, a loudspeaker announced "the Shah's instruction that Mossaddiq be dismissed has been carried out. The new Prime Minister, General Fazlollah Zahedi, is now in office. His Imperial Majesty is on his way home".

This lies, which Roosevelt called a "pre truth", preceded a nine-hour battle and but for U.S. help, the pro-Shah forces would have lost. Major General George C. Stewart, Director of the Office of Military Assistance in Iran, testified before the Congress:

'When . . . thing was about to collapse, we violated our normal criteria. Among other things we provided the army with blankets, boots, uniforms, electric generators and medical supplies (so) they could support the Shah. The guns . . . the trucks . . . the armoured cars . . . and the radio communications that permitted the control were all furnished through the Military Defense Assistance Programme.'"[20]

"In 1953 John Foster Dulles became alarmed at events in Iran, where Premier, Mohammad Mossaddiq, had deposed the Shah with the help of the local communist Tudeh Party and the Soviet Union, and nationalized the British-owned Anglo-Iranian Oil Company. The CIA was instructed to mount a covert operation to restore the Shah to power. To Iran went a clandestine operative called Kermit Roosevelt, who was grandson of the late President. With him he took a small operational force and - by CIA accounting terms - the comparatively small budget of $2,000,000, not all of which he spent. Mossaddiq did not have popular political backing and Roosevelt had little difficulty recruiting an opposition. He hired organizers to foment anti-Mossaddiq street demonstration, further to weaken the Premier's fading support. Officers still loyal to the Shah were instructed how to seize the radio station, always the first and most vital requirement of a coup. The operation was practically bloodless and for its success Roosevelt was secretly awarded the National Security Medal and personally summoned to the White House to receive praise from President Eisenhower. (When Dwight Eisenhower became President of the United States in 1953, he appointed Allen Dulles, Director of CIA. Dulles brother, John Foster, became Secretary of State).[21]

I was told by Akhavi that on 15th August the Shah would issue two separate decrees in which he would oust Mossaddiq from power and would appoint Zahedi as the new prime minister. The Shah's decree was a coordinated coup anticipated to be carried out in the evening of 15th as follows:

1. General Nasiri who was a colonel at the time and the commander of Javidan Guard was assigned to hand over a Shah's decree to both Mossaddiq and Zahedi.

2. Nasiri had been ordered to hand over Shah's decree to Mossaddiq at ten in the evening. Two armed soldiers would protect him against any possible threats.

The plotters of the coup had anticipated two situations:

A. Mossaddiq would accept to resign peacefully and therefore Zahedi would take office as the new head of government.
B. He would refuse and in this case the coup would at once be carried out.

Three military units had been put on full alert each of them with the capacity of a regiment to launch the coup. Regiment commanders announced their commitment to swiftly occupy the sensitive departments should Mossaddiq refuse to resign. Nasiri's protectors were to inform their superiors by radio if that happened. One regiment had been assigned to surround Mossaddiq's residence and arrest him. The second regiment would capture the radio and TV broadcasting stations and the third would remain on full alert to assist the other two regiments should they need support.

Zahedi was leading the coup. Regiment commanders had to start upon a telephone order from Zahedi. Mossaddiq refused to step down. Zahedi ordered the regiment commanders to go ahead but none of the regiments abided the order. Having understood the units had refused to carry out his orders, Zahedi went into hiding in his office until the 19th.

Brigadier General Reyahi, a Mossaddiq supporter, discovered the coup plot and without any hesitation dispatched forces loyal to Mossaddiq where the three regiments had already been stationed and disarmed all of them without any bloodshed. Reyahi, commander of the air force General Sepahpour and gendarmerie commander Brigadier General Mahmoud Amini rushed to the three garrisons to monitor the disarming of the coup troops.

The Shah together with his pilot Major Khatami, his court servant Atabai who later became deputy court minister and his wife Thoraia had already flown to the southern port city of Nowshahr and waited to see if the coup would succeed. In the early morning of 16 August, the Shah without killing the time fled to Baghdad with his entourage when he was told that Zahedi's coup had failed.

Later, the three regiment commanders were questioned to

explain the reasons behind the coup failure. They admitted that Shah's departure to Nowshahr, which was interpreted as a preparatory move to escape abroad, greatly discouraged them and therefore they decided to put arms down and stop the operation.

The reasons behind the coup failure could be enumerated as follows:

1. Many people were aware of the coup attempt including several officers of the regiments who were very anxious to know the reason behind their unprecedented gathering on the eve of the coup.
2. The timing, ten in the evening, was not appropriate. Of course, it was a good time to deliver the Shah's decree to Mossaddiq though darkness of night caused some difficulties for the coup plotters.
3. Coup leaders did not anticipate a concerted and timely reaction from Reyahi, Sepahour and Amini, all of them well-known for their pro-Mossaddiq tendencies.
4. Lack of determination on the part of coup plotters especially Zahedi who failed to show up in the public during the operation and encourage his subordinates to occupy Mossaddi's residence. If Zahedi personally showed up before his troops, their morale would have been strengthened and they could have fought firmly for the Shah.
5. Shah's failure to remain in the capital greatly demoralized his supporters and left a negative impact on the troops.

Colonel Momtaz, a close friend of Nasiri, was commanding Mossaddiq's special guard. Momtaz and Nasiri were classmates at Officers Collage during their study there. Nasiri said that he rushed to Mossaddiq residence and asked for permission to meet Momtaz. After pleasantries were exchanged, Nasiri handed over Shah's written decree to Momtaz to be immediately passed to Mossaddiq. Momtaz asked him to wait for response. Mossaddiq in reaction to Shah's decree ordered Momtaz to arrest Nasiri and put him in jail. Nasiri recalled the good old days they had and requested him to ignore the order but Momtaz threw him a false smile and said, "the past is the past. His Excellency Dr. Mossaddiq would ring Riyahi to inform him of your arrest. You will remain in jail until further notice".

The Shah, whose plane had landed at Baghdad's airport, flew to Rome after refuelling. Iran's Ambassador to Iraq Mozaffar Alam had received strict orders from Tehran to avoid meeting the Shah. In Italy, the Iranian Ambassador Gholamali Khajenouri, too, refused to meet the Shah. Khajenouri's refusal annoyed the Shah since they had been close friends for a long time. Khajenouri was always moving in the Royal Palace before being appointed ambassador to Italy. He only allowed the Embassy's Commercial Attache called Sadeq to meet Mohammad Reza in his hotel in Rome.

The Shah asked Sadeq to prepare the car he always used to get from the embassy. Khajenouri asked for permission and Mossaddiq categorically turned down Shah's request. Mohammad Reza stayed for two days in Rome. During his stay in the Italian capital, a number of British and American authorities were in constant touch with him.

As the news of Shah's departure was publicly announced, members and supporters of the Tudeh Party took to the streets and dismantled Shah's statues erected in his honour and chanted slogans in support of a 'republican' system of government.

> "When the Shah and his Empress Soraya heard in Rome that the people were tearing down his statues and portraits in Tehran, he lost his hope of returning to Iran. Soraya says in her memoirs that she asked him, 'Where would you like to go?' and he replied, 'probably America' and suggested that he would like to buy a farm there.
>
> When an Associated Press correspondent brought in a wire report that he had been rehabilitated by 'the friends', Soraya says, 'the king went so pale I feared he might faint.' Soraya gave him a drink, and he confessed: 'I did not play any role in the fight.'"[22]

I doubt they were real Tudeh Party supporters. To me, if they were representing the real Tudeh Party, they would have come to a compromise with Mossaddiq government and would have not waited for the U.S. intervention and the subsequent coup attempt.

The supporters of the Tudeh Party whether they were real sympathizers who in this case failed to play an effective role or a British-backed group who in this case handled their mission successfully, persuaded Mossaddiq to regain power.

For three days after the 16 coup failed, an essentially 'revolutionary state' prevailed in Tehran. Tudeh sympathizers had captured the capital and were in full control of all strategic government buildings.

Mossaddiq, in a meeting with U.S. ambassador, also acknowledged that he could not bring the situation under control. The ambassador conferred with the State Department officials in Washington on the alarming situation in Iran and U.S. representatives were discussing the situation with the Shah in Rome. The Shah was also briefed on the unstable situation in the country by the Iranian ambassador.

On the 19th, there appeared from the south Tehran Bazaars a pro-Shah mob led by Shaban Bimokh (brainless). It gathered strength as it moved. The army joined forces in the afternoon, and by evening again controlled Tehran in the name of the Shah. Mossaddiq had given in to pressures and was forced to quit power.

The downfall of Mossaddiq, after three years of prime-ministership, revived Shah's authority. Later, Head of the MI-6 in London told me that the Shah was reluctant to return to Iran and proposed to the Americans to appoint a military figure as the new head of state. I was in London for my special intelligence training course. The Americans believed Mohammad Reza's rule had come to an end and that tampering with the Constitution may bring more troubles later and did not insist on his return to power but the British insisted he should be reinstated. He said it was London that convinced the Americans to participate in the coup to reinstate the Shah because if they were late in saving the Pahlavi dynasty, Iran would fall to the communists.

Despite all the developments the ambiguity still remains as to who first engineered the coup? The Americans described Zahedi the mastermind and the winner of the coup who did not spend much money despite receiving $ 5 million from the CIA.

Honestly, the truth was that accurate planning of Brigadier General Akhavi paved the way for the successful execution of the coup and removal of Mossaddiq from power. As the coup forces launched their offensive, Akhavi, in an attempt to escape responsibility if the coup failed, pretended to have gotten sick and was hospitalized at the army's hospital number two. Later, as a sign of appreciation, Mohammad Reza appointed Akhavi Minister of Agriculture.

Akhavi, a committed anti-communist, was the mastermind of the Arfa team. He did not follow Zahedi during the coup operation and preferred to act independently. His coup plan was accurately observed and helped Zahedi succeed in toppling the Mossaddiq government.

The main elements who helped the coup succeed were Rashidian brothers whose father, Habib Rashidian, was a staffer of the British Embassy. Rashidian's three sons, Seif, Ghodrat and Assad were also serving the British. They were a wealthy family and possessed many houses in Tehran. The younger brother, Assad, was more active and could be witnessed at the Palace almost daily. He was an influential personality in Tehran bazaar. The three brothers had no higher education and could not be trusted.

Their role in the coup was to invite civilians and *bazaaris* to take to the streets in support of the Shah. Reportedly, they gathered around five to six thousand people in the capital's streets. A woman called princess Etezadi who was an expert on instigating people delivered an enthusiastic speech with her chador tied around her waist. The crowd moved towards Mossaddiq's residence. Major General Khosravani who later became the Head of Physical Training Organization gathered a number of athletes led by Shaban Bimokh (brainless) and headed the same direction. Bimokh was later awarded by the Shah a showplace (zorkhaneh) for his support of the dynasty.

Javidan Guard troops who were disarmed by Reyahi during the aborted 15 August coup joined the crowd.

The 19 August coup leaders had anticipated the following:

— Different groups would be formed in designated areas in the capital led by figures assigned by coup leaders.
— All the groups would move towards Shah-Naderi street so that demonstrators get to the destination simultaneously.
— The demonstrators would chant slogans in support of Mohammad Reza's monarchy.
— Javidan Guard forces would join the demonstrators and would arm them with light weapons.
— A tank company armed to the teeth would join the crowd and would move towards Mossaddiq's residence. They would also surround his house and arrest him.
— A platoon would capture the Tehran radio station.

— Mossaddiq's arrest would be broadcast on the radio.
— Zahedi, accompanied by a tank company would rush to the Royal Palace and would introduce his cabinet.
— Finally, Mohammad Reza would be cordially requested to return home. The new cabinet ministers would be at the airport to accord a red carpet welcome upon his arrival.

Everything went like a clockwork. Pro-Mossaddiq forces did not intervene and remained in their barracks. The demonstrators rushed to Mossaddiq residence. A colonel called Rahimi ordered shelling of Mossaddiq's house with tanks. Mossaddiq took refuge in a neighbouring house but finally found no option but to surrender.

> "All those who contributed to the 1953 coup were rewarded in one way or another. Colonel Nasiri who had delivered to Mossaddiq the message dismissing him, was promoted to General and put in charge of SAVAK; General Fadhlollah Zahedi who had led the coup became first Prime Minister after its success; his son, Ardeshir who was believed to have acted as liasion with Kermit Roosevelt, was given the Shah's daughter Shahnaz as bride and he was eventually made ambassador to London and Washington; Captain Khatami who had piloted the plane which took the Shah to Baghdad and Rome was made Commander of the Air Force and married Shah's sister Princess Fatemeh after her divorce from her first American husband...
>
> ... Mossaddiq was sentenced to three years imprisonment on charges of treason, and after he had served his sentence, was kept under house arrest for the rest of his life."[23]

Rumours spread in the capital on Zahedi's embezzlements. Some said that the Americans had provided Zahedi with $ 5 million and others put the amount at $700 thousand. The prevailing view confirmed the first figure. Gossips were also circulated in the city that Zahedi had spent little money to cultivate support for the monarchy and kept the rest for himself.

CIA's Roosevelt and his people were closely following the developments. The Shah finally returned home. From the very beginning it was clear he could not tolerate Zahedi's popularity. As he arrived in Tehran's Meharabad airport, he chewed Zahedi's ears off as soon as he learned that Zahedi had given Nasiri the rank of colonel. Nasiri was a Major before the coup

During Zahedi's government, Assadollah Alam was the contact between the Shah and Zahedi as was Ala during Mossaddiq's time. Alam routinely met the Shah to receive his orders on state affairs and he then conveyed them to Zahedi. It became clear that Zahedi was following a line independent of the Shah. Of course, there was no doubt that he had adopted such a stance after consultations with the Americans. Alam who was in routine touch with the British and American embassies made effective efforts in removing Zahedi from the top place on Iran's pyramid of power. Alam remained Iran's number two until his death.

About one and half years after the coup, Zahedi was dismissed and sent to Geneva. The MI-6 Chief was right in arguing that it was the British who brought Reza Khan to power unseated him on 16 September 1941, and saved his son in 1953.

> "The British had a not undeserved reputation for interfering in Iran's domestic affairs for over a century. We were alleged to have helped to bring the Shah's father to the throne and we had of course been directly involved in his abdication in 1941 and his son's succession."[24]

> "Whatever interpretation one chooses to place on the objectives and consequences of Operation Ajax, it abruptly and permanently ended America's political innocence with respect to Iran...the direct intervention in 1953 cast the United States in the role so common in Iranian history of the cynical external power prepared to manipulate Iranian political circumstances for its own benefit...it is unfortunately true that after 1953 the United States would never again be able to enjoy the presumption of benign objectives and entightened self-interest when engaging itself in the affairs of Iran."[25]

BIOGRAPHY OF MOSSADDIQ

Mohammad Mossaddiq, Iranian political leader who nationalized the huge British oil holdings in Iran, was born in Tehran in 1880. The son of Mirza Hedayat, a former minister of finance, Mossaddiq grew up as a member of Iran's ruling elite.

After serving for a period as treasurer of Khorasan Province, Mossaddiq went to Neuchatel, Switzerland (c. 1908), where he studied law, obtaining the degree of Docteure en Droit for his thesis Le Testament en droit musulman (secte chyite) (Paris, 1914).

On his return to Persia in 1914 he was appointed Governor General of the important Fars Province. He showed both energy and tact in the performance of his duties. He refused to recognize the new regime established in Feb. 1921 by Seyed Zia-ad-Din and Reza Khan, but when Qavam al-Saltaneh became Prime Minister later in the year Mossaddiq was appointed Minister of Finance. He introduced some much-needed reforms. In 1922 he became Governor General of Azerbaijan, but soon resigned owing to differences with the military authorities. He was appointed Minister of Foreign Affairs in 1923 but relinquished that post later in the year on being elected to the Majlis as a deputy for Tehran. He opposed the change of regime in 1925 and, disliked by Reza Shah in consequence, retired into private life for a time.

Mossaddiq re-entered public service in 1944, following Reza Shah's forced abdication in 1941, and was elected again to the Majlis. An outspoken advocate of nationalism, he soon played a leading part in successfully opposing the grant to the Soviet Union of an oil concession for northern Iran similar to an existing British concession in southern Iran. He built considerable political strength, based largely on his call to nationalize the concession and installations in Iran of the British-owned Anglo-Iranian Oil Company. In March 1951 the Majlis passed his oil nationalization act, and his power had grown so great that the Shah, Mohammad Reza Pahlavi, was virtually forced to appoint him premier.

The nationalization resulted in a deepening crisis in Iran, both politically and economically. Mossaddiq and his National Front continued to gain power but alienated many supporters, particularly among the ruling elite and in the Western nations. The British soon withdrew completely from the Iranian oil market, and economic problems increased when Mossaddiq could not readily find alternate oil markets.

A continuing struggle for control of the Iranian government developed between Mossaddiq and the Shah. In August 1953, when the Shah attempted to dismiss the Premier, mobs of Mossaddiq followers took to the streets and forced the Shah to leave the country. Within a few days, however, Mossaddiq's opponents, with U.S. support, overthrew his regime and restored the Shah to power. Mossaddiq was sentenced to three years' imprisonment for treason and, after he had served his sentence, was kept under house arrest for the rest of his life. He died on March 5, 1967. The Iranian oil-production facilities remained under control of the Iranian government.

Mossaddiq's personal behaviour, which included wearning pajamas for numerous public appearances; speeches to the Majlis from his bed, which was brought into the chambers; and frequent bouts of public weeping, helped focus world attention upon him during his premiership. Supporters claim the behaviour was a result of illness; detractors say he had a shrewd sense of public relations.[26]

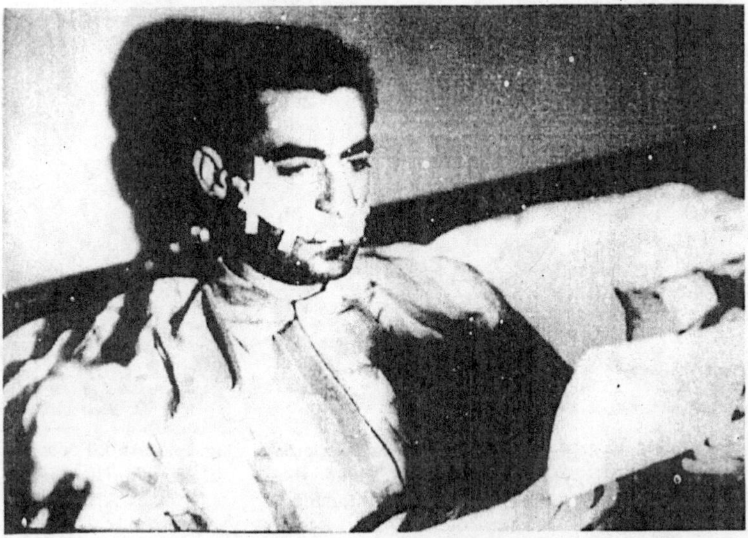

Fig. 10: An abortive assassination attempt on the life of Mohammad Reza Shah Pahlavi in 1949

Fig. 11: Mohammad Reza Shah with British Prime Minister Winston Churchil, Tehran Conference

Fig. 12: Dr. Mohammad Mossaddiq, Iran's popular prime minister who had warned the Shah in the early 50s of the tearful end of his dictatorship

Fig. 13: Kermit Roosevelt, CIA's man who guided Operation Ajax which unseated Mossaddiq

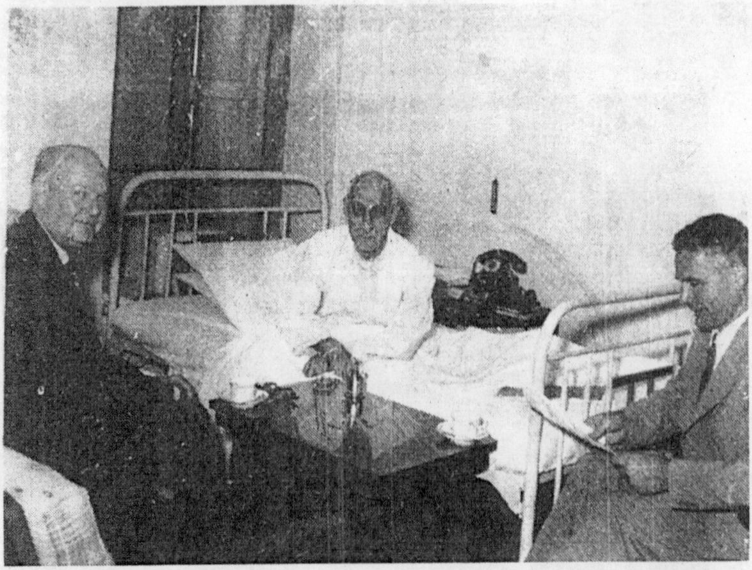

Fig. 14: Mossaddiq, a politician who nationalized Iran's oil industry and kicked Mohammad Reza Shah Pahlavi out of Iran. His government was overthrown by a coup masterminded by the CIA

Chapter 3

The Shah and the Royal Court

EARNEST PROUN'S DEATH

Proun enjoyed undisputable influence in government departments. He lobbied ministers to give his friends posts in high places and fire those who ran against him. For low-rank officials, it was Proun's orders they had to carry out. His self-made instructions included commuting or even forgiving the sentences of culprits. He intervened in every Iranian domestic affair he wished without consulting Mohammad Reza except in parliamentary elections and formation of cabinet.

He even intervened in Shah's private life. His speech swayed Shah's opinions on domestic or foreign policy issues and even on his personal life. Even Mohammad Reza's friends were chosen by Proun. He was the closest man to the Shah after me. The Shah usually had his meals with Fawzia, Proun and I. It was Proun who made Taqi Emami, a relative of Seyed Hasan Emami, Tehran's Friday prayer leader, and Fathollah Amiralai, Chief of the Pahlavi Foundation hotels, friends to the Shah. Proun helped both men financially after persuading the Shah to allow them make use of government funds.

Proun had struck up a close friendship with Crown Prince Mohammad Reza when we were studying in Switzerland. He had been employed in the school three months before the start of the academic year and it was evident that he was in permanent contact with the British and was spying for them. Although his manoeuvreing was limited during Reza Shah's rule for being a gay, he found the way open for his activities in the Court after Reza Shah's abdication.

Wealthy families were honoured to receive Proun in their homes. Almost all high-ranking authorities enjoyed close relations with him and he was their consultant if a problem emerged. He gathered all the information he had been ordered to acquire during his meetings with the Iranian officials and passed them to the Embassy.

He behaved the Shah from the position of strength and was outspoken before him. Despite his bullying behaviour, the Shah, to my surprise, showed tolerance and did not take any punitive measures against him.

Some two years after Mohammad Reza married Thoraia, Proun got kidney stones and his right leg was paralyzed. He was not able to walk without a walking stick. He was taken to Switzerland for treatment. A few weeks after he was hospitalized, Iran's Ambassador to Italy Hormuz Qarib disclosed that Proun had succumbed to his illness. Mohammad Reza made no certain reaction to the death of his long-time friend. There was no sign of grief on his face. Perhaps, Proun's death was a good news for him who found a trouble-maker gone.

PROUN AND FREEMASONRY

Proun was one of the founders of Freemasonry and the Pahlavi Lodge in Iran. I guess it was in 1954 when one day Proun took me to a man's house in Naderi street. On our way to his house, Proun told me that he was the Leader of the Middle East Freemasonry Movement and urged me to kiss his hands when we meet him.

We were directed along a walk to a room at the bottom of a garden. A tall, hard-faced man with an incredible width of shoulder was enjoying a smoke of hubble-bubble pipe. Proun with his right hand on his heart bowed before him and kissed his hand but I only shook hands with him. Proun had already spoken to him about me.

"His Excellency has accepted that you be admitted into the Freemasonry and this is a great honour for you to join us", Proun told me.

He said that a good number of politicians and senior government officials including some top ranking military officers such as Chief of Police Mehdiqoli Alavimoqqaddam had registered in the organization.

It was a courtesy call on the leader of Freemasonry and nothing in particular was discussed. After the meeting, Proun said that the man was a native of Iraq who led the Freemasonry but did not give his name to me and instead kept insisting that I join the organization.

Some time later, I learned that the man was Mohammad Khalil Javaheri who was also leading the Pahlavi Lodge established with Shah's consent. I informed the Shah of my meeting with Javaheri.

"I know Javaheri well. It is better if you join the organization but it is up to you", the Shah shrugged his shoulders.

However, I never joined the Freemasonry since I was not interested in its establishments. My refusal to join the organization angered Proun but there was nothing he could do against me.

DIVORCE OF FAWZIA

As I said in the previous chapter, Fawzia, a very gracious woman but languidly shy, was reluctant to show up in public meetings while the Shah, by nature, was fond of talkative women. The Shah liked his wife to chum up with his guests and show up in banquets. Despite their differences, Fawzia showed tolerance and was faithful to Mohammad Reza. Fawzia's characteristics openly ran against Shah's desires. They had their first kid, a pretty girl named Shahnaz in 1940, when the British decided to remove Farouq from power in Egypt because of widespread corruption within his administration.[1] Accordingly, they decided to get Mohammad Reza divorce Fawzia perhaps to avoid any undesirable consequences that could threaten Iran's monarch. Proun played the main role in separating Fawzia from Mohammad Reza.

Unlike Fawzia, Mohammad Reza was not faithful to their matrimonial life. He had picked up a girlfriend called Divsalar. He spent part of his lesiure time having love with her. The Shah had kept Fawzia in the dark but Proun found it enough troublesome to sow discord between them.

Fawzia lost her tolerance after Proun spilled the beans about Shah's girlfriend before her. His motive was obvious. After consultations with the Embassy, he had been told that they must be divorced. He tried to conceal the plan from me and only revealed the information he wanted me to know, not more not less. Although he had kept his thumb on the Shah, he was not aware of Shah's every private affair. He received the girl's address and her meeting schedules with the Shah from the Embassy. He had been told to assure Fawzia that the charges were true.

Colonel Rafatian, a close friend of Proun, drove to the girl's house after it had turned dark. Proun and Fawzia were seated in the back. Fawzia and Proun remained in the car. Proun ordered Rafatian to fire into the third floor of a four-storey flat with his pistol. A scream came out of the window. The girl came to the window, broken by the bullets, stretched her head out and stared around hastily. A few minutes later, the Shah walked out of the building and disappeared in the dark. It was enough to persuade Fawzia that the Shah had betrayed her.

The same night, the Shah, Fawzia, Proun and I dined together. Fawzia was absolutely silent. It was not difficult to read anger and disappointment in her face.

She remained mute for a few days, receiving only Egyptian ambassador and his family. After a week, I learned that she was about to leave Iran for Egypt. When I asked her motive she said she was homesick and wanted to go on leave for a month or so. She left for Egypt but returned earlier as expected. Perhaps she had been convinced by her mother not to leave her husband.

The return of Fawzia was not a good piece of news for Proun since his plan did not come into fruition. As a next plot, Proun accused Fawzia of betraying Shah's trust in her. This time, when Fawzia learned of the allegations, left Iran for her native country and never returned. In November 1948, King Farouq decided that Fawzia had endured sufficient misery. He wrote to Mohammad Reza and asked for divorce of his sister and the Shah agreed.[2]

PROUN'S HOMOSEXUALITY

Proun's female sentiments were strong. Since Reza Shah hated him for his gay behaviour he was not allowed to make his activities public at the Court. After Reza Shah's collapse there was nothing to prevent him. He set up a gay team at the Imperial Court.

Proun, a poet, was also fond of fine arts and showed a great inclination to theatre and decorative works. Every morning he used to tell Mohammad Reza all the stories which happened to him in the nights. He together with the Commercial Attache of the Swiss Embassy who was also a gay, had rented a house in northern Tehran. The Swiss embassy official had remained in Tehran since 1936 until his death in 1976. Both were single and never married. Proun once confirmed that all those whom he had brought to the Court including Taqi Imami were gays.

Anyhow, Proun got ill and was hospitalized abroad and finally succumbed to his illness in 1961.

AYADI, COURT'S RASPUTIN

After the death of Proun, Brigadier General Abdulkarim Ayadi took his place at the court. He was later known as Iran's Rasputin.[3] His difference with Proun was that he was polite and less violent.

When Soraya Esfandiari was Shah's wife, I had no strong presence at the Court but Ayadi had won Soraya's support and was respected by all Bakhteyaris. He was aware of every affair of Mohammad Reza's private life. Ayadi and his agents were in constant touch with the MI-6 station in the British Embassy. Of course, during this time, British did not need me as a source of information and they came to me just to facilitate their job.

So, it becomes clear that the British were aware of Mohammad Reza's private life since his childhood. First, they appointed Afra and Proun to the Swiss school prior to our arrival in Switzerland and after Proun's death, Ayadi took his place to closely study the Shah's character and his actions and then pass to the British, the same Soleiman Behbudi did about Reza Shah.

Ayadi entered Shah's private life as a doctor but actually was a British spy. Shah's brother, Ali Reza, was suffering from microphobia and needed a special physician. Ali Reza did not usually take part in a party or a public gathering or if he did he left the place soon. He had married a poor Polish woman in Paris. She was among those refugees who had immigrated to Iran during the Second World War. They had a son called Ali Patrik. Ali Reza always felt that some diseases were threatening him. Mohammad Reza was also suffering from microphobia but it was not so severe as Ali Reza had.

Prince Ali Reza's only friend was Hassan Shekarchi, an illiterate guard of the royal hunting grounds. So, Ayadi came to the Court as a doctor to treat the two brothers but he was secretly in touch with the British intelligence officers. Ayadi's father was a Bahai leader and had inherited the title. He had studied veterinary science for two years in Paris and then changed the course of his study into medical sciences. He remained Ali Reza's doctor until his death. Ali Reza always carried with him syrups and tablets of different vitamins. Ayadi's prescriptions not only did not cure him but also quickened his death.

I had been left in no doubt that the British had already chosen Ayadi to spy for them. He possessed all the qualities for a seasoned spy and therefore was helped to foothold in the Court. For the west, he was playing a bigger role than any other spy. Ayadi had influence in any government department. He was appointed as the head of the regular army and disciplinary forces cooperative shops. All the requirements had to be purchased upon his order. Any goods, even if the country was a producer, had to be imported from abroad mostly from Britain and the U.S.

Ayadi was controlling all segments of the army. Even he was appointing the cooperative shops bosses and determined their rationing system. The medicinal organizations were also under his command. They were not allowed to purchase or sell any products without his permission. The fishing centres in the south were under his control. His posts exceeded 80. All government officials respected him and carried out his orders without any objection. Through his efforts, some Bahais were appointed as ministers during Hoveida premiership who himself happened to be a Bahai. The ministers did not also dare to take any decisions without his consent. There were no jobless Bahais during his stay at the Court and the Bahai population was said to have tripled during this time. All Iranians whether living in Iran or abroad were of the opinion that Ayadi was the real ruler of Iran but did not dare to acknowledge that openly. He was always accompanying Mohammad Reza on his foreign trips. Ayadi left Iran prior to the victory of the 1979 Islamic revolution.

MOHAMMAD REZA AND WOMEN

Mohammad Reza did not have a pure matrimonial life. He betrayed the trust of his wives by sleeping around. I wrote about his scandalous links with a girl during our study in Switzerland in the previous chapter.

Since our return home from Switzerland in 1936, Reza Shah was watchful of his son not to let him be entrapped or lured by prostitutes. To ease his worries, Reza Shah decided to get him a wife. Firuzeh, a young woman just divorced from an army physician after a year of matrimonial life, was said to be the prettiest in the capital. She was living with her aunt and only sister, Sabireh. Unlike Firuzeh, Sabireh was not pretty at all. Her aunt was a physician educated in Caucasia. Firuzeh's uncle was Saed Maraqei, a once prime minister.

Initial preparations were made and after consultations with Firuzeh's aunt, I was asked to drive to the clinic of Firuzeh's aunt in Lalehzar street in central Tehran and take the bride to the Palace. After waiting for about two hours, the bride, in all white wedding dress and marvelously made up, sat in the back seat of my car. I drove north without any hesitation directly to Mohammad Reza's residence. The bride and ihe groom stared at each other for a few seconds. Then, Mohammad Reza, dressed in a conservative suit and tie, came over to Firuzeh and put his right arm around her. They seemed to be quiet happy and started to live as a couple.

Reza Shah used to call on Firuzeh every other time and take a walk with her in the garden. He was trying to give a formal appearance to their relations. Firuzeh received 300 tumans a month in addition to her personal expenses. Reza Shah was happy with the new couple. Mohammd Reza's relations with Firuzeh remained loving until his father, upon the British recommendations, proposed to marry Fawzia, sister of the Egyptian King Faruq.

One day, Mohammad Reza asked me to take Firuzeh's personal belongings to her aunt's house and tell her not to return to the palace again. I followed his order. Firuzeh got angry and requested to leave Iran. Mohammad Reza agreed and gave her some jewellery and large amount of cash. She left Tehran for Rome, Italy. There she was married to an Italian merchant. Later, she got divorced and was married to Fereidyun Jam, the former husband of Princess Shams.

After leaving Fawzia, Mohammad Reza asked me to get a girl for him. By chance, I met a pretty girl called Pary Ghaffari in a dinner party. She had attended the party with her mother. Pary did not look more than 17 at the most. She was tall and firm-breasted with fair hairs. When I went to them to propose marriage on behalf of Mohammad Reza, they treated me like a royal guest. They stared at me with bulging eyes at first after I introduced myself to them thinking I was proposing marriage for myself. The girl became more happy when she learned the Crown Prince would be her future husband. I got their address and a few days later, I drove the girl and her mother to a garden in suburbs of Tehran where Mohammad

Reza was already waiting. The Prince and Pary went for a walk. They were all smiles when they returned after an hour. It was clear that they had agreed on their terms. For a few days, I took Pary to Mohammad Reza's residence and after that Prince's driver did it. Mohammad Reza donated Pary a large beautiful house in northern Tehran. He, of course, left her after he married Soraya.

Before he married Soraya, he was planning to get a girl from the European monarch families. He, therefore, invited the daughter of the deposed Italian head of state along with her brother to Tehran. Mohammad Reza's mother and his two sisters advised him against marrying a Christian. The girl was warned that she would get in trouble if she married Mohammad Reza. Finally, the girl got disappointed and left Iran.

Later, Bakhteyaris received a position at the Court but contrary to Farah Diba's relatives, Soraya's relatives did not use their position to increase their influence in the Court. During Mossaddiq premiership, Mohammad Reza used to eat his meal in private or only with Soraya, Proun and I but after the 19 August coup between 100 to 150 Bakhteyaris attended dinners at the Palace on holidays. No one was invited without Soraya's permission. Mohammad Reza's mother, Taj ol Moluk and his elder sister Princess Shams gradually became her enemies for her uncompromising stance and humiliating behaviour towards them. Their disputes continued to the last day when Mohammad Reza divorced her.

Soraya and her associates were treating me very friendly. At the time, I was a colonel teaching at "War University". For a time, I was denied to be listed to attend the parties regularly held at Shah's residence on holidays. So, one Friday, I went to the Palace without invitation. Mohammad Reza made a row when he learned that I had been denied to the parties. After the incident, I was greatly respected even by officers with a higher rank. There had remained no doubt for me that university lecturers and high ranking officers had learned of the incident. Since then invitations poured in inviting me for dinner or lunch.

Soraya, too, was extremely pretty but languidly shy and diffident. After a long time, it became clear that Soraya could not give birth to any child. Mohammad Reza was not also interested to have a son so soon because he was afraid to be assassinated if there was a successor. In the following years, he was even afraid of his elder son, Reza who was approaching maturity. Once, Mohammad

Reza privately voiced his concern over a successor to me. Anyhow, Soraya who borne no children was divorced in 1958 and later left Iran with a lot of jewellery and money for Germany and resided there.

After divorcing Soraya, he whiled away his leisure hours with Giti Khatir, one of his remote relatives. Giti was a widow. Mohammad Reza's relations with Giti remained warm until he married Farah Diba.

Both before and after he married Farah, Mohammad Reza had ilicit relations with many women who were mostly staffers of the foreign airlines based in Tehran. His sister, Ashraf, was the pimp. In his trips to the United States, Mohammad Reza had love with some women and donated them thousands of dollars. A 19-year old American beauty queen whose name I have forgotten was his favourite during his Washington visits. In December 1959, the Shah married Farah Diba, who bore him a son and heir in 1961.

DIBA FAMILY AT THE COURT

The father of Farah, Sohrab Diba, was a graduate officer from France. He was born in Tabriz, married Farideh in 1932 and died of tuberculosis in 1943 when he was a Captain.

Farideh Diba, Farah's mother, did not marry after her husband's death and was living with her engineer brother, Mohammad Ali Gotbi. They were from Rasht, the capital of the northern Gilan province. Farideh was poor and had to work for her brother to feed her only child. Gotbi sent Farah to France to study fine arts but could not send her enough money to meet her requirements.

At the time of her study in France, Farah and her close associate and Iranian classmate Leila Arjmand took Communist tendencies. I did know a number of students who were studying with Farah who were strong supporters of Communism. One of the students once told me that they boycotted anyone without leftist tendencies at the university. Her economic problems had also created a favourable ground for such a tendency. Farah maintained her thoughts after she married the Shah and turned her office into a propagation centre of Communism. With her blessings, many pro-Communist agents were employed in her office.

With the little money she received from Gotbi made it impossible to continue studying, Farah appealed to whoever could help her.

She accidentally went to Ardashir Zahedi for financial assistance. Zahedi possessed a big villa in Hesarak in suburbs of Karaj, western Tehran. He had turned her private villa into a brothel. He picked up girls and women and took them to his villa. There, he raped those with nice figures and passed those who were not to his taste to his inferiors.

Being aware of Zahedi's character, Farah appealed to him for money which meant selling herself. Farah's appearance did not receive Zahedi's favour. That was perhaps the reason he telephoned Mohammad Reza to get rid of the girl. Mohammad Reza, without probing her past history, proposed marriage. The waiting Farah immediately accepted the proposal and they married in December in 1959. And the poor Farah was elevated to the rank of Iran's First Lady and was crowned as the "Empress" as all the people might have watched in their television.[4]

Having been married to the Shah, the poor girl became a wealthy woman and her position gave her the opportunity to back all her friends and families named "Diba". Within a short period of time, Gotbi's wealth exceeded billions of rials. All families under the surname of "Diba" were regularly invited to the Palace every Friday. Her mother, Farideh was given a palace next to their Majesties. Farideh pretended to observe the religious obligations and usually appeared with covering (hijab) in the public.

Empress Farah was in a good position to form her own judgement. She regularly saw members of her family and had her own circle of friends. Many people felt they had a better chance of getting their point of view listened to if they spoke to her than if they made a direct approach to the Shah. She was a proud and intelligent woman.

During this period, Leila Arjmand, Farah's classmate in France, was her advisor. Her previous doomed history had persuaded Farah to establish friendly relations with Leila. Leila's warm relations with Farah allowed her husband, Amir Arjmand, to receive a good position and become a confident of the Shah's private life. Amir Arjmand was a professor at Tehran University. He along with a number of his friends were columnists at Tehran's major Persian daily *Ettela'at*. His articles supported leftists. The secret police or SAVAK in its daily secret bulletins once quoted a part of Arjmand's articles and said that Communists had infiltrated

Ettela'at and had formed a powerful faction. SAVAK's bulletin believed that restrictions had to be imposed on them to limit their activities and expel the undesirable elements and make a purge within the publishing institute.

As the wealth of the Imperial Family increased with the blessings of the hike in oil prices, a great portion of it naturally went to the Empress. Surprisingly, in 1971, Major General Firuzmand who was in charge of all military probing missions informed me that the Shah had ordered an all-out investigation of Farah's office. Firuzmand appointed my brother, Nosratollah, to follow the investigation. Nosratollah's probing made it clear that over 600 people were working at Empress Farah's office, most of them foreign ministry employees with some expertise knowledge about fine arts. She had ordered her employees to identify historical buildings with antiques and introduce them to her. Later, she sized the buildings, by force if necessary.

She spent a lot of money to broaden her office and possess more properties. What her activities were aimed at? She did all these things just for amusement and nothing else.

The Empress allocated millions of rials to her children and to repair Neyavaran Palace. Heavy expenses were also devoted to Their Majesties foreign trips. The most expensive antiques were unnecessarily donated to the host countries head of state and their families.

The Shah's coronation ceremonies received a large portion of government's revenues, all ordered by the Empress.

Billions of rials were also spent for the annual Shiraz International Cultural Festival and other unnecessary ceremonies. Farah's relatives and close friends transferred billions of rials to their foreign bank accounts. Their assets were really what they had plundered the wealth of the nation.

Since Hoveida's premiership, Mohammad Reza and Empress Farah brought every thing under their control, something usual during the Qajar period. Whatever remained out of the revenues at the Court were given to the Court Minister, Assadollah Alam. Americans and Britons were also pillaging the army by selling billions of doallars worth of arms. To this conclusion, it will not be any exaggeration if we describe this period as the height of corruption and plunder at the Court.

THE SHAH AND MONEY

As the Shah was helped in the consolidation of his position, to his fortune the price of oil dramatically increased and the country's economy was booming. As the Shah saw it, the Persian Gulf was becoming the most important economic and strategic area in the world and control of it would have to be exercised by Iran. This was when Britain had left the Persian Gulf and the Shah had started to play his role of policeman in the region.

> "The Shah celebrated his thirty years on the throne in 1971, but it was a year later that the climax of his reign was reached. This was in October 1972, when two and a half thousand years of monarchy were commemorated among the ruins of the former Achaemenian capital, Persepolis. Sixty-eight kings, princes and heads of state attended[5]... Persepolis had become a city of tents, one for each country's representative. Units of the Iranian forces of earlier periods, clad in the costumes and uniforms of those times, marched past the massive remains of the site. Catering had been put into the hands of best Persian cooks, but if any of the guests preferred their national dishes to the luxury foods prepared by Parisian chefs their own cooks were flown in at the Shah's expense. As it was, mountains of caviare and other delicacies were consumed by the bigwigs, the members of their party and by lesser fry like journalists. The equipment needed to prepare and maintain this jomboree can be imagined. Numerous power stations had to be erected in the desert to serve the refrigerators and air-conditioning units, as well as telephones, television, transport and so forth. The whole three-day affair cost the Iranian taxpayer $ 120 million, contrary to the official estimates of $ 40 million. The Shah felt that Persepolis had put the seal of legitimacy on the Pahlavi dynasty...
>
> (Hours of parades, by soldiers in uniforms of the past, celebrated the centuries of Iran's military triumphs. Standing at the tomb of Cyrus the Great, the ancient warrior who created the Persian Empire, the Shah addressed his predecessor in confident tones. "Rest in peace," he cried out, "the Iranian flag is flying today as triumphantly as ever in the past".)
>
> Another example was on the anniversary of Shah's forty-eighth birthday on October 20, 1967 in Gulestan Palace where

Mohammad Reza like his father placed the crown on his own head. Then he placed smaller crowns on the heads of his wife, Farah who was proclaimed Empress and on his son. There were 3,380 jewels in the crown which he put on his own head and rather fewer in the other two crowns...

Unfortunately, it was not only entertainment that was on a lavish scale in Iran during the late 1960s and early 1970s, this was the time when everybody began to get their fingers into the pie. The Shah was treating Iran as if it was his private property, and first pickings naturally went to his family. The Queen mother was interested in real estate, land and buildings. She maintained an impressive office in a building in Takhtitavus Street, which after the Revolution became the office of the Ministry of Revolutionary Affairs. The Shah's brother, Prince Mahmoud Reza, concentrated on mining, including cobalt, bauxite and turquoise; he was the principal shareholder in the Firouz Mining Company, the Shaharand Industrial Company and many others. Princess Ashraf was involved in banking, paper mills, and lotteries, and so on. Loyal friends were not forgotten. General Zahedi's son, Ardeshir, who had married Shah's daughter and the had been made ambassador to Washington, took over the controlling interest in the motor industry, and innumerable former politicians, diplomats, soldiers and businessmen were similarly rewarded, as were officials of the CIA who had proved helpful."[5]

"Ayatollah Ruhollah Khomeini from his exile in Najaf, Iraq, on October 31, 1971 denounced Shah's plans to impose on the nation the celebration of two-and-a-half millenia of monarchy. Although Khomeini's condemnation of the Shah and his declaration that the monarchy was not compatible with Islam was not taken seriously, it laid the basis for his future revolution. A summarized part of his speech follows:

"I feel it is my duty on certain occasions to draw attention to some aspects of the problems facing the people of Islam, and it may be that you will consider it your duty also to attempt to aid your Muslim brothers, even if only by way of declarations, telegrams, and letters...

Now, according to numerous letters and reports I have

received, one of the unfortunate aspects of the present situation in Iran is that a large number of people have died of hunger. While these tragic circumstances and conditions prevail, millions of tumans are to be spent celebrating in honour of the monarchy. According to reports, 80 million tumans are to be spent on decorating and lighting up Tehran alone. Experts have been invited from Israel to take care of the arrangements - from Israel, that stubborn enemy of Islam and the Qoran which a few years ago attempted to corrupt the text of the Qoran, and now imputes to the Qoran unworthy statements, which our students abroad vigorously refute and deny (may God strengthen them). Israel, which is at war with the Muslims and plans to occupy all the lands of Islam up to Iraq and (God forbid) to destroy the noble shrines of Islam! Israel, which set fire to the Masjid al-Aqsa, a crime that the Iranian regime tried to cover up with all sorts of propagandistic proposals to rebuild the mosque! Israel, which has turned more than a million Muslims into refugees and occupied the lands of Muslims! That state is now to arrange the celebrations for the Iranian monarchy, and that state is supplied with Iranian oil by tankers. Ought the people of Iran to celebrate the rule of a traitor to Islam and the interests of the Muslims who gives oil to Israel?...

What benefit have our people ever derived from such rulers that we should now celebrate and light up our cities? Are we to commemorate Agha Mohammad Qajar, that bloodthirsty savage? Or the monarch who massacred people in the mosque of Gowharshad in such number that the walls were stained with blood and the gates of the mosque had to be closed so that none might see the spectacle?...

Tradition relates that the Prophet (upon whom be peace) said that the title of King of Kings, which is borne by the monarchs of Iran, is the most hated of all titles in the sight of God. Islam is fundamentally opposed to the whole notion of monarchy. Anyone who studies the manner in which the Prophet established the government of Islam will realize that Islam came in order to destroy these palaces of tyranny. Monarchy is one of the most shameful and disgraceful reactionary manifestations.

Are millions of tumans of the people's wealth to be spent on these frivolous and absurd celebrations? Are the people of Iran to have a festival for those whose behaviour has been a scandal throughout history and who are a cause of crime and oppression, of abomination and corruption, in the present age?

Only recently, because of a slogan uttered in the university that ran counter to his lowly inclinations, he sent his bandits to the university and had them beat the students atrociously. According to reports that reached here, some female students needed surgery as a result of the blows and wounds they received. Their only crime was opposing the twenty-five hundredth anniversary celebrations and saying, "We have no need of this festival. Put an end to the hunger of our people; do not celebrate over the corpses of our people"...

People address themselves to us constantly from all over Iran, asking permission to use the charitable taxes demanded by Islam for the building of bathhouses, for they are without baths. What has happened to all those gilded promises, those pretentious claims that Iran is progressing on the same level as the more developed countries of the world, that the people are prosperous and content? Are the people prosperous when they sell their children because of hunger?...

If the Ulema of Qom, Mashhad, Tabriz, Isfahan, Shiraz, and other cities in Iran were to protest collectively today against this scandalous festival, to condemn these extravagances that are destroying the people and the nation, be assured that results would be forthcoming. There are more than 150,000 students and scholars of the religious sciences in Iran. If all these scholars, authorities, proofs of Islam, and Ayatollahs were to break the seal of silence and make a collective protest to remove the endorsements of their silence from the list of crimes committed by the regime, would they not achieve their aims? Would the authorities arrest them all, imprison and banish them, destroy them? If they were able to, they would destroy me before anyone else, but their interests do not permit them to do so...

This is the situation in our ruined homeland. Does not all this need to be said? Must not these atrocities be exposed? I consider it my duty to cry out with all the strength at my command and to write and publish with whatever power my pen may have. Let my colleagues do the same - if they consider it proper, if they regard themselves as belonging to the nation of Islam, if they consider themselves to be Shi'a - let them give some thought to what needs to be done. And if they do not consider it proper, they must decide for themselves, and may God Almighty forgive them. What are we to do in the face of all these problems? Under these circumstances, when the foundations of Islam are being destroyed and every last possession of the deprived and poverty-stricken people of Iran is being plundered for the sake of this abominable festival, is there really no path of action open to us?...

Come to your senses; awaken Najaf! Let the voice of the oppressed people of Iran be heard throughout the world. Protest to the government of Iran by letter and telegram. It costs nothing to write a letter; for God's sake, write to the Iranian government. Tell them to abandon this abominable festival, these scandalous extravagances. If these latest excesses are not prevented, still worse misfortunes will descend upon us and we will be confronted with even more distasteful events. Every day new events are created, new disasters for the wretched people of Iran. They even have a special expert for dreaming up these events, these idiotic spectacles. If matters continue on their present course, we will be faced with events in the near future that none of us can even imagine...

I proclaim to the governments and heads of state that mean to take part in this abominable festival that it has no connection with the people of Iran, and that to participate in it is to participate in the murder of the oppressed people of Iran. Let all Muslim heads of state take note in particular that this festival is anti-Islamic and that it is being arranged by Israeli experts and engineers; they should therefore shun all participation in it.

It is the duty of the Muslim people of Iran to refrain from participation in this illegitimate festival, to engage in passive struggle against it, to remain indoors during the days of the festival, and to express by any means possible their disgust and aversion for anyone who contributes to the organization of celebration of the festival..."[6]

In 1972 Iran was believed to have accumulated debts of $ 3 billion, but by the end of 1973, all the debts had been repaid. This transformation was due to the quadrupling of the price of oil, which promised to raise Iran's oil revenue from $ 5 billion a year to the staggering figure of $ 19 billion.

The Pahlavi Foundation had been set up in 1958, ostensibly as a charitable organization, funded by the sale of crown lands to the tenants. Independent of the government, its tentacles reached out deep into many aspects of the economy, both at home and abroad. The Foundation was originally established with its own Bank Omran (development) in order to put to good use the revenues from the sale of the crown lands. Beyond that it became to all intents and purposes a separate empire within the state. By 1979 its assets were estimated at around $ 3 billion.

Bank Omran which was affiliated to the Pahlavi Foundation was mainly engaged in developing the Shah's fortune. Although as a charitable organization, it was really the chief vehicle for the family's finances.

Since I was not directly involved in the financial affairs, my judgement is totally based on what I heard. There were a few people who had accurate information about the Shah's wealth. They were Mostafaqoli Ram, Jafar Behbahanian, Hassan Tufanian and Jafar Sharif-Emami who was for many years the Chairman of the Pahlavi Foundation.

Ram was the chief of Bank Melli for some time and later was given the presidency of Bank Omran, owned by the Shah. Upon Shah's order he put Shahrak Gharb lands in northwestern Tehran on sale and added to the bank's deposits. He was also aware of the Shah's accounts in foreign banks since he was responsible for Mohammad Reza's bank affairs abroad.

Behbahanian who was in charge of financial affairs at the Court was Shah's agent to buy lands and, therefore, had accurate information on Shah's properties.

Ram and Behbahanian were informed of a large number of amount the Shah had deposited in his foreign accounts. Of course, their information did not apply to Shah's money launderings and appropriations at home.

Tufanian and Sharif-Emami had also adequate information about Shah's wealth.

As I said earlier, Reza Shah transferred all his movable and immovable properties to Mohammad Reza before he was sent to exile. The young Shah donated each of his younger brothers ten million rials in cash and his father's remaining palaces. Only the net revenues from the sale of Reza Shah's lands in the north exceeded 620 million rials per year. Mohammad Reza was really wasting the revenues gained from his inherited wealth, mostly purchasing jewellery and donating them to his mistresses. All these expenses were in addition to the budget devoted to the Court.

In a decree the Shah had appointed Mansur Mozaian, a retired army General to sell the properties of the Pahlavi Foundation in Gorgan, northern Iran. He embezzled a lot of money and passed the rest to the Shah. The land transactions attracted many high-ranking officials, businessmen and wealthy people to rush to Gorgan to get lands. Mozaian gradually created on organization and occupied many lands under the pretext that they belonged to the Shah and had to put them on sale.

Those landholders who possessed documents lodged complaints with the local courts against Mozaian but finally they were convinced to pay bribes to Mozaian himself to get back their lands. And those who possessed no supported documents or had no influence in the government, lost their lands and let Mozaian occupy and sell them for the Shah.

I usually received hundreds of complaints at the Special Information Bureau (SIB). The farmers and local residents were very dissatisfied with Mozaian's conduct. I remember to have sent numerous officers to Gorgan to investigate the cases but Mohammad Reza finally ordered all complaints back to Mozaian to decide.

A few years before the victory of the Islamic Revolution in 1979, I ordered an officer to investigate how many hectares of land the Imperial Family had occupied and why in spite of selling them over the past decade they still possessed many lands. Mozaian had replied that the Shah's lands were extended to the Iran-Soviet border!. Accurate local investigations disclosed that Mozaian for nine years out of ten had been selling wastelands. According to the estate laws, the lands were national and belonged to the government and not the Imperial Family.

The officer's findings were handed over to Mohammad Reza. The Shah asked Mozaian to give explanation. Mozaian protested to me and complained to the Shah that the officer's report was not accurate and was based on wrong judgement. He believed that the lands, according to authentic documents (there were no documents at all) belonged to the Shah. He was the first man who lodged a complaint to the Shah against me and protested my decision to investigate the land cases in the north. All this happened after the Shah had declared all the wastelands as national. He sold the occupied fertile properties and transferred the money to foreign banks.

Another case of money laundering was in arms agreements. Field Marshal Hassan Tufanian had received international reputation for his role in arms deals and was described as a major arms dealer. He was Iran's special agent to buy weapons from abroad for ten years.

I guess the Americans had introduced him to Mohammad Reza. Tufanian had studied military in the U.S. and enjoyed close relations with the American military attaches in Iran. He went on a shopping spree and bought any toy the Shah ordered him to buy from the United States, Britain and Israel. But how was it possible for the Shah to distinguish the kind of weapons or order such weapons? The procedure was that, upon military experts recommendations, the commanders of the armed and disciplinary forces passed requests to the head of the joint staff of the armed forces to be delivered to Mohammad Reza for approval. The number of weapons were also proposed by the military experts.

The Shah usually approved requests if there was no opposition from Washington and London. Of course, it was the British and Americans who dictated their terms for the Shah's weapons programmes. After the Shah's approval, Tufanian ordered for the already prepared list of weapons. Though Tufanian was an influential agent at the Court and the Shah usually did not reject his offers, he was not the decision-maker.

It was certain that the arms suppliers were paying commissions to Tufanian. Of course, it was an ordinary and acceptable international principle in arms transactions. The supplier country usually devoted two per cent in a major arms deal to the agent and five per cent to an ordinary order. Tufanian had let Mohammad Reza know of the percentage. The Shah gave a part of the cash to Tufanian and ordered the rest to be paid to his own desired people. Of course, the Shah paid the share of the U.S. and its allies in his arms deals. It was clear that if Tufanian had received just half a per cent in any arms deal, over the ten years he had become a billionaire.

Tufanian was arrested during the climax of the revolution. My brother Nosratollah told me after he was released from prison that a few agents came to the Qasr Prison and took Tufanian to Lavisan where documents pertaining to arms deals were kept. Tufanian reportedly handed over the documents to an American agent and then left Iran with him. At the time, rumours spread that the Americans had taken Tufanian and I out of Iran. Why the Americans saved Tufanian and secured his release from prison? The answer is that some of the U.S. authorities were involved in the arms deal and if Tufanian and the documents pertaining to the arms deals reached the hands of the revolutionary regime, they would disclose them, and their disclosure would certainly lead to a big scandal worse than that of the watergate.

The Shah sometimes played the role of a broker or an arms dealer. Due to a deterioration in the relations between Saudi Arabia and Germany, the Bonn government turned down a request from Riyadh for arms. The Shah asked me to order the equipment the Saudis had demanded from Germany. I flew to Geneva to conduct the 32-million dollar deal. We got the weapons and then re-sold them to Saudi Arabia with a higher price. We earned 800,000 Swiss Francs. The Shah asked me to pass the money to Nasiri to help the poor students.

I would like to cite a memory to portray a more accurate impression of the financial corruptions in arms deals during Mohammad Reza's rule in Iran.

It was around 1970. One day, the then Premier Amir Abbass Hoveida rang me and asked me to meet him in the next morning at the Budget Organization building. I met his request and arrived on time. I was invited to hear the decisions about the country's budget and economic programmes. Head of the Budget Organization Majidi and other economic experts were to make speeches to elaborate on government's budget policies. As far as I can remember, the statistics announced at the meeting showed the following:

Revenues	*Amount (in billion rials)*
Oil revenues	1600
Others	600
Total	2200

Revenues	*Amount (in billion rials)*
Military Budget	
Army	560
Jandarmerie	80
Disciplinary forces	50
Total	690

A speedy calculation would indicate that one third of the country's total budget went to the army and disciplinary forces. If the army devoted just fifty per cent of its budget to arms agreements, (totally 300 billion rials) it could purchase weapons exceeding five billion dollars per year. Moreover, the total people employed in the army was quoted at 400,000 but the real number did not exceed 180,000. Personally, I guess even the latter number was an overestimation and it could not go beyond 160,000. The documents filed at the joint staff could prove my judgement. A portion of the budget was allocated to weapons industries and the rest was earmarked to import arms from abroad. Now, it has to be asked who was spending the large-scale budget. There was no one but the Shah himself.

> "Early in 1973, Iran contracted to buy $ 2 billion worth U.S. arms, the biggest ever arms deal which the United States had signed with any country before. The Shah spelled out his line of policy in an interview given to *Newsweek*, where he said: "Not only do we have national and regional responsibilities but also a world role as guardian and protector of 60 per cent of the world's oil resources ... what we are buying is a deterrent that will be credible to all our neighbours."[7]

A SATAN CALLED ASHRAF

Studying the personal character of Princess Ashraf, Shah's twin sister, is of special importance since she played a significant role both in domestic and foreign policy affairs during her brother's reign.

Among members of the Imperial Family, Princess Ashraf had

an exceptionally strong personality which sometimes led to ill-feeling between her and the Shah.

> "Princess Ashraf was a woman with a very strong personality, and ... in her presence Reza Shah, who greatly admired the toughness of her character, so like, he felt, to his own, had once protested that nature must have made a mix-up in the womb of his wife, because Ashraf ought to have been the boy and Mohammad Reza the girl."[8]

Ashraf was not liked by her father and that caused moral pressure on her. She was not pretty at all but always pretended to be the prettiest. She was not afraid of making risks in her life, no matter if it led to scandals or damaged the credibility of the royal family. She was very serious and Mohammad Reza counted on her in solving the country's political crises. To portray the true picture of Ashraf, I would like to cite some memories.

As I mentioned earlier, Prime Minister Qavam al-Saltaneh used to meet Mohammad Reza daily but the Shah was concerned about his increasing power. One night, Shah's brother, Prince Abdolreza, Princess Ashraf and I attended a dinner at Shah's residence in Sa'adabad Palace. The Shah began complaining about other's interference in his affairs. He was very critical of Qavam for making vital decisions without first consulting him. During a trip to Moscow, Qavam had signed an oil agreement with the Soviets with full rights in the Caspian. The Shah who no longer could tolerate Qavam's behaviour finally decided to abdicate. Princess Ashraf got upset and chewed Shah's ears off for being so intolerant. Abdolreza tried to condole the Shah but in vain. The Shah returned to his sleeping room with grief and we got out of the Palace. In the premises of the Palace, Princess Ashraf, angry over Shah's decision, suggested that Prince Abdolreza seize power immediately if Mohammad Reza was firm on his decision to resign. She adamantly believed that her family must not give up the throne easily. She pushed Abdolreza to accept her offer and promised to make preparations for his succession but Abdolreza turned down the offer and urged her to try to convince Mohammad Reza to stay in power. Princess Ashraf threatened that Gholamreza would succeed the Shah if he insisted in rejecting the offer. The frightened Abdolreza, thus, accepted to do accordingly.

Of course, the Princess was not talking on her own. She had cordial relations with the British Embassy. Diplomats from the Embassy were coming every day to the Palace to meet her. Their meetings always took place in a private room unknown to the government.

Princess Ashraf got in her car and disappeared. It seemed to me that she went to see the British officials to discuss her brother's decision. From that night onwards, the Princess kept a very watchful eye on the developments in the Court to see if the Shah was still intent on his decision to abdicate. There had remained no doubt that the British were considering to remove Mohammad Reza if he politically remained weak. After the collapse of Qavam cabinet, the situation changed and Mohammad Reza changed his decision.

Of course it would occupy thousands of pages to truly disclose the role Princess Ashraf played during his brother's rule especially during Mossaddiq premiership. I just suffice to mention that she had formed a team to step up efforts to remove Mossaddiq from power. Following the downfall of Mossaddiq until the victory of the 1979 Islamic Revolution, she established a political faction and invited all the influential figures who had been dismisssed from their posts by Mohammad Reza to her party. In other words, she employed all those Mohammad Reza had sacked from power. It is interesting to say that the majority of them were pro-British agents who returned to power after a period of diplomatic campaign.

After Reza Shah was sent to exile in South Africa, Princess Ashraf got divorced. After separation, she travelled to South Africa to meet her ailing father. Then, she flew to Egypt. There, she fell in love with a man called Ahmad Shafiq.[9] For a time, the Princess fell in love with Hushang Teimourtash, son of the former court minister. Mohammad Reza opposed their marriage but their relations remained warm for sometime. The misfortune for husbands of Princess Ashraf was that she resented them after some time. Ashraf got divorced from Shafiq and later was married, after Shah's approval, to Mehdi Bushehri, a wealthy Iranian she fell in love with during a trip to Paris. Of course Mohammad Reza's approval of their marriage was a formality. They had no child. After a year, the Princess said she was fed up with him and wanted a new husband. Bushehri was clever enough to leave her but remain her husband by name. That helped him extort billions of rials from governmental agencies just for carrying the title of Princess Ashraf's husband.

This was all about Ashraf's husbands but she betrayed them and slept around with her boy friends whenever possible. Of course, it would take many pages to disclose the dirty life she started after her father's death. She whiled away her hours with tall and young men. I can claim that Ashraf herself cannot remember the names of all the men she has slept with.

For a time, she was a mistress of Taqi Imami, the famous Freemason. In her trip to Egypt, she stayed with King Faruq for a few weeks.

When I was studying in Paris in 1952-3, Princesses Ashraf, Shams and the Queen mother were staying in the French capital to remain safe in case the Shah was toppled during the nationalization of oil crisis. Princess Ashraf had rented a separate room in their well-appointed hotel and invited her friends there. I used to see her two or three days a week, taking her out for a walk or cinema and doing her shoppings sometimes. There were three men I saw intermittently in her room, two French and a Yugoslav. The latter was a young officer and a former aide-de-camp of the Yugoslav leader who had sought political asylum in France. Whenever I went to see Princess Ashraf, one of the three were in her room. She was straight with me and never tried to conceal things from me.

Once, I was an hour early when I got to her room. It was around 9 in the morning. The Yugoslav man had laid his hands clasped beneath his head in the bed staring at the ceiling. He was half-naked. Ashraf was just awake. She had worn the skimpiest of an underwear, two narrow strips of nothing. The lines of sleep were still on her face. She made no attempt to cover herself. She did not need to explain that the man had slept with her the night before. She introduced him to me and then we went shopping.

For a time, she was a mistress of Qolamhussein Jahanshahi who was the chief of her office and commerce minister during Alam cabinet. She whiled away her hours with the then Pakistani Foreign Minister Zolfaqar Ali Bhutto during the latter's trips to Tehran. I would like to cite three more examples to give an accurate understanding of Princess Ashraf's character.

Once, Managing Director of Bank Omran (development) complained to the Shah and said ihat Princess Ashraf had received 3,000 million rials from the bank for construction of some buildings and now she was requesting for another 3,000 million rials. Mohammad Reza appointed the head of his office Nosratollah

Moinian to investigate the case. I summoned Jahanshahi to accurately explain the story. He was afraid of trial and maintained he was innocent. He confirmed that Princess Ashraf had passed the money to a young man to accomplish the building projects. Jahanshahi took the man to my office. He was tall and handsome, around 23. Later, Jahanshahi revealed the details of the story and said that she had donated the money to the young man because of his good face. I informed Mohammad Reza of the story and he ordered not to pay her any more money.

Another interesting affair was Princess Ashraf's relations with Parviz Raji. A man in his late 20s, Raji was appointed the chief of the prime minister's office during Hoveida Cabinet. The Princess, after her first encounter with him, fell in love with Raji. Their friendship allowed Raji to be quickly promoted to high posts. When he was just 32, he was appointed Iran's ambassador to Britain. He kept his post before Bakhteyar was appointed Prime Minister as Shah's last hope to save the Pahlavi monarchy.

During this period, I was the deputy chief of the secret intelligence service, SAVAK. One day, Princess Ashraf telephoned me and asked to eavesdrop Raji's telephone conversations and closely watch his activities. She also ordered to chase him and report his relations with women and take photographs and pass these to her. This made me wonder because many people in SAVAK would learn about Princess Ashraf's sex-scandals. I wrote to the Shah inquiring him what to do. With great surprise, he ordered to meet her sister's request. The Shah did not care even if all the people learned about his sister's illegal relations with men. After all, Princes Ashraf's order was carried out. I usually received a 200 to 300-page report daily. The documents were very interesting. They included all telephone conversations between Raji, Princess Ashraf and their friends. The papers might still be available in SAVAK.

When Raji was appointed ambassador to Britain, Princess Ashraf used to travel to London once a week to meet him. Raji himself has acknowledged to his illegal relations with the Princess in his written memoirs.

Another affair related to Princess Ashraf was the tragic murder of Palancheyan for rejecting her love offer. I had not seen Palancheyan by face but only through photographs. To Princess Ashraf, he was the most lovely boy friend she had been looking for years. Palancheyan belonged to an Armenian well-to-do family.

The trouble for Palancheyan came after he refused to accept the Princess's love offer. One day, the telephone rang. It was my superior boss Nasiri, the chief of SAVAK. The call was unprecedented since we did not usually interfere in the affairs of each other. He called me to his office to consult about an order. Princess Ashraf had ordered Nasiri to arrest Palancheyan. Nasiri was afraid he might be questioned by the Shah if he carried out the order. Surprisingly, Mohammad Reza approved his sister's order irrespective of its possible consequences. Thus, upon Shah's permission, SAVAK arrested Palancheyan and put him into jail.

Princess Ashraf had made tangible offers to him ranging from money to high place jobs hoping he would welcome her offer the next time but contrary to her expectations he again turned down her request. This time, the Princess, as a last-ditch attempt to lure him into friendship, ordered Majid Bakhteyar, a close friend of Palancheyan to invite him to a party in the southern port city of Nowshahr. It was the same city where the Shah escaped to from Baghdad following the 1953 crisis in the country.

The party, as I have heard, was arranged but Princess Ashraf asked Bakhteyar not to let Palancheyan understand that she was also there. Palancheyan had flown to Nowshahr along with Bakhteyar in his private two-engine plane. Upon the Princess's order, Bakhteyar and a number of girls made him drunk and then directed him to a private room in the upper floor. The door was suddenly opened and Princess Ashraf, wearing a skimpy dress, got in. She made no hesitation to clung to Palancheyan. She said she was mad for him. The shameless Ashraf grabbed the drunk man's right arm and thrust him beneath her and swayed over him but Palancheyan pushed her away and left the room. Princess Ashraf lost her tolerance and this time decided to kill him. She ordered SAVAK agents to tamper the engine of his plane. She anticipated that he would take off the day after and would crash mid-way. She had also decided to inform Bakhteyar of her decision and invite him to accompany her in order to avoid the accident. Contrary to her calculation, Palancheyan decided to have a short flight over the sea for enjoyment. The poor Bakhteyar accepted Palancheyan's invitation to get on the plane together. They took off but the plane shortly crashed into the sea killing both on the spot. This was just a part of Ashraf's corruptions. I am sure there are many other sex-related scandals about her which I may not be aware of.

Of course, she did not only plunge into sexual corruption but she was worse in financial affairs. She was fond of two things in her life: men and money. She was a professional gambler. She had invited a man called Eskandari to join her team. The man was a relative of Iraj Eskandari, leader of the Tudeh Party. Eskandari through playing tricks had possessed the Mahrabad Airport lands and got these officially registered in his name. Later, he sold the lands to the government at sky-rocketing prices and became a milionnaire. Princess Ashraf, Eskandari and Mohammad Reza usually played cards together. Another famous gambler Hajebi who was an agent of Ayadi sometimes joined the team. Eskandari and Ashraf played tricks to win the games. Mohammad Reza usually lost between 400 to 500m rials every night. Princes Ashraf received more than half of the cash and gave the rest to Eskandari and Hajebi.

Princess Ashraf was an international drug trafficker and according to some documents she had links with the U.S. mafia groups. She always carried heroins in her bags and smuggled drugs wherever she travelled. She bypassed airport security without any inspections since no one dared to check her bags. Some customs officers passed reports to me about her illegal actions. I informed the Shah and he reluctantly suggested to persuade her not to carry narcotics. Of course, when Mohammad Reza himself did not dare to prevent her from carrying drugs, there was no one to talk to her about the case.

Gradually Princess Ashraf's relations with mafia groups became open. Later, scandals erupted and caused disclosures of her drug smuggling. The scandals received extensive coverage in the foreign press. One scandal occurred only two years before the victory of the 1979 Islamic Revolution when she was in France.

I have heard that once Princess Ashraf was driving back home in the early morning from a gambling house. In her car was Foruq Khajenouri, a close friend of her. As they were driving home, a car suddenly appeared in front of them and made them to stop. Immediately, some shots were fired at Foruq and she died on the spot. Later, it was revealed that the assailants were mafia agents and had planned to get rid of Foruq since she was considered an obstacle for their direct transactions with Ashraf. In brief, the Princess was tired of an ordinary life and enjoyed these affairs.

This was the character of Princess Ashraf, a woman with extreme sexual thirst and the most powerful female member of the Pahlavi family. She was truly the "most corrupt woman in the world". In the history of the world's corrupt women, I have never witnessed any as corrupt as Ashraf. An addict, a drug trafficker, a member of the U.S. mafia and a woman who, according to herself, could not go to sleep before meeting a new man in her bed.

MOHAMMAD REZA'S FAMILY

Taj-ol-Moluk, Mohammad Reza's mother, had come from a land-owning family, had married Reza Khan soon after he became an officer, and retained a great influence over him. She bitterly resented it when later he married two more wives though she accompanied him on his exile to South Africa and was with him when he died.

Taj-ol-Moluk was one of the pillars of power at the Court during her son's reign. She hated Soraya, Shah's second official wife, but was very kind to Farah Diba from the day she was married to the Shah. The reason perhaps was that Empress Farah always came to her room and greeted her. Farah also used to give her a ring daily and tell her regards to her. Empress Farah's good behaviour enhanced her character and credibility before Taj-ol-Moluk.

Prime Minister Assadollah Alam had employed some of his Shirazi relatives at the Court. They formed a powerful pressure group there. Through Alam mediation, Taj-ol-Moluk was privately married to a man called Sabah Yavani who was a relative of Alam. His sister penetrated into the Court and seized many powers there. Her powers were to the extent that she was able to invite any one at the Court. It could be said that Taj-ol-Moluk's palace was under the influence of the Alams.

The Shah's many sisters and brothers were deployed in the area of the Court, each with responsibility for an organization, independent of the government. Princess Ashraf, among many responsibilities was the Head of the Imperial Organization for Social Services. Princess Shams, Shah's elder sister, ran the Iranian Red Crescent while the half-brothers had lesser areas of responsibility. It was difficult, if not impossible, to secure contracts without the intervention of this prince or that princess.

Princess Shams had been married to Freidun Jam but later was divorced. She was in no way like her younger sister Princess Ashraf. She tried to keep good links with all the factions at the Court. She avoided politics and preferred to remain neutral when political differences erupted. Princess Shams later converted to Christianity. Her conversion angered the Shah who saw it a weak point in the Imperial Family. However, he did not take any measures against her but ordered to keep it secret.

A friend of Princess Shams was Mahin Khadivi whose husband was deputy minister of agriculture for some time. I learned that Khadivi had embezzled large amounts of money. I made a file against him which resulted in his dismissal.

Princess Shams was also leading some charity organizations. She had adopted some girls from a nursery and took them to her Palace. One of them was Mahasti, the daughter of an army Captain who had already died. Her family could not meet their expenses and therefore took her to the nursery. Mahasti was pretty and very intelligent. She became her jester and was invited to all parties at the Court.

And then there was Prince Abdolreza who enjoyed the support of the Qajars. He had studied political science at Harvard University and was respected very much in the Pahlavi family. He was the one the British were contemplating to put on the throne should Mohammad Reza be swept from power in the 1940s but was mysteriously killed in a plane crash. Suspicious fingers were pointed to the Shah himself but he kept silent and did not react to rumours. I cannot rule out or rule in the allegation since I have no information about the accident. But that could be similar to the incident which happened for Palancheyan in the hands of Princess Ashraf.

Apart from Prince Gholamreza who was not active at all, Princess Fatema, Shah's youngest half-sister, was the cause of many troubles. Prince Abdolreza had been studying in California and brought an American friend called Vincent Hillyer back with him for vacation. Princess Fatema met Hillyer and they fell in love. She announced her intention of going to California to study, and did so, but promptly got married. The fact that her husband was not only an American but also showed no intention of becoming a Muslim caused outrage. The marriage proved an unhappy one and ended in divorce. They had two children, Keivan and Darius.

General Mohammad Khatami, the husband of Princess Fatema, succeeded Gilanshah as the private pilot of the Shah after the latter was killed in a plane crash. Then, he became the commander of the air force. It was Khatami who commanded the plane which took

Mohammad Reza out of the country during the August 1953 coup de'tat.

Khatami, a physically strong man, married Princess Fatema after she had been divorced from her American husband. He remained as the commander of the air force for 15 years until he was killed in a plane crash.

FEREIDYUN JAM

Brigadier General Fereidyun Jam was the husband of Princess Shams, Shah's elder sister. He was fond of military affairs since he was drafted into the army. He spent much of his time studying military tactics and all his discussions with his friends centred mainly on military affairs. He had a strong memory and memorized poems in the little leisure time left for him. He was faithful to his wife and did most of the housework and let his wife rest. There were tens of guests he happily entertained every day in his house. I was one of the close circle of his friends. He was very kind to his friends and behaved with good will. Betrayal had no meaning for him since he never did so. He was not offended even if he was betrayed. He had no enemies.

It was around 1961 when the Shah consulted me about his imminent decision to grant Jam a new posting. Within a few days I told Jam that the post of a division commander in Mahabad, western Iran, was awaiting for him. Soon he left for his new posting but was dissatisfied because he could not take his wife with him. The division was deployed in a mountainous region of Mahabad and the city's health system was not good at all. After a year, he telephoned me and requested a new posting somewhere else. When I conveyed his request to the Shah, he agreed to give him a new posting in Shiraz. When Jam arrived in Tehran from Mahabad to leave for Shiraz, he learned that the Shah had changed his mind and had decided to oust Bahram Aryana from the post of Chief of Staff and instead appoint Jam in his place. Jam had struck up friendship with an American military advisor who had an attractive wife. The couple dropped in Jam's house intermittently and soon they invited Jam for a countryside visit to the United States. The advisor and Jam had become intimate friends and discussed arms purchases and the two country's military capabilities.

Once the Shah ordered the purchase from Britain of 2,000

Chieften tanks. The tank's engine was American-made and the rest were totally manufactured in England. The American advisor went to work persistently telling Jam that the tanks were not good. He played up the tank's deficiencies and convinced Jam to encourage the Shah to cancel the order. Mohammad Reza was firm in his decision and turned down Jam's proposal to scrap the deal.

Soon an incident took place which was more or less like a conspiracy to oust Jam from his top post. A top general had invited many Iranian and foreign officers at a reception in his house. I was also invited. Nazem and Jam were talking together while other officers were chatting in groups. I was playing my favourite play-card, bridge, with a few friends. An officer came to me and said he had heard that Nazem was telling Jam to agree to a coup plan. The frightened Jam, he said, told Nazem that it was not a good place to talk about that. It came to me as a surprise but I did not take it seriously because my understanding of Jam and Nazem's characters was that they would not engage in such a dangerous play. I was confident that the officer had reported his hearings to the army's intelligence. Shortly, Nazem was made to retire despite his young age and Jam lost his post. He was succeeded by Brigadier General Azhari. After his ouster, with my blessings, he was appointed Iran's ambassador to Spain. In Spain he learned Spanish and became a close friend of the Spanish dictator General Franco and King Den Carlos. All this happened after he had divorced Shams. He departed to take on his new assignment in Madrid along with his new wife, Firuzeh, a former mistress of the Shah.

Jam was a friend of Shahpour J., a difinite British spy in Iran, but had no relations with secret intelligence agencies.

STATESMEN OF THE PAHLAVI PERIOD

Here I would like to give you a general understanding about the character of the high-ranking government officials especially prime ministers during Mohammad Reza's reign. I can claim that all the premiers who took office during Mohammad Reza's leadership were pro-British or pro-American. Politicians with close links with the British and American embassies had a greater chance of promotion to key posts.

After the August 19, 1953 coup Britain's influence which had already declined in other parts of the world after the World War II started to decline in Iran too and the Americans took their place. Being new to the game, the Americans lacked subtlety with which the more experienced British manipulated Iranian politics and politicians. However, the British maintained a lesser role in the Iranian politics.

The elderly politician **Foroughi** was a top Freemason. He was the first Prime Minister after Mohammad Reza was put on the peacock throne after his father's abdication on September 16, 1941. Foroughi was the one who had made the succession to power of Mohammad Reza possible through consultations with the British. Since he was not interested to be a power behind and not be involved in executive affairs he stepped down.

Ali Soheili, a British-trained politician took over and appointed his own trusted men in key positions. It did not take long before he found himself ambassador to London after he had left his post.

Qavam al-Saltaneh, a politician of the Qajar period, did not fear to play gambles with the Russians while he maintained his close connections with both the Americans and the British.

The next Prime Minister was **Mohammad Saed Maraghei**. Being a British puppet, he was also a favourite of the Russians. He had lived for many years in the Caucasia and Moscow had some influence on him. In October 1944, the Russians had demanded an oil concession from Iran. The Russians did not capitalize on him after they failed in securing the concessions they expected from Iran.

> "In spite of intense Russian pressure and the activities of the Tudeh Party, Prime Minister Maraghei refused to be browbeaten into granting oil concessions to the Russians in the Caspian until the conclusion of peace. This stand was strengthened after the resignation of Maraghei who was succeeded by Morteza Qoli Bayat by a bill introduced by Mossaddiq."[10]

Ebrahim Hakimi, Mohsen Sadr, and Abdol Hussein Hajir performed briefly in their posts but **Ali Mansur**, an elderly politician, who was supported by the Americans became Prime Minister in two intervals.

Mansur government which lasted from April until the end of June 1950, set up a special committee to examine the oil bill so that one committee took the place of the usual three.

In June 1950, the Shah appointed General **Ali Razmara** Prime Minister. I have examined about the role of Razmara and his successor Hussein Ala in the previous chapter.

It was **Mohammad Mossaddiq** who emerged as a popular leader in the height of the oil crisis. I have no doubt that Mohammad Mossaddiq was a Freemason and had connections with the British. To me, because of certain purposes, Mossaddiq was urged by the Americans to seek nationalization of oil. He belonged to a Qajar family and had a deep-rooted grudge against the Pahlavi family and the very person of Mohammad Reza. In 1951 he became Prime Minister but was ousted about three years later when Tudehis gained influence in the government. Mossaddiq had no well-organized group supporters. It was just the support of a group of people which made Mossaddiq a leader and it was the withdrawal of their support that led to Mossaddiq's fall.

General **Fadhlollah Zahedi** who masterminded the August 19, 1953 coup against Mossaddiq succeeded him as Prime Minister. Zahedi, relying on U.S. support, tried to act independent of Mohammad Reza and weaken the Shah's position but he was forced to resign after Assadollah Alam intervened, and both London and Washington made it clear that he must go. Zahedi spent the rest of his life in Switzerland womanizing and resting.

Both Fadhlollah and his son, Ardeshir who later became ambassador to London and Washington respectively, used to devote much of their time womanizing. Ardeshir who was given Shah's daughter Princess Shahnaz as bride, remained Iran's ambassador to Washington up to the 1979 Islamic Revolution. He tried to play the role of his father as the saver of Shah's regime in 1979 but there was nothing he could do.

In April 1957 the Shah named **Manuchehr Eqbal** as Prime Minister. While Eqbal was to remain in the post for a record of 1,245 days, his appointment marked a period in which the Shah took charge of the operation of the government. In the political arena, the Shah sponsored the formation of two political parties the Melliyun, or Nationalist Party in 1958, and the Mardom, or People's Party. The first was headed by Eqbal, and the second by Alam, a long time associate of the Shah.

Eqbal, an ambitious premier, started his public life since he was working for the Iranian oil company. Later, he received Princess Ashraf's favour and through his own efforts was elected head of the Cabinet. Like other top ranking authorities, he was a supporter of both the British and Americans. He entered politics early when he was in his 20s. First he was Health Minister and then was appointed Prime Minister. He resigned and was succeeded by Jafar Sharif-Emami but I failed to discover the reasons behind his collapse.

After his resignation, he left Tehran for Paris. After living for many years in France, he returned home and was appointed the Chairman of the National Iranian Oil Company (NIOC). He kept his post until his death. During his tenure of office, embezzlements increased in the government organizations especially in NIOC. I informed the Shah of the main cases. Some officials lost their posts and were prosecuted as a result but no definite files were made against them.

Jafar Sharif-Emami was appointed Prime Minister for two terms. Before his appointment to the top executive post, Sharif-Emami was the Speaker of the Senate and the Head of the Pahlavi Foundation. He also had been the Head of the Iranian Engineers Organization and led many other money-making posts. He was the leader of the Freemasons in Iran. A very intelligent figure, Sharif-Emami dominated all the state affairs and was considered the most seasoned stateman of his time.

> "He made a come back to power when the revolution was coming to a climax in 1978. By then, Shari-Emami was viewed as a pale and inefficient figure of the past. Although he promised freedom of political participation to opposition parties, abandoned the imperial calendar (which calculated years from the time of Cyrus the Great) in favour of the Islamic calendar (which began with the Holy Prophet Mohammad's flight from Mecca in 622 A.D.), closed gambling casinos and some other gregarious symbols of Westernization and undertook a number of other steps intended to appeal to the religious community, his programme failed to gain widespread support or credibility. The new Prime Minister himself was viewed as a loyal courtier and was generally believed to have shared in the corrupt practices of the past. I was told that he transferred over 17 million dollars to foreign banks in his accounts when he escaped abroad before the victory of the 1979 Islamic Revolution...
>
> Sharif-Emami was replaced by Ali Amini at the instance of

> the Kennedy administration. The Shah, feeling himself under pressure "too strong to resist" appointed Amini Prime Minister in May 1961. Amini who belonged to one of the great landholding families in the country was always tagged as "Washington's man" while the Shah recognized in Amini a potentially serious rival for real power and reacted accordingly...
>
> Born in 1903, he brought with him a long tradition of public service both by inheritance and by personal experience. He had been a cabinet minister under Mossaddiq and again under General Zahedi. He had spent three years as the Iranian ambassador to Washington, where he impressed observers as an intelligent, moderate, reform-minded and pro-western political figure. President Kennedy and some of his advisors made no secret of their belief that Amini would be the ideal individual to carry out a meaningful and badly needed reform programme."[11]

He entered into a contract with a multinational consortium which helped the Americans achieve their long-awaited political and economic objectives in Iran and received the lion's share in the consortium. The British were also satisfied with the trend of developments in Iran. The U.S. and British strong presence in Iran prevented the penetration of Communism in Iran and allowed them to freely exercise influence in the Iranian politics. This was Amini who paved the way for the implementation of U.S. policies.

Early in 1962, **Ali Amini**'s government amended the 1960 land law, making it into a new law. It shifted the limitation on land ownership from a specified acreage to one village and transferred lands to peasants already working in those fields etc.

After 15 months, the Shah dismissed Amini and introduced his own programme of land reforms which he called the "White Revolution". Never again would he permit a potential rival so close to the seat of power.

Amini reappeared as a key advisor to the Shah as the revolution came to a climax in late 1978 but held no official post.

> "And then there was Assadollah Alam, the man of power who succeeded Amini. The only son of Mohammad Ebrahim (1881-1944), Alam came of an ancient, aristocratic family from Birjand in Khorasan province, eastern Iran. Born in Agusut 1919 only two months before the Shah, Alam was educated at the school

established by his father in Birjand. His family had for generations been Anglophiles because they judged that friendship with Britain was in the best interests of Iran.

In response to Shah's fear of provincial conspiracy, Alam's father took residence in Tehran, leaving all the management of his vast estates to his son. Mohammad Ebrahim's loyalty was rewarded with his appointment as Governor of Fars, and subsequently as Minister of Posts and Telecommunications. For many years, the Alams had faithfully served the ruling dynasty.

Alam married Malektaj, daughter of Ebrahim Qavam in 1939. It was a match intended to strengthen links between the royal family and the non-Qajar aristocracy since Qavam's son Ali was already married to Princess Ashraf, Shah's twin sister."[12]

Alam's political role appeared after the August 19 coup. He was an intermediate between Mohammad Reza and the British as well as American Embassies. The British and Americans had installed many an agent in different parts of Iran and the government but to me there were only four men who played a sensitive role and helped them materialize their long term political objectives in Iran. The four were Earnest Proun, Abdolkarim Ayadi, Shahpour J. and Alam.

Alam's role was not confined to a limited scope of affairs. He was the topmost advisor to the Shah on domestic affairs. Of course, Alam himself was implementing the terms dictated by the British and the Americans. That is to say, the decision on Iran's internal affairs were made in London and Washington and Alam was vested with the responsibility to implement the instructions.

In 1950, Alam was appointed Minister of Interior and subsequently Minister of Agriculture. Between 1953-62 he held a variety of high offices both at the Court and as a minister. At the Shah's bidding, he founded the Mardom, or people's Party which comprised people and groups trusted by the regime. When he was appointed Prime Minister in July 1962, he was given two principle objectives: to quell the mounting opposition to land reforms and at the same time to subsume it within the so-called "White Revolution". So it was that he exterminated Fars clans.

He had created the big circle of his friends around him and had installed all his supporters to key posts in the provinces. Khorasan, Sistan-Baluchestan and Fars provinces were his strong bastion.

During Mohammad Reza's reign, the central government was powerful. Tehran enjoyed good relations with its powerful northern neighbour, the Soviet Union. There was nothing to threaten Khorasan and Sistan. So what was Alam's role in this part of the country? I should say this was London's traditional policy to make plans for a long future. The British ignore time and insist on their principles. There were no reasons to abandon their support of Alam and Qavam families although they did not need them immediately. The British had also won the support of many people in these two provinces and certainly would lose their influence if they broke relations with Alam. Later, the Americans learned this British strategy and planned accordingly.

During these years, a three-member committee, set up on orders from the Shah, was responsible to approve the eligibility of the candidates who were to run for the parliamentary elections. The three were Alam, Mansur and I. Alam exercised the most influence.

Alam was a wealthy man as well. He possessed many properties in Khorasan, Sistan and Fars provinces. He was responsible to administer the lands of his father-in-law, Qavam in Shiraz. He seized fertile lands in northern Minab by force. He deposited millions of dollars in foreign banks and possessed many unique antiques and jewelled articles.

To me, people such as Hajir and Soheili who were assets of London were more intelligent than Alam but what made Alam distinguished to the British was his father's traditional connections with London as a tribe leader of Birjand and the influence of his wife's family. Alam died of leukaemia in early 1978.

Amir Abbass Hoveida succeeded Alam and served the Shah faithfully as Prime Minister for nearly thirteen consecutive years and as Minister of Court for one year more.

Hoveida used the stick to implement Shah's orders. As prime minister, he was not a decision maker since the Shah was in the years of his absolute power. This period was the worst time of Mohammad Reza's leadership.

Hoveida and Nematollah Nasiri who served for fifteen years as Director of SAVAK were arrested with more than a dozen other former top ranking authorities in the last week before the victory of the revolution. They remained in prison briefly and later were executed after trials.

DRUG SMUGGLING AND FINANCIAL CORRUPTION

During Mohammad Reza's reign, much ballyhoo was made by the government against drug trafficking and a number of petty agents were executed but that was only a show to conceal the strong smell of corruption from the ruling family.

Princess Ashraf was actively involved in the smuggling of drugs. Her financial corruption and narcotics smuggling caused a great scandal and received an extensive coverage in the Western press.

A campaign plan against poppy cultivation in Iran was launched during Jahanshah Saleh's tenure of office as Health Minister. The plan, recommended by Washington, was aimed at supporting the governments of Turkey and Afghanistan whose drug trade was a main source of foreign currency income for them. However, the plan neither eradicated drug addiction nor the smuggling of narcotics in Iran.

Fliks Aqayah undoubtedly was a drug trafficker who had acquired international fame. His father Alexander was the number one man among the Armenian minorities and was the South Armenians representative in the Parliament until his death. Fliks, Alexander's eldest son, succeeded his father and kept his role in the Parliament before he was appointed Senator by the Shah.

Fliks was a politician and an expert on Iranian and international affairs. He had connections with the CIA, the Federal Bureau of Investigation (FBI) and the mafia groups. He also enjoyed close personal relations with Mohammad Reza and surpassed all the corrupt people in embezzlement.

During the World War II, Fliks came to an agreement with a U.S. army logistics commander and appropriated all the surplus properties which remained in the stores. A number of American sergeants were also involved in the complicity. The two embezzled millions of dollars without the knowledge of army commanders and shared it between themselves. Fliks even did not spare articles like sugar and stealed tons of it and sold it abroad. He concluded sugar transactions with Britain but forged documents and defamed Shahpour J. He had already made similar transactions with the French. He came to terms with Princess Ashraf and persuaded her to receive a definite share but she was always the losing party in any deal in their bilateral relations.

Amirhushang Dolu, who belonged to a Qajar family, was another top drug trafficker and distributer in Iran. He was known as the leader of Iran's caviar. A man fond of Paris, Dolu had already been living in France. He became a confident of the Shah after his first meeting with him. He knew many Iranian and French pretty girls and took them to Shah's residence and this was enough to have influence at the Court. Top ranking officials were meeting him daily and made their requests to him. Dolu passed all the requests to the Shah and the latter approved them without any exception.

Army General Gholamali Oweisi could be named the third major smuggler of narcotics in the government. He lacked a good general knowledge but approached the Shah through collusion and quickly was promoted to high posts. He siezed a portion of the opium imports from Afghanistan and Turkey when he was the commander of gendarmerie. He also confiscated the drugs discovered by his officers and secretly sold them. Oweisi embezzled over 50 billion rials during his tenure and transferred the money in foreign currency to his bank accounts abroad.

In the years of my post at the Imperial Investigations and SIB, I discovered thousands of cases of embezzlement and bribery among top ranking government officials. It was there when I learned that embezzlement and money laundering was commonplace in almost every government department.

In the last decade of Shah's rule, over 3,750 cases of worngdoings were reported to the Justice Ministry but all were filed upon a verbal order by Prime Minister Hoveida and no action was taken against the culprits. The Shah was also reluctant to comment and usually paid no attention to the matter.

One case pertained to a man called Farmanfarmanian. He was a contractor who built the biggest Tehran stadium. Later, engineers reported that he had played tricks and did not employ all the necessary materials he had already received. Mohammad Reza did not order to punish him but urged him to complete the construction work and repair it. He did accordingly.

At the time when cement was hardly available in the domestic market, thousands of cement sacks were discovered. After investigations it was disclosed that the hoarded material belonged to Majid Alam, a close friend of the Shah. A report on the hoarding materials with documentary pictures were delivered to the Shah but unexpectedly, it was returned to me the day after without any response. That meant reports should go to archive's files.

One of the interesting cases I followed was the embezzlement of General Parviz Khosravani and his friends. Leader of Taj Sports Club, and appointed Head of Physical Training Organization by Hoveida, Khosravani had seized fertile lands in suburbs of Tehran from the local owners through coercion and registered these in his name.

The Ninth Department of SAVAK in a detailed report presented a complete list of the registered lands and economic installations belonging to Khosravani throughout the country. I remember the number of his properties exceeded 200. I passed the report to the Shah but he ordered it to be studied by Alam. Finally, a small part of his lands were donated to the Pahlavi Foundation and no decision was made for the rest and he kept them for himself.

Another scandalous affair related to Khosravani was gambling parties in his house. Ahancheyan, a famous bazzari, and Naser Golsorkhi, Minister of Natural Resources were also attending the parties. Ahancheyan and Golsorkhi conspired together and siezed many lands in the suburbs of the capital. The Shah got informed of this and asked me to fully brief him of their plans. I confirmed the reports and also their gambling parties. The same day, Mohammad Reza ordered the dismissal of three ministers and Khosravani.

Prior to the victory of the 1979 Islamic Revolution, once Khosravani came to my office for valediction. He said he planned to live in Turkey but later my brother, Nosratollah, informed me that he had resided in Spain.

SHAH'S WHITE REVOLUTION

In 1963, the Shah began to promulgate a series of measures for reshaping the political, social and economic life of Iran that he called the "White Revolution" (to distinguish it from the Marxist, or Red variety).

To do this, he changed the very basis of the society similar to what Kemal Ataturk had done in Turkey on a larger scale. The programme was approved by a fraudulent referendum held on January 26, 1963. However, the measures were correctly perceived by a large segment of Iranian society as being imposed on the country by the United States and designed to bring about intensification of U.S. dominance over Iran, which had been instituted with the CIA-inspired August 19, 1953 coup de'tat which toppled the popular Mohammad Mossaddiq government.

> "The Shah's six-point programme of land reform, female suffrage, forest conservation, denationalization of state-owned industries, profit sharing for industrial workers, and rural literacy. . . White Revolution corresponded perfectly with the philosophy of economic and cultural development then in vogue in U.S. academic circles."[13]

The largest estates were broken up at the instance of the Kennedy administration but the peasants remained as landless as ever. He distributed land to the peasants to keep them happy, but he destroyed their life support system. The reforms introduced a more inefficient agricultural operation. The farmers were granted no credits, no fertilizer supplies and no marketing system.

> "Shah's "Land Reform" programmes broke up the old feudal holdings. He struck a blow for greater economic independence for the peasant farmers, but he also broke an agricultural system that had been successful for centuries. By destroying the link between the capital supply that the feudal landowners could provide the peasants and the marketing network that they controlled, the Shah's reform introduced a vastly more inefficient agricultural operation. Although his intentions were good, he failed to complete the reform process by arranging for credit to the farmers, for fertilizer supplies, and for an efficient marketing system...
>
> The net result was that the problems for agriculture, which had already begun to assert themselves because of the pressure of population on arable land, became compounded as that arable land was farmed less efficiently. Families living in the farming areas began to recognize that they could not support themselves with the resources available, and it soon became standard practice for younger male members of the family to leave the farms and seek employment in the cities.
>
> The Shah's industrialization programme added to the pressures for migration. The availability of attractive jobs in the small industries in and near the provincial cities and even Tehran provided an additional impulse that complemented the

> pressures that were forcing young men off the land... Because of the oil boom of 1973, Iran began to earn about twenty-two billion dollars a year in hard currencies from selling its crude petroleum overseas. The Shah determined that he would plunge almost all of that back into the industrialization of his country, so that by the year 2,000 it would be "fifth-largest industrial entity on the face of the earth".[14]

The Kennedy administration had calculated that a farmer would keep a strong motivation to work if he possessed lands and a motivation to defend land would mean struggle against Communism. The Americans had little knowledge of the structure of the Iranian society and their proposed reforms in Iran destroyed Iran's agriculture. I am convinced that the British might have been involved in recommending the plan.

> "In 1956, 29 per cent of the people lived in towns, while in 1966 this figure had attained 38 per cent. Thus, in 1966 the rural population was 62 per cent of the total and included farmers and craftsmen living in 60,000 villages and the migratory and semi-nomadic tribes. The migration from the villages to the cities continued to dramatically grow in the 70s as families moved to urban areas in search of employment, and to enjoy the amenities not to be found in the villages. Tehran, the capital, attracted the largest number of migrants."[15]

As the population grew, and the cities began to spread, the country became greatly dependent to foreign imports for foodstuff. With the economy totally dependent to foreign imports, the Shah concentrated on the military not food production. As a result Iran, once self-sufficient in food, became one of the world's largest food importers. And it was the western companies which received the largest profit from the economic opportunities in Iran.

Over 2,000,000 tons of wheat were annually imported from the United States. Millions of dollars went to the import of frozen meat from Australia and foodstuffs from Argentina and Bulgaria. Sometimes, over 800 ships were waiting to get their consignment unloaded at the southern port cities which required compensation from the part of the Iranian government for delays.

The oil price increase was a catastrophe. While the four-fold increase in the price of crude oil could turn Iran into an economically developed nation, Shah's favourite projects were absurdly unrealistic and irrelevant to the country's needs.

From 1975 onward, the government had a budgetary deficit of nearly $2 billion. As the recession in the west deepened, the demand for oil fell. Corruption, the flight of capital abroad, and infrastructure bottlenecks compounded the problems. All this was the result of the Shah's "White Revolution".

> "The philosophy of the Shah-People Revolution contained a prescription for a time when the people became dissatisfied with the Shah's policies. But I still did not believe that there was a serious risk of the Shah being overthrown. He had vast experience, the armed forces remained loyal, and he had lived through more difficult periods over the past thirty-seven years. He would continue his policy of liberalization, confident that he could clamp down again without difficulty if need be. It if came to a clamp-down the armed forces would do their duty as they did in 1963 when the tribal kans and the religious leaders raised the standard of revolt against land reform."[16]

> "Iran suffers from undigested economic growth, hastened onwards by the quadrupling of oil prices in 1973 and by the Shah's determination to create a modern society within the span of his reign. The growth has led to an advance in the living standards of most Persian and to the foundation of an industrialized economy that should be able to survive the eventual emptying of Iran's oil wells. The diet is basically healthy. The indigestion has been caused by some profligate and showy waste, a hollow infrastructure (especially the lack of trained men and women), the huge wealth of a relative few and the largely unfulfilled expectations of many. Add to this a dash of xenophobia and the way is clear for Iran's religious leaders, distressed lest foreign-slanted materialism could be trampling traditional Islamic values under foot, and determined to have an authoritative voice in the new Iran, to recruit the disgruntled to their cause - and some three quarters of Iran's 35m people are devout followers of Shia Islam."[17]

> "Mohamad Reza Shah's 25 years of strong control was based on

a number of factors. In the early stages U.S. support, itself partly based on oil interests and seconded by the British and others, was of importance. It was the Americans who transferred FBI training methods to Iran, later seconded by the Israelis. Many Iranians were apt pupils in intelligence and secret police methods, and this aptitude had some basis in money, which in turn had its base in oil. Both the large size of the various Iranian police, intelligence, and secret police organizations, and their and the government's disposal.

Governmental strategy toward the economy, especially since the 1960s, was rapidly to develop large enterprises, using as much modern and labour-saving technology as possible. Despite a few showy 'crack-downs' extremely large profits were encouraged for both domestic and foreign companies, while little was done for those on the bottom rungs of the economic scale.... more seriously, the impetus given by oil to the dramatic economic boom experienced by Iran from 1963 until the late 1970s, with her per capita GNP rising from ca. $200 to $1000 in real terms, and with one of the highest growth rates in recent history for a sizable country, did not lead to a narrowing of the already wide income gap between the rich and the poor, but quite the contrary. Gains were concentrated at the upper levels, and this was largely the result of government policies."[18]

PROBLEMS OF TEHRAN

"Wonderfully situated at the foot of the towering, snow-capped Albroz range of mountains, Tehran in 1974 was a monument to all that is worst in the achievements of modern man. Ugly, sprawling, shoddy, undistinguished, polluting with cars and people, buried under a cloud of pollution, must have been one of the most repulsive capital cities in the world.

The city pulsated with activity of all kinds, construction, demolition, commerce, industry, government, all the indicators of a booming economy... The Shah had invented the phrase, Great Civilization, in 1972 and had subsequently declared that it would be achieved by the end of 1980s. It was essentially materialistic, the realization of the Shah's vision of Iran as a fully developed, industrial state, the Japan of Central Asia. But it was more than that. In the Shah's mind, Iran was part of western civilization, separated by an accident of geography from its natural partners and equals. The Iranians in his view were Aryan, not semitic, and their innate talents and abilities had been suffocated by the blanket of the Arab invasion 1,200 years previously and its spiritual concomitant, Islam. He saw it as his mission to lift this blanket and to restore Iran to its former grandeur among the Great Powers."[19]

With the oil price increasing four-fold, the government had enough cash to turn the capital into a paradise in the Middle East but the Shah did the worst.

Although the city has snowfalls in the winter, usually the snow melts fairly soon. According to accurate reports released by the official sources, the underground waters in Tehran had bubbled up as a result of rain and running waters and was an imminent danger for sky scrapers. As soon as the snow of the Albroz range of mountains metled in spring and summer, it made streams. Some streams joined the Jajrud and Karaj rivers in eastern and western Tehran and some others rolled down into the city and made lake in southern Tehran. In southern Tehran, some houses were inhabitable as these were wet in all seasons. Many pictures were taken and might be still available in the SIB.

The capital was beset by the problems of large cities everywhere, and by some special ones. In the latter category, the city lacked a proper sewage system. There were no plans for development of big cities and this caused an outsized development of the capital and a great disorder in building constructions.

Traffic jams tend to build up on many of its streets. With more than 660 factories and 1,800 smaller industrial units in 1976, air pollution was an increasing problem. The generative workforce was employed for non-infrastructure projects and the society was driven into consumption.

Contrary to Shah's claim his land reforms deteriorated the living conditions of the villagers and made the poor farmers poorer. The reforms pushed the young male members of the families to rush to big cities in search of jobs. The population of Tehran and provincial capital cities dramatically increased as a result and caused a population explosion.

In 1976, a study conducted by SIB suggested that only within five years, 2,700,000 people were added to Tehran's population,

500,000 to Mashhad, 500,000 to Isfahan and 300,000 to Shiraz.

Despite traffic jams becoming an intricate problem, still vehicle imports continued unabated. There were no adequate regulations to prevent immigration to Tehran and vehicle imports. Everybody was thinking of his own interests. Many appropriated millions of rials through establishment of Iran National Company which assembled Paykan cars. The government did not think of the consequences of its policies. In fact, it was not important what would happen in the coming decade.

In short, Tehran itself was an indication of the great disorder and corruption of the regime. Why the population of Tehran suddenly increased from 1.5 to 4 million in 1961? Where can anyone see a similar phenamenon?

I can say with certainty that the chaos and confusion in the country was the result of Mohammad Reza's economic and social policies.

Another problem for Tehran was the lack of a subway system. Construction of a subway was repeatedly discussed during Shah's reign but no concrete results were achieved. It was wondering that many world cities even some Asian capitals enjoyed subway but Tehran lacked it despite huge oil revenues.

The French offered a project to construct a subway. To me the plan was the most dangerous, useless and expensive of its kind. It was dangerous because the proposed subway was 20 meters deep under the ground and lacked an urgent electricity system. It was useless because passengers had to walk some 3 to 4 kilometers to get the immediate station while in Paris there is a station every 500 meters and it was expensive because it could eat millions and even billions of dollars and make the French firms happy.

Japanese firms proposed another plan to construct an air-way but it was again useless although its safety had been guaranteed by the respective firms.

Anyhow, Tehran which could be described as the symbol of Mohammad Reza's land reforms had turned into an ugly city. Buildings had been constructed but without any standard plans for a modern city.

It is a principle that destruction is easy but construction is difficult. Mohammad Reza destroyed the whole structure of the society; he did the simple and easy task.

Fig. 15: Mohammad Reza Shah's wife, Empress Farah

Fig. 16: Amir Abbas Hoveida, a prime minister who remained in office for 13 years

Fig. 17: (Second from left in front row) Chief of Savak Teimour Bakhteyar. (first from right) Shahpour J. Others are British intelligence officials

"O Cyrus, Great King, King of Kings, Achaemenian King, King of the Land of Iran!

"We vow to ever safeguard the traditions of humanism and benevolence on which thou founded the Persian Empire, and to remain for the people of the world the bearers of the message of world brotherhood and truth..."

Mohammad Reza Shah Pahlavi, Shahanshah of Iran, before the tomb of Cyrus, Pasargade, October 12, 1971

Fig. 18: Mohammad Reza Shah Pahlavi celebrated his 30 years on the throne in 1971 but it was a year later when two and a half thousand years of monarchy were commemorated on a grandiose scale among the ruins of the former Achaemenian capital, Persepolis. The Shah felt that Persepolis had put the seal of legitimacy on the Pahlavi dynasty

Chapter 4

Pahlavi Regime, The West's Espionage Bastion

BRITISH AND AMERICAN AGENTS IN IRAN

When the Indian sub-continent became a British colony, Iran and Afghanistan were given special treatment in the British overseas diplomatic desks because of common borders with Britain's traditional arch rival, the Russian Czar and later the Soviet Union.

For London, the two countries were effective instruments to curb Russia's ambitions on the much coveted Iran. The Britons had made arrangements in southern and central Iran to fight the influence of the Soviets and protect Iran against a possible Russian invasion.

If the Russians could control Iran, they would control the Persian Gulf. This had been their dreams since the days of Peter the Great, and they were unable to achieve it without occupying Afghanistan and Iran's Baluchestan Province.

During the Qajar period, Britain was making all-out efforts to exert its influence in Iran and Afghanistan by setting up espionage networks and doing everything necessary to win the loyalty of local chiefs and tribal leaders.

Over the years the British, through the Anglo-Iranian Oil Company (AIOC) had built up a highly efficient intelligence service. Many politicians, and local powerful chiefs from all corners of Iran were on their payroll, safeguarding their interests in this country.

In the oil-rich Khuzestan province they had their puppets Sheikh Khazal and Sheikh Mohamareh who created an autonomous government for a period of time. Before and during World War I, the British supported Sheikh Khazal financially and militarily, and he was encouraged to think of independence of Reza Khan and to hope for British support in this. It was only after Reza Khan consolidated his power in 1924 that Khazal was told to be loyal to the central government which he was. Khazal transferred all his money and jewels abroad and left his immovable property to his children. Shahpour J. had repeatedly explained that Britain never forgets its friends, it was true. Sheikh Khazal's son, Ahmad, was awarded later. He became the aid-de-camp of Mohammad Reza for a time.

The British did enjoy the loyalty of the Qavam Shirazi family in Fars. Ahmad Qavam, son of Qavam Shirazi, married Shams, the elder daughter of Reza Shah. Qavam was a trusted intermediary between Reza Shah and the British. He was the main power broker in the time of crisis. He shuttled back and forth between Reza Shah's Palace and the British Embassy conveying messages between the two parties although he failed in his last attempt to keep Reza Khan in power in 1941.

In Khorasan and Sistan-Baluchestan provinces, the British had put everything in the hands of the Alam family. British and Iranian troops had been stationed in the northern frontier to deter any Soviet invasion of northern Iran.

Saram-ol-Dowleh was installed with full powers in the ancient central city of Isfahan. His prime objective was to carry out the British recommendations in his realm. In return he was supported politically and awarded by his masters. He inherited a great wealth from his father, Zal-ol-Soltan, son of Nasereddin Shah of Qajar.

In the northern Gorgan province, the Akbar family was well-known British agents. The family played an important role in bringing Reza Khan to the throne.

The British also enjoyed a deep influence among the Bakhteyari tribes, and maintained the same privileges in Hamedan Province. They had trained some Iranian politicians for these purposes. Of course, the British influence in Iran dates back prior to the rise to power of Reza Khan.

Before the Communist Bolshevik revolution, the Russians exerted their influence in Iran through their Cossack Brigade stationed in northern Iran. After their revolution, they changed course. They exercised secret infiltration and set up parties in the sphere of their influence.

The Soviet leaders were privately engaged in a power struggle and the policy makers focused their attention on internal problems rather than seeking adventurism abroad. This provided the British with a golden opportunity to establish a centralized powerful military government in Iran, to protect their interests in the Indian sub-continent. Reza Khan was chosen to play this role.

After World War II, Britain's power dramatically declined and the United States which had virtually remained safe from the war emerged as a new world power. Post-war Britain was in no position, militarily or politically, to challenge Russia single-handed in Iran. So, the Americans who were more prepared took this risk after Stalin died in March 1953.

The first time America interfered in Iran was when the domestic politics heated up over the controversial bill to nationalize the oil industry. The Americans supported the move led by Mossaddiq with the aim of receiving a share in Iran's oil later and entered into partnership with the British.

During the August 19, 1953 coup, the British pushed for Mohammad Reza to succeed his father. Their objective: to prevent the Americans from suddenly seizing all the influence over Iran. The British believed that a monarchical regime was the best for Iran, and they acted accordingly.

Gradually the British formed a strategic relationship with the United States and allowed Washington the role they used to play in Iran prior to the war. They introduced many of their agents such as Assadollah Alam, Hassan Ali Mansur, Amir Abbass Hoveida, Jafar Sharif-Emami, etc. to the Americans. Iranian politicians who were on the British payroll also extended their cooperation to the Americans while keeping their good links with their traditional masters in London.

In 1953 the Shah was back in his Palace and the supporters of Mossaddiq were being suppressed or were hiding. The real seat of authority in Tehran in those days was the American Embassy rather than Niavaran Palace. It was the CIA with the coordination of British intelligence which had staged the coup and were now supervising the aftermath.

To me, what the Americans are doing today in any part of the world is not possible without the help of the British. Post-war Britain has followed Washington as its firm supporter in all international disputes and the Americans, in return, are the first to support British interests all over the world.

The two friends believed that they were the custodians of Iran and therefore came to a mutual agreement to establish a well-organized intelligence agency to safeguard their interests.

The Central Intelligence Agency (CIA) was empowered to set up SAVAK, the Persian acronym of the Iranian National Security and Intelligence Organization, and the British Intelligence Service was assigned the task to create the Special Information Bureau (SIB) on the basis of their Joint Intelligence Committee (JIC). This way, the Iranian secret services started extensive activities both at home and abroad as a wing of the West's secret agencies. Later, Israel's Mossad also joined the other two and even took the lead in intelligence operations in Iran.

THE BRITISH AND FORMATION OF SIB

I was teaching at War University, when a guard officer in 1959 came to my office and said that I had been summoned by the Shah. I rushed to Mohammad Reza's Marmar Palace. It was a short visit, as I entered his room the Shah came straight to the point.

"A man is waiting for you at Nasiri's office. Go and meet him and carry out his orders without any questions", the Shah ordered.

I immediately went to Nasiri's office. The man waiting was Shahpour J. whom I had repeatedly seen at banquets but had not asked his name. He told me that at a banquet given in Shah's honour during his 1959 state visit to Britain, the Shah had asked the Queen how she was informed of domestic and world developments. The Queen replied that it was a very easy task. She told the Iranian monarch that Britain had established a special organization some 70 years ago to provide up-to-date reports to the top-ranking authorities. The Queen suggested that a reliable person be dispatched to London for special training. The Shah welcomed the proposal and the Queen ordered J. to go ahead with the task.

At first, Nasiri had proposed General Samadianpour, Chief of Police and Mowatheqi to undertake special training in Britain for that purpose but the Shah happily accepted J.'s offer when he rejected Nasiri's suggestion on the grounds that the two were not qualified for such a sensitive mission and instead introduced me for the trip.

SIR SHAHPOUR REPORTER, BRITAIN'S TOP SPY IN IRAN

Once I asked J. "Why are you so kind to me?"

"I have known you for years now. I have taught at War University for five years and almost all the students share the opinion that you are one of their best teachers and quite popular. That is enough for us", he said, as he showed me a file picture of him and his students.

J. asked me to give a date to travel to Britain. The day after, I flew to London.

Shahpour J. was 55 at the time of the revolution. He asserted that he was a Zoroastrian. His family had lived in India but later migrated to Iran. His father, Ardashir J. was one of the founders of Freemasonary in Iran. He was the man who proposed Reza Khan, commander of the Persian Cossack Brigade, to the British which subsequently London had the 1921 coup carried out by Reza Khan and Seyed Zia-o-ddin Tabatabai, a journalist, that ended the previous Qajar dynasty.

I don't know Shahpour's educational background, but he seemed to be the most seasoned intelligence asset Britain had at its disposal in Iran and others ranked inferior to him. He had access, as he himself claimed, to all British secrets regarding Iran. He had a magnetic personality and was able to easily win one's confidence. I was in no doubt that he had undergone professional training courses, but he never disclosed his role to the Iranians. In meetings he was friendly and calm and did not surrender to arguments. 'Speak less and listen more' was his policy and when asked he gave the shortest possible answer. He never took notes in meetings, thanks to his excellent memory.

Shahpour was clearly superior to the Chief of the MI-6 station in Iran but kept no official post. A chief of MI-6 station remained in Iran only for four years and then was replaced with a new chief, but J. was a permanent agent of MI-6 who had no substitutes. J. claimed that he enjoyed friendly personal relations with the Queen and attended annual meetings between the Shah and the Head of MI-6 held during winter sports games in Switzerland.

J. had become so close to the Shah that he had been allowed to teach English to Her Majesty, Shahbanou Farah after the latter was married to the Shah. Later he became personal English teacher to the Shah's heir apparent to the throne, Prince Reza.

Although he was fully infomed of all the affairs at the Court, J. was always inviting me to give him some information concerning Mohammad Reza's private life, his girl friends and the people gathered around him. He showed great interest in learning these things. He used to play up the British power in the world and believed that London's superiority had not declined even after World War II. Shahpour J. had relationships with many influential people.

Brigadier-General Ali Motazed, Deputy of SAVAK and later Iran's Ambassador to Syria prior to the victory of the 1979 Islamic Revolution, was in close touch with Shahpour. Brigadier-General Hashemi who was the Head of SAVAK in Khorasan Province and later Director of the 8th Department, was another contact for him. Among military figures Major-General Kamal and Brigadier-General Alavikia had received J.'s attention and enjoyed cordial links with him. Shahpour had also attracted the confidence of some influential families such as Farmanfarmayan, Bakhteyari and Qashqaies.

I had never seen J. disappointed. The first and the only time I saw him distressed and angry was in 1972 when the Shah surprisingly ordered my report on a 300 million-tuman transaction with a British company to be published in the Persian daily *Ettelaat*. Although Flix Aqayan, the Armenian billionaire, was behind the deal, Shahpour was identified in the report as the broker in the transaction that had gained some profit. The relatively small deal compared to big deals in which millions of tumans were embezzled, were overlooked. After the publication, Shahpour came to my office angry and upset and asked why Mohammad Reza had ordered the reports of embezzlements involving his friends to be carried in the press. I expressed regret and tried to calm him.

Shahpour had brought a book with him to my office. He said that the book revealed his father, Ardashir, had proposed Reza Khan to the British. He pointed to me and clearly but slowly said that I knew who chose the Shah to succeed his father. He left the book for me to study but in fact he meant that I should pass the book to the Shah so he would understand that Shahpour could disclose many secrets.

After a short period of time, Shahpour in a splendid ceremony was honoured with the title of "Sir", a title accorded only to ministers and those who had offered great public services to Britain. The title was the second in importance after "Lord" which was given down to royal and distinguished family members on a hereditary basis. Shahpour's promotion was published in *Ettela'at* upon the Shah's order. *Ettela'at* was chosen perhaps to compensate for the embarrassment caused over the suger deal.

Later Shahpour kept his promise and in an article carried by the influential *Daily Express* revealed that his father was behind the installation of Reza Khan to power.

INTELLIGENCE TRAINING IN BRITAIN

I undertook three courses of intelligence training in Britain, the first of which was for the creation of the Special Information Bureau (SIB).

I had collected my personal belongings and was ready for the fateful flight to London. J. did not give me any address and said a 'friend' would be at the London airport to take me to my hotel. The plane calmly landed at the Heathrow airport. As I was looking around to see the 'friend', I noticed an aged man was walking to me.

"Colonel Fardust?" he asked politely but without any exchange of pleasantries. "Yes" was my brief answer. He introduced himself as hotel waiter.

Later, I learned that he was a retired MI-6 agent who had been vested the responsibility to handle these affairs. It was the first lesson for me to understand that it was the best method with the least expenses for the MI-6 and similar organizations to keep their retired personnel active.

The waiter (MI-6 agent) took me to my five-star hotel in central London. Behind the hotel was a palace. He gave me the room's key. He told me that I could order whatever I liked and whenever I wished. It was a well-furnished room with all the amenities required for a modern flat. He told me that I was allowed to take a walk out of my hotel in the park but I had no permission to go to the Iranian Embassy.

During my four-month stay in London, he called on me several times, and invited me to theatre and restaurant. Even once he invited me for a dinner at his home.

I was in no doubt that I was under surveillance. That was necessary for MI-6 to study my character and reactions since I was to create a modern intelligence organ in a strategic country like Iran and would assume the topmost intelligence post upon returning home.

He took me to a place with many skyscrapers. There were about 20 buildings, each with 10 floors and each floor with about 50 rooms. The lifts took us a few floors up. We got out and stopped in front of a room. The waiter said an MI-6 retired old woman is living in this flat. She owns no house and, therefore, she cleans hotel rooms. She also prepares delicious coffee!. The man knocked at the door. The old woman inside the room asked to identify himself. The waiter uttered a code word, the door opened and we got in. The waiter brought me a pencil and a leaflet to fill in and cautioned that the papers had to be kept inside the room.

They bade me goodbye and left me alone. My training had started.

I was trained by three teachers. My teachers spoke a fluent Persian. Only one of them could not easily communicate in Persian and an interpreter was always at hand to facilitate his job. The waiter had already told me the schedule: five days a week. Saturday and Sunday off. Classes would start at 9 a.m. and would end at 5 p.m. In between I had one hour break to eat my lunch with the teacher. After the class, I was directed to my hotel.

Throughout the period of my training, I was not allowed access to any documents and I was even denied to bring my personal notes back home at the end of my course.

After finishing the first course, two other teachers, a Communist professional teacher and an expert on Iran's economic affairs, started teaching special lessons. My Communist teacher commented on Communism as a theology and only devoted the whole course explaining its social and economic system. My economic expert was a British Iranologist. During the whole course, he maintained a tough tone against the Shah. He was very critical of Iran's economic conditions and believed that Mohammad Reza had to make some fundamental reforms otherwise his government could not remain in power for long.

He believed Iran had a great potential to grow all agricultural products and if the Shah's government embarked on a long-term plan, the country would become self-sufficient in food production and agricultural goods in a short span of time.

The teacher believed that Iran should avoid money-consuming big industrial projects and instead implement small and medium-sized projects in order to save hard currency and create as many jobs as possible to solve one of the country's big problems, unemployment. He said that Iranian government should construct small dams on rivers to make the water for irrigation available throughout the country. He wanted me to pass his recommendations to the Shah.

The teacher's proposals ran exactly against Shah's "White Revolution" which was implemented a few years later at the instigation of the Kennedy administration.

In the 1960s, London and Washington made every effort to receive more shares in Iran's oil and keep Iran dependent to themselves economically. To achieve their objectives, they plundered the Iranian oil, injected assembling industries into Iran, imposed big and expensive projects and destroyed Iran's agriculture. The United States exported wheat and Australia meat to Iran and in return, they imported crude oil from Iran.

One day, I was invited to the MI-6 documents centre. As the Centre's President was explaining the files, suddenly Shahpour J. dropped in. His unexpected presence in London was a surprise to me. He explained that different files on all countries, even Britain itself, were available at the centre. The centre was considered an important source of accurate information. He then asked me if I liked to see films about Reza Shah from childhood to his seizure of power.

It was a memorable film I saw about Reza Khan since he chose to go into the soldiering trade up to crowning himself the Shah. I requested to see the film about Mohammad Reza but Shahpour, despite his earlier consent, turned down my request and said it was too early for me to see the film.

After finishing the course, I received 48 hours of special military training at Plymouth, a port city in southwestern England. The training included destruction operations. I underwent gun-shooting special training by a military expert. He used to carefully explain all parts of the pistols and pledged that whoever was trained there would be easily able to carry out accurate assassinations even if strict security measures were imposed. It was clear for me that some agents from all over the world were receiving special training for terrorist and sabotage activities. The trainees returned to their home countries and waited to receive orders to carry out their designated job.

After finishing the whole course, I was informed that a meeting had been arranged for me with my British counterpart, the Head of Joint Intelligence Committee (JIC). After the meeting, he said the training was over and it was time to manage the affairs in action. I stayed in his office for two days and he personally gave me the necessary instructions.

During the period of training, the waiter invited me to restaurants and theatres but did not allow me to pay the bills. He said I was his guest and I was not expected to pay. When I returned home, I learned that all the expenses even the theatres I had been invited as a guest had already been paid by the Iranian government. The expenses were estimated around 3,000 pounds. The invitation perhaps was a British kind of invitation extended to their guests!.

I submitted a comprehensive report about the training I undertook in Britain to the Shah and he approved all the requirements I requested to set up the bureau. I told the Shah that the British welcomed me cordially and respected me too much. "They have to. They make a lot of gains from this country", was Shah's answer.

I found that Mohammad Reza was aware of my training schedule and my teachers were. He rejected the instructions of my Iranologist teacher and said, "He has nothing to do with our policies. It is none of his business". Without any waste of time, I started to make the preparations for the establishment of SIB.

After assuming office as Deputy Chief of SAVAK in 1961, again I was despatched to Britain to receive a four-month long training, again at the instigation of Shahpour. SAVAK's educational programme was poor. Shah felt that it was needed for improving his agency's efficiency. Contrary to my previous training, ironically it was educationally poor with little to learn. When I complained to a responsible official he replied that that was all they could offer. Once during this period, Head of MI-6 Middle East Branch invited me to his house for a dinner. The chief of the MI-6 Sir Dick White, a number of MI-6 agents, and a few attractive women were also in attendance. The women had worn as little as decency required, revealing just enough of themselves to pique any man's desire for more. White expressed satisfaction with the training and offered me a book, with no signature of course, as gift. I returned his favour with a valuable Persian handicraft. I met White two more times in Iran later.

The Middle East Branch Head of MI-6 said that those who retired from the MI-6 mostly got a post somewhere, a commercial ship for instance, and met the secret agents of the MI-6 at target ports and passed over all the collected intelligence to the London office.

The Head of MI-6 station in Iran once also invited me for a dinner. An unidentified guest was also with us. After dinner, we had all kinds of beverages and beer. I felt a headache. The unidentified guest urged me to give him some information on the condition that the Shah would not be informed. I immediately understood that he was suggesting to employ me. I got afraid and reasoned that the Shah has allowed all the governmental organizations to provide the British with any information they required but it was impossible not to inform him. The guest did not insist and changed the subject.

The third and the last training I received in Britain was in 1963. The travel was put forward by the British. Brigadier-General Mahutian the then Deputy Chief of SAVAK and Samadianpour, the then Deputy of Police, were also invited to receive the training. There was nothing new for me.

During the period, once we were invited to visit the Scotland Yard Criminal Museum. They showed us a film. The film had much to see. I have to state that rape and sexual abuse in Britain is widespread. Police have created special branches to investigate the cases of sex abuse. A film was also screened in the museum which identified the ways to arrest criminals. The pictures shown in the film were obscene and disgusting.

The head of a special branch said that more than a thousand cases of rape and murder are committed every night in Britain. He also disclosed that some exemplary punishment cases have usually been reported and some research was under way to scrutinize the root cause of the criminal acts.

BRITISH INTELLIGENCE AND ITS ESTABLISHMENTS

Contrary to U.S. secret agencies, the British intelligence apparatus has traditionally observed maximum secrecy even for its name and structure. Personally, I have never seen any memories by the senior members of the British secret services or top government officials but there are lots by the CIA and FIB former heads.

That is why the CIA and FBI, and even the National Security Agency are known internationally, while the people have been kept in the dark about the structure of the British intelligence services.

It is said that the first ever modern secret organization which served the British authorities was set up during the reign of Queen Elizabeth the First in the 16th century. The organization was known as "Her Majesty's Secret Service". Before the outbreak of WWII, when there was no sunset in the possessions of the British Empire, vast intelligence services were required to ensure the continuation of the British domination over its colonies.

So, for four and a half centuries, the British had established an "intelligence aristocracy" to protect their interests around the world. The members of the world-wide network were mostly local influential figures or wealthy people who actually ran the affairs in the region of their influence.

Up to the 19th century, Freemasonary organizations all over the world especially in their colonies like India and regions of their influence like Iran were the main source of information gathering for the British but in the 20th century and especially after Britain's power declined in post-WW II, the British changed their mind and turned Freemasonary organizations into political institutes to train politicians.

In Iran, the British had this role carried out by influential families of Qavam Shirazi, Alam, Sheikh Khazal, Bakhteyari, Khan Akbar, Saram-ol-Dowleh, Qaraguzlu etc. As long as Britain maintained direct control over its colonies, the world-wide network was run by the British Colonies Office and the British agents in Iran got the instructions from the British Indian ruler.

During World War II, the British formed the Special Operative Executive which operated under the umbrella of the British intelligence apparatus. The SOE was charged with setting up intelligence, political, and partisan groups to operate against the Germans. SOE was very active in Iran especially in the tribal regions of south and southwestern Iran. The Germans tried a lot to penetrate into SOE but in vain. SOE was the basis of the British intelligence operations in Iran later.

The developments after the war made the British adapt themselves to the international climate and therefore decided to create new organizations to meet their intelligence requirements both at home and abroad.

The secret services were divided into separate organizations responsible for foreign intelligence and domestic security.

Section 5 of the Military Intelligence which during the war carried out counter-espionage missions was assigned to look after the domestic security. MI-5 was not a widespread organization but a department with a limited scope of activities and a few personnel, all with a degree higher than B.A. MI-5 was responsible for counter-espionage, domestic security, and political parties. MI-5 operates under the direct supervision of Prime Minister. It controls anti-government political activities. Maximum secrecy requires that MI-5 agents operate under the cover of Scotland Yard officers. For that a "Special Branch" has been set up in the central Scotland Yard headquarters which commands MI-5 operations.

Little information has leaked out about the activities of the MI-5. It has branches in every British county. The branches are empowered to put all government employees under surveillance and pass reports on any suspicious moves. Members of the "Special Branch" which were estimated at about 300 showed up in civilian clothes at duty. They would accompany British authorities on their foreign or domestic trips. So, it can be said that MI-5 and the Scotland Yard Special Branch are the counterpart of FBI in the United States. Of course, they are different in structure. FBI coordinates operations between the police departments of all the states while MI-5 does not interfere in police affairs.

A special organization known as Defense Intelligence Staff was responsible for all the military intelligence and counter-intelligence affairs in the British army. Of course, it was functioning under the army's general staff. All the qualified officers were chosen and received a two-year special training and then were given a post as an intelligence officer.

DIS had set up many external branches abroad which performed their responsibilities through the Section 6 of Military Intelligence.

MI-6 was responsible for military intelligence during the war. It became an independent intelligence organization known as the British Secret Intelligence Service after the war.

Industrialized nations such as the United States, Britain, France, and even Israel have an independent external secret service such as America's CIA which not only gathers information from all over the world but also watches certain political groups which in certain cases hatch plots to overthrow governments which do not come in agreement with U.S. policies. Of course, it does not apply to the Soviet Union. KGB is the intelligence and counter-intelligence organization within and outside the Soviet Union, and GRU is the military intelligence again in and out of the country. So, both the KGB and GRU are charged with both internal and external operations. The two are directed by a joint committee under the supervision of the politbureau of the Communist Party. That is why all Soviet Embassies house large numbers of KGB and GRU agents.

Economic recession caused by war made it clear that MI-6 was not able to manage its world-wide network. Although the British traditionally do not have a good attitude towards the Americans, they gradually came to the conclusion that there was no option left to them but to devote some parts to them and therefore the Americans received parts of the British powerful networks all over the world and this led to a political and intelligence cooperation between the MI-6 and CIA.

Later, the emergence of the Israeli intelligence agency, Mossad, allowed it to receive a share and therefore met a part of the expenses.

Excluding the maximum secrecy applied to MI-6, there are a lot of similarities between MI-6 and CIA in operational affairs. The main responsibilities of MI-6 are setting up spy networks in target countries, collection of a wide range of foreign intelligence including the activities of the pro-government or opposition parties in the countries of residence.

The MI-6 central bureau is operating under the supervision of the Foreign Office but is functioning independently. Unlike CIA, MI-6 chiefs are selected from within the secret network and are appointed by Prime Minister, and their names are preferably kept secret. The organization has got agents in any country, the number of which depends on the strategic importance of that country and the existing political relations. The number of MI-6 agents in the British Embassy in Tehran was not more than five or six while KGB and GRU agents at the Soviet Embassy were estimated at 50 or so. This was perhaps in line with a British policy of "maximum work with the least personnel and expense". Later, I observed this practice in the SIB.

MI-6 agents are required to inform British ambassadors of their activities only in principle but are not necessarily expected to disclose all the details. Even, in some cases, the ambassador is denied access to some special information carried by MI-6 agents. Sometimes, MI-6 is forced to carry out operations which are contrary to the policies of the Foreign Office. The ambassadors usually do not interfere in MI-6 affairs. Moreover, MI-6 station staffers are not obliged to carry out ambassadors' instructions unless orders are officially received from the central bureau. The reports carried by MI-6 agents are directly mailed to the central bureau while in the public they are officially identified as Foreign Office employees.

In the central bureau, there are departments responsible for looking after the affairs of the world's five continents. Every department is divided into different sections, each section dealing with a number of countries, for instance, Horn of Africa etc. And every section is subdivided into desks, each responsible for a country. Should a country be of no great importance to Britain, the MI-6 desk in charge of the neighbouring country would look after the affairs of that country too. Members of each desk are required to speak in the language of the country they are assigned to.

All the MI-6 agents work for 20 years with a desk and become specialized in the sphere of their assigned responsibilities and usually make research or get a job at university after retirement. I followed this policy in SIB. Every member of a desk gets a four-year mission to the target country, and his mission may be repeated during his 20 years of service. For instance, an Iran Desk agent is assigned to the MI-6 station in Tehran for four years. During his stay, he gets a comprehensive knowledge about Iran, and after he is back to his desk at home, he is a reliable analyst on Iranian affairs. In exceptional cases, agents are promoted to a higher rank. A member of Iran Desk may become Chief of Middle East Section in the last years of his service. Of course, desk chiefs are proud of their post since it is considered an important post.

During my training in Britain, I met all those in charge of Iranian affairs including MI-6 Chief, Asia Department Chief, Middle East Section Chief, and Head of Iran Desk as well as members of the desk. All members of the desk spoke fluent Persian. There were at least two permanent agents on Iranian affairs at work. One is the Head of MI-6 station in Tehran, and the other his deputy. The two have connections with the Section Chiefs in Britain, SIB, SAVAK, army's intelligence, and their agents in the Iranian government departments and individuals. All the files about Iran since 300 years ago were in the hands of the Head of Iran Desk. As I said, desk agents would retire after 20 years of service, and section chiefs after 30 years. After retirement, they usually teach at universities or do research.

As I have stated earlier, MI-6 followed a clandestine policy. During my three trips to Britain, the British were always playing safe in their statements and did not talk in detail. I learned about many of the untold secrets later when I was given the post of Chief of SIB. It was during these trips that I understood that, contrary to the British, Americans followed an open policy in intelligence affairs as they did in setting up SAVAK in Iran. Of course, it was not possible for me to break up the system functioning in SAVAK and change it into a secret-organized system. Moreover, Iranian government officials preferred SAVAK's open establishments which used to show power and threaten the opponents.

In addition to MI-6, there is another intelligence service in Britain called Government Communications Centre which is similar to that of the American National Security Agency. GCC is mostly concentrating on the technical aspect of the domestic and foreign intelligence such as setting up radar networks, or listening posts, etc.

All the British intelligence affairs are fixed and decided by "Special Bureau" at the Joint Intelligence Committee. SIB Chief is the Secretary of JIC. During my special training in Britain, SIB Chief informed me that, without any exception, all the personnel at the bureau were military officers. He also explained that all the British intelligence activities were coordinated by JIC in its weekly meetings at its central office. The agenda at the talks are provided by the Special Bureau and signed by all the members present at the meeting. A copy of the approved items is sent to the Prime Minister and a second to the Queen. Prime Minister is required to read the reports and issue orders for implementation. The practice of sending a copy of the reports to the Queen is just a formality but, anyhow, that helps the Queen to consult the Prime Minister on important matters.

SIB Chief also revealed that besides intelligence officers, Home Office Minister, Foreign Secretary, and the Plenipotentiary Minister of Colonies were attending the weekly meetings. When I asked if Britain still possessed any colonies, he said that he was responsible to follow up the affairs in the former British colonies.

Upon returning to Iran, I informed the Shah of the British intelligence system. Soon Coordination Council was set up to perform the same role of the British JIC and was elected the Head of SIB and Secretary of the Coordination Council. All the chiefs of secret services including SIB, SAVAK, army's intelligence etc. attended the meetings. The Shah had exempted cabinet ministers from attending the meetings.

TRAINING AT BRITISH SECRET INTELLIGENCE SERVICE

Here, I would like to briefly explain the training I undertook during my three trips to Britain:

Special Bureau Organizing Training

SIB Chief who was also Secretary of JIC briefed me on the structure of SIB and the way it functioned. He believed that except the branches functioning in the British commonwealth member states, the whole structure could be fully translated into action in Iran. He also informed me of the weekly meetings of JIC and those allowed to participate at the meetings as well as the topics discussed in the meetings.

Summarization and Report Assessment Training

Making a resume of the reports was the basis to handle the daily work at SIB. We used to sum up hundreds of reports and make an informative leaflet after accurate investigations and pass it on to the Shah. Of course, no important parts could be either omitted or any personal judgements be attached to the report.

I started practicing how to summarize reports and my British instructor corrected my errors. The prime objectives in summarization was to give the main substance of the report without altering the meaning. Since I was not fluent in English, I looked up the terms and words which I did not know in the dictionary before the class commenced. Later, I taught employees of SIB in Iran how to summarize reports and some of them became valuable assets to SIB.

Evaluation was the second principle in making reports. My instructor was always telling me that a report without scrutinized evaluation was not useful and could not be relied on.

Moreover, I was also taught how to write a well calculated report and bring what matters into full attention. We did not prepare identical reports for all the top government authorities because it did depend on their posts and ranks.

Protection Training

The training included personnel, building and document protection. Personnel protection training was to ensure that all the personnel from the top boss to the cleaner had a clean personal and political record or did not commit any wrongdoing during his service.

Building protection was entirely aimed at safeguarding the buildings of the intelligence services and taking adequate measures to prevent attacks, penetration, planting of listening devices or bombs, etc. The measures even included placing iron bars on the windows, using sophisticated locks etc., and using closed-circuit television networks and other electronic devices to ensure the security and safety of the buildings.

Document protection training specifies how the documents be categorized in terms of sensitivity, subject etc. and where they be kept.

Investigation Training

I was trained to read the reports word by word and take notes of the sources mentioned in the reports in a separate paper before conducting an investigation. You read the available documents, interview different sources and selected individuals, etc.

Report Writing

The instructor delivered a speech about a particular subject and then asked me to write a detailed report on the subject. Then I summarized the report in order to be submitted to the responsible authorities. Of course, detailed reports with all the possible additional information and documents were sent to judiciary officials in order to facilitate decision-making for them.

Secret Networks Training

SIB Chief was arguing that his bureau was Britain's intelligence brain. He meant that the government could not hold its authority without it. He explained that the bureau had to bring all the governmental and private organizations and even intelligence and counter-intelligence departments under full surveillance in order to protect the country against any possible domestic or foreign threats.

SIB was also responsible to discover corruptions and take

measures if deemed necessary. Upon arrival in Iran, I informed the Shah of the system operating in Britain, and he ordered setting up of independent intelligence networks like the one led by Sahapour.

What I stated above was what I learned during my first trip and what follows are the experiences I collected during the second and third trips.

Recruitment Training

I undertook special lessons on how to evaluate the personalities and the characteristics of the candidates applying for a post at SIB in two sessions. My Iranologist instructor gave me a paper which included the personal history of some applicants. At first, I got surprised because I did not expect the British to provide me with such documents but later I understood that they had been allowed to do that. It was a well calculated investigation form made and completed within decades.

Applicants under 22 years of age were not recruited. Every applicant was required to introduce two recommenders within the secret service whose post should be chief of a section or higher. Should the applicant qualify for the conditions, he is asked to fill a form and SAVAK's First Department starts studying the applicant's life to ensure a clean record.

It was pretty clear that the form had been completed within years. Upon arrival, I ordered Colonel Khodadad who was in charge of SAVAK's First Department to employ the applicants on the basis of the same conditions.

Should the study prove the applicant's clean record and eligibility, necessary documents are asked for a two-year temporary employment. After two years, the department will carefully discuss his permanent employment. All employees were retired at 60.

The instructor explained that MI-6 employees did not remain idle after retirement and got a high post under the cover of a company manager etc. in a foreign country. Those employees who become specialized in a certain field are invited to universities. Oxford University is usually the pioneer in employing the retired MI-6 agents. Mrs. Lazmbton, a top member of the MI-6 who is an Iranologist, could be described as a good example.

The top agents at MI-6 are called "eminance grise". Legacy is a principle closely observed in recruiting agents but unidentified people may have a chance if recommended by reliable agents. For instance, Abbass Aram, a British agent, held the post of Foreign Minister for long. When he was Tehran's Ambassador to Japan, he found Hushang Ansari, a staffer of the Embassy, a good agent with outstanding characteristics and, therefore, introduced him to the British. Ansari was immediately promoted to high posts and assumed the post of Information Minister. Later, he was assigned as Iran's Ambassador to the United States. After his tenure expired, he held the posts of Finance Minister and Managing-Director of the National Iranian Oil Company. He was a candidate for the post of Prime Minister but the regime's days came to an end and the revolution triumphed.

Shahpour Reporter was an English teacher at War University since 1954. One may ask why he took that job? Certainly his post at the university was symbolic and his main task was to identify the elite officers and introduce them to MI-6. After receiving approval from the MI-6, the elected officers received different courses of special trainings and later were accorded posts.

Of course, some of the facts I am revealing are the result of my friendly chats with Shahpour Reporter, and my achievements during years of work.

Intelligence and Counter-Intelligence Training

There existed two ways to gather intelligence from abroad. They were extraterritorial means for setting up of bases in the target country. Establishment of a base in target country is similar to that of an extraterritorial base but it first needs to be fully protected, for instance a shop in a border town in northern Iran.

The MI-6 had established many such bases in Iran. Of course, it could be also established through an Embassy, for example, a military attache of a British friendly Embassy such as Turkey or Pakistan. The military attache would meet Iranian military officers and in between, he would have got his required information, or he would have been invited to watch a parade and he would learn about the kind of weapons on display and the style as well as the uniforms of the military personnel etc. All these are "information" for a military attache.

My teacher laid a great emphasis on reading newspapers and studying the public opinion of the target country which he described as "open information". He quoted top CIA experts as saying that nearly 95 per cent of the information required by the agency was collected from the mass media and only the remaining five per cent were classified. Of course, classified documents, perhaps, are less valuable compared to the information received from public channels. Therefore, seizing documents and private information must be carried out when only a sensitive issue is engaged.

MI-6 agents who are dispatched as British or embassty staffers of a friendly country must undergo intelligence and counter-intelligence training in the army. The period is in the form of vindication. An agent has to carefully behave, make friends according to the instructions taught to him, meet friends and participate at public ceremonies and get information as much as possible, carefully review the newspapers and magazines, listen to the radio and watch the television regularly and closely follow all the developments happening in the target country. In short, a MI-6 agent has to be very active, intelligent and enjoy a good political wisdom and many other special characteristics which are required for a politician.

An agent, during his training period, learns how to safeguard the personnel, buildings and documents. He also becomes an expert on how to launch espionage activities and how to foil counter-intelligence campaigns.

I also undertook special anti-government covert training. My instructor told me that the government should do everything to keep the population happy and avoid public measures which could dissatisfy the people. The secret services should be at work to penetrate into opposition groups and foil the spread of public discontent with the government. He also said for countries like Iran whose foreign intelligence requirements are met by the CIA and MI-6, there was no need for an independent secret service abroad. In SAVAK, only the Second and Seventh Departments were in charge of collecting and analyzing foreign intelligence respectively.

Another topic I was trained was "psychological war" training. It has mostly been extracted from the experiences of WW II. "Psychological war" is aimed at weakening the enemy through different means including spreading rumours. The Americans made a good use of this method during the Cold War era against their rival, the Soviet Union. Here I would like to comment on the

British Broadcasting Corporation which is effective in influencing the public opinion.

Contrary to the public understanding, BBC does not function under MI-6. BBC is a limited and specialized corporation administered by a Supreme Council. Members of the council are seasoned politicians, mostly MPs. But that does not mean it is an independent body as well. Of course, it has coordinations with MI-6 about on presentation its programmes. In council meetings, one or two MI-6 representatives are in attendance. BBC has special desks for all the countries it airs or broadcasts programmes most.

Of course occasional differences in the stance of the British government and that of BBC is only a matter of recommendation by council members. A similar system is also applied to the Voice of America.

THE BRITISH AND QARANEI COUP

During the nineteen years of my service at the country's intelligence apparatus since the establishment of SIB in 1960 until the victory of the 1979 Islamic Revolution, the British or American officials never identified Mohammad Reza's opponents to me or any other intelligence officials like the Head of SAVAK or the Head of Army's Intelligence.

This was obviously the strategy of the intelligence agencies not to identify the opponents of the head of state to him but to exploit them for their own interests. The only rare case divulged by MI-6 was the one related to Major-General Qaranei.

Colonel Qaranei was one of the officers who took part in the August 1953 coup against the Mossaddiq government. He received the confidence of the Americans and soon assumed the post of Chief of Army's Intelligence with the rank of Major-General. His post was the highest intelligence position in the country since SAVAK had not been established yet, and the police was too weak and disorganized to ensure that everything was under control. So, first-hand information reached Qaranei and this paved the way for him to seek greater powers in the country. As his image improved, his ambition of seizing the top seat of power grew as well.

It was not too late that MI-6 revealed to the Shah that he should expect an imminent coup de'tat by Qaranei. For months, Qaranei who had won the support and confidence of the Americans, had been making plans to overthrow Shah in a military coup and form a military government. The plan had been masterminded by CIA station in Athens, Greece, and the U.S. Embassy in Tehran was not involved in the plot so as not to infuriate the Shah. Qaranei had selected few elite officers to carry out the coup. Esfandiar Bozorgmehr, a civilian whom Qaranei had a real trust was the contact between him and the CIA station in Athens. He shuttled between Tehran and Athens to make the necessary coordinations.

The Shah ordered to closely watch their activities but let them go ahead until it was necessary to stop them. A special team went to work. Bozorgmehr was arrested at Mehrabad airport upon arrival from Athens but the news of his arrest remained secret to ensure the success of anti-coup operation.

The documents MI-6 had provided the Shah were strong enough to implicate Bozorgmehr in the plot. Bozorgmehr confessed to his complicity and revealed the names of others involved in the coup conspiracy. Soon, Qaranei and his men were arrested. The Shah did not protest to the Americans. Qaranei was sentenced to three years of imprisonment but was shortly set free after his wife came to me and begged that her husband be forgiven. Qaranei owed his life to me, and he helped me a lot in post-revolution years especially in the weeks after the fall of Shah's government.

The coup made it clear that Americans did not attach great importance to Mohammad Reza's throne in the early years after the 1953 coup but on the contrary, the British policy was aimed at saving Pahlavi dynasty and consolidate Shah's strength and power.

Washington's lack of interest in the Shah became clearer during Amini government. It was after Richard Nixon had taken office as president that the United States placed all its trust in Shah's regime as its closest ally in the strategic Persian Gulf region.

To me, the Qaranei affair left two general impacts: One was that Mohammad Reza, since then, made many efforts to win Washington's confidence and maintain cordial relations with the newly emerged superpower, and; secondly, Americans learned that they were not able to implement any plan without the consent of London, and this led to a closer intelligence cooperation with the British.

MOHAMMAD REZA AND INTELLIGENCE AGENCIES

During 34 years of his rule over Iran, Mohammad Reza maintained regular contact with British and American intelligence representatives in Tehran. The meetings were held at different levels. He used to receive U.S. and British ambassadors separately every two weeks. Regular meetings also took place with MI-6 and CIA station chiefs every fortnight.

> "The Shah used to see the head of the Tehran CIA station once a week; Saturday morning at 9 o'clock was the time set aside for their two-hour meeting. But as the Shah grew more confident, relations between him and the Embassy began to change. He felt the Americans needed him more than he needed them..."[1]

Weekly meetings were also arranged with Shahpour J. He was in London every time prior to Shah's trips there to make the necessary consultations with British authorities and pass the latest information to MI-6 Headquarters.

Mohammad Reza's relations with the two agencies were not limited to meeting their agents in Iran. As I stated earlier, he used to participate in winter games in Switzerland every year and arrangements were made for him to meet MI-6 Middle East Branch Chief. Similar contacts also existed with CIA agents. The Shah had no private meetings with the Russians. His meetings with other ambassadors were public.

During Mohammad Reza's leadership, unauthorized contacts with U.S. Embassy advisors had sharply increased. There was no control over contacts with the embassy. However, to remove any shortcomings, the Shah had established links at the highest level. Officially, a few people were allowed to remain in open touch with foreign intelligence officers for certain purposes. They were Court Minister, Prime Minister, Chief of SAVAK and a few of its designated officers, Head of the army's intelligence and I. Mohammad Reza had empowered us to keep relations with the intelligence officers and repeatedly insisted to allow them access to any required information.

There were lots of U.S. and British operatives active at the Royal Court who gave the guidelines to their subordinates. Abdolkarim

Ayadi and Assadollah Alam were the valuable assets to the British and the Americans. The moles included the circle of Mohammad Reza's close friends as well as foreign diplomats. Here I would like to cite two interesting incidents.

The Brazilian ambassador always showed up at the parties with his wife at diplomatic functions and the parties at the Royal Court. Shortly, the Shah fell in love with the ambassador's wife. The woman, of course, was very anxious to get to the Shah and become his mistress. The ambassador's close relations with the Shah and his influence at the Court facilitated the way for the ambassador to remain in Iran for a longer time after his four-year term expired.

At the end of his second term, the ambassador invited many officials to a farewell party including the Shah and other members of the Royal family. I was also among the invites. We had a lot of drinks. Drunken, the ambassador and I went to the garden. We talked on different subjects. Then, he asked me if I was aware of the reasons behind the extension of his mission. I told him that since his government was satisfied with his good offices to protect his country's interests in Iran, it was quite natural to have his tenure extended. He smiled and said that his country had little interests in Iran and, therefore, it was not the main reason. He explicitly said Washington favoured him to stay, and recommended the Brazilian government to extend his tenure and his government did not see any reason to oppose the suggestion of a friendly government. This way, I learned that the ambassador and his wife had been working for the CIA.

The French Military Attache and his wife were also among the guests usually invited to the Court. They had been posted to Iran after the Brazilian ambassador and his wife had left the country. The attache, a colonel, and his wife remained for 8 years in Iran like the Brazilian couple. When I travelled to France to study law at the doctorate level in 1953, Qarabaqi who was on a Paris visit gave me the address of the former attache. I went to a meeting with him. He had retired with the rank of Colonel. He was working in a real estate agency. He said he had wanted to stay in Iran longer but he had been asked by the French military officials to return home. I asked him why, despite remaining for 8 years in Iran, he got immediately retired. He replied that it was not the French but the Americans who helped him stay in Iran for a longer time.

Of special interests was a "Top Secret" news bulletin the Shah regularly received from the U.S. Embassy. The bulletin was delivered to him during his regular meetings with the ambassador. The news bulletin was published monthly in 10 to 20 pages and a copy was received by all the head of states who had strategic relationships with Washington. A red seal of "Top Secret" was marked on the bottom of every page. It covered the latest international and regional political developments and those of special interest to the recepient countries. The monthly bulletin was sent to SIB after the Shah had studied it, to be destroyed. About two years before the fall of Shah's government, the bulletin stopped coming to SIB. I do not know the reason. Perhaps the Shah did not see it necessary to pass it on to me.

One of the interesting subjects raised in the bulletins was the Caspian Sea oil reserves. The bulletin said that oil experts have discovered large oil reserves in the Caspian Sea close to Baku, extending southward to the Iranian coast. It said should Iran start exploiting the oil, the reserves close to Iran would remain intact since the flow of oil was southward but oil reserves near Baku would start to dry up soon.

More important which I could have never forgotten was the bugging by CIA of Mohammad Reza's private telephone conversations and that of other top ranking authorities. Once, the U.S. Embassy in an attempt to convince the Shah to accept its proposal, in a statement cautioned that his telephone had been tapped and information had leaked out. The Embassy offered a 10-number switchboard independent of the city hot lines. The Shah accepted the offer and the telephone lines were set up. I had accurate information indicating that there existed a red line centre in the U.S. Embassy which could bug all the conversations. Those who were connected with the red lines were the Shah, Court Minister, Prime Minister, Commander of the Royal Guard, Chief of the army's intelligence, Chief of Army's Joint Staff, Chief of SAVAK, Commander of Gendarmerie, Chief of Police, and Head of SIB (I). It became clear to me that Americans would never offer anything if they were not beneficiaries.

CIA IN IRAN

Since the establishment of SIB, I was in direct touch with the CIA station chief in the U.S. Embassy, Colonel Gratian Yatsovic until the end of his mission in Iran. Of course, I had regular meetings with Shahpour J. and the MI-6 station chief at the British Embassy.

Yatsovic was a Yugoslav air force officer who had flown in to the United States with his plane during WWII and sought political asylum there. He was granted U.S. citizenship. He might have had a good intelligence aptitude since he was soon recruited by the CIA and was rapidly promoted to a high rank. It did not take him a long time to become Chief of CIA station in Iran. A CIA posting in Iran was a coveted one since the country was America's closest ally in the region.

During his stay in Iran from 1957 to 1964, he held regular meetings with Iranian authorities and gave parties at his residence but after all he did not have an accurate understanding of Iran as Shahpour J. had.

It was during Yatsovic's posting to Iran that SAVAK was established and he kept American advisors in different SAVAK departments up to 1963 which enabled CIA to closely control the secret service. It was also during his tenure that an American-designed new brigade was formed, its members scattered in the army, SAVAK, and the police. The brigade officers were constantly in touch with American advisors and attended banquets in their homes. The more contacts you had with the Americans, the easier it was for you to grasp a higher position."Spying" did not apply to connections with CIA station chief and exchange of information with him and his subordinates but any unofficial links with Russians, even a staff member of the Embassy, was forbidden. If the composition of an army platoon was revealed to Russians, it was considered an act of "espionage" and the "spy" would be severely punished. The Soviets never objected to the behaviour of the Iranian authorities. Of course, Russians got their required intelligence up to the 1954 through the military and political wings of the Tudeh Party and after the party was eliminated, they relied on their own spies.

"The two superpowers ranged against each other in Iran, with sharply conflicting interests and aims in the area. In other parts of the world the superpowers may find a common interest in maintaining the existing balance, but not so in Iran and the (Persian) Gulf. In this area the Americans used to have virtually everything they wanted; they had the oil and the authority; they were the people in possession, and so they wished at all costs to preserve the status quo. The Russians, on the other hand, had been excluded from the area, economically and strategically. Yet it was an area on their borders and where their influence had once been considerable. It was therefore in their interests to see the status quo upset - not violently upset, perhaps, because the Russians are not keen to see violent revolutions on their doorstep - but altered gradually in their favour. So in Iran it was the Russians who looked for change; the Americans who resisted it....

So it was that the American Embassy in Tehran became the nerve centre for the control of the whole area. When Iran began to play the role of policeman in the (Persian) Gulf region, it was the American Embassy which became the police station. The function of the Embassy staff was more than simply to maintain diplomatic relations with the Shah's government; it was rather to act as protector of his regime. This meant that, though power was divided between the Shah in his Niavaran Palace and the Americans, it was the Embassy compound which became in effect the most important single spot in the whole of Iran..... No body (in the government) questioned that what saved the Shah's throne for him in 1953 was intervention by the CIA, and all the American ambassadors who came to Iran after that had CIA connections, until 1973 when the logical conclusion was reached and the then head of the CIA, Richard Helms, was appointed ambassador."[2]

I have kept two interesting incidents in my mind concerning CIA activities in Iran.

It was around 1971. I had just been appointed Chief of the Imperial Investigations Organization. One day a man who identified himself as a staffer of the U.S. Embassy telephoned me and requested an appointment. I asked permission from the Shah if I was allowed to receive him.

"If he asked about your organization, give him whatever

information you wish but avoid revealing anything else", the Shah told me on telephone.

I received him in my office. His questions centered on my job but at once he changed the subject and asked a suspicious question. I immediately understood that he had been only looking for that. Moqaddam had been appointed Head of Army's Intelligence.

"Would he obey Nasiri's orders or would he act independent of him?" he asked.

Despite Mohammad Reza's strict order, I decided to tell him the fact about Moqaddam.

"He acts very much independent of Nasiri. I know Moqaddam well. He is not a man to obey Nasiri", I disclosed.

The staffer became very happy with my answer. He gave me a big smile as a sign of appreciation and thanked me for the reply and left. I could not understand the reason for his joy with my response but later I learned that they had been trying to establish direct links with Moqaddam but feared that he might inform Nasiri of his links with the CIA.

Then I reported to the Shah that I had not obeyed his order. He did not chastise me for that.

Another memory was about the National Front. Yatsovic and I experienced our first cooperation over that affair. It was 1961. Yatsovic came to my office and said "I informed His Majesty of a problem, and he ordered that I come to you for action".

"What is the problem", I asked.

"We are interested to know more about the National Front. Members of the front are mostly well-educated people and the front itself is growing fast. We want to know if any Tudeh Party members had infiltrated into the party", he asked.

He provided me a list of between 600 to 700 names, mostly university teachers and students with full identifications and requested me to carefully investigate the personal records of all the persons. The Shah confirmed the request and ordered me to see to the Yatsovic's demand.

The outcome of scrutinized investigations revealed that about 30 per cent of the names were Tudeh members. I reported our findings to Yatsovic and he passed the results to CIA Central Headquarters. Soon, CIA's order came. National Front leaders were told to purge the party and repeat it every few years to identify the new infiltrators and expel them from the party.

Yatsovic's superiors gave him a medal of honour for his excellent job. He showed the medal to me and said his superiors have also thanked me for my contribution. I jokingly said, "I did the job and you got the medal!".

Even when he was transferred to Greece, Yatsovic kept visiting Iran regularly and I saw him several times in Alam's house. Two others replaced Yatsovic at the U.S. Embassy. I had repeatedly met Richard Helms during his visits to Iran. When he first visited Tehran, he was CIA Deputy Director. The next time he arrived in Tehran, he was in the capacity of CIA Director. Soon, he was appointed Ambassador to Tehran.

During his first visit to Tehran, Helms said that his younger brother had been a classmate of the Shah and I in Switzerland. I could not exactly remember. Helm's brother was working in a granary in the United States. He was invited to Iran and soon he arrived with his wife. He requested a meeting with me and I did not hesitate to receive him. He showed me some pictures of his school age. In the pictures, Mohammad Reza and I could be seen in the background. He paid a courtesy call to the Shah the same day and left Iran the day after.

During his tenure of office in Tehran, Richard Helms carefully followed the developments in the southern Persian Gulf littoral states and always travelled to Arab countries to hold negotiations with their leaders. He repeatedly invited my wife and I to dinner banquets at his residence but every time I refused under different pretexts.

My reluctance to socialize with him while many people such as Qarabaqi were proud to attend the parties, had made the Americans wonder, and perhaps it was the reason that the last U.S. Ambassador to Iran William Sullivan has described me as "mysterious" in his memoirs.[3]

An important responsibility was to monitor Russian activities in their soil. Radars had been installed in the border region when I became Deputy Chief of SAVAK in 1961. Brigadier Kangarlu, Director of the Fourth Department was responsible to provide adequate protection to the radars. CIA bases in north Iran had between 30 to 40 Americans each. The bases were in jungle areas where barbed-wire and other protective means had been laid with a range of 20,000 meters and a height of about three meters. There were warning bells that could ring throughout the base should someone attempt to penetrate into the base. There were 20 armed troops guarding each base.

Americans had installed powerful radars in north Iran capable of covering all southern Soviet republics with a range of 5,000 kilometers.

All the intelligence gathered by the bases were passed on to the station in the Embassy and nothing was reported to SAVAK.

Of course, the scope of CIA activities in Iran was much wider and I was not aware of many other CIA activities because the responsibilities had been divided between different top security officials by the Shah. Nasiri was coordinating the connection of the CIA and the Iranian intelligence services.

MY MEETINGS WITH MI-6 CHIEF

I have to explicitly acknowledge that during Mohammad Reza's reign no one was given high posts unless he received the prior approval of the British or American Embassies. The more subservient you were to them, the more chances you had to get a post. I was not an exception from this rule too.

Let me give an account of my past political life and the reasons behind my promotions and positions close to the real seat of power. Shortly after I was appointed Head of SIB, Shahpour J. told me that the British government has, for long, been studying my character and capabilities. He admired my past public life and argued that since I had committed no offences to hurt the interests of Britain, there was no reason to keep me away or prevent me from maintaining a strong presence at the Court.

Sometime later, the "Supreme Coordination Council" was established corresponding to that of the British JIC and I became the council's secretary with the rank of Colonel.

A year after SIB was established, while keeping my title, I succeeded Alavikia as Deputy Chief of SAVAK. Of course, the new post was proposed by Shahpour J. A few days later, he came to me and asked, "Are you satisfied with the new post?" He wanted me to understand that he had lobbied for my promotion. During my tenure of office at SAVAK, J. used to come to my office every other day and talk in private. He held similar meetings with Nasiri. Of course, the Shah had no objection to my promotions. I was his confidant and, to him, very talented who deserved such promotions.

After I got the SIB post, upon Shah's order, I continued my regular meetings with MI-6 station chief every fortnight. Shahpour J. usually was interested to know more concerning Shah's private life and Head of MI-6 station was willing to discuss different political and economic topics with me. We usually spent a few minutes warming up and then MI-6 station chief went to ask me a repetitive question. "What's up?" was his question as an introduction to our political discussions.

J. was of the opinion that a potential danger was always threatening the southwestern Khuzestan Province. When I answered that Arab settlers in Khuzestan had no power to rise up against the central government, J. questioned that where did I know that the southern Arab littoral states were not supplying their fellow Arabs with economic and military assistance.

The statement indicated that the British, since long time ago, had planned to bring Iran-Iraq at odds, and to achieve that end, they had already created the ground for disputes and the pretext for an Iraqi attack against Iran, if necessary. In fact, they made a coal under ash to make it erupt whenever their interests demanded.

I continued to regularly meet the British and American station chiefs until 1963. After that, the Shah ordered Nasiri to do the job and I ceased having contacts with them.

I met the Head of MI-6 three times. As I explained earlier, our first meeting was in London during my training. The second meeting took place during the latter's visit to Iran. His colleague at the Embassy gave a banquet in his honour in which I was also invited. After dinner, he shook my hand and suggested to me to keep in close touch with the British girls and said, "British girls are very pretty, do not lose them and keep chatting with them". I met some of them but I found them itching for something. The third meeting was also in Iran in 1970 in the British Embassy at a banquet in his honour.

The MI-6 station chief had only invited Nasiri, Chief of Army's Intelligence General Kamal, Chief of Police General Mobser, Director of the 7th Department of SAVAK General Motazed, and I to the party at his residence.

Shahpour J. as usual made a round of chatting with the quests and then translated all his discussions for the big boss. During the banquet, I learned that MI-6 station chief was more friendly to Motazed but I couldn't understand the reason. It did not take me a long time to learn the reason. Soon, Motazed succeeded me as Deputy Chief of SAVAK. I was then appointed Chief of the Imperial Investigation Organization while maintaining my SIB post.

> "In 1958, I established, as part of my court, the Imperial Investigation Organization. One of its major tasks was to look into the complaints of ordinary citizens. Although I had been in the habit of personally reading all the letters addressed to me, or at least abstracts of them, I naturally had to refer them to appropriate authorities for action. Increasingly I noted one serious shortcoming in the way the complaints or petitions were disposed of ...
>
> Although the gendarmerie as well as our other agencies of government often handle internal self-discipline very well, experience showed the need for an investigating authority. That is what my Imperial Investigation Organization provides. Its staff can go anywhere and without fear or favour or red tape investigate any alleged injustice. Citizens can with complete confidence bring their grievances or their pleas directly to me and my personal staff."[4]

MAHUTIAN NETWORK

As I said earlier, the British, unlike Americans, favoured a decentralized intelligence network with many tiny branches where maximum secrecy would be maintained.

Northern Iran was of special importance to the British because of Iran's joint border with the rival power, Soviet Union.

The British used to collect their required intelligence through two channels. One was the official SAVAK network which followed the American style of a centralized and threatening agency. SAVAK was supplying any kind of information MI-6, CIA and the Israeli Mossad wished to get.

And the second channel was a secret network led by Brigadier-General Mahutian. The network was proposed and established by MI-6. It was the first British-organized secret network which was put under my supervision. After I was appointed Deputy Chief of SAVAK, Mahutian who was also a top SAVAK official disclosed to me that he had established a secret network operating in north Iran.

He said, "the network under my command has rapidly grown and it has been financed by your predecessor Brigadier-General Alavikia who deducted the amount from SAVAK's secret budget. Now that you have succeeded him you should supervise our activities and pay our required budget."

The British could have asked Chief of SAVAK Pakravan to supervise the activities of the network but Shahpour J. again had recommended that I assume the responsibility for that.

Since any deduction from SAVAK's budget was subject to the approval of Chief of SAVAK, I requested Pakravan to pay the required money to the network as before.

Mahutian was reluctant to explain about the activities of the network but he did when I asked him if there was anything preventing him from telling me all the facts. He spoke slowly since there were microphones and other listening devices planted in my room. He said the network's main responsibility was to penetrate into KGB, identify KGB agents and lure them into spying for MI-6 or act as a double agent.

Mahutian said that his network was active in both Mazandaran and Gilan provinces and some 15 shops were already operating in the border towns.

MI-6 station chief suggested that the best way to gather information was to set up a shop in a border town and install a puppet agent as a shopkeeper to provide the MI-6 with the necessary secret information. Of course, the decision was made after lengthy debates by the intelligence experts at the embassy. He believed that customers would get acquainted with the shopkeeper and gradually would become friends. Therefore, close relations with the people would allow the shopkeeper to get the necessary information and pass them on to MI-6.

He also explained that the shopkeeper, or better to say the spy, known as "conscious "agent would visit Tehran every other time and would consult with MI-6 station chief and get the necessary instructions. In certain cases, an agent would be dispatched to the border town to make the necessary coordinations.

Mahutian said Pakravan had been kept in the dark about the network's inside activities. He refused to comment when I requested to go into details nor was he willing to let me know what kind of information they collected and for what reason. All the intelligence directly reached the station chief but the expenses for running the network was paid from SAVAK's secret budget. Even the salaries of agents were paid by SAVAK. It was solely a British intelligence network manned by Iranians and financed by SAVAK.

Recruitment in the network required a complicated procedure which existed in many of the intelligence agencies. An applicant for a post was brought under strict surveillance for a long period of time to ensure his capabilities. He would get employed only if he received a security clearance. Moreover, he had to undergo special training for the post.

Every member of the network was paid 4,500 tumans a month. Mahutian said he was considering to expand the network and set up more shops and asked for 400,000 tumans. I informed Pakravan of the demand. He was confused and reluctant to agree to the demand.

"I don't know what this network is doing and it is eating a huge budget. I do not want to turn down their request but let me make it clear that I'll not agree for any more budget without knowing about their activities", he said with an angry face. Pakravan was right to protest the demand for increasing payments. At the time, SAVAK's secret budget was about 5 million tumans. It was increased to 20 million tumans in 1971. The next time Mahutian requested a higher budget, Pakravan turned down the request outright. Mahutian did not insist too.

It did not take a long time when Nasiri succeeded Pakravan. Mahutian asked for retirement, perhaps recommended by MI-6, and I reluctantly agreed to his retirement. I am certain that Nasiri continued to allocate a budget to the network up to the 1979 Islamic Revolution. This was coincided with the boom in oil prices. As Iran's oil revenues increased, SAVAK's secret budget increased too.

Mahutian did not speak too much and did not show his talent to his inferiors. He used to give a short answer to questions usually "no" or "yes". To me, he was a reliable asset. He was talented enough to lead a vast intelligence network.

Mahutian was single and never married, and I did not hear any love affair related to him. His network was a clear example of the deep influence of British intelligence services.

Of course, the British believed that SAVAK had to function with a British style and maximum secrecy must be maintained but the

Iranian government's favour of showing power and American support persuaded London to stop pressing him to change the style.

SECRET RADIO STATIONS IN IRAN

It was around 1966. In one of our regular Friday meetings, the Shah told me, "there exists a secret network at the General Staff of the Armed Forces. I want you to administer the network. Provide adequate accommodation, financial support, and administrative facilities to members of the network". I ordered my deputy at SIB, Abdollah Eshqipour, to meet the Chief of Staffs of the Armed Forces to inform him of the Shah's order and do the necessary coordination.

A week later, three officers were introduced to me. They were Colonels Maqsudi, Nuranian, and Fruzin. I asked them to brief me on the activities of the network. Maqsudi said, "German army's advances during WWII had caused fear of an imminent occupation of France by the Hitler army. The French army set up a nationwide secret radio station. The network continued to function even after the Germans pushed their way into France. Army units were positioned around each station and General de Guell led partisan resistance operations from London against German troops. The British who liked the system decided to introduce the same network in their army after the war. And our network is similar to that".

I guess during Shah's trip to Britain the Queen and Shahpour J. had proposed the establishment of both the Mahutian network as well as the radio station and Mohammad Reza had accepted the offer.

For years, the secret network had been operating under the army's General Staff and for some reasons, the Shah decided to delegate the responsibility of the administration of the network to SIB. What was the reason for this change? The were several reasons. One was the change of seats at the General Staff. The change would lessen and reduce the secrecy required to be exercised in the stations. As long as the network was operating under the army, there was always fear of information to be leaked out. There was also growing fear of a Soviet infiltration into the SAVAK and the General Staff. The British did not like the system practised in SAVAK and believed that SIB was a secure organ to handle the job. They had complete confidence in me and they liked my style since I had been trained in Britain and acted accordingly. Moreover,

SIB was the only secret organ in the country where maximum secrecy was observed and its chief was never removed or replaced. Of course, again Shahpour J. had suggested me to administer the network. It operated under my command up to the 1979 Islamic Revolution.

As I said, the first ever station appeared in Britain and Ireland on the basis of the experiences achieved during the French resistance movement and later, the British spread the stations in their desired countries.

The conditions of the articles of association of the network stipulated that at the time of peace, underground houses should be set up to launch activities without letting anybody learn about their existence. One or two powerful long-range clandestine radio stations were set up in any of the houses and an agent was assigned to live with his family so that the work went ahead as already planned. Gradually, special places were identified and treasures including weapons and jewellery were hidden at special spots. In case of any invasion of the country by any belligerent state, the radio station would start operation as a secret liberation army unit in all corners of the country. The head station in Cyprus would inform its subordinate stations in Iran of the required information about the sites of the treasures in order to meet their financial and military needs and help them start partisan operations.

The plan, proposed by London, was aimed at countering any Soviet invasion of northern Iran and prevent the collapse of the central government in Tehran. This way, secret radio stations were set up under the supervision of MI-6 in Mashhad, Gorgan, Sari, Rasht, Tabriz, and Isfahan. The stations were monitored by and remained in constant touch with MI-6 station in Cyprus. The central station in Iran was in Tehran to coordinate the activities and issue instructions during peace time.

The British recommended the central ancient city of Isfahan as an alternative station to re-organize and lead the operation in case Tehran and northern cities were occupied by the Soviets. They had anticipated that Isfahan would not be captured by the Soviets because of its geographical distance and, therefore, Western military forces or pro-West groups would be immediately deployed in the city to resist any advancement of the Soviets. In this case, Isfahan would be the main office to coordinate and lead the operations and would also remain in contact with MI-6 station in Cyprus.

Moreover, Cyprus would stand the last choice to keep radio links with the stations inside the country and help prepare the liberation army units if Isfahan was also sieged or captured by the Soviets.

In the first get-acquainted session with the assigned officers, I learned that a man called "doctor" was the most influential figure who was chairing the weekly meetings of the central office of the radio stations. A British Embassy agent was always attending the meetings. I immediately asked for a meeting with doctor. He came to my office the following morning. The man was Dr. Javad Mahiman who was the strong man in the network. The meetings usually were presided over by Mahiman and he was the only one in charge of tackling the affairs in consultation with British Embassy MI-6 chief. The latter attached a great significance to Mahiman's views in running the affairs.

Mahiman diligently carried out the plan and identified appropriate sites to hide the treasures. Some treasures were hidden in the mountains in suburbs of Karaj. Mahiman prepared accurate maps of the sites and delivered them to the British agent which later were passed on to London. A map of the treasure sites was also made available to the related radio stations.

Mahiman explained that treasures included 500,000 tumans worth of gold, 250,000 tumans in cash, 50 light weapons, and other individual military means. The secret budget of the network and SIB were requested through a letter annually. The secret budget of SIB in 1978 was 750,000 tumans, and that of network was 1,200,000 tumans. Fruzin prepared a monthly report about the expenses of the network. Network's secret budget was increased by one million tumans after MI-6 station chief personally intervened to request a higher budget.

The radio stations had assumed the responsibility to help the Shah leave the country in case of emergency. It was scheduled that Mohammad Reza would be taken to the emergency airfield near Kahrizak, in suburbs of Tehran, and get on board a plane and immediately get out of the country. It was also predicted that Mohammad Reza would flee to Pakistan if the whole country falls to the enemy and would fly to one of the Persian Gulf islands, most probably to Kish, in case only northern Iran is occupied by invaders.

The stations were normally functioning prior to the victory of the Islamic Revolution. In December 1978, Colonel Fruzin handed over a message to me in which the British agent had requested delivery of all the documents available at SIB or the radio central building and all the correspondence with Cyprus. I ordered to vacate all the documents and pass them to the British. Since then, I have no information about the fate of radio stations.

MOSSAD EXTRATERRITORIAL OPERATIONS IN IRAN

During Mohmmad Reza's reign, the Israeli intelligence agency, Mossad, was the most active foreign intelligence agency operating in Iran after CIA and MI-6. Here, let me give you an account of my conversations with a top member of Mossad about the sphere of the agency's operations and intentions. Later, Director of the 8th Department of SAVAK told me that he was Deputy Head of Mossad's external relations.

There are two major intelligence networks in Israel. One is responsible for internal security which probably is affiliated to the Prime Minister's office and is equivalent to Iran's Third and Eighth SAVAK departments. The Israeli internal security agency (Shin Beth) comprises nine departments as follows:

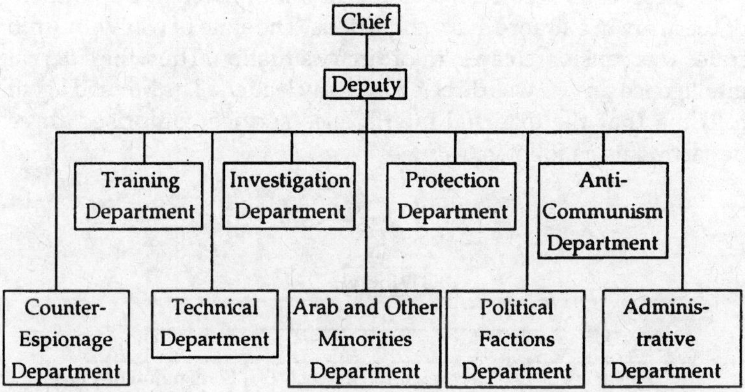

Each department was also sub-divided into different sections and each section into smaller units. SAVAK's Investigation Department had been copied from that of the Israeli internal security agency.

"Shin Beth has the responsibility in Israel for counter-espionage

> and internal security and the service is basically internally oriented. Shin Beth is primarily responsible for collecting information on foreign intelligence organizations, both hostile and friendly, and their activities; protecting the security of Israeli officials and installations abroad; and investigating all forms of subversion directed by either internal or external forces, including sabotage and terrorism in Israel and abroad. Shin Beth evaluates all information developed, collates it with other material routinely and overtly available from both Israeli and foreign sources, and submits evaluated reports to the appropriate government agencies for action. Shin Beth operates to combat two main adversaries: Arabs and the Soviet Union as well as Eastern European intelligence services.
>
> Shin Beth is organized into eight operational and functional departments: (1) Arab Affairs; (2) Non-Arab Affairs; (3) Protective Security; (4) Operational Support; (5) Technology; (6) Interrogation and Legal Counsel; (7) Coordination and Planning; and (8) Administration."[5]

The external intelligence network functions independent of the internal security service. It operates under the Second Department of the army in extraordinary conditions. The state of war with Arab states was considered an extraordinary situation. Thus, the external intelligence service was directed by army leaders. The Mossad agent told me that the external intelligence service comprised three departments as follows:

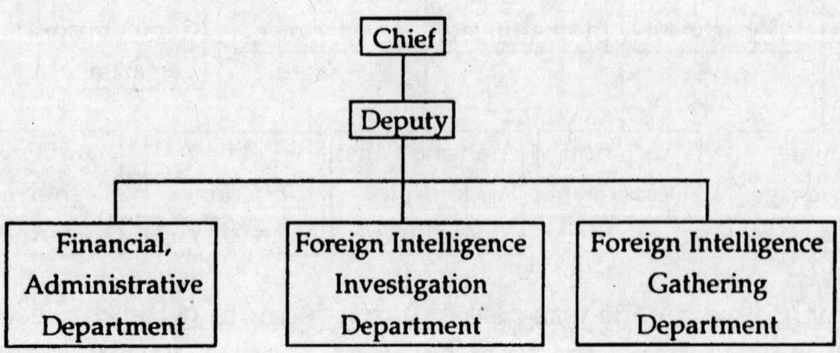

The external intelligence service was equivalent to that of the Second and Seventh Departments at SAVAK. He believed that Mossad's extraterritorial operations were of vital importance to the very existence of Israel and insisted that the Israeli government had to acquire the latest and most accurate information about its neighbouring Arab foes as well as the developments in the entire Middle East. At the time, Egypt, Lebanon, Syria, Jordan, Iraq, and Saudi Arabia required special attention respectively.

He said Israel's foreign and internal intelligence services had been successful and that the government was satisfied with their functioning. He explained that since Jews had been scattered all over the world, especially in Europe and North America, they had achieved great progress. Moreover, the situation allowed them to capture key intelligence posts and gain valuable experience in this field.

> "Mossad is responsible for foreign intelligence collection, political action and counterterrorism. In carrying out its mission to collect positive intelligence, the principal function of Mossad is to conduct agent operations against the Arab nations and their official representatives and installations throughout the world, particularly in Western Europe and the United States, where the national interests of the Arabs in the Near East conflict with Israeli interest. Mossad collects information on the disposition, morale, armaments, equipment and state of leadership of every Arab Army that could be called into action in the case of another round of fighting; and all the information that illuminates Arab internal politics and relationships among the principal Arab leaders and the diplomatic activity of all countries in the Arab world."[6]

Following the creation and establishment of Israel in 1948, all Jews with different skills were invited to join the newly-created intelligence posts. Therefore, it becomes clear that from the very beginning, the Israeli intelligence and security agencies enjoyed professional members and well-organized establishments. Now, I would like to draw your attention to the wide-ranging extraterritorial operations of Mossad in Iran.

Immediately after I joined SAVAK in 1961, Brigadier-General Alavikia, Deputy Chief of SAVAK, introduced Yaacov Nimrodi, an Israeli intelligence expert, to me and said that the Shah has allowed him to remain in touch with him for exchange of intelligence with SAVAK. Nimrodi at the time was a Lieutanent-

Colonel and headed Mossad's station in the secret Israeli Embassy in Tehran.

A few weeks later, Nimrodi came to my office. He bade me a good morning and offered me a sum of over 60,000 tumans.

"What is this money for?", I asked.

"Since the establishment of Israel's extraterritorial bases in Iran, we have paid this much on a monthly basis to Alavikia for his cooperation with us, and we continue to do so to you as his successor", he said.

I rejected his offer. Then, I directly went to Alavikia's residence to inquire about the issue. He confirmed that payments had been made. He accepted my view that it was amounted bribe. However, I refused to accept the money and Nimrodi did not insist.

Anyhow, since probably 1958 Israel had established three bases in Iran. The bases were in Ahvaz in Khuzestan Province, Ilam in Ilam Province, and Baneh and Marivan in Kurdestan Province. In all these areas, SAVAK had its stations too. The targets were Iraq and the southern littoral Arab states. The bases recruited local agents in order to better carry out their espionage missions. The recruited agents were mostly Iraqis but later, agents from Kuwait, Bahrain, United Arab Emirates, and even Saudi Arabia were recruited to the Ahvaz base. The bases were gathering the latest information on the internal situation in Iraq and especially on the government-owned organizations. A copy of the reports prepared by the Israeli bases was sent to SAVAK's Second Department.

Iraq was of special importance to Israel and, therefore, great attention was paid to the developments taking place in that country. Gradually, the bases, which enjoyed all kinds of facilities, extended their activities to the southern Arab states.

> "Mossad stations outside Arab areas in the Near East are generally under diplomatic cover within the embassies and consulates of Israel. There are stations in the United States, most of the European capitals, Turkey, Iran (during the Shah's time) and strategic centres in Latin America, Africa and the Far East. Operations range from formal liaison exchanges with host services through unilateral projects to special executive actions directed against Arab terrorists. There are also smaller stations, which run mostly unilateral operations and handle local liaison on such matters as Arab terrorists....

The principal targets of the Israeli Intelligence and security service are: (1) the Arab states - their capabilities and intentions toward Israel, their relations with the USSR and other powers, their official installations and representatives throughout the world, their leaders, internal and inter-Arab politics, morale, military preparedness and other order of battle; (2) collection of information on secret U.S. policy or decisions, if any, concerning Israel; (3) collection of scientific intelligence in the U.S. and other developed countries; (4) determination of government policy toward Israel in the USSR and East European nations and the problem of Jewish emigration from these areas; (5) close monitoring of anti-Zionist activity throughout the world; and (6) collection of political and economic intelligence in other areas of interest to them, such as Africa."[7]

SAVAK had also established ten extraterritorial bases abroad to monitor the domestic situation in Iraq and other Arab states but their efficiency was even less than the three Israeli bases because of lack of experience on the part of SAVAK agents.

The bases continued operations until 1967-8. Some 300 Israelis were active in these bases. By 1968, Israeli leaders decided to shut down their bases in Iran, and Mossad, since then, directly operated from inside Israel for collecting intelligence on Iraq.

However, Mossad continued to operate in Iran and Nimrodi remained in constant touch with SAVAK. After the bases were removed, Nimrodi continued his exchange of intelligence not with me but with Motazed after he succeeded me. Nimrodi had the most extensive connections with SAVAK but in no way the Americans complained about this. As I stated earlier, CIA and MI-6 had deliberately encouraged SAVAK to turn to Mossad.

I met Nimrodi two times in Tehran after the bases had been withdrawn. He was on a mission to Tehran. He was continuing his job in Israel.[8]

FREEMASONARY, BAHAISM, AND BRITISH TUDEHIS

Freemasonary, since its establishment in Iran, was functioning as a pro-British political organization. Its influence had deepened to the extent that the majority of the statesmen and high ranking authorities had registered in the organization or did so when appointed to a key post. It could easily be claimed that Freemasonary organizations were the most important political groups which administered the affairs in the country for a long time. Wealthy families and many distinguished personalities joined the new setup and carried out the recommendations and the designs of British leaders.

Freemasonary in Iran came into existence under the title of "Pahlavi Lodge" led by Javaheri with the approval of the Shah. Earnest Proun who was a conduit between Mohammad Reza and the Lodge was the most influential figure in the group. As I said earlier, Proun took me to Javaheri's residence for a meeting, and tried to convince me to join the organization but I refused since I was not interested to align with them.

Since the very first day of SAVAK's birth, Americans assigned the 3rd Department to collect information about the activities and investigate the role of foreign bureaus or international organizations operating in Iran. The investigation included Freemasonary and Bahaism as well. The American advisor at the 3rd Department was closely supervising the study and passed the required information on to CIA station chief. A permanent two-member section within the 3rd Department was charged with supervising Freemason and a few other groups operating in the country. The section released two bulletins a year about Freemasons. Although the Shah was aware of Freemasonary activities in Iran, a copy of the bulletin was sent to him through SIB to study.

The unfavourable reputation of Freemasons and a growing opposition to the activities of the group forced the Shah to keep his relations with them strictly covert but he always backed them in a way or another.

The Shah was regularly kept up to date on the latest function of the organization. For their part, Freemasons always expressed loyalty to Mohammad Reza and supported his throne.

The publication of a three-volume book under the title of "Freemason's Lodge and Freemasonary in Iran" written by Ismael Rain inflicted a heavy blow to the organization because it disclosed the names of many of its members. I understand that the disclosure was orchestrated by the Americans to reveal the strong hold the British had over the Iranian ruling clique. Americans had two clear intentions behind the disclosure: first, to lay the blame of past mistakes at the feet of the British and Freemasons and to bring both into ill repute; secondly, to gradually isolate British policy-makers in order to pave the way for U.S.-backed agents to seize key posts.

Bahais were another sect under the surveillance of the 3rd Department. The department prepared a comprehensive report about the activities of Bahais every three months. The Shah was fully aware of Bahai establishments and of high level posts held by Bahais, and he used to show his goodwill to them.

Bahais were in prominance even during Reza Shah. The former monarch appointed Assadollah Sanie, a famous Bahai, his aid-de-camp. Sanie's influence increased during Alam, Mansure, and especially Hoveida. He was War Minister during Hoveida's cabinet for some time. The most prominent Bahai during Pahlavis was Abdolkarim Ayadi. Abdolkarim's father had chosen the surname "Ayadi" meaning "elements or hands" because he was one of "Ayadi Amrollah" (Elements of God's Order), a close group to Abbass Afandi. Abdolkarim's blessings helped many other Bahais to seize top posts during Mohammad Reza's reign. He played a decisive role in having Amir Abbass Hoveida, a Bahai, appointed Prime Minister. Hoveida's father had also been one of the close associates and special writers of Afandi.

The activities of Bahais were jeopardized only once when Hojjatoleslam Falsafi, a famous preacher, lashed out at the sect. In an attempt to pacify public wrath, Mohammad Reza ordered the demolition of Hazirat-al-Qods, a holy place for Bahais, in Tehran. The Shah ordered Ayadi to leave the country for a short time. He stayed in Italy for nine months, and returned home after the situation returned to normal.

Bahais are not allowed to assume political posts without the prior permission of their top leader in Aka, a Bahai holy site in Israel. They are required to confine their activities to trade and agriculture.

"So, why have you accepted a political post?", once I asked Sani.

"Leader permits us to accept political posts in exceptional cases", he replied.

Bahais believe that Iran is the "Promised Land" for Bahais and therefore assuming political posts in Iran was not prohibited. All the Bahais I have met do not have a feeling of being Iranians. It was clear to me that they were spies. The Shah not only did not show any sensitivity towards the growing power of Bahais in Iran but also he explicitly disclosed that he was happy to see them in important posts because they did not conspire against him. The powerful Bahais did everything to improve their financial position and take the upper hand in handling the country's economic affairs. I did not know any poor Bahai during this period. Many districts in Tehran were under Bahai's virtual control.

In 1975, Shah's personal office (under Moinian) handed over to SIB a complaint. The letter said Hojabr Yazdani, a wealthy influential individual, had confiscated lands of sheperds and villagers in Sangsar. The Shah ordered to investigate the case and report back to him the outcome. I dispatched two SIB officers and a SAVAK photographer to the area. The officers reported that inhabitants of Nazaranabad in the mountains of Sangsar are all Bahais. Yazdani was their leader. They had seized lands of nieghbouring Muslim-inhabited village. The evidence was collected, and was handed over to the Shah. The following morning, Ayadi telephoned me and said Mohammad Reza had shown him the report. He said the report was biased, and urged the Shah to dispatch an unbiased team of experts to re-investigate the case!. I said the documented report was accurate, and that there was no need for a re-investigation. Anyhow, nothing was done to return the lands to their Muslim owners. A year later, I learned that Yazdani was engaged in big land transactions in Tehran. He was always escorted by his two bodyguards.

During the reign of last Pahlavi monarch, Bahais launched an extensive campaign propagating Bahaism in Iran. They used girls as means of luring men to convert to Bahaism. They also prescribed marriages between Bahais and Muslims. Iran had the biggest Bahai population in the world after the United States. Bahais who are mostly living in Chicago, U.S. are a powerful community. During the height of Bahais power in Iran, Bahaism was among the religions mentioned in employment application forms in government departments but it was dropped from the forms after their holy site was demolished in Tehran. Since then, they were introducing themselves as Muslims!

> "With the advent of neo-colonialism and the introduction of imperialists to remote countries, a flood of researchers from imperialistic governments, particularly Britain and the Czarist Russia, began pouring into Islamic countries and, under various

pretexts, primarily set to learning the different dimensions of the culture of the Islamic nations and peoples. Mr. Hemfer (founder of Wahabism and the instigator of Mohammad Ben Abdul-Wahab), in his memoirs, says: "The British Foreign Secretary told me that about 5,000 spies and experts on cultural issues had been deployed in the remotest parts of the world to obtain sufficient intelligence on nations and their customs and traditions". On the other hand, the Ottoman Empire which was gradually being weakened, had turned into a field of rivalries between the British and the Russians, each trying to pave the way for its own future domination by penetrating into intellectual, political and social groups.

One of the best known conspiracies by the imperialists in this connection was this same issue of "religion making, sectarianism and creating gaps in the Muslim ranks", just as the history of coming into existence of many of the present beliefs, concepts and parties in the Islamic countries go back to those days (such as Zionism in the Middle East, Babism, Bahaism and Kasravism in Iran, etc.).

Bahaism was a rather successful experience by imperialism and the enemies of Islam, although it did not prove much benefit to its original promoter, Russia. Since its genesis, however, it has acted as a political party, opposed to Islam, disuniting people and paving the way for the superpowers' penetration into Islamic countries, especially Iran. Here, we shall endeavour to describe the background which caused the Russian government to exploit it to create a new faith called Bahaism.

Following the death in 1825 of Sheikh Ehsaee who had managed to launch a new school of thought, called Sheikhia, in Iraq's Shia teaching centres during the tumultous atmosphere of the time between the Osoolis (those believing in rational principles to understand the rules of scripture) and the Akhbaris (those who believed in traditional narratives without applying intellect or rational principles), the ground-work had been laid by Ehsaee for misuse by imposters by virtue of omitting two precepts, namely "resurrection" and "justice", from the religious precepts and their replacement by a fourth precept called "the fourth pillar" (belief in the existence of a deputy and direct link between the Imam and the people during the Imam's absence). Following his death, his disciple, Seyed Kazem Rashti, attempted to propagate his ideas, thereby gradually increasing the gap between the mullas of the new sect and those of Shi'ism. Rashti, who, according to many historians and history books, was not from Rasht but from Vladivostok in Russia and was a political agent of the Russian government, had in his class a young man from Shiraz, named Mirza Ali Mohammad.

After Seyed Kazem's death, Ali Mohammad Shirazi claimed deputyship and attracted some people around himself in Iraq. Among his disciples, there was a man by the name of Sheikh Issa Landarani whose real name, according to his own confessions and the documents published by Czarist Russia, was Kiniaz Dolgorouki who, in the beginning, during the rule of Fath Ali Shah, had been an employee and a translator of the Russian Embassy in Tehran. He had then gone to Russsia and, upon his return to Gilan, had introduced himself as a Muslim by the name of Issa Lankarani. Wearing the clergy attire, he went to Iraq on an intelligence mission for his government to gather intelligence about the situation in the Iraqi religious teaching centres. There he attended the classes taught by Ali Mohammad Shirazi who claimed to be the deputy of the absent Imam Mahdi. This same person (by the fictitious name of Sheikh Issa) was later sent to Tehran as the Russian Ambassador, at which time he supported the Bahai movement in Iran and, according to admissions by Bahais, was the cause of Bahai's release from prison.

Shirazi's psychological disorder, his strong ambitions for leadership, continual instigations by Sheikh Issa Dolgorouki, and the susceptible circumstances created by Rashti all united to induce Ali Mohammad to proclaim himself the justice-administering world saviour by pretending to be the "Promised Mahdi of Islam", and thereby attract the wretched and oppressed people to his beguiling mirage, which caused three civil wars in three sensitive regions of our country and shed much blood.

In his confessions in this respect, Dolgorouki has written: "... I gradually approached him and became one of his closest friends. I invited him to my house several times, where I mixed his water-pipe tobacco with Indian hemp juice and hashish. During his ecstatic moods I encouraged him to stand up against the Shia mullahs and to claim superiority."

Such circumstances gave rise to Ali Mohammad's claim of Mahdism and even prophecy and divinity and so a new sect called "Babism" (which later changed to Bahaism by Hossein Ali Mirza's claim) was created by Shirazi and, in fact, under the leadership of the Russian spy. Ali Mohammad Bab's propagation of superstitious and sacreligious ideas sent him to prison. However, he was released from prison by Manouchehr Khan Motamedodoleh, the governor of Isfahan who was born an Armenia and was from Georgia in Russia and, with the Russian Government's help, had penetrated the Qajar establishment as an enemy and had a deep dislike for Isfahan's Shia mullahs. Manouchehr Khan brought Bab to Isfahan and provided him with propaganda facilities. As stated in "Summorised History" by Nabid Zarandi, "Manouchehr Khan himself endeavoured hard to spread the faith". Dolgorouki has written in his book: "As soon as I received information that Bab had arrived in Isfahan, I wrote a friendly letter to Isfahan Governor Motamedodoleh, asking him to protect him as my good, respected friend."

As is evident, the agents of Czarist Russian government spared no effort to protect him and to spread the new faith. Even when, under pressure from Iranian mullahs and the people of Isfahan, ordered him to arrest and exile Bab to Maku, northwestern Iran, Manoucher Khan refused to enforce the order. "Sayyah's Personal Memoirs", a book written by Abass Afandi (the third Bahai leader), states on page 16:"... Manouchehr Khan sent him out of Isfahan with a group of his riders. When they reached Mourchehkhort, they were secretly ordered to return to Isfahan, where he securely sheltered him in his own house."

This fact was divulged after Manouchehr Khan's death, when Bab was exiled to Maku. After some time he was imprisoned in the Chehrig Castle, and finally in 1850, he was hanged in Tabriz after trial. Although Bab expressly repented twice, his real instigators, the Russian agents, did not allow the disturbance to die down and, even to his death, encouraged him to make baseless claims of disuniting effect.

During Shirazi's imprisonment, unpleasant events took place at the hands of Babis in Zanjan, Ghazvin, and Mazandaran at foreign instigation and by the makings of people such as Mirza Hossein Ali (a pleasure-seeking Iranian who took over the leadership of this new religion, claimed Babism and later claimed to be Baha Ullah, or Glory of God, and even God) as well as a prostitute by the name of Qaralein. History is ashamed to relate such events. The blood of hundreds of innocent men, women and children was spilled. The political disorder at the time, the Shah's chronic illness, repercussions of the instability of his reign, the Qajar family's quarrels over the throne, the existence of ignorant and oppressive governors and incompetent clergy, prevalence of religious gains, the uprising by the Afghan people, British support for separation of the Afghani region, dispersion of Iran's 60 thousand men army as a result of British threats, expansion of the influence exercised by the Russian, British and French embassies in Iran, and riots by the people of Khorasan against the ruling class created such an atmosphere that enabled the Babis to strengthen themselves and thereby give rise to the bloody events at Sheikh Tabassi Castle as well as the tragic events in Tabriz and Zanjan. Amir Kabir who sensed British and Russian imperialism to be behind such events, decided to crush them. However, in the wake of his death, foreign embassies proceeded with their schemes until August 1952 when the Babis tried in vain to assassinate Nasserddin Shah. Following this attempt, Baha Ullah was arrested, convicted and sentenced to death. However, he was released from prison at the Russian Ambassador's support and mediation and was saved from certain death at the recommendation of Emperor Nicolevic Alexander KK, whereupon he was exiled to Iraq with the remnants of the Babis. During their ten years in Baghdad, they continued with their sedition, causing disunity and diversity among the Muslim community as well as committing crimes, most of which are recorded in history books. They were finally summoned to Constantinople by the Ottoman Government. The fact is that the Ottoman Government initially sought to use them as a means to weaken the Iranian Government. But, as soon as it found out about their secret connections with the Russian and British embassies in Turkey, it put a stop to their activities, and finally, under pressure from the people who had grown impatient with their atrocities, it divided them into two groups one of which, called Babia, headed by Sobhe Azai, was exiled to Cyprus, and the other group, headed by Baha Ullah, was exiled to Akka in Palestine. The Babia group in Cyprus abandoned its activities and is now almost extinct. But Baha Ullah in Palestine, with the help of the British government, who were at war with the Ottoman Government, as well as Abass Afandi's activities and his trips to Europe and America and the support he received from the Zionists who contemplated to set up a government and to occupy Palestine, was able to set up an organization in Palestine, modelled on European political parties, at a site called "Beitol Adl" (House of Justice) in Haifa. This same establishment gradually became an authority for taking decisions on Bahai activities in all countries, and was turned into a fundamental pillar for establishment and entrenchment of the regime occupying Qods (Jerusalem). Following Baha Ullah's death, Abbass Afandi and Shoghi Afandi respectively took over the leadership of the affiliated party."[9]

Here let me explain about the term "British Tudehis". It became a common phrase on the lips of the people during Mohammad Reza's reign. I have little knowledge about its foundation and its leaders, but certainly, British intelligence agents were behind the party. Most likely, Assadollah Alam was the topmost member and leader of the party. The party came into prominence after August 19, 1953 coup. Alam did nothing without receiving orders from the British, and certainly a large number of its members had previously been agents of London who had performed great services, and, therefore, deserved posts of a ministerial nature or the like at the Court.

Chapter 5

Secret Agencies During Pahlavis

SECRET AGENCIES DURING PAHLAVIS

During the reign of Qajars, no organized intelligence or security agencies existed in Iran. Reza Shah, too, did not take serious measures to establish secret services. Britain could perhaps be blamed for this. The British may have deliberately discouraged the creation of intelligence agencies at that time and may have even sabotaged efforts in that respect.

During both Qajars and Reza Shah 'intelligence' did not cover collection of intelligence information from the rival and target countries. Nazmieh (as it was called) which later was changed into Shahrbani (police) acted as Reza Shah's "eyes and ears".

Shahrbani was charged with counter-espionage and suppression of opponents. In fact, its fundamental mission was to protect the authority of the throne, a mission it was not fully prepared for. That was why Reza Shah was not totally dependent on Shahrbani to keep his throne. He had created fear among the people through brutality to maintain order and provide internal security.

Of course, Iranian embassies abroad were collecting as much information as they could about the country of their residence and sent them on to Reza Shah through the Ministry of Foreign Affairs. The collected intelligence were not comprehensive and clearly lacked an analytical order. It was sporadic information the embassies acquired from different sources.

The army's intelligence was weak too. No adequate definition of 'intelligence' had been given and the sphere of army's intelligence activities was confined to making sure that soldiers were in good shape and there was enough food for the personnel and alike. Gendarmerie, although with autonomous powers, was acting under the patronage of the army.

It was only after well-experienced French teachers were brought into the country that Iranians learned the ABC of intelligence at the newly-established War University. French officers taught Iranians how to collect information about the enemy's army, their positions and plans, and how to contain enemy's penetration attempts etc. The manuals were also translated into Persian to be taught by Iranian teachers later. They left Iran just before the outbreak of World War II.

So, it could be claimed that Iran had been deprived of an efficient intelligence organ during Reza Shah and this remained so after Reza's abdication. That is when U.S. influence overrided that of the British in the country. To be specific, it was after August 1953 coup that the first ever organized intelligence establishment came into being in Iran. During this period, two officers in particular became proficient in intelligence affairs and acquired valuable experience and information. The two were Brigadier-General Deyhami and Major-General Hassan Akhavi.

After the August coup and the consequent U.S. domination over Iran, Washington adopted certain strategic policies in order to turn Iran into its prime base in the region. For that, they first helped establish a counter-intelligence network within the army and later proposed the creation of SAVAK, the Persian acronym of State Intelligence and Security Organization.

It was evident that a country without efficient intelligence agencies could not function as America's pillar of diplomacy in the strategic Persian Gulf region and, therefore, decisions were made to act immediately. Moreover, since Iran bordered America's arch rival, the Soviet Union, a pro-U.S. regime had to be installed to serve U.S. interests and counter possible Soviet threats.

Furthermore, establishment of an active intelligence agency by the U.S. would allow Washington to further stabilize its foothold in the region in general and in Iran in particular.

Americans insisted that counter-intelligence directorates within the army be immediately established and after much effort the proposed plan was translated into action and the army was equipped with intelligence units. The counter-intelligence directorates were established on the basis of U.S. strategic policies and its intelligence structures.

Brigadier-General Tajbakhsh and Major-General Qajar were the most experienced intelligence officers I had ever known. The two chaired army's counter-intelligence directorate respectively. Tajbakhsh was my student at War University in 1955 when I was teaching there. I found him fond of intelligence affairs. He was not a wealthy man and was suffering from economic hardships.

He used to make files for high ranking authorities, keeping the papers in his drawer to use them against his rivals at the required time. Let me cite an example: I suppose it was in early 1960 that I learned he had fabricated a file against Abbass Qarabaqi alleging that he was spying for the KGB. He handed over his documents to the Shah. The Shah passed on the case to the Supreme Coordination Council and I was its secretary for investigation. General Oweisi and a few others defended Qarabaqi and the council finally dismissed the allegations. I did believe that it was unlikely that a cautious Qarabaqi might have spied for the Soviets.

Tajbakhsh soon showed his capabilities and was employed by Americans. He successfully completed his studies and graduated from the university. Later, he received special high intelligence training and was appointed head of army's counter-intelligence directorate. After assuming his post, all army officers did not dare disobey or offend him.

Promotion to high posts in a short period of time was a rare occurrence. Tajbakhsh's appointment to this key post indicated America's great interest in him.

He was a man who appeared to have a heart of stone. I never saw him express regret. He did not seem to have any feelings. Execution did not grieve him and he enjoyed torturing prison inmates and telling the stories of their suffering to his friends. Sometimes, he invited me to accompany him during his missions if anything highly important was predicted to happen. And I did in a few cases. Once he invited me to see the body of Reza Shamsabadi who had been killed by SAVAK after he was found responsible for the assassination attempt against the Shah in March 1965. He wore gloves touching the bleeding spots of his body curiously looking for something.

"This man (Shamsabadi) had lost his nerves. The stories about him say that he had dived into a lake in his village when he was very young and by accident his head would struck a sharp stone and would leave him partially demented. The brain damage seems to be the main reason behind his failed attempt against His Majesty's life", he charged.

Of course, no one could believe all these nonsense but no body was willing to have a dispute with him because of the trouble he would create for them later.

Americans always met his wishes and never left him disappointed, perhaps it was aimed at luring him into their service. I had never seen an intelligence chief with such powers and characteristics. On Tajbakhsh's recommendation, a 10-member American expert team arrived in Iran to train Iranian officers in up-to-date counter-espionage methods. After the training period had expired, a series of books on intelligence work were donated to SAVAK. The donation surprised me and I gradually learned that Tajbakhsh's links with Americans were beyond what I had imagined.

Later, Tajbakhsh requested permission to retire on grounds of ill-health and the need to go abroad for treatment. I was told he was in good health and all that was a pretext to get out of Iran. However, his request was granted and he immediately left Iran. The Americans had promised him a good job. CIA did not want to lose a valuable asset for its own use in America.

Upon assuming the leadership of army's counter-intelligence, Brigadier-General Qajar accumulated immense wealth. I greatly doubted his honesty. Later, like his predecessor, he applied for retirement. And it was agreed. After retirement, he either emigrated to the United States or was invited there by the CIA.

> "From the times of Cyrus the Great, Persian Shahs had always been served by organizations that acted as their "eyes and ears" These institutions functioned in many ways to preserve and protect the authority of the throne. They were usually clandestine in nature and involved agents who travelled around the kingdom in various disguises. . . In order to assert authority and to command respect for the power of the Shahs, these organizations acted with stealth, zeal, and brutality. Secret arrests in the middle of the night, abductions and imprisonment, and, above all, torture were the marks of their profession. They tried to establish methods of operation that inspired among the general populace an awe for their ubiquitous presence and knowledge, a fear of their harsh retribution, and a deference to their final authority. Over the centuries, this system served the Shahs and sustained their dynasties.

Reza Shah, although employing such a system, was not particularly dependent on it for his authority. He was fearsome enough in his own right, he was constantly on the move as his own eyes and ears, and he had at his command a far more respected organization in his precious army. However, when he left the throne and when his army collapsed, there was little in the way of an invisible institution to serve the new young Shah, Mohammad Reza. Indeed, during the period of World War II, while Iran was under Allied occupation, he had very few "eyes and ears" of his own.

It thus came as a considerable shock to him and to his government to discover, in the aftermath of the Mossaddiq assault on the authority of the throne, that the Soviet Union, during its occupation of Iranian territory, had built up a large espionage organization that reached deep into the upper echelons of the Iranian armed forces. In reacting to this, he sought assistance from his American friends in establishing a modern intelligence organization that would guard against the technologically proficient KGB and GRU organizations that were functioning under Soviet direction in Iran.

In 1957, after considerable organizational effort by the CIA, the United States government devised for the Shah a framework of a modern intelligence system and helped him establish it. It was given the name Sazman-e Ettela'at Va Amniyat-e Keshvar (Iranian State Intelligence and Security Organization) and, from the initials of this title, soon became known by the acronym SAVAK. Recruits who were designated for his new service were given training in intelligence and counter-intelligence methods in the United States and, later, in Israel. They were trained not only in fundamental police work but also in the analysis of Soviet techniques and, above all, in the detection of sophisticated Soviet electronic espionage.

Whatever the quality of the information exchange, our intelligence collaboration with Iran was more than justified, in Washington's view, by Iran's willingness to let us position two major listening posts on Iranian soil overlooking the rocket-and-missile-launching facilities that the Soviets maintained in their central-Asian republics. From these stations, we would monitor every electronic activity at those facilities, as well as Soviet military activity in the whole area of territory facing toward the

Persian Gulf. They were essentially simple antennae with tape-recording devices, manned by civilian technicians who lived in barren isolation, but their product was the most sophisticated compendium of military intelligence in the entire watching brief that we maintained on the Soviet threat."[1]

A HISTORY OF SUPREME COORDINATION COUNCIL

The poor performance of Iran's outdated intelligence services during Reza Shah and even after the latter's abdication could not guarantee the stability of the regime.

Keeping Mohammad Reza in power and safeguarding America's pillar of diplomacy required the creation of an efficient security and intelligence system in the country. Moreover, the British were not willing to relinquish all their interests and facilities in Iran or hand them over to the Americans and, therefore, they insisted on receiving a share in the new security and intelligence system.

Later, British policy makers succeeded in securing Mohammad Reza's consent in this matter during the latter's state visit to Britain in 1959. Subsequently, I was assigned to travel to Britain and make preparations for the creation of SIB. During my stay in Britain, I familiarized myself with the British intelligence system and its functions. Upon arrival home, I received clearance from the Shah to establish the SIB in late 1959, similar to that of Britain's SIB.

So, the concept of a security and intelligence network for the country was propounded in 1960 with the creation of the Supreme Coordination Council (SCC) and SIB.

After receiving the go-ahead from the Shah to establish the network, I immediately started training the designated officers for the anticipated posts. All were set, and after three months of hard work, SIB started operations.

In compliance with British JIC, I was empowered to establish the State Security Council (SSC). Upon Mohammad Reza's order, weekly meetings were held in an inner building of the Marmar Palace which was also the venue of the army's intelligence. The Shah banned participation of all cabinet ministers in these meetings. The first meeting was attended by Chief of Army's Intelligence Major-General Hajali Kia, Chief of SAVAK Major-General Teimur Bakhteyar, Chief of police Major-General Mehdiqoli

Alavimoqqaddam, Commander of Gendarmerie, a Brigadier-General most likely Moqbeli Malek, Chief of SIB and Director of the Council Hussein Fardust (I).

The attendance of Teimur Bakhteyar and Kia created some problems from the very beginning. Teimur did not attend all the meetings and if he did, he would either give orders, insult his opponents or walk out in protest. In short, SSC meetings began and ended with disputes and outrage. Finally, I lost my patience and informed Mohammad Reza of their behaviour. The next day, Bakhteyar and Kia were given the choice to either retire or be dismissed. Kia was victimized in order to avert rumours and objections and Bakhteyar accepted to retire. Of course, Bakhteyar's retirement (or better to say dismissal) was not only because of his behaviour at SSC meetings. The Shah had for a long time been seeking an excuse to rid himself of him and my complaint gave him the pretext.

Soon, Major-General Kamal replaced Kia and Brigadier-General Pakravan took Bakhteyar's seat. Kamal usually did not show up at the meetings but he appointed Alavikia to fill his vacant seat. No objection was raised to Kamal's representative. Sometime later, Alavikia was dismissed from his post of Deputy Chief of SAVAK on charges of (financial) misappropriations. I took his seat. Later, Pakravan also resigned and Nasiri succeeded him as Chief of SAVAK. However, SSC meetings continued without any achievements. The meetings did not satisfy the British because no important issues were raised and instead the participants usually made jokes and enjoyed themselves. The reason, of course, was that in order to win Shah's favour, the participants preferred to directly address him in their private meetings. The Prime Minister used to meet the Shah twice a week, except in special cases; all cabinet ministers had direct access to the Shah, Directors of SAVAK, army's intelligence, police, and Gendarmerie were honoured two times a week and a court minister as well as Chief of SIB were entitled to meet the Shah every day. Consequently, all the problems were settled and solved in direct meetings with the Shah.

The government did not send any reports to SIB and the security and intelligence networks did not have anything new to say. This trend continued until 1960. So, to summarize, until 1960, a concerted security and intelligence network was not fully materialized and everything was sorted out through the Shah and not through a special responsible organ.

One morning in 1969, Mohammad Reza summoned his War Minister (soon Defence Minister) General Azimi, Chief of the General Staff of the Armed Forces, Jam or Azhari (I do not remember, most likely it was Jam), Chief of SAVAK Nasiri, Chief of Army's Intelligence Palizban, Chief of Police Mobser, and Commander of Gendarmerie General Oweisi, to Marmar Palace. For some reason, I did not attend the meeting.

The participants unexpectedly saw Shahpour J. at Shah's residence. First J., as representative of the British government delivered a speech and officials took notes. Shahpour said, "As you know, SSC can play a vital role in maintaining the security of the country and it can predict and avert catastrophes at a high level. Therefore, I have received orders from London to remind His Majesty of the importance of SSC (J. refused to name the British official who gave the order but it should have been the Prime Minister) and His Majesty preferred to have this matter discussed in his presence. First of all, SSC meetings have to be held regularly. Second, all important international and domestic security and political issues have to be propounded at the meetings. Third, if any of SSC members have already informed the Shahanshah of a matter, it does not mean that they do not have to raise it at the meetings. The minutes must regularly be made available to His Majesty and all orders must be accurately carried out. Informing the Shahanshah immediately of the developments and events is one aspect and discussing all the problems at the meetings is another. And fourth, British officials have recommended that, apart from SCC, a new council with the membership of deputies of disciplinary, security and intelligence networks together with SCC Chief, be formed. Minutes of the new council have to be handed over to His Majesty and SSC".

After Shahpour's address, the Shah elaborated on the importance of SSC and the new council and emphatically called on SCC members to reiterate their loyalty to the state and threatened that all those who refuse to obey the orders would be dismissed.

"We can, in no way, ignore any deficiencies or lack of cooperation of any member. Without any doubt, if any deficiencies are observed, the guilty will be chastised and sacked," the Shah warned.

He also made it clear that both councils will be held under the supervision of SIB and it has to report any decisions made at the meeting to him. Therefore, the following changes were made:

- The Chief of General Staff of the armed forces joined the council and SSC was changed into "Supreme Coordination Council (SCC) and later was known as the First-Grade Coordination Council (FGCC).
- A new council known as the Second-Grade Coordination Council (SGCC) was established in which deputies of all security and intelligence networks took part.
- The venue of the meetings and the responsibility of both councils would lay with SIB.
- It was determined that SCC would be presided over by the person of the Shah at his residence only in urgent cases.

Since I was not present at the meeting, Nasiri informed me of the decisions made at the meeting the same day. The Shah confirmed Nasiri's remarks. Then, I requested the Shah to give the necessary orders for the establishment of the SGCC. The Shah commenting on the council wrote, "O.K. Do it and pay careful attention". On SGCC he wrote, "You prepare it and choose the members. Hold regular meetings like those of FGCC and pass the minutes to me."

The SGCC was formed comprising Directors of the Third and Eighth Departments of SAVAK, chiefs of the army's intelligence and counter-intelligence departments, chiefs of police intelligence and counter-intelligence, chiefs of Genarmerie intelligence and counter-intelligence, an officer of SIB, and Director of the Council.

At the opening ceremonies of the SGCC, I read out Shah's orders to the members and answered the questions raised by them. I stated that any officer of any rank could be summoned to the council and that he would be obliged to respond any questions put to him. The council was empowered to summon any civilian, even a minister, and if he refused, the council would inform me immediately. The same procedure applied to the FGCC. I did not participate in the later sessions but I appointed the chief of my office to supervise the sessions. This way, coordination council meetings were regularly held every week on Saturdays. The FGCC meeting was held on a Saturday, and SGCC on the following Saturday.

The minutes were passed on to the Shah and one copy each was unofficially handed over to the British and American embassies. The minutes of SGCC contained first hand information. The FGCC meetings were regularly held but members again were informing Mohammad Reza of the top stories earlier before the meeting (they were trying to boast about their efforts). Though important matters were usually discussed at the meeting, they had lost importance. The remarks were included in the minutes and passed on to the Shah but they were mere repetition of what the Shah had heard from his subjects. The meetings of SGCC were regularly held and were attended by all members. All the domestic and international developments were reviewed in great detail. Any decisions made at the meeting had to be implemented and supervised by the man in charge. He had to declare the results in the next session; if he failed to do so, he would be chastised, however, if the mistake was repeated. I was informed of the matter. It was my duty to order him to abide by the regulations and if he refused he would be dismissed. Of course, during all the years of the council's existence, no deficiencies were reported. Once, in order to put the loyalty of the members to test, I summoned the man in charge and informed him that he would be replaced. He obeyed the order and gave the necessary response to the council. The active role of SGCC was in stark contrast to the inactive role of its superior council. The minutes of both councils for the preceding six months were stored at SIB and the chief of my office, Nejati, looked after them closely.

At the time of the 1979 Islamic Revolution, Colonel Memar Sadeqi (officer of administrative affairs) was delegated by the office of Prime Minister Bakhteyar to get all the documents and deliver them to the Prime Minister's office.

The changes which occurred in the system of the security and intelligence networks after the August 1953 coup with the guidance of the U.S. and British secret agencies and with the consequent help of the Israeli Mossad could be categorized as follows:

1. The police force was relieved of the task of counter-espionage and anti-government activities, and the responsibility was delegated to SAVAK. Consequently, the Third Department of SAVAK was assigned the task of countering anti-government operations and the Eighth Department discovering and foiling espionage activities. During the period, the police handled only inter-

organizational anti-sabotage and anti-espionage operations. Later, the police intelligence became responsible for collecting information and the counter-intelligence department of police looked after the efforts to counter inter-police espionage and anti-government activities emanating from within the police force.

2. Army's intelligence was relieved of the duty of acquiring non-military intelligence from target countries and the Second Department of SAVAK took over the task. Of course, the responsibility of the army's intelligence for gathering military information through Iranian military attaches remained intact.
   SAVAK's 7th Department was made responsible for investigating and reviewing the information gathered by the Second Department.
3. Gendarmerie's intelligence was detached from the army and was delegated to look after the efforts countering anti-government and espionage operations within its institutes. Later, Gendarmerie's intelligence was made responsible for gathering the required information from its specific area of operation, and the counter-intelligence department took on the task of countering espionage activities within Gendarmerie.
4. Army's intelligence network was divided into two intelligence and counter-intelligence departments, and these took on the responsibility of carrying out intelligence operations in target countries. Later, it was decided that even if any army officer was arrested for espionage activities his case had to be followed up by counter-intelligence department.
5. Creation of coordination councils was mainly aimed at encouraging coordination in planning, and an organized system in security and intelligence networks.
6. The SIB was the supervisor and director of the two councils and was considered as the brain of the country's security and intelligence networks. All the subordinate networks were required to report their activities to SIB and, if necessary, SIB would exchange information with the networks. The former Information Ministry collected articles

and radio newsreels about Iran published or aired by the world mass media and delivered them to SIB.

Although the efforts and steps taken to create an organized intelligence agency were effective, neither SSC nor SIB succeeded in playing their role as the heart and brain of the country's intelligence networks, and they were no more than a caricature of an intelligence and security organization. Here, I would like to explain the reasons for the failure.

As I stated earlier, JIC led all security networks in Britain. JIC always received the required information from its specialized departments and, therefore, dominated all the affairs and outlined all the domestic and foreign policies of the government. It seems certain that the Prime Minister was the most important decision-making figure but he never allowed himself to interfere in the affairs of the intelligence networks unless the two followed different policies or contradictions occurred.

It was impossible to translate the system into action in Iran. Mohammad Reza's absolute power was the main obstacle. Moreover, chiefs of intelligence networks, especially SAVAK, followed arbitrary policies. Mohammad Reza's selfishness prevented SIB from becoming the heart of the country's intelligence organ. Directors of SIB's subordinate networks were in direct touch with the Shah and decisions were usually made at private talks. These decisions were never subject of special discourse at the meetings of FGCC and SGCC.

The numerous organs which were able to provide up-to-date information did not join the coordination councils. In Britain, related ministers had joined JIC while the Shah had prohibited his ministers from taking part in the meetings of the coordination councils and he had established direct links with his ministers. Intelligence networks lacked specialized departments. Inadequacies had caused the networks to turn into departments for transferring information to the Shah instead of determining the strategies of the state. It was Mohammad Reza who made the decisions which in actual fact were those dictated to him by the American and British governments. The Shah did not understand the role which SIB had to play, and the Americans and or the British also did not mind that their installed Shah did not care because the existing networks were meeting their objectives and enabled them to gather information about Iran's domestic situation easily.

Therefore, it could be concluded that all the establishments did not constitute a real responsible intelligence system. All organs were directly dependent on the Shah and disorganized information was rushed to him. He had to verify all the information in his mind. Moreover, he had no time to ponder and, therefore, was not able to settle everything himself.

I repeatedly requested the Shah to allow his Foreign Minister to participate at the meetings of FGCC but every time he turned down my appeal. Of course, the Foreign Minister was among the few officials who had the right to meet the Shah twice a week. Any organized system disturbed the Shah. When I received the post of Head of the Imperial Investigation Organization, the military special investigation department, under Major-General Firuzmand, received my responsibilities. There was no change in the status quo until the 1979 Islamic Revolution. Firuzmand was always boasting and did not report the truth. Therefore officers under my command did not enjoy much power and SIB failed to achieve its expected objectives and carry out its responsibilities.

SIB, ITS FUNCTIONS AND RESPONSIBILITIES

The power structure at SIB was as follows:

A President and a Vice-President headed the SIB. During all the years of its existence until the 1979 Islamic Revolution, I was the President. Keeping a reliable individual in a top position was a fundamental practice strictly observed in Britain. Samadianpour, Eshqipour and Nejati were the three vice-presidents respectively during this period.

The First Department looked after all the administrative and financial affairs. Allocating a budget for SIB's secret activities was excluded from the department's responsibilities. Instead, Vice-President of SIB was responsible for the job. Nautrally, this department had more employees than any other department in SIB. One top officer, 20 other military personnel and a typist were working in this department.

The Second Department was responsible for state affairs. All the Information received from different government departments were studied and summarized, and then a report was prepared by the department. If any orders pertaining to this report were issued, the Second Department was responsible to follow up the matter in coordination with the departments concerned, and prepare a comprehensive and objective final report on the matter. Four officers and a typist were posted at this department.

The Third Department was charged with taking care of political affairs. It was responsible for studying and summarizing information and preparing reports on political issues which were usually obtained from the army's intelligence and the Third Department of SAVAK. Again if any orders pertaining to these reports were issued, the Third Department had to contact the relevant departments, extract further explanations and prepare a report with the help of the Second Department. Four officers and a typist worked in this department.

The Fourth Department looked after military and police affairs. This department procured and summarized reports about the army, police forces and gendarmerie. Four officers and a typist were also involved in the operations.

The Fifth Department was engaged in investigations. Initially, this department did not exist but was formed at a later date. The reason for its formation was to satisfy Mohammad Reza's desire that certain cases be looked into more thoroughly. Any kind of investigation required by any administrative, military or police department was carried out by this department. Because of the heavy workload, six officers and a typist were involved in the operation.

SIB employees were few, but their efficiency was great. SIB carried out its tasks independently, and was not subject to the authority of any other department. Only the Imperial Guard was entitled to intervene in our affairs, and that too for giving clearance for employment of our required personnel and monthly salaries. SIB's secret budget amounted to 7,500,000 rials, supplied by the Joint Staff of the Armed Forces. However, every year, as a regular procedure in the army, the number of personnel and the secret budget were reviewed. So, SIB was not allowed to recruit people itself, rather applications had to be passed on to the Ground Force Headquarters and the necessary procedure was carried out there. Promotion was possible if the headquarters approved the proposals.

Administrative posts were made available in the bureau for officers with ranks of higher than colonel.

The officers at SIB were held in higher esteem than the regular army officers and usually were given key posts after 10-15 years of service. Immediately after the formation of SIB, upon Shah's order, Samadianpour and Moseqi joined the SIB. Nasiri informed me of the order and stated that Samadianpour's unofficial and secret duty was to provide a copy of the reports available at SIB to Shahpour J. Later, Samadianpour, with the help of Nasiri, was promoted to the rank of Major-General and was appointed chief of police. Some officers at SIB who later, after promotion, received highly sensitive positions are as follows: Naser Moqaddam became Major-General and chief of military intelligence. He was appointed chief of SAVAK after Nasiri's resignation.

Khatami was promoted to the rank of Brigadier-General and was appointed commander of the counter-intelligence directorate of the Imperial Guard.

Firuzmand became Major-General and head of special military investigations. Nasratollah Fardust became Major-General and succeeded Firuzmand as head of special military investigations.

Broumand Jazi was promoted to the rank of Major-General and succeeded Moqaddam as chief of military intelligence. Mahmoudi became Brigadier-General and commander of a garrison in Isfahan. Naji became Major-General and commander of a garrison and military governor of Isfahan. He was executed after the 1979 Islamic Revolution.

Eshqipour became Brigadier-General and chief of special military investigations. Najati, became Brigadier-General and succeeded Eshqipour. Shaker became Brigadier-General and president of the officer's college. Jafari became Major-General and Chief of Police at the time of the revolution. Afshani became Major-General and commander of the counter-intelligence directorate of Gendarmeri. Amini Afshar became Brigadier-General and Chief of Army's Intelligence. Zandipour became Brigadier-General and Chief of Joint Staff Committee of SAVAK and the police. He was assassinated before the revolution. Parnianfar, Brigadier-General and chief of SAVAK in Tehran.

These officers were admired me for my successful leadership of SIB and accepted any suggestions I made to them. All the officers, after their promotion and receiving their new posts, showed up in

SIB office to help their colleagues and received a share of the benefits that the bureau could offer.

As I stated earlier, one of the main responsibilities of SIB was to investigate daily reports, confirm their accuracy, summarize them, and then pass them on to the Shah. I have already explained the deficiencies which existed in the system. Here I would like to reiterate that operational information was not dispatched to SIB. If police or Gendarmerie, by accident, discovered any reports pertaining to operations in case it related to the military, they would send them to the army's intelligence and if civilians were involved, they would pass them on to SAVAK. This was the policy agreed to by the above-mentioned departments. SAVAK and army's intelligence took the operational information to Mohammad Reza and, therefore, did not pass it on to SIB. (By operations here, I mean phone tapping surveillance, installing listening devices and other similar intelligence operations).

The reports which were delivered to SIB were as follows:

1. The military intelligence sent a bulletin to SIB every day, each bulletin approximately 20 pages in length which included information about the army, borders, the latest developments in the armies of target countries and some miscellaneous information. It also dispatched a rotary report every month or once every two months about the military status of a target country including all the specific required information.
2. The Third Department of SAVAK provided SIB with a daily bulletin covering all the developments in the country. Every month or every two months and in some cases once every three months or six months, a separate bulletin was dispatched to my office. The bulletin covered the activities of the tribes, religious minorities, Freemasons, Bahais, opposition factions both at home and abroad etc.
3. The Seventh Department of SAVAK sent a daily bulletin which included reports on target countries and its extraterritorial operations. It usually acquired the information from the Second Department and published its press release after corrections and verifications. The information regarding target countries was received from

the Second Department and the rest were extracted from newspapers and radio newsreels.

4. The Eighth Department of SAVAK provided SIB with a daily bulletin on the activities of foreign diplomatic missions in Tehran. Every three months a rotary bulletin was released on the department's own functions.
5. SAVAK's Tehran Department also sent a daily bulletin on its functions and the sphere of its operations.
6. The police also submitted a 30-page bulletin to SIB every day.
7. Gendarmerie also sent a 30-page daily bulletin.
8. The former Information Ministry sent a daily bulletin of 20-30 pages covering radio broadcasts from all over the world and another bulletin on articles published in foreign media about Iran.
9. The Kook organization too sent the reports it had received from other sources.
10. The SIB was usually apt to get information from its secret networks.

On the whole, a 50-page daily report and at least two bulletins (totalling 70 pages) were sent by different departments of SAVAK to SIB. In addition, some reports were acquired from other sources which increased the total number of pages to 250. Prior to the formation of SIB, the 250-page report was mailed directly to the Shah but he did not read many of them and ordered that it be destroyed.

Soon after SIB started operations, I attempted to give some kind of order to the reports. At the first few meetings, I made it clear that all the reports had to be summarized and each one had to be written on a separate piece of paper with a heading. I also recommended that the emblem of all departments be attached to their reports. My recommendations were taken seriously, and from that date onward, various departments observed the new procedure. Therefore, the 250-page report was reduced to between two to five pages daily.

The officers, after many years, became experienced in summarizing the reports and became specialists in their task. I read the final few pages of the reports and sometimes summarized them and even in some cases dropped them completely if they were not sensitive enough to be read by the monarch. Then, the reports were prepared and typed on special papers and passed on to the Shah. This facilitated Shah's understanding of the developments happening inside and outside the country within a few minutes.

In emergency cases, reports were given to SIB over telephone. The Military Police (MP) at SIB enjoyed the right to contact the MP stationed at the Palace and the latter was obliged to pass the reports on to Mohammad Reza at once and inform SIB of Shah's instructions.

Another prime responsibility of SIB was to administer the SSC which was later transferred to FGCC and SGCC. The sessions were more or less being held until the 1979 Islamic Revolution and the minutes were passed on to the Shah, all members of the council also received a copy.

Since no serious or sensitive issues were raised in FGCC meetings, the minutes radically decreased and these sessions became less frequent and were held only if a member requested or I found it necessary to do so.

The third important task of SIB was to set up secret networks in the army, SAVAK, and police forces. The pre-mentioned tasks were SIB's official responsibilities but few people were aware of the secret networks functioning under SIB. Even SIB employees, SAVAK, police and army officers were not aware of these secret networks and their agents remained unidentified. Part of SIB's annual budget was devoted to its administered secret networks without the knowledge of others.

SECRET NETWORKS OF SIB

When I was undertaking training in Britain, my teacher urged me to insist to the Shah that in addition to the existing counter - intelligence networks and the military intelligence, SIB required to secretly monitor these forces and foil any penetration attempts by opposition groups and individual political opponents. When I returned to Iran, I directly took the proposal to the Shah. As I had anticipated, the proposal made the Shah happy. On his orders, the Kook network, run by Army's Intelligence Chief Major-General Kia, was set up to meet part of SIB's objectives. After his retirement, Major-General Homayuni took Kia's seat. Later, the seat was given to me. The reports provided by Kook were passed on to the Shah via SIB. Kook was responsible for discovering and reporting public discontent in the society. SIB's Second Department cooked Kook's reports and analyzed them in order to facilitate decision-making at higher level.

When I was serving as SAVAK's Deputy Chief, I was in touch with General Mahutain's network. Soon, all the responsibilities of radio network communications were delegated to me. As chief of the network, I was informed of the links existing between the radio network and MI-6. The Mahutian network had been planned and founded by the British, but Kook was American-oriented and this made it difficult for me to find out about its foreign connections.

After getting clearance from the Shah, I began to implement the plans which had already been drawn up. A year after the formation of SIB, I decided to set up secret networks in the army, Gendarmerie and police. The trainings I had undertaken in Britain were sufficient to enable me to get the plan off the ground. Therefore, I did not hesitate to speed up efforts in that respect. I was certain that if the plan was disclosed or the agents were identified, all my efforts would be foiled and SAVAK's counter -intelligence department would oppose the plan. For this very reason, secrecy was accorded top priority and the plan was implemented step by step to evade possible disclosure. Even the agents were not aware of their friends' membership in the network.

Major Safapour, the head of a counter-intelligence unit in Abbasabad garrison, north Tehran seemed to be a competent officer for administrating the networks in the army and police forces. I kept a close watch on his activities in order to examine his abilities and characteristics. Gradually, I was convinced that he was the best choice for the job. I briefed him on our activities and my plan to monitor Iran's secret services. He was pleased that he had been given this chance and pledged to do all he could to achieve our ends. The plan to be implemented by Safapour anticipated the following:

- — The recruited agents will infiltrate into the army, police and gendarmerie.
- — Agents will be chosen from among low-ranking personnel so that they can attain the required information without causing suspicion.

— All agents, regardless of rank and occupation must be committed and of high calibre.
— Agents will be expected to carry out their duties even when they are transferred to another unit.
— After retirement, agents should continue to work and not cut links with the network.
— Accurate investigations about the past public life of the agents have to be carried out with a copy of each report stored in SIB files.
— Meetings with the leader of the network should be held in safe houses, and he is expected to make the necessary briefings there. Meetings can be held at SIB but only in urgent cases.
— If an agent is stationed in a remote city, he has to mail his reports to the addresses determined by the leader of the network.
— The monthly salary of the officer agents was 2,500 rials, and agents with lower military ranks 1,500 rials.
— If a member of the network is transferred to another department or if he retires, he would be still obliged to carry out his responsibilities at the network. Safapour began operations slowly with a meticulousness based on his own style. In the beginning, the first problem we faced with was that some of the recruited agents were shocked to learn about their new responsibilities, and some of them could not believe what Safapour told them. Therefore, I decided to meet these agents to assure them that everything was okay. It was decided that a recruited agent would show up at SIB as a complainant (so as not to cause any suspicion). Then, they would request an appointment with me to raise their complain. Because I had been given their names in advance, I would receive them and talk to them and would corroborate what Safapour had told them about their duties. Then the agents would accept the job and would meet Safapour in a safe house, and begin their activities.

Gradually, Safapour's network spread through the army, police gendarmerie and penetrated into most sensitive departments. Later, it expanded its networks to 35 branches.

Safapour was an expert in report writing and was very

experienced in his field of work. When he was promoted to the rank of Brigadier-General, I transferred him to the special military investigations which accommodated for his rank and above. Of course, he kept his post as leader of the network at the same time. After five years, I helped him get the rank of Major-General and still he cooperated with the network. When I was appointed chief of special military investigations, he would work with me round the clock. He had good managerial abilities and was adept to solve all the problems. He was responsible for investigations and many other administrative jobs. Safapour's network, however, did not pacify Shah's fears. The Shah ordered that SAVAK was to be brought under watch.

The reports carried by the network were divided into two separate categories including general information and activities which were considered harmful and jeopardizing. The latter reports were passed on to the counter intelligence department and processed there. General information, if necessary, was sent to the person in charge of the department concerned. A monthly report on the activities of the network was also prepared and passed on to the Shah.

MY MISSION AT SAVAK

One and a half years after SIB commenced operations, the Shah empowered me to re-organize SAVAK. From 1962 to 1972, while keeping my position at SIB, I worked as Deputy Head of SAVAK. Major-General Hassan Pakravan was the agency's chief. In 1964-65 Nematollah Nasiri replaced Pakravan as Head of SAVAK.

One Friday, I went to the palace as usual. The guests, most of them friends and relatives of Empress Farah, were present at the weekly reception and, as always, only a few friends of Mohammad Reza had been invited. Nasiri was also among the invites. It was here that Nasiri informed me of my new post. When I asked the Shah if the information was true, he said "yes".

"SAVAK not only lacks organization, it has also become the center for all kinds of abuse. You exercise authority in your work and you get the best results from the officers around you. I have decided that you keep your thumb directly on SAVAK".

He asked me to prepare a report on my findings in SAVAK within twenty days. Later, I became aware that someone in authority had reported that my predecessor, Alavikia, had been abusing his position and had established private trade links with Iran's southern Arab neighbours.

The next morning, I showed up at SAVAK's Headquarters and introduced myself to Pakravan. I then went on to Alavikia's office. He greeted me and left the seat for me. He was, however, very concerned about his future especially about the report I was to give to the Shah. Alavikia then was appointed Head of SAVAK's branch in West Germany. He became engaged in arms deals and commenced intelligence cooperation with western secret agencies.

On assuming my post, I immediately began my investigations. Colonel Kangarlu, Director of the Fourth Department, proved to be the most honest and daring figure whom I could count on his abilities. I called him to my office to get what I needed to know. He told me whatever he knew with documented evidence, and when he could not answer my questions, he introduced someone to me who could supply the appropriate answers.

During the course of my investigations, it became obvious that the person who had reported Alavikia's activities to the Shah, had a high position in SAVAK. Later, I came to believe that he was the head of the American advisory team attached to SAVAK.

According to my calculations, Alavikia had embezzled 250 to 300 million rials, the main portion of which he had given to Bakhteyar. Consequently, during 5-6 years of his service, Alavikia had stolen approximately 1,500 million rials.

Within twenty days, I prepared a report and passed it on to Mohammad Reza. In the report, I informed the Shah that the organizational chart, drawn up by the American advisory team, existed on paper only and it had not been implemented. In reality, five to six men were running SAVAK. I disclosed all the cases of mishandling including those of Alavikia. I told the Shah that if concrete evidence was required to convince him of the wrongdoings, it would probably take months to gather evidence because of the business transactions in which the parties concerned were involved. Fortunately, the contents of my report convinced the Shah that his secret agency needed to be reshuffled.

"You are empowered to rectify the prevailing state of affairs in SAVAK and do not pay any attention to the orders issued by Pakravan. Pakravan will be ordered to avoid interfering in your affairs", he added.

Pakravan did not interfere in my affairs after Shah's order and only he continued to oversee operational affairs.

Since 1956-57, ten American advisors organized SAVAK along lines laid down by their own intelligence system. Intelligence in its universal sense means foreign intelligence. SAVAK was gathering both foreign intelligence and taking care of domestic security. In short, SAVAK was acting as America's CIA and FBI. The Third and Eighth Departments were equivalent to FIB, and the Second and Seventh Departments to CIA.

General Teimur Bakhteyar was the first Chief of SAVAK. He took the agency's leadership sometime after the August 1953 coup when he had became Military Governor of Tehran. Until the creation of SAVAK, he, along with his subordinates, for three and a half years gained operational experience in intelligence work and developed a harshness that came with this experience. During these three and a half years, this team which later formed the core of SAVAK carried out important operations such as discovering the military wing of the Tudeh Party, and Fadaeyan-e-Islam Group, and liquidating Shah's opponents. The performance of Bakhteyar and his team was a prelude to the establishment of the modern SAVAK.

Bakhteyar kept his post until 1960. Pakravan was the first acting chief and Alavikia acted as second acting chief. From 1960 Pakravan took Bakhteyar's seat but no first acting chief was appointed and Alavikia continued to work as the only deputy of SAVAK. This small deviation from the rules laid out in the American chart did not create any problems.

The American advisory team had, during five years since the establishment of SAVAK, dictated their training system, but they did not allow any of their books to be translated.

Having carefully studied SAVAK's points of strength and deficiency, I prepared myself to reorganize the agency. The trainings I had received in Britain were not compatible with SAVAK's American style. There was, however, no other option left for me but to do what I could to improve the agency's efficiency. I did not make fundamental changes in SAVAK's structural system, but gradually I made some minor reforms and encouraged order. American advisors did not object to my policies, rather they cooperated with me and lauded my efforts.

When I became certain that Colonel Kangarlu was one of the most eligible figures who could promote my reform plan, I decided to choose other members of my "reform team". The second member was approved upon his recommendation, and the third was selected by the first two. This process continued until seven people had been selected. The 7-man team formed the "Supreme Commission of SAVAK" and the most senior member of this team administered the meetings. I spelled out the reasons behind the creation of SAVAK and the agency's grave responsibilities at the opening session of the Commission. Then I assigned the commission to study how best the reforms could be introduced. The Commission, upon consultations with department directors and intelligence advisors, determined the mechanism for achieving our goals. I then asked the Commission to categorize the responsibilities of the team members and assign each of them to a particular department for best results. Consequently, new sections were created within the departments and in some cases redundant sections were eliminated. An organizational chart was also drawn up. The Commission had to assess the volume of the work involved and, accordingly, the number of personnel to be employed, and determine the kind of training the personnel of each section had to undergo - this being based on the ties of their own individual sections. It was also decided that a number of storehouses, workshops and the like would be needed for the use of the section. The equipments required by each section were gradually procured. I gave directors the right to disagree with the advice of the Supreme Commission should they find any of its decisions harmful to their department or section. If any dispute erupted between directors and the commission, the commission would convene to sort out the dispute. If not, my order was the final verdict. Having completed its primary "reform" mission, the later was delegated the responsibility of dealing with the problems raised by SAVAK departments and of appointing qualified agents to sensitive posts. I had already given the Commission a list of sensitive posts which were to be filled by highly qualified SAVAK agents. This Commission carried out its functions with adequate authority throughout the entire tenure of my office in SAVAK, that is until 1970.

Gradually SAVAK recruited its required agents. Some were employed and some others were transferred from the army. Retirement from the army did not relieve those army personnel working in SAVAK of their responsibilities. SAVAK became a vast organization, with about 5,000 personnel throughout Iran and its foreign stations.

After some time, I decided that there was no longer a need for the 10 American advisors to continue working for SAVAK. They did not carry out their responsibilities, either they did not know what they had to do or how to do it, or they pretended not to know. The Americans advisory team showed interest in the affairs of the Third and Eighth Departments and their presence in other Departments was merely a formality. I requested that they devote more time to the training aspect of their mission but all, except one advisor at the Third Department, refused. In reality, only two of them were able to train our personnel and the rest were not useful any more. I consulted Mohammad Reza, and insisted that they were no longer any help to SAVAK. Mohammad Reza supported my judgement. The American team, with the exception of the advisor at the Third Department who requested that his stay be extended for another six months, were told to leave. A farewell party was held in their honour at a SAVAK club, and the team left Iran in 1963.

To improve training, we invited teachers from Israel and America to work in the counter-intelligence department of the army to help Tajbakhsh complete and improve his training programmes. First hand educational books and training manuals, which had previously been impossible to obtain, were procured and given to Tajbakhsh. As part of my reform plan, I created a new department in SAVAK, increasing the number of departments to nine. The department was responsible for investigations. SAVAK's buildings were located in different streets. I was afraid this could undermine the agency's security measures and its operations. To improve security protection, I ordered the construction of new buildings in Saltanabad after Shah's initial approval. The new headquarter was built in an area of 400,000 square meters. Soon, half of the personnel were transferred there. At the time when I was transferred to the Special Military Investigations Department, two other buildings were also under construction. The CIA central building map was copied to construct the buildings to ensure security.

During the entire tenure of my office at SAVAK, I did not allow any one to change his field of expertise. Promotion was allowed for people only in their own specialized fields. This procedure helped experts gain experience and become more professional. During the period, I was the person who approved decisions. Chief of SAVAK (Pakravan and later Nasiri) simply looked after the operational affairs.

Day by day I became more professional in my field of work. I would study the training literature and discuss any problems I had with the experts. I strove to establish the importance of consultation within the agency, and so I ordered that, besides the Supreme Commission which consulted only with me, other commissions be set up in different departments. My endeavours, to a certain extent, proved successful, and by 1970-1 a number of Middle Eastern countries were dispatching their intelligence and security agents to Tehran for training.

Nevertheless, I have to acknowledge that even with all the efforts made, with the high-level training given, the provision of equipment, the employment of 5,000 personnel and tens of thousands of agents and informers, SAVAK was not successful in discovering all subversive and covert activities. The more it grew, the more proud it became, just leaving a frightening picture of itself.

Directors of SAVAK were more proud of their position rather than trying to discover the root causes of opposition groups and public discontent in the society. SAVAK aimed its activities at creating terror and fear in the hearts of the people, thus, this massive agency became the most despised in the country, and all the hate which developed in the society against Mohammad Reza and his regime, was directed against SAVAK.

TEIMUR BAKHTEYAR, FIRST CHIEF OF SAVAK

I met Teimur Bakhteyar for the first time in his house. Major-General Mahmoud Eram, an officer of the Arfa group, was a close friend of Teimur and I. It was Eram who took me to Bakhteyar's residence at the insistence of Teimur.

Bakhteyar's house was located in a side street off Kakh avenue. It was a double-room apartment on the second floor of an old two-story house. He lived there, in poverty, with his Bakhteyari wife and a young daughter. The 30 year-old Bakhteyar was tall and very handsome. He greeted us warmly and showed us into one of the rooms which was separated from the other by a curtain and furnished with old, third-rate furniture.

Throughout the visit, Teimur spoke mostly about his huntings in Bakhteyari mountains, West Iran. He showed a great predilection for danger. He was very interested in guns and showed us some of his prized collection. Though he was from a family of Bakhteyari tribal leaders, he had little wealth. He made his life with a normal monthly salary. He was a pure tribesman who had been a witness to many tribal fightings within the Bakhteyari tribes during his childhood. I understood that he wanted me to see how he was living and tell Mohammad Reza of his deplorable situation in the hope that he would be provided with a better house. It was obvious that he was strongly attached to his wife and little daughter and was determined to give them a better kind of life. Of course, Teimur himself said nothing of this, and his pride did not allow him to do so. We failed to see each other for a second time. However, I informed the Shah of his situation and capabilities.

When the Soviet-backed Iranian communists went to establish an autonomous republic in Iran's Azerbaijan immediately after the end of World War II, Bakhteyari voluntarily joined the army under Major-General Zarrabi near Tabriz to crush the rebellion. Fierce fighting reportedly broke out, and Teimur's group, with the help of tribal Zolfaqaries, crushed the Democrat Party's rebellion, killing scores of them and forcing others to flee. Teimur got his award for courageously fighting the Moscow-backed secessionists. He was promoted to the rank of Lieutenant-Colonel.

When Moqaddam came to power, Teimur, now a Colonel, was commander of an armoured brigade stationed in the western provincial capital of Kermanshah. The British had kept a close watch on Teimur. Being a courageous Bakhteyari was enough reason for Britain to keep him as their man. Having seen his boldness in crushing the rebellion in Azerbaijan, the British got him involved in the 1953 coup that unseated Mossaddiq.

Teimur's character won him approval from the Americans too. On the night before the coup, the unit under Teimur's command rushed to Tehran. His unit was the most powerful and most orderly military force. The head of MI-6 Tehran station told me that Americans intended to help a military dictator seize power after the coup but they dissuaded them from doing this insisting that no officer in the Iranian army commanded the support of the whole army. Teimur was the most likely candidate for the American's plan and certainly he himself was not averse to this idea. In reality, he could have actually seized power in the August 1953 coup if Britain did not intervene. No obstacle was in his way, and no other officer could match his power and character. Even Zahedi could not have stopped him. In my opinion, the British were completely mistaken in their analysis. A bold and determined officer could have quickly become acceptable to everyone and could have rallied the support of other officers. We only need to look to Reza Shah as an example, how did he come to power? An irresolute, weak commander is always rejected by the army. A powerful Cossack Brigade commander was quickly crowned Reza Shah under the support of the army and foreign supporters but the same Reza Shah was abandoned in September 1941 when he exposed his weaknesses. His army commanders disobeyed his orders and acted independently. The very same Sergent Bouzarjmehri, an illiterate man who, with the help of Reza Shah, was promoted to the rank of Major-General and who on the orders of Reza Shah took possession of people's lands in Shahriar, south Tehran, and made his two sons the inheritors of this land, and who administered Reza Shah's lands in the north during those tragic events, was not prepared to provide even five containers of petrol out of an existing stock of 80,000 on September 11th, 1941 to enable Reza Shah to escape. If Mohammad Reza had not intervened it is difficult to imagine how Reza Shah could have got his car to Isfahan.

Once I heard that a Colonel named Samadi had gathered about 8,000 officers in the amphitheater of the Officer's College, and had spoken against the Shah. The officers had clapped in applause.. When the Shah was reinstated after the coup, these same officers kissed Mohammad Reza's hand. I informed Mohammad Reza of Samadi's speech, but he urged me to forget about it. He said, "this has been a regular practice in Iran and Iranians are very sensitive, one day they set a person on a pedestal, the next they knock him to the ground." He was, I interpreted referring to the case of Mossaddiq. In the morning, the mob were chanting slogans in support of Mossaddiq, in the afternoon, they wanted him ousted. If Teimur had taken power after the coup, he could have secured the support of his fellow officers and Mohammad Reza would have not even thought of returning to Iran.

After the coup, Teimur immediately established the Military Governorship in Tehran, thanks to the support of the Americans. He executed whoever the Americans, British or Mohammad Reza wanted to get rid of. He suppressed the Communists, savagely executed members of the "Fadaeyan Islam", and committed many atrocities against prisoners, male and female. He did not even refrain from abusing old, respected men like Ayatollah Kashani. In short, his tribal primitiveness gave way to savagery in the shadow of his absolute power.

Teimur, now a Major-General, was greatly favoured by the American advisors at the Second Department. It was upon their recommendation that in 1956, he was appointed the first Head of SAVAK. After assuming the post, he strengthened his collaboration with the then War Minister Field Marshal Hedayat (the first who was given the rank of Field Marshal in Iran) and was promoted to the rank of General. In reality it was Mohammad Reza who masterminded his appointment as head of SAVAK in order to take him away from military affairs. However, the Shah was afraid of Bakhteyar's temperament and his lust for power. Teimur banked on Soraia and hoped that in the immediate future he could become prime minister or chief of the general staff of the armed forces.

During his reign of power at SAVAK, Bakhteyar accumulated a fortune, thus making up for his childhood poverty. In my position as deputy head of SAVAK, I saw examples of hundreds of his deeds in the files. He fabricated a file against a wealthy bazaar tradesman accusing him of being a Communist and had him throne into jail. Alavikia, his deputy, met with the poor prisoner and upon receiving a million tumans had him set free. Bakhteyar also accepted good farming land as bribes. Within a few years, his wealth reached the billion tumans mark and his collection of jewels, gold and antiques was unequalled. He let Alavikia to have his nail into the pie.

During Bakhteyar's leadership, SAVAK, in effect, existed only on paper. Its personnel did not exceed 150 and Bakhteyar, Alavikia and the Amjadi brothers at the Third Department were in reality running the whole organization. The budget devoted to SAVAK was misappropriated and squandered. Bakhteyar came to believe that only money spoke, and he strove to make money in order to attain power and realize his hopes. He was very arrogant and bold. The 10-man American advisory team were his advisors and consultants and they counted on him to be there for them if they should need him.

Power changed Teimur, he was no longer the devoted husband and father, and his personality changed so much that it was difficult to see him as the same man I had met years before.

He flaunted his illicit affair with Pouran, singer, driving through crowded streets in his military uniform with her by his side. At a later date, he fell in love with Qodrat, Yumni's wife, and forced Yumni, with threats, to divorce her. Yumni was a retired colonel and at the time was in charge of the Aram newspaper. He emulated Bakhteyar in arrogance. One day, angry Yumni came to me asking, "what kind of a country is this? Bakhteyar has taken my wife from me!" I reprimanded him and reminded him that he was not much better than Bakhteyar, and that through his newspaper he cheated people and got enormous amounts of money from people by threatening them. He said, "even if that is so, it does not mean that he is entitled to take my wife from me". I blamed him for his sorry state of affairs.

Teimur soon realized that Yumni had complained to me. The next day, Teimur forced him on a plane and sent him out of the country. He married Qodrat but did not divorce his first wife. His daughter, now an adult, married the son of General Yazdanpanah. Teimur sought to secure my friendship, and this he achieved. He always wanted something and was never satisfied. I really did not know what would become of him and therefore in our meetings I did not set any value on his promises. In 1960 when the State Security Council was established (later known as the Supreme Coordination Council) (SCC) under my leadership, Bakhteyar either refrained from attending the meetings, or when he did attend he merely quarrelled with Kia. When I finally had enough of their bickering, I informed the Shah of their behaviour. The next day, the Shah who was looking for an excuse to rid himself of the two, ordered their retirement.

Bakhteyar built a large beautiful house next to Shah's Sa'adabad Palace and decorated it with valuable furniture. He usually invited Arab ambassadors, members of the Senate and National Consultative Assemblies, ministers and high-ranking military officials to his house and gave parties in their honour. The name, rank and position of the guests were deliberately called on the loudspeaker when entering and leaving the house so that Mohammad Reza could hear the names!. I was always among those invited. Bakhteyar always received me warmly, but he never asked any favours of me at that time. In return, I would keep silent since I was aware of his aims, he was striving to become Prime Minister.

He paid newspapers to print a large picture of him with the caption beneath reading "Iran's next Prime Minister". When Amini was elected premier, he began to deride and defame him. Bakhteyar established friendly links with Princess Ashraf, Shah's twin sister, and kept in close contact with her. For her part Princess Ashraf was interested only in three things: jewels, money and man, and Bakhteyar satisfied all three. For a time Ashraf tried to persuade the Shah to accept Bakhteyar's premiership but he was reluctant and did not reply to her requests. Gradually, Bakhteyar intensified his verbal attacks on Amini to the extent that Amini complained about him to Mohammad Reza. The Shah, who was aware of Washington's firm support of Amini, ordered Bakhteyar to be taken under guard to the airport and put on a flight to Europe.

Bakhteyar, along with Qodrat, his new wife, and his two children went to Geneva. There he openly voiced his opposition to Shah's government and began cooperating with certain circles operating in Britain and America. At the time, SAVAK's Geneva station chief was Colonel Haqiqi, a fanatical Bahai who was loyal to Bakhteyar. SAVAK, aware of Haqiqi's close relationship with Bakhteyar, sent a team to Geneva to watch Bakhteyar without Haqiqi's knowledge. In 1960, I travelled to Geneva for the new year holidays. Haqiqi came to welcome me at the airport. I asked about Bakhteyar, he said, "just speak well of him and do not ask me any questions". At that time, Bakhteyar had left Geneva for the south of France. During my stay in Geneva, Haqiqi served me well and was very devoted to me. Later, when he died, Haqiqi left 32 million Swiss Francs in his bank account. He was not a wealthy man and it was obvious that this money was Bakhteyar's which he had given to Haqiqi in trust. SAVAK in a letter to the Swiss bank, claimed the money belonged to Iran, but the bank did not even reply to the letter.

When Teimur went to France, the French government, upholding a promise given to Mohammad Reza, put Bakhteyar under surveillance of its secret police and reported his activities on a daily basis to SAVAK. Bakhteyar later travelled to Lebanon and from there to Iraq. During all his time abroad he was a problem for the Shah's government, and SAVAK had secret agents watch him round the clock. Bakhteyar spent large sums of money to set up close links with British and American officials, and in turn they saw him as a possible alternative to Mohammad Reza. No one could predict future developments, one day perhaps it would be necessary for another military coup to take place in Iran and Bakhteyar was the ideal person to lead the coup. In principle, this was the way the British and American intelligence agencies worked, even though they had good relations with Mohammad Reza and were happy with his regime, they did not want to lose people who could succeed him if it was required.

One day Dr. Jafar Shahid came to see me. He published a weekly magazine for youths which was affiliated to the army, consequently he received large sums of money from the army for this cause. He had previously accepted money from Bakhteyar and had propagated his cause in his magazine. Shahid said that he had met Bakhteyar in Geneva and had then departed for London to attend an important party. At the party, Director of British Petroleum Company, who was considered a critic of the Shah's regime in Britain, described Bakhteyar as a capable person and went on, "we would dearly like to see him become Prime Minister". He urged Shahid to pass his message on, through a Court official, to Mohammad Reza. Shahid replied that I (Fardust), as a close friend of the Shah, was the best person to take the message and he agreed. I explained to Shahid that this kind of talk would jeopardize his own position and that it was best for him to leave the matter well alone. I do not know if Shahid was telling me the truth or if Bakhteyar had told him to tell me this. Had the British wanted Bakhteyar to become prime minister they could have passed this request on to Mohammad Reza through Shahpour J., thus the mediation of Shahid in this matter seemed ludicurous to me. I did not tell Mohammad Reza of this, had I done so Shahid would surely have been throne into jail.

Bakhteyar left southern France for Beirut with SAVAK at his heels. His trip took place just before the June 1963 uprising. SAVAK had taken a picture of Bakhteyar with an unidentified man on the beach. Moqaddam later claimed that Bakhteyar had paid 20 million rials to the man to instigate the uprisings of 1963.

Bakhteyar's activities reached their zenith when he was in Baghdad. According to SAVAK's reports, Bakhteyar enjoyed the use of the extensive facilities the Baathist regime had to offer, and a company of soldiers was even assigned to protect him.

Fugitive and retired army officers and civilian personalities gathered around him. Through Saddam Hussein's intervention, Bakhteyar set up relations with Dr. Radmanesh, the Secretary

General of the Tudeh Party, and members of his own clique consisted of some Communists. SAVAK, who had many informants in Bakhteyar's circle of friends and acquaintances, said that he was planning open revolt against the Shah and that he proposed to enter Iran through the western borders and gather a force together in the Bakhteyari mountains to embark on partisan attacks against the central government. Before launching his extensive antigovernment operations, Bakhteyar was killed by one of his aides. Bakhteyar's assassination plan was hatched by SAVAK. Nasiri, who supervised all operational affairs, did not utter a word about the plan to me, this was because in SAVAK each person was in charge of his own designated tasks, and just as he did not interfere in my affairs I did not interfere in his. When the assassination was carried out, I had already moved to the Imperial Investigation Organization and did not hold any position at SAVAK. No report was dispatched to the SIB either, the plan was decided upon in meetings between Mohammad Reza and Nasiri. However, Sabeti who came to the office every fifteen days to attend the meetings of the Second Grade Coordination Council told me what had happened. At the time, Sabeti was the head of SAVAK's Third Department. According to him, SAVAK was able through Shahriari, the head of a secret branch of the Tudeh Party and a SAVAK agent, to make contact with a Communist fugitive officer. Teimur was deeply fond of this officer who was a former air force Major. SAVAK promised to pay him a large amount of money and send him to South America if he succeeded in killing Bakhteyar. The officer accepted the task.

One day, the two went out hunting. Bakhteyar ordered his Iraqi escort to wait their return and the two continued searching for prey. As the guards lost sight of them, the officer shot Bakhteyar and fled to Iran. SAVAK, in return, fulfilled its promise and sent him to South America with the proposed amount of money. In this way, the Shah rid himself of Bakhteyar.

SAVAK, FROM PAKRAVAN TO MOQADDAM

If one is going to write a history of SAVAK from beginning to end, then one has to categorize it into four periods. The first period begins with the creation of SAVAK in 1956, by American advisors and covers the leadership of the man they chose to lead the organization,

Teimur Bakhteyar. In reality, during this period, SAVAK lacked all semblance of a true organization and with only about 150 personnel undertook its duties as laid down by the Shah, these included the brutal repression of his opponents. Gradually, the power acquired by Bakhteyar in this post, and his close relationship with the 10-man American advisory team attached to SAVAK, troubled Mohammad Reza and he subsequently dismissed him in 1960.

The second period of SAVAK's history begins with the appointment of Pakravan as Chief of SAVAK, and actually with the beginning of my tenure of office in the organization. During this period, Mohammad Reza's aims were firstly to purge SAVAK of Bakhteyar's supporters and change it into an organization which was fully loyal to him, and secondly to organize SAVAK such that it could protect his monarchy. Consequently, old friends of Bakhteyar such as Amjadi and Zibai were gradually discharged, and the American advisory team, which in effect was the real leader of SAVAK, left the organization on amicable terms and Israeli teachers eagerly took its place. Eventually Pakravan, who came to be seen as a man of weak disposition and who consequently lost favour in Mohammad Reza's eyes, was also sacked, and Nasiri, a loyal officer to the Shah, took his place. During this period, SAVAK was turned into a powerful organization with a personnel force of approximately 5,000. Therefore this period, which lasted until 1971, could be described as the period of training and organization.

The third period of SAVAK's history begins when Moqaddam and myself left in 1971, and the organization, which we had created, was virtually handed over to Nasiri, Motazed and Sabeti. This was SAVAK's period of aggression and power, and it was during this period that the organization became the centre for all political intrigues and reached the height of its infamy.

The fourth period, which was the period of its decline and fall, coincided with the last months of Mohammad Reza's monarchy and begins with the dismissal of Nasiri and Motazed and the installation of Moqaddam as Head. Finally the history of SAVAK which spanned approximately 22 years, ends with the triumph of the 1979 Islamic Revolution.

When I entered SAVAK, Bakhteyar enjoyed immense popularity there. The high-ranking officials and directors enjoyed a good period under his leadership and aided and abetted him in his thieving. Brigadier General Alavikia was Bakhteyar's reliable middle man. The Amjadi brothers were his devotees and aides. Pakravan himself also had a special liking for Bakhteyar and respected him as a brave officer. In effect, all the important people at SAVAK had formed one clique and I was the outsider who had joined them. The reason for the establishment of this clique was purely for the misappropriation of funds and the abuse of power. SAVAK's budget was carelessly squandered and embezzled, files were fabricated and huge bribes were taken. During my tenure of office at SAVAK, controls were established in the Sixth Department and the embezzlement of money greatly decreased. However, Brigadier General Zengani, Director of the Sixth Department (financial affairs), and his subordinates, continued to embezzle funds and Zengani officially announced his embezzlements to be legal up to five per cent. His opinion reached the ears of Nasiri but he did not oppose Zengani's actions. It was natural that, in such an environment, my joining SAVAK was not greeted with enthusiasm, and even though previously the directors and especially General Moulavi, the Head of SAVAK in Tehran, queued up every day outside Pakravan's office, they rarely came to see me. Whatever, everyone knew me well and were forced to condescend to my wishes.

A few days after assuming my post, I asked Kangarlu about Colonel Zibai. At that time Zibai, a strong supporter of Bakhteyar, was infamous for his callousness and for using brutal methods of torture against prisoners. Kangarlu confirmed the allegations. Consequently, I brought an end to Zibai's term of service in SAVAK. This action on my part pleased Pakravan greatly, for he had wanted to rid himself of the man but did not have the nerve to do so.

Colonel Zibai was a distant relative of mine, my sister's (who was called Iran) son was married to the colonel's niece, and the colonel's nephew was married to Iran's daughter. Colonel Zibai had accumulated great wealth during Bakhteyar's period at SAVAK, and his brother too was a wealthy factory owner who also owned several skyscrapers in Tehran. Despite my relationship with the colonel, his dismissal was a necessary and wise move from every point of view, even though it brought a hail of protest from my sister. I later learnt from my sister that both the Zibai brothers had gone to America. The factory owner had gone to live in New Jersey where he was engaged in trade, and Colonel Zibai had gone to live in a small village in America, but he was so afraid of Iranian students in the States that he did not even give his address to his own brother.

The dismissal of Mustafa Amjadi was next on my agenda. I did not relish the task because I had been friends with both brothers for many years and I had been a guest in both their homes many times. Both were students of mine when I was a teacher at the War University, and I was especially close to Mustafa. However, the June 1963 uprising and SAVAK's inability to predict and prevent the riots had prompted Mohammad Reza's discontent. At the time, Bakhteyar was in Beirut and the Shah was afraid that the domestic turmoil would lead to a coup and Mustafa Amjadi, who was the Director of the Third Department and thus directly responsible for the security of the state and who did not hide his strong support for Bakhteyar, many have deliberately refused to inform him of the conspiracy against him. About 8 p.m. on the evening of June 5, 1963, Oweisi and I had a meeting with Mohammad Reza, and in this meeting he ordered the dismissal of Amjadi. The next day, I replaced Amjadi with Moqaddam. However, I promised Amjadi that after a few months I would give him a suitable job in another area. I kept my promise and after a time I arranged his new job and he kept it for many years and became very wealthy from it. At this time, Naser Moqaddam was a Colonel and an officer of the SIB. Along with my brother, Nosratollah, he administered the affairs of the third branch of the bureau. Moqaddam was the only officer I brought with me from the bureau to SAVAK, and I re-organized the Third Department there through him. On the whole, the Amjadi affair was settled without any major upsets, and I was happy that Mohammad Reza happy with his dismissal and did not order a more severe punishment for him.

After a time, Pakravan was also dismissed from SAVAK and Nasiri took his place. I asked Mohammad Reza to appoint Pakravan to another suitable post, he agreed and consequently Pakravan became Minister of Information in Hoveida's cabinet. Later, Pakravan served for three years in the Iranian Embassy in Pakistan and then went on to become Iran's ambassador to France for a term. When his term in France ended, I gave him a prestigious job in an organization in charge of literacy training.

Nasiri thus became Head of SAVAK, but as long as I was Deputy Head his powers were limited. At first he did not mind this curtailment of his authority, but gradually his attitude changed and he sought complete authority over the organization. In this period, Motazed who was well-known for his cajolery, and Sabeti was an opportunist, both worked closely with Nasiri. When Moqaddam and I left SAVAK, Nasiri realized his desire, Motazed took my place and became the Deputy Head of SAVAK and Sabeti became Director of the Third Department.

As I explained before, when Hasan Akhavi recommended Nasiri to me for the post of Head of the Imperial Guard, his only qualification was that he was loyal to the Shah. Akhavi told me that he was the only suitable candidate for this post because he was not very bright and for this post that did not matter. Akhavi's assessment was correct and later this weakness in Nasiri's character was to rear its head on many occasions in all the positions he held. Nevertheless, the events of August 1953 made him famous and he found favour with Mohammad Reza. His uncouthness and unawareness were thus compensated by his loyalty.

Gradually, however, Mohammad Reza ran out of patience with him and ordered his dismissal. For a while, he was out of work, but later he became the Chief of Police. In reality though, others administered Nasiri's affairs. Later, the Shah sent Nasiri to SAVAK, he probably felt that it would serve his interests to have a person like Nasiri in SAVAK's leadership. In SAVAK too Nasiri gradually came under the influence of Motazed and Sabeti. When Moqaddam and I left the organization Nasiri, Motazed and Sabeti took over the reins of power and during their time there these three individuals became extremely wealthy and abused their power greatly.

One day in 1971, the Shah summoned me to his Palace and told me that he had decided to give me a more important job: Head of the Imperial Investigation Organization. He asked me whom I recommended to take my place in SAVAK and I suggested Moqaddam. I left the Palace and went straight to SAVAK. After collecting my personal belongings I made my way to Nasiri's home in Lavisan, north Tehran. I told him what had happened and while he expressed his sorrow to see me leave, he refused to accept Moqaddam as my replacement claiming that he could not work with him. He added, "that aside, what can I tell Motazed who has served the organization from the beginning". I told him to contact Mohammad Reza and tell him his view on the matter, this he did and the Shah accepted his request. The next day, Major-General Motazed was appointed Deputy Chief of SAVAK.

After this event, on the orders of Mohammad Reza, a commission was set up to deal with the disputes and problems occurring in SAVAK. General Palizban, Nasiri, myself and the Chief of the Joint Staff of the Armed Forces were members of the commission. Palizban was the head of the military intelligence, and, according to the Shah, was not worthy of the post. The commission heard Palizban's explanations, prepared a report and passed it on to Mohammad Reza. He, on the recommendations of the commission, agreed to appoint a more experienced person to deal with the affairs of military intelligence, and I suggested Moqaddam, who at the time did not have an official post. Thus Moqaddam became head of military intelligence. Palizban later became a Senator.

These developments in fact signified a change in the security and intelligence policies of the country. As I explained earlier, Shahpour J. actually strengthened the role of SIB and my role as coordinator of the security forces when, in 1970 at the Palace and in the presence of Mohammad Reza, he reminded officials of the security forces of the importance of the security council and of establishing secondary cooperation councils. My appointment to the post of head of the Imperial Investigation Organization, taking over from General Yazdanpanah, and subsequently my changing the organization from one of disorder and disunity into one of efficiency; the appointment of Moqaddam as head of military intelligence and consequently the strengthening of its role; and finally the effective role played by Nasiri, Motazed and Sabeti in SAVAK, were all changes dictated by America and England. The aim of the two powers in bringing about these changes was to strengthen Mohammad Reza's position in the new circumstances of the region.

Moqaddam was able to make some changes in military intelligence, just as he had done previously in the Third Department of SAVAK. I, for my part, did not hold back on my support to him, and I put the best officers at his disposal. Up until this time, Moqaddam had been a very modest and humble man, and because of this everybody liked him and he had a good reputation. However, when he became head of military intelligence, his character changed and he became very pompous and ostentatious. For example, he held a wedding party for his son. As usual, I didn't attend, but some of the guests told me that they had never before experienced such a grand affair. Apart from the food, drinks, singers and location, the attendance of 1,000 people including high ranking officials such as the Prime Minister, cabinet ministers, members of the legislative assembly and the judiciary, officials from the military, the mayor's office and the police and other important figures made for an unprecedented occasion. The building and the area surrounding it had been decorated with baskets of the most beautiful types of flowers. It was obvious that millions of tumans had been spent on the wedding party. A trip to America, a few meetings with American Embassy officials and some American advisors, along with a few promises for the future, had completely changed Moqaddam.

Moqaddam attained the rank of General and at the time of the revolution, Mohammad Reza made him Head of SAVAK in the hope that his good name would help give the organization a better face and thus draw attention from past atrocities. Nasiri was made Iran's ambassador to Pakistan, and Motazed was dispatched to Iran's Embassy in Damascus. Moqaddam established relations with the Iranian National Front and tried to crush the revolution but without success. The appointment of Moqaddam as Head of SAVAK not only did not solve any problems, it also cost him his life.

ORGANIZATION OF SAVAK AND TRAINING

I explained earlier that SAVAK had two main responsibilities; they were foreign intelligence and state security which in reality were a combination of the CIA and FBI introduced by the American advisors during their stay in Iran. Here, I would like to explain the establishments that existed in SAVAK.

Chairmanship's Sphere of Control

The central ranking structure of SAVAK was as follows: Chief, Deputy Chief, Head of Foreign Intelligence, Director of Department, Deputy Director of Department, Head of Section and Head of Branch.

As far as I can remember, SAVAK's Chief had the following area of control:

SAVAK Investigation: Brigadier General Ansari ran the section. Upon regulations drawn up by the investigation experts and approved by me, this section was assigned to carry out the task of investigation at SAVAK departments at home and its stations abroad. Ansari himself was responsible for the affair and, therefore no staff were required except two as his aides.

In order to follow up his responsibilities at SAVAK stations abroad, Ansari had to make many foreign trips. According to the regulations, he had to look at the details very carefully and, therefore, he spent about 20 days on every visit to SAVAK's main branches in provincial capitals. His reports and the precision excercised in the reports had facilitated the job and I, in the meantime, issued the necessary orders.

Nasiri gave my orders to the responsible branches and later briefed me on the steps taken by them. He also accepted complaints, if any, from any branches and passed them on to the responsible body upon my orders.

Complaints Section: Brigadier-General Zaltash was chief of the section and was fond of his job. He had put a box in a safe place for complaints in order to allow all his staff to file their objection against whoever offended them, even their chief. Zeltash held the key and opened the box every morning. He looked into the complaints very carefully and insisted on meeting the complainant personally in order to learn the root cause of the problem. He came to my office once a week and read out a summary of the complaints and the measures taken to close the cases along with a series of proposals. Most of his proposals were sound and, therefore, I approved of them. The approval was then passed on to the relative departments with request that action be taken. He then met the complainant again to make sure that his demands had been seen to. If there were any unjustified and illegal requests, he persuaded the complainant to drop his complaint. The procedure was designed so as to allow the staff to get their problems off their chest and prevent any unpleasant consequences.

SAVAK's public prosecutor's office was also within the sphere of the chairman's control. A public prosecutor and a number of assistants handled the affairs and fixed any administrative offenses.

SAVAK's primary court comprised five members of staff and the court of review of seven members.

The staff of the three judicial bodies were proposed by the "Supreme Commission of SAVAK" and were allowed to start work after approval was given. I studied the verdicts passed by the court of review. According to the regulations which applied to all ministers, I was entitled to enhance any sentences passed. I always made use of my powers and that helped me to gain popularity.

Accountancy: An expert accountant with the rank of Major-General looked after the accounts of the Sixth Department. This was another part of chairman's sphere of control.

Annual Budget: Major Shahsta was in charge of the annual budget section. Any payments had to meet the approval of Chief of SAVAK and no one else was entitled to order any payments to be made. During my tenure of office, I did the job. Whenever I wanted to take money from the treasury, I would ask Major Shahsta and after receiving permission from the Chief of SAVAK (Pakravan and later Nasiri) he would meet my request. My requests were always approved of. When I left SAVAK in 1971, the annual budget had reached about 20 million tumans and could be increased every year upon the approval of Mohammad Reza who usually agreed.

Since Shahsta was old and could not handle the affairs appropriately, his brother helped him to run the affairs for a period of time but, responsibility for the budget lay with him.

The motor unit and health department led by Major-General Badaie and Brigadier-General Latifi respectively was another area under the control of the Chief of SAVAK.

SAVAK's Provincial Bureaus: The set-up of SAVAK offices in provinces as regards personnel was in proportion to the population and the activities of the bureau in the province. In border provinces, an extraterritorial branch also functioned. Internal security, which existed in all SAVAK branches had two sub-divisions, every division had a specific responsibility. One division was to check covert activities and the other reported public discontent. An intelligence section also functioned but branches in some provincial capitals had set up anti-espionage sections. The investigation section was also an integral part of any SAVAK branch.

The structure of SAVAK offices in the provinces included a chief, two or three advisors and a number of guards.

Administrative Department of SAVAK

The administrative organization of SAVAK, like any other intelligence or non-intelligence, military or civilian network was drawn up on the basis of the regulations approved by the secret agency. The regulation predicted 13 or 14 responsibilities for any member and defined the tasks of all the staff from employment to retirement.

As far as I can remember the staff department regulations at SAVAK were as follows:

Employment: Any engagement of the personnel in SAVAK was under two categories: Employment and contract. During the whole of SAVAK's existence, the procedure did not change. Any civilian wishing to be employed in SAVAK had to be introduced and recommended by someone already working for SAVAK and no one was employed upon personal application. Since all members of staff wished their relatives to join them, recommendations were not in short supply. The personnel department registered the names of all applicants and recalled them in sequence of priority, if any new members of staff were required. Of course, employment in the MI-6 in Britain required two recommendations from an official not lower than chief of a department. I failed to set up the same conditions in SAVAK but a similar procedure applied to the SIB. If anyone was to be employed all SIB officers gathered in the conference hall and selected three officers with the rank of Major and Lieutenant-Colonel on the basis of information obtained in a directory. An officer was assigned to put under investigation all his personal records and his past political life. The officer was also asked to obtain information from five officers who knew him and then write the name of the three officers down in order of priority. The three officers were then introduced to the Commander of the Ground Force for approval.

Investigation: According to an approved document the Fourth Department was responsible for political and non-political (ordinary) investigations. If a clean record was given, the applicants were introduced to the Personnel Department to undergo some tests and present their educational qualifications. When the procedure was completed, a final approval by the Chief of SAVAK was required. Of course, during my tenure of office there, my signature was enough for the approval.

Some contract employees were also working for SAVAK. They were commissioned or non-commissioned officers. Again, the Fourth Department handled the investigation and handed over the results to the Personnel Department. If a clean record was given, the army was requested to allow the applicant to be posted to SAVAK. In order not to waste time and effort the army was contacted in advance and if consent was given, the Fourth Department commenced its investigations.

Promotions: For civilians, there were nine grades. Before getting a grade, some conditions had to be met. First, the Chief of SAVAK or the related director had to ask for the promotion to be granted and, second, the Personnel Department had to agree to the promotion. For instance, a clerk (the lowest job) could be promoted to grade four but could not be granted a higher grade unless he was the Chief of the Section.

To better distinguish the positions and ranks, an article was included in the regulations to give the military and the civilians a position corresponding to their capabilities. For example, a Colonel was equal in rank with a civilian holding the grade nine. Promotions for non-commissioned officers were allowed by the Chief of SAVAK (during my post there, I did the job) who later reported the promotion to the army. For commissioned or high ranking officers, the Chief of SAVAK only made a request and if the army approved, promotion was accorded.

Job Assignment: The Personnel Department introduced the applicants to the related sections and they started work. The "Supreme Commission of SAVAK" which comprised seven members had to approve the key posts. The commission fulfilled its responsibility until I stepped out of the organization.

Training: Intelligence officers received nine months of training. The Fourth Department also trained guard officers for three months. The training period for technicians lasted only one month.

Specialization: Since getting specialized staff was difficult, experts were allowed to receive promotions within their own range of command. Of course, some facilities were anticipated for their promotions.

Administrative Offences: A public procedure and a court (five members) as well as a court of review (seven members) were responsible for administrative malfunctions. They had to follow the regulations approved by the cabinet ministers.

Incentives: Upon proposals by the Chief of SAVAK or the related director, incentives were granted to those only who deserved encouragement.

Salary: Salary was paid according to the regulations approved by the cabinet ministers. Any officers with the rank of Colonel or lower were paid by the army and when they were promoted to the rank of Brigadier-General, SAVAK paid their salary.

Retirement: As long as I worked there, because SAVAK was a newly-founded organization, no one retired. If contract employees were retired by the army, they were still allowed to work for SAVAK, if they so desired.

I carefully supervised and checked any changers in SAVAK and the Chief of SAVAK did not interfere in the administrative affairs.

The Chief of SAVAK's sphere of responsibility at the time was operational affairs and if promotion was requested, he left the matter with me.

First Department

The First Department of SAVAK under Brigadier-General Seifollah Frouzin handled the administrative affairs. As far as I can remember, the Department comprised a personnel and communication section and a section which dealt with visiting guests.

The Personnel Department was of special importance to SAVAK and was chaired by Captain Khodadad, a retired officer. He was proficient in his work and in many ways he was even better than his boss, Frouzin. Because of the importance of the Personnel Department, I personally looked after each one of the files, and even though this was a very time consuming job, I did not leave it for others to do.

The communication section was run by a Major who had a good command over his job. He administered all the internal and external networks operating in SAVAK and supervised all telephone switchboards. He also set up a radio network system in all corners of the country, and proposed a central telephone switchboard for SAVAK bureaus in the provinces, after approval these were established under his supervision.

Any radio or telephone maintenance requirements were met by this section. I played an effective role in the development and provision of the communication system, in the training of the personnel and in providing maintenance facilities in this section.

Second Department

The Second Department was responsible for collection of foreign intelligence including the theft of secret information of all types which it then passed onto the Eighth Department for investigation. Mansour Qadr was in charge of the department who in 1948 was appointed Iran's ambassador to Jordan. He was succeeded by his deputy Brigadier-General Farazian.

Farazian lacked competence in his job, but he was an obedient officer and was thus able to administer the department in an organized manner.

The training for the Second Department was carried out by Israeli instructors, particularly by the leader of the Israeli extra-territorial base in Khuzestan Province in the south of the country who contributed greatly towards improving the quality of this department.

The Second Department acquired information through two channels: first, through the extra-territorial bases. Therefore, they had a branch in all the SAVAK border stations and despite deficiencies, they were able to establish networks along the Iranian border with Iraq and Afghanistan and were very active in acquiring intelligence. In fact, Iran's extra-territorial facilities, especially regarding the Arab states, were usually employed by the Israeli extra-territorial bases and later instructions came from Tel Aviv and SAVAK really gained nothing. The second channel was setting up bases in the targeted countries. Most of the intelligence was acquired through this means.

The post of the first secretary of Iranian embassies abroad or similar posts were the cover for the agents of the Second Department to operate. They participated in ceremonies in order to make friends with others like them in other embassies, they travelled to different cities to see the situation of the people, studied news and sent back reports to central headquarters. By using these open methods they could guarantee 90 per cent of the Second Department's intelligence needs.

If we believe the words of the intelligence agency instructor that 95% of CIA's information is extracted from public sources and only 5% is classified information of the targeted countries, it has to be said that the Second Department could not even guarantee 1% of its intelligence from classified intelligence, therefore it can be said that more than 99% of the Second Department's required intelligence were collected from public sources provided by SAVAK agents in targeted countries. Nevertheless, when the above information was sent to SIB in the form of Seven Department's bulletins and was combined with the information sent from military intelligence, it gave a comprehensive social picture of the country in question.

The Second Department, like other SAVAK departments employed its personnel after careful selection and appointed acceptable people for sensitive jobs and jobs suitable for their duties and training. Extra-territorial training was a brief specialized training period and was a pre-requisite for extra-territorial officers. Various branches and sections of the Second Department were in charge of dealing with the affairs of one or two certain countries, naturally, the personnel became experts on the affairs of these countries after years of experience.

Third Department

The Third Department administered the vast apparatus of internal security that reached into every city, town and even villages. It was widely despised among SAVAK officers because of its methods and had the most extensive facilities placed at its disposal.

The basic mission of the department was to thwart attempts to topple the government and to preserve and expand the power of the monarchy by essentially clandestine means. It also carried out anti-espionage operations and had other responsibilities similar to those of the FBI in the United States and MI-5 in Britain. It was supervised by the Chief of SAVAK. The department was also empowered to carry out certain secret political missions abroad, the assassination of Teimur Bakhteyar serves as an example.

Directors of the Third Department were Brigadier-General Mostafa Amjadi (until the 1963 uprising), Colonel Nasser Moqaddam who was promoted to the rank of Major-General (until 1971) and Parviz Sabeti, respectively.

The important section within the department which formed the core of SAVAK's internal operations was charged with identifying anti-government groups and individuals and counter attempts to overthrow the government in all parts of the country including those seeking autonomy or secession.

Naturally, any political opposition to the Shah was included in the list of this section, from ordinary political activities to the setting up of anti-government groups or organizing armed uprising and assassination attempts. The section was sub-divided into several branches with specific responsibilities based on SAVAK's requirements. Because of the importance of the department's responsibilities, when I entered SAVAK I immediately met all its requirements including personnel, training, equipment, annual budget, etc. naturally, the Shah wished to see internal security duties carried out at the highest level, but this was not achieved while I was in SAVAK. Moqaddam who once was director of the department also acknowledged to me that he only achieved partial success, because of the difficulty of the operations.

I invited British and American instructors to teach counter-subversion operations in order to improve the state of affairs in the department but they refused my request since it was not in their interests. Again, I was forced to turn to Israel for help.

Upon my request, Nimrodi dispatched an Israeli expert to Tehran to train Iranians on how to counter anti-government activities. The chief instructor was the same man who was appointed deputy chief of the Israeli security agency. The training lasted three months and about thirty students attended his classes. The instructor brought a book with him which was translated and given to the Training Department and the students. During his stay in Tehran, I carefully studied the book and consulted him to clear up any difficulties I had with it.

In the preface of the book brought by the Israeli instructor, an attractively written sentence decorated the page and read 'if a country is to counter the activities of subversive, secret groups, its first priority must be to create public gratification'. Experience has shown that even countries such as Britain, U.S. or the Soviet Union which are equipped with the most modern security appratus are not able to achieve complete success in identifying and neutralizing the subversive networks. Therefore, with this in mind and upon the recommendation of the Israeli instructor, a second section within the department was established.

The section was actually SAVAK's social department and one of its responsibilities was to obviate social discontent and conduct regular testing of the government's popularity. It was required to check the level of public satisfaction or dissatisfaction, investigate and discover the reasons for public discontent and offer its suggestions to the concerned authorities. SAVAK handed over its reports to SIB and to other responsible bodies. The section was subdivided into different parts on the basis of the various social classes. Later, following the spread of strikes in the universities, an independent organ under the name of the "department of universities and students abroad" was set up because the disturbances created by the students had turned into a very important domestic problem. Several branches were created within the section such as the religious minorities.

Perhaps the above explanations on the responsibilities of the second section appear a little ridiculous since the 1979 Islamic revolution demonstrated the deep dissatisfaction of people of all walks of life towards the Shah's regime. However, in my opinion, its establishment was a completely valid act and if this section failed to discover the public discontent it was for several reasons, the main ones being Mohammad Reza's dictatorship, the depth of foreign influence in the country and the corrupt administration. The result of such a system was that the Third Department pretended to play up a social content, praise the government and play down public dissatisfaction in its reports. As far as I was concerned, however, I reflected any dissatisfaction I witnessed and even did not evade sending the letter of a top religious leader Musa Sadr which was full of abuses, to the Shah.

From 1971, when I went into Imperial Investigation Organization, I increased the number of personnel from 150 idle and old employees to 1500 active staff. About 250 investigators helped me discover 4,000 cases of misappropriation and embezzlement which involved amounts in excess of ten million tumans to the time of the revolution; all were reported to the Shah. He handed over all the cases to the justice department where they remained in the archives and nothing was done about them. However, I continued to pursue the cases even though I achieved nothing. I even did not evade disclosing the embezzlements of Majid Alam, a close friend of the Shah. The important figures in the country knew my mentality, and all of them, without exception, took notice of what I said and did. Therefore, no one can claim that Mohammad Reza was unaware of the corrupt nature of his regime or of the prevalent public discontent, and no one can claim that he was the innocent party and blame me for the bad state of affairs. Whatever I did I did because the Shah personally wanted me to do it, and I did not shirk my duty in the slightest. I presume the explanations I have given about Mohammad Reza's public and private life and those around him have revealed many of the untold facts.

To return to the main topic, the Third Department, having the most sensitive responsibility of all SAVAK departments, that is looking after the security of the state, was the largest section in the Shah's secret organization and therefore had many employees placed at its disposal and also agents abroad were charged with meeting its needs. Its facilities and powers gave the Third Department a special place in SAVAK and its director much fame and power.

When such an organization, headed by an ambitious individual like Sabeti, and administered by people like Nasiri, and when the head of the state expects them to provide absolute security without answering to the calls of the disgruntled factors of society, then naturally disastrous consequences result.

From 1971 onwards, mountain-climbing troups who appeared in the mountains of northern Tehran at the weekend received the attention of the department. SAVAK claimed that these groups of youth were formed by those who had been trained abroad, and were taking part in partisan exercises. Once the issue became very sensitive when an army major went to the Imperial Guard's headquarters to claim that he had heard some shots fired when he was out hunting in the Lashkarak mountains of northern Tehran. According to him, he drew closer and saw a number of people training, climbing up the mountain and shooting. The head of the group calmly invited him to chat and informed him that their number was great and that they used to come there to train their members. The commander of the Imperial Guard informed the Shah of the officer's allegations and he delegated the army chief of staff Azhari, to investigate the issue and report his findings. Azhari came to the conclusion that the officer had lied and he was simply looking for attention. Azhari's view on the matter was conveyed to the Shah and he ordered the chief of the Imperial Guard to search the area by helicopter along with the major reconnaissance flights but found nothing. Nothing was heard of the officer again and the truth, falsity or exaggeration of his claim was never discovered.

Another issue was the control the Shah exerted over top-ranking officials through SAVAK. Where the members of the royal family were concerned this control was excercised with the help of the court staff and the drivers. Counter-intelligence agents of the army also watched the activities of officers who held key posts. Upon Mohammad Reza's order, SAVAK approached the family members or close friends of the officers under observation to achieve its objectives.

In my own case, my driver, who was an agent of the army's counter-intelligence section, was secretly watching me from the time that I became the head of SIB. Later, Sabeti informed me of the agent and I did not object since it was normal. After 1971, Sabeti in a meeting with me revealed that Nasiri had appointed his secretary and the secretary of Major-General Motazed, the deputy chief of SAVAK, to set up friendly relations with my wife Tala and in this way he was able to acquire from her information he required. Although it was true, I tried to convince myself that Tala did not realize what she was doing and was acting as an 'unwitting agent". I was used to these kind of things after many years of living with intelligence affairs.

Where civil servants were concerned, SAVAK established relations with their friends or wives in order to keep an eye on them and acquire information. In the prime minister's office, a number of officials, employees and all of the security guards were SAVAK agents who gathered information for SAVAK. Security guards and employees at the home of the prime minister were also used by SAVAK. In the ministries and independent organizations, security guards were used from the ministry's office of security; all of them were SAVAK agents. Other agents also watched key officials. As a whole, the Third, Eighth and Ninth departments were jointly involved in meeting SAVAK's objectives.

Fourth Department

It was charged with SAVAK's security. The department, under the directorship of Brigadier-General Kangarlu, was divided into three sections on the basis of its three-fold security responsibilities: personnel security, site security and document security. A sub-divided branch dealt with guards. The heads of provincial SAVAK bureaus for security guards were also under the command of the Fourth Department.

Personnel Security: This in no way meant that the department would protect SAVAK personnel against physical attacks from opposition groups. Rather, personnel security meant that the past life of the personnel, prior to their employment in SAVAK, was investigated along with those they were acquainted with according to methods approved by the Personnel Department. The staff selection procedure was such that SAVAK could not be penetrated by enemy agents or opposition elements. However, the department for personnel security and to check any suspicious moves and give SAVAK employees complete briefings on their responsibilities and on precautionary measures that must be taken. The briefings were aimed at training the personnel. For example, suppose an agent of the targeted agencies or one of the secret opposition groups planned to get information from SAVAK, he would first of all approach an employee of SAVAK and establish friendly links with him and gradually he would acquire the necessary information from him. In this way, the employee would become an unwitting agent for these agencies and groups.

Site Security: This included physical and human security. Physical security meant that buildings and entrance gates had to be checked and equipment such as iron doors, strong, secure locks, alarms, closed-circuit TVs and the like were in place to ensure the safety of the buildings. Human security meant securing the sites and equipment by employing SAVAK guards.

Document Security: Documents were categorized into classified and ordinary documents on the basis of their importance, and each one was filed in a special way. Although the Personnel Department was expected to look after the security of the documents, the Fourth Department was in charge of ensuring that the task was carried out correctly.

Guards Department: Guards were employed to protect SAVAK buildings in Tehran and the provinces as well as SAVAK stations abroad. These guards were selected from among those who had done their military service and who were physically fit. They worked in four shifts. The first shift worked a 24-hour day and three guards were in charge of each post, the guard changed every eight hours. The second shift was put on alert for unexpected incidents and stayed at SAVAK. The third shift received all kinds of practical and theoretical training, and members of the fourth shift were on leave. Expertise in driving was an obligation for the guards as was familiarity with technical matters.

The department's provincial bureaus also had a number of guards in proportion to the size of the bureaus. The guards of the department were also responsible for the security of the prisons. Security for the U.S. radar bases in northern Iran also lay with the Fourth Department, but the personnel working within the bases were all American subjects. The radar installations had vast fences around them, and the security of these fences was in the hands of the department under the supervision of the American head of the base. I do not remember the exact number of SAVAK guards but they should have been about 800. The guards were organized like the army and were divided into units such as battalions, companies, and platoons but did not use such titles. Strict regulations existed for these security units and their commanders were officers.

The Fourth Department also taught the staff of government organizations the principles of security and set up security offices in each organization. Sometimes, SAVAK personnel were appointed to head or form the staff of these offices. For example, Brigadier-General Hariri, the former chief of SAVAK bureau in Fars Province, was sent to work in the offices of the Tehran municipality.

Fifth Department

The Fifth Department commanded by Brigadier-General Saedi was responsible for technical affairs. Saedi, despite lacking expert knowledge, was an efficient manager. When I entered SAVAK, the Department was more like an antique museum than a SAVAK department responsible for technical affairs. The only pieces of equipment there were 2-3 worthless tape recorders, 4 microphones and about 6 cameras and other similar things.

Each piece of equipment was old and did not meet even a thousandth of SAVAK's needs. I soon learned that Brigadier-General Alavikia had also embezzled money from this Department. In the annual budget, he had asked for five million tumans to be given to the section for the purchase of technical equipment but only 10,000 tumans had been spent, the rest he had taken for his own use. During my time at SAVAK, I rectified the shortcomings of the Fifth Department into an active and efficient one. Its subdivided sections were also improved. Equipment was purchased to meet the needs of the Department in Tehran, the provincial capitals and stations abroad, and always one-third was stored in the department's stocks.

Every six months, Saedi brought me a list of his department's requirements including the price and the supply source for my approval. I, in turn, approved all of his recommendations without exception. He managed to import all the required goods through the Sixth Department and reported every item to me. In this way, the Fifth Department was equipped with the modern technical tools. The principles of intelligence activities dictated that approximately ten per cent of the discovery of secret organizations was made possible only with the use of technical devices and 20 per cent through agents infiltrating the organization. Infiltration did however have its setbacks. The smallest mistake on the part of the agent would mean his exposure or even death. Of course, the superior role of the infiltrators could not be denied, however, technical devices greatly helped them in their missions.

The Fifth Department was subdivided into the following sections:

Surveillance Section: Surveillance teams were a part of the Fifth Department since the time that I stepped into SAVAK. At first, I was surprised that the department, despite its great deficiencies and lack of technical tools, had trained and seasoned experts for surveillance purposes and had been provided with all the necessary equipment and their missions often ended in success.

When I asked the Department's Director to explain how he had such expert teams at his command he gave an ambiguous answer. However, the reason was clear enough for me. The American advisors perhaps wanted the teams for some purpose and therefore trained them and provided them with all the necessary equipment, payment for which came from the annual budget of SAVAK. Members of the surveillance team were carefully selected and given the best and most complete training. Each team was equipped with three vehicles and each vehicle carried three members. The vehicles were all equipped with radios and were in different size and colours so as to avert any suspicion and avoid possible disclosure. The leader of the team was in constant touch with the section headquarters. Team members were also quite familiar with the codes.

During my time at SAVAK, the number of teams was tripled and SAVAK bureaus in the provincial capitals were provided with one or more teams. Once through Lieutenant-Colonel Yacob Nimrodi, an Israeli, the best surveillance team leader was invited from Israel. The invitee worked with a number of teams for a month and became acquainted with the training system and the problems the teams here faced. At the end of his visit, he provided me with a detailed report in which he described the SAVAK teams as one of the best in the world.

Phone Tapping Section: This section was also a part of the Fifth Department and had a telepone network which was independent of the main communication section. Because it was in their interest to see to the efficiency of this section, the American advisors had chosen the best personnel for this section and had given them the best training.

When I entered SAVAK, one hundred telephone lines were being tapped and the conversations recorded round-the-clock. The machine began recording when the telephone conversation commenced and stopped when the receiver was hung up. At the end of my mission at SAVAK, the number of telephone lines which were being tapped had increased from 100 to 400. In addition, agents placed at the communication centre could also bug telephone lines. Conversations were recorded and tapes were passed on to the Sixth Department for investigation. Gradually, the number of personnel in this section and the supply of facilities for phone tapping operations abroad was increased. However, the groundwork of the plans was planned by the American advisors.

Censorship Section: This section was established before I entered SAVAK and its main office was located at the Central Post Office. The personnel who worked here were all well-trained experts but there was no advanced equipment available. After much investigation, it was decided that the most sophisticated devices from this line of work were made in Germany. Consequently, these were purchased and were put at the disposal of the personnel of this section.

At the central office the personnel of this section had a special room where they would check letters, opening and resealing the envelops and taking photocopies of the contents in such a way that no one could tell they had been tampered with. Despite the huge number of letters, the apparatus did its job well. SAVAK branches in the provinces were also provided with less advanced equipment to censor letters and take copies.

Lock Section: Soon after the establishment of SAVAK, it was discovered, through the police that the most skilled locksmiths could be located in the vicinity of what was then the Shah Mosque. With the help of the police, two of them were employed. They were able to make any kind of lock and unlock any lock easily but their tools were outdated and their methods were old fashioned and they were not able to break open safes with a six digit combination lock or the such like.

Gradually, more locksmiths were recruited and the personnel of this section reached seven. I had the most updated implements imported for them from the U.S., Germany and Japan, and I sent two of the most talented from amongst them to the U.S. for training. The reason behind this was to train them with the latest methods so that they could break the combination of any safe. In this I was successful but of course they needed some special instruments, for instance, some devices which would increase the volume of sound 100,000 times to enable the agent to discover the safe's code. This amplifier would help to break the combination lock of a safe by allowing him to hear the particular sound which is made when the correct code number for opening the safe is reached. The safe cracker is always after this particular sound. At a later date, safes with combination locks were built in America which needed a device which would amplify the sound one million times in order for that special click to be heard. It is interesting to note that at the same time as these safes were built, the necessary amplifier was also created by the same firm. Apparently, however, the sale of these devices was under the control of the government and they were only sold to those intelligence, security and military organizations which were U.S. clients. The two men whom I sent to America for training were also taught how to open safes with explosives and by melting the lock. The latter two methods were very quick but the main problem was that the break-in was obvious whereas with the amplifier the safe could be opened and the documents copied without anyone realizing they had been touched. Breaking the combination of safes is the method widely used by the secret agencies whereas melting the lock or the use of explosives is the normal method of bank robbers.

At a later date, I also sent two other talented employees to Japan for up-to-date training. The Japanese intelligence agency taught the two the most modern methods of safe breaking and made them first-class experts in their field. Japanese technology was very advanced, and the Japanese had invented a lock which when one tried to open it with anything other than its own special key it would not open and could not be opened again. Although this was an extraordinary discovery, and a few of these locks were brought to Tehran, still they were of no real practical use. The team sent to Japan was instructed to bring two or three samples of any device they deemed suitable back to Iran. These samples were then subject to stringtent tests in Tehran and, if they passed these tests, a large number was ordered and given to the relative intelligence agency.

Photography: Great achievements had been made in the photography industry by Japan, some western European countries and the United States. Some members from this section were sent to Japan and other countries for training and they were provided with the best equipment in their field of work. Equipment which was made available to SAVAK at that time consisted of cameras which could take a clear picture of a man, to the extent that he could be recognized, from a distance of six kilometers. Other cameras were also supplied which could take pictures from the closest distance, even ten centimeters. These cameras were widely used for taking pictures of documents in foreign embassies.

Other photographic equipment including infra-red cameras were also supplied to this section.

Electronic Surveillance Section: This was one of the most secretive of all in the Fifth Department. The head of this section was the Deputy Director of the Department. He was employed before my tenure of office began at SAVAK. He possessed a doctorate degree of the highest level in electronics and he gathered around himself an experienced team of electronic experts. The members of this team were either technicians, electronic engineers or held M.S. degrees in electronics. The section was equipped with transmitting sets and receivers, radios and closed-circuit TVs to give additional security to sensitive sites and any other type of electronic device needed by SAVAK.

Of special importance were the microphones which were planted in the meeting rooms of secret groups and the houses of influential figures or suspects, or in foreign diplomatic missions. Upon the orders of Mohammad Reza, microphones were also sometimes installed in the houses of some top-level government officials and he was briefed on all their activities. These microphones were installed in such a way that they could not be discovered. Of course, there were devices which could detect the microphones. One was a pocket-sized device which detected the sound waves coming from the microphones and thus revealed approximately where the microphone was hidden. Secret networks in Iran did not have such devices and there has never been a case where the hidden microphones have been found. The influential figures and suspects were never aware of the existence of such devices and never realized that they were being listened to. SAVAK used different types of hidden microphones on its missions and the most advanced technology of the time was placed at its disposal.

In this section, a special team was assigned to discover transmitters and to find ways to stop microphones from being found. SAVAK installed transmitters in targeted embassies by hiring the local staff, but in some cases they were discovered. Of course, the embassies of Kuwait and Saudi Arabia and the like did not even think that a secret microphone would be planted in their building so the thought never crossed their mind to search for one!. Thus, in these embassies the microphones were put to their full use. However, the embassies of the (former) Soviet Union and the East Block countries were constantly looking for listening devices and they created problems for the Fifth Department.

Receivers were usually set up in the vicinity of the place where the transmitters were planted, that is in a nearby building or in a car parked in an adjacent street. Upon the recommendation of the American advisors, a number of houses in the vicinity of the Soviet Embassy were rented for this purpose.

Tape recorders used by SAVAK had to have three specialities: first, they should not be able to be heard from a short distance even of half a meter. The Japanese-made recorders were usually turned on and off by means of a wire which was brought through the sleeve of the agent's shirt. Second, they should be small in size, the smaller the better, and third, the cassette should be able to record for a long period of time.

The problem with the very small transmitters was that those which were rechargeable did not work for more than 24-48 hours, the battery operated transmitters worked for one month and the electric transmitters worked permanently. So agents had to secretly enter the building every other day to charge the rechargeable ones. Sometimes infiltrators such as servants were employed to handle the job. If meetings were held in open areas such as a garden, tiny transmitters in the shape of a thin strip of wire which could not be seen even from a distance of ten centimeters, were used. These microphones were "shot" on to the branch of a tree at the meeting place. They were useful as long as they were not discovered. The very reason behind the establishment of the electronic surveillance section within the sphere of the Fifth Department was to carry out such delicate and skillful activities.

Members of the teams had to familiarize themselves with all

these technical skills including unlocking doors, entering buildings, planting transmitters, copying documents and other operations.

Closed-circuit TVs had a special section in the Fifth Department. These were used to protect important, sensitive sites. Although electric fences and alarms were in use at such sites, closed-circuit TVs did a more thorough job. The TVs were fixed in designated places and watched all activity inside and outside the walls of the building. I also set up a graphology section in the Fifth Department.

As I explained earlier, the training of SAVAK personnel was very inadequate when I entered the organization. From the time I first began work at SAVAK my attention was directed towards improving the training and promoting it to the highest level. This I did upon Mohammad Reza's orders.

The main problem I faced was SAVAK's lack of experience in implementing its tasks. Prior to the establishment of SAVAK, the police and for a time the Military Governorate (after the August 1953 coup) carried out these tasks in their own way and with inexperienced staff. Therefore, in order to set up a well-organized secret network, it was necessary to acquire training from the intelligence agency of a country which was well experienced and expert in this field of work. The training which the American advisors had given the Iranians during the first five years of SAVAK's existence was in no way sufficient, and it became apparent that they were not ready to cooperate fully. Indeed, they were not allowed to, and some of the advisors did not have the qualifications required to improve the level of training.

Sixth Department

It was charged with SAVAK's financial affairs. Director of the Department was Brigadier-General Zanganeh. He was not a good Administrator and was very unreliable in financial matters. He openly embezzled five per cent of the budget seeing it as his legal right. The Department spent only the official budget which came from the Presidential Bureau and the Ministry of War (Defense) so that no budget would go to the Parliament in the name of SAVAK. An expert accountant supervised all the accounts of the Sixth Department.

The Department was subdivided into a few sections. The accounts section determined and estimated the annual budget and was responsible for payments. The supply section provided everything from stationery to technical tools of clandestine operations as requested by the Fifth Department.

All the materials required including concealment devices, self-destructive containers for transporting secret documents and films, special cameras, secret wiring etc. were supplied either from the domestic market or were imported from abroad by this section. The clubs section was looked after SAVAK's clubs and the parties held in the clubs. It also prepared food for the guests and the guards who worked 24 hours a day. I once sent the head of this section to Paris to become familiar with the procedure operating in the French restaurants mainly to learn how to prepare special trays for food. These trays would make the serving of the food much easier.

Seventh Department

Its task was to study, analyze and disseminate the intelligence clandestinely collected by the Second Department in raw form. Brigadier-General Kaveh, a seasoned intelligence asset with an excellent command over his job, was leading this sensitive department.

Since the responsibilities of the two departments were inter-related, they were organized along the same lines. For instance, a section in charge of collecting intelligence on neighbouring Iraq in the Second Department had a counterpart in the Seventh Department responsible for studying the gathered information. The only difference between the two departments was that the Seventh Department did not have an extraterritorial network.

The Seventh Department published a daily and also a monthly summary of current events and regularly submitted forecasts of future world developments to the relative section of SIB. These bulletins provided a monthly account of the situation in the targeted countries and were compared with similar bulletins and reports from the army's intelligence. The main difference between bulletins from the army's intelligence and the Seventh Department was that the first covered only military matters while the latter brought up political, economic, cultural and social affairs. The SIB finally collected all the reports of these two organs. In addition, the Seventh Department and the army's intelligence also exchanged bulletins so that both could gain a comprehensive knowledge of the targeted countries.

Although the Seventh Department during the 70s grew to be one of the largest departments in SAVAK, it nevertheless lacked the manpower to digest the huge glut of intelligence gathered overtly. The Department also provided an annual evaluation of the overall reporting of each targeted country

The targeted countries were classified in both the Seventh Department and the army's intelligence on the basis of importance. Neighbouring countries were in the first class, regional states in the second and other targeted countries in the third. The Ministry of Foreign Affairs was also required to pass on to these departments, in the form of bulletins, any useful information it received from Iran's diplomatic missions abroad.

Eighth Department

Carefully organized by the Americans, it was responsible for counter-espionage and control of the civilian population throughout the country.

The department was of special concern to the West and both the Head of MI-6 station in the British Embassy and the CIA station Chief in the U.S. Embassy were in constant touch with the department and received useful information on a regular basis. When I was working there, Brigadier-General Hashemi was in charge of the department. He lacked competence in his job but his deputy, Qajar, was an experienced person who later became Major-General and emigrated to the United States.

The Eighth Department was granted a measure of autonomy, empowered to initiate surveillances on its own initiative. It had set up counter-espionage sections in SAVAK bureaus throughout the country. The bureaus were reinforced if a new development took place. For instance, the Isfahan bureau was reinforced after the iron smelting factory began operations.

The activities of the Eighth Department were as follows:

— Identification of intelligence personnel and agents of foreign diplomatic missions in Iran. The Soviet Embassy had the largest number of intelligence personnel from both the KGB and GRU. The department estimated the number of active agents at 50.
— Checking the arrival and departure of the staff of the targeted embassies to and from Iran and finding out if the person

under observation had finished his tenure of office, had been replaced, or was on his way home to deliver his reports.

— Renting houses in the vicinity of the targeted embassies in order to keep a watchful eye on the building. We always had problems with the Soviet Embassy because they quickly discovered our base and created trouble for SAVAK agents.

— Checking the arrival and departure of the staff of foreign embassies and people going to and from the embassy. This was done by erecting stands opposite the main entrance to the embassy and using cameras and other devices or controlling the entrance door from a canvas-covered truck watching through a slit in the canvas. The Soviets knew of both these methods and, therefore, they only allowed ordinary clients to use the main entrance door.

— Surveillance of certain members of the embassy or visitors to the embassy. In many cases, the people under observation were employees of the intelligence section of the embassy who had appointments with their own Iranian spies for consultations. It was not difficult to keep watch on these employees except where the Soviets were concerned. They usually thwarted SAVAK's efforts or suspended the meetings when they realized that they were being watched. However, in some cases, SAVAK's plan worked against the Soviets and it managed to obtain useful information.

— Approaching the people who had met the embassy intelligence agents. Usually they agreed to work with SAVAK and became double agents. The Eighth Department, after arresting them, set them free and allowed an exchange of information to take place since this favoured both sides.

— Identification of Iranian local staff in the targeted embassies and making use of them. The department preferred to use Iranian personnel who were working in the foreign embassies and who were trusted. All the staffers at the Soviet Embassy from the ambassador down to the cleaner were natives of the Soviet Union and that made it difficult for SAVAK to penetrate into the embassy but Iranian local employees at the Iran-Soviet Cultural Relations Society were in close touch with the department. The Soviets were aware of this contact but kept quiet and seemed to favour double agents. The same applied to the embassies of the Eastern European countries.

I remember one interesting case in particular. The Iraqi Embassy had employed an Iranian cleaner who cleaned the rooms after embassy staff had left. The Iraqis trusted the man since he was illiterate and they never suspected him of spying. He was hired by the Eighth Department. The man passed information and documents on to SAVAK after being briefed in advance. He handed over the documents at a particular hour to SAVAK agents who were waiting in a car outside the embassy building. The documents were returned to him after they had been copied, and he put them back in their place that same night.

After a period of time, documents inside iron safes were required. The cleaner was briefed on how to search for the combination of the lock. He searched a desk drawer and handed over all the numbers he found there to a SAVAK agent who was always close at hand. One of the sequence of numbers seemed to be the correct combination. The cleaner had been taught how to break open a combination lock, and so he returned to the embassy and tried the sequence of numbers the agent had given him and by chance, the safe opened. He handed over the documents to the SAVAK agent and put them carefully back when he had finished with them.

Another similar case happened in the Kuwaiti Embassy where the Iranian porter was hired to work for the department. It was easy to carry out such operations against the embassies of such countries but impossible in the case of the well-equipped embassies like the Soviet Embassy.

— Contacts with the intelligence agents of friendly embassies: top-level contacts existed between SAVAK and the U.S., British and Israeli embassies. The Eighth Department placed its most useful intelligence at their disposal and carried out instructions issued by MI-6 and the CIA. In the case of the embassies of friendly Arab countries, since the heads of SAVAK missions always had relations with the security officials of these countries, the department also enjoyed close relations with their intelligence agents working in the embassies of Iran. SAVAK always tried to receive useful information from them and not to give it. It was common practice for intelligence to be appropriated from these embassies and all the useful information to be passed onto Nimrodi.

— Approaching Iranian nationals who had friendly relations with a member of the embassy staff and employing them as double agents. Even though the Soviets were aware that the person they were speaking to was a double agent, they still showed great interest in meeting them and extracted whatever information they could get from them. They were always ready to talk to their Iranian friends about anything, they got information and sometimes deliberately gave information in order to keep the relationship going. The procedure was an old practice adopted by the Soviet and British embassies.

Hajir was a British double agent who worked as a secretary in the Soviet Embassy. Saed Maraqei was also a double agent. Major-General Amanollah Jahanbani, who became the chief of the Iran-Soviet Cultural Relations Society also had this role. The department followed the same procedure and had a number of agents who established friendly relations with the staffers of the Soviet Embassy. Their best agent was Saedi, the husband of Nayereh Saedi, who was a previous employee of the railway and later found his way to the Parliament as reward for services rendered. Certainly, the Soviets knew that he was a SAVAK agent but still they met him in his house once a week. They were very respectful towards him, and for years this contact continued.

Another activity of the Eighth Department was surveillance of the religious minorities and controlling their contacts, especially with the Soviet Embassy. The Armenians in particular were regular visitors to the embassy, although they did not refer directly to the embassy but to buildings in nearby streets. The aim of the Armenians was to get a visa and travel to Armenia. Middle-class and poor Armenians, who held sympathetic tendencies towards the Russian Armenia and who had relatives there were the targets of the KGB, GRU and SAVAK.

Here, I would like to explain and define the terms "counter-intelligence" and "counter-espionage". In the army, every effort is made to protect military secrets and adopt a defensive position. For instance, a division in general is the target of the rival countries from its building to its personnel and documents, and thus all of these have to be protected; the best way to do this is to thwart or block any intelligence intrusion by rivals and defend ones own intelligence.

Therefore, counter-intelligence could be defined as efforts to protect military secrets from falling into enemy hands. Since society does not have a special organization dealing with this kinds of protection, the Eighth Department became responsible for counter-intelligence throughout the whole of the country except in the army and security forces. Naturally, not everybody could be put under surveillance, therefore, one had to concentrate on finding the spies, and in order to thwart their operations, counter-espionage activities had to be carried out. Therefore, the term counter -espionage was attributed to organizations like the Eighth Department.

The training of the members of the department to certain extent was carried out by the British but most of the training was given by the American advisors. Once, the relative expert was invited from Israel to teach and some people were also sent to the United States for training. However, the most skilful and comprehensive training was given by the American advisory team with the help of Brigadier-General Tajbakhsh and together this training helped improve the competence of the department.

From the point of view of training matters, there was a constant exchange of information between the army's counter-intelligence section and the Eighth Department, because counter-intelligence and counter-espionage training is really one and the same, the difference between the two lies only in their names. Whenever the counter-intelligence section of the army held training classes, a number of people from the Eighth Department also attended. The police and gendarmerie's counter-intelligence agents also received their training in these classes.

When I worked in SAVAK, Major-General Ali Motazed headed SAVAK's foreign intelligence organization. He had three deputies, but they were gradually removed one by one. The Second and Seventh Departments were also under the command of Motazed. This was the arrangement given to the foreign intelligence organization by the American advisors and modelled on the CIA.

Later, in talks with top-ranking Israeli intelligence officials, I learned that it was also run along the same lines as the Israeli intelligence agency, with the difference that in Britain and the

United States the foreign intelligence organization is independent from the security organization but in Israel it is affiliated to the general staff of the army. This is because the Israelis see themselves to be in a state of war and naturally their main objective acquiring military intelligence.

In the Soviet Union, the system was totally different, the overseas and internal intelligence organizations were under the umbrella of the KGB, while military intelligence and counter-intelligence came under another organization called GRU. In SAVAK, the American advisors set up foreign intelligence organization in the form of the Second and Seventh Departments alongside the security organization, because Iran did not need to acquire extensive foreign intelligence. In order to create coordination between the two departments, a foreign intelligence chief was appointed as their head; his official title was deputy foreign intelligence chief of SAVAK.

Ninth Department

Mohammad Reza sometimes turned over certain cases to SIB for investigation. So, on the basis of the training I had received in Britain, I set aside some officers for investigation purposes. In this way, the fifth section of SIB was formed. However, it occurred to me that investigation was most certainly a speciality which we did not have, and each speciality has some principles. A lot of cases came up in SAVAK which needed investigating, and each department and branch carried out the job in their own way using their own methods.

One day, I asked Nimrodi if investigation was considered to be a speciality in his country or not. He replied that it was not only seen to be a speciality but that in the Israeli intelligence agency a department existed which was concerned purely with investigation. Upon my request, he invited the director general of the department to Tehran. I convened a meeting of a number of SAVAK's directors or their deputies, members of the Supreme Commission of SAVAK and the Israeli director general. The Israeli who showed a lot of interest in the subject brought much literature with him and, as he spoke in French, I personally translated what he said into Persian. Everybody was obliged to take notes from his talks. At first, he spoke about why the Israeli intelligence agency needed such a department and then he went on to explain, from the organizational chart, the responsibilities of each of the sections and how they carried out their work. Later, I got his charts off him along with a brochure which described in detail the process of an investigation from beginning to end. Before his departure, I gave the director a present as a sign of my appreciation for the work he had done.

The training he had given had impressed everyone, and when it had finished I immediately ordered the Supreme Commission to establish a Ninth Department to carry out investigations. The Supreme Commission suggested Colonel Zarabi who later became Brigadier-General, to lead the new department and I approved.

I then asked the newly established department to write a book on investigation using the charts and documents I had acquired from the Israeli instructor and the notes taken from his lectures. The book was written in coordination with the training department, and after closely studying it, I approved it totally.

One of the responsibilities of the new department, on the advice of the Israeli instructor, was investigating people. On that basis, a special investigation training course was provided and most of SAVAK's personnel attended the course. Some investigation officers began work in the provincial capitals, their number depending on the population of the province. The members of the Ninth Department had agents in different organizations and in the various strata of society, however, they were described as "colleagues" and not "agents" and their duty was to help SAVAK in its investigations.

ISRAEL AND TRAINING SAVAK

Although my training in Britain for SIB was of the highest standard, it was intended for something other than the work that SAVAK was involved with. I, therefore, decided to seek help again from the British.

First of all I went to London alone, and then Samadianpour and Mahoutian accompanied me for updated training. However, the training received there was not sufficient for the British were also reluctant to teach SAVAK new methods and they openly stated that it was not possible for them to train us further. I then sent about six people for three periods of training to the United States. When they returned home, it became clear that the Americans had nothing useful to offer either.

At the time, Iran had recognized Israel as a de facto state and Tel Aviv had opened an informal diplomatic mission in Tehran. The intelligence officer at the Israeli Embassy was Lieutenant-Colonel Yaqub Nimrodi who, with the approval of the Shah, had active relations with SAVAK. I had information that the Israeli intelligence network was very strong because some Jews occupied very sensitive intelligence posts in Europe and North America and after the creation of Israel in 1948, they had set up Israeli intelligence and security organizations. Therefore, with the help of Nimrodi, I organized a programme of training for SAVAK which led to the establishment of Training Department under the leadership of Brigadier-General Keyvani.

> "As a result of the establishment of diplomatic relations in the late 1960s between Iran and Israel, the Iranians had a full embassy in Ramat Gan with a SAVAK representative, a military attache, a commercial attache, a consul, and an ambassador. But it wasn't officially designated as an embassy and it did not have a sign on the door or flagpole. Officially, the Iranians had an interests section in the Swiss Embassy in Tel Aviv, but it did not really exist, and callers in the Swiss Embassy who asked for it would be referred to the unofficial Iranian Embassy in Ramat Gan.
>
> Israel had the same unofficial status in Tehran. The building on Kakh Avenue had no sign on the door, but everyone knew what it was. The reason for this elaborate charade was. The Shah's concern that his relationship with Arab nations would be disrupted."[2]

The reluctance of the American and British intelligence agencies to provide updated training was encouraged by the CIA and MI-6 who had devised a calculated plan to lead SAVAK towards Israel and pave the way for the influence of Zionists in Iran. One should bear in mind that Zionists had penetrated the Western intelligence agencies to the extent that they could be described as the coordinators of Western secret agencies.[3]

At the beginning, about three teams, each with ten members from the Second, Third, and Eighth Department, were sent to Israel. The training lasted about two years and was very successful. This indicated that the Israeli valued Mohammad Reza's friendship greatly and banked heavily on the future role of SAVAK in the region. Thus, I preferred to invite Israeli teachers to Tehran. Nimrodi helped in the arrangements and invited the necessary teachers. About thirty-five students were chosen to attend each class. At the conclusion of the class, I asked the teachers to provide me with a list of people present at the class giving priority to the most talented and skilful. These orders were carried out and I chose the first three top students of the class to train others. The Israeli teachers brought the necessary training books and manuals with them, something which the British and Americans had never done and which had placed SAVAK in a severely strained position. The books were translated into Persian and were very effective in giving order to the training programmes. The Israeli teachers were all outstanding instructors in their field. The instructor who trained SAVAK personnel in security measures was the most experienced in his field at that time in Israel. Later, I learnt from the Eighth Department that he became the deputy chief of the Israeli security agency. Perhaps that was why Attapour and other SAVAK agents were given employment in Israel after the revolution. His lessons covered the problems of security, subversion and counter-subversion techniques. The books he taught from were translated into Persian and notes were taken from his lectures.

The teacher in interrogation matters was also the best in Israel. His training manual was also translated and notes taken from his lectures. The teacher in the Imperial Investigation Organization was the best in Israel and it was upon his suggestions that the Ninth Department was established. As I explained previously, SAVAK's instructor in foreign information was also the chief of the Israeli extraterritorial base in Khuzestan Province and was more experienced than even Nimrodi.

SAVAK saw the most updated training in counter-espionage activities after the establishment of the Training Department. Brigadier-General Tajbakhsh, the chief of the counter-intelligence unit, informed me that a ten-member team of counter-intelligence experts, who were officers in the U.S. army, had come to Tehran upon his invitation. Consequently, I sent eight officers to the army to be trained by them. The training was excellent and I was very grateful to Tajbakhsh for his efforts in this regard. This team also provided SAVAK with a series of books in English which was handed over to Kiavani, Director of the Training Department. I soon came to realize that the army was the number one target for the Americans in Iran and SAVAK stood second on their list of priorities. As I explained earlier, the presence of the American advisory team in SAVAK was pointless and therefore I asked them to leave Iran. This they did willingly. This happened at the same time as the number of American advisors working in the army was increasing every day. The Americans and the British were deliberately denying SAVAK their services so that it was forced to turn more and more towards Israel for help. Their policy was very beneficial for Israel. Nimrodi always proudly described Iran as the best friend of Israel in the region.

Gradually SAVAK attained self-sufficiency in training its personnel, but at the same time it did not cut its relations with Israel and sometimes Israeli instructors were invited to Tehran or a five or six member delegation was sent to Israel in cases where the instructor could not come to Tehran. Permanent instructors were chosen from amongst the best personnel and each one trained in a wide range of subjects and was made a specialist in one or more fields. Some of the Israeli teachers who had been invited to Iran were also the best experts in their field. The training programme consisted of the following:

1. Courses on the duties and regulations of the First Department. These were taught by the Director of the Personnel Department Captain Khodadad.
2. Courses on communications and SAVAK's facilities in this field which were taught by the Chief of SAVAK's Communication Section.
3. Extraterritorial training by the instructors of SAVAK's Ninth Department.
4. Training the heads of SAVAK stations abroad by instructors of the highest level invited to Iran for this purpose.
5. Training in methods of counter-subversion given by the teacher of the Ninth Department.
6. Briefing sessions on subversive activities and measures to counter such subversion given by the heads of the various sections of Third Department.
7. Training on the security of personnel, sites and documents given by the instructor of the Ninth Department.
8. General information on technical affairs and SAVAK's

technical facilities given by the Director of the Fifth Department.
9. General information on the financial affairs of SAVAK taught by the representative of the Sixth Department.
10. Training in the study of foreign information given by the instructor of the Ninth Department.
11. Training in investigation techniques also given by the instructor of the Ninth Department.

The training period for the above subjects including the training exercises lasted nine months. The Ninth Department was able to organize two classes with 35 students in each. During my time at SAVAK, about sixty per cent of the personnel attended the classes. Ranking officers only needed to attend specialized courses in their own field of study. These courses were taught by me after the Ninth Department had approved of the notes. About half of the personnel did not need to attend the special training course. Intensive four-month training courses were also provided for high-ranking SAVAK figures (such as directors etc.) who could not stay away from their place of work for a long period of time. The Ninth Department was in close touch with the intelligence and counter-intelligence units of the army and exchanged books and training documents.

GRAPHOLOGY TRAINING

After I entered SAVAK, I gradually learnt that one of the small problems which the Third Department had to tackle was the lack of graphologists. Sometimes, during operations, letters were discovered which had been deliberately written in a different style of hand writing so as to make it difficult to say who had written the letter. Naser Moqaddam, Director of the Third Department, requested my assistance to overcome this problem.

There was no graphologist in SAVAK, but I was informed that the police had personnel in this field. I contacted the police headquarters and learned that they had only one person whom it was said was a graphologist. The man was questioned and he claimed that he had been appointed to the post and he was doing this work based on his own personal experience. He did however make many claims and when his chief was asked if he could confirm his remarks, he rejected his claims as pure exaggeration. He explained that he was always making mistakes in his work and had created many problems for the police.

"Since there was a vacant post for a graphologist he was appointed to the post but he is not an expert," his chief told me.

I was very disappointed and therefore turned my attention to the Justice Department where it was believed that a specialist could be found. After investigations, it became clear that the graphologist was no better than the one in the police. I thus came to the conclusion that a seasoned graphologist did not exist in Iran.

Brigadier-General Alavikia who, with the blessings of the Shah, had been made the head of SAVAK station in West Germany was told to find out where in Europe a college which taught graphology existed. After investigations, he informed me that there was a college of graphology in Lausanne in Switzerland which offered studies up to doctorate level in this field. This came as a surprise to me. I asked him to send me the subjects of the course taught there to make sure he was correct. The subjects disclosed that the college was teaching hieroglyphics! Alavikia had also disappointed me.

The next time I turned to the chief of MI-6 station in Iran for help. After months of delay, he claimed that the agency had no such speciality. I did not believe him. I then asked the CIA station chief in Iran and he also, after a delay in replying, claimed that they did not have a graphology department. At a later date, I received information which proved that both MI-6 and the CIA had the most experienced graphologists in their service. I complained to both of them but in vain. Thus, once again, I turned to the Israelis for help.

In my meetings with Nimrodi, I always held the upper hand. It was usual for him to say at first either that he could not help me or give me excuses as to why my request could not be met. My reaction to this was always the same. I immediately ordered that all SAVAK departments desist from giving intelligence information to Nimrodi and refuse meetings with him (after consultations with Nasiri on the matter). Consequently, in the first meeting I had with Nimrodi afterwards, he would announce that the best experts would be sent. I would then lift the ban on the exchange of foreign intelligence with him.

Nimrodi dispatched one of the top graphologists in the world to Tehran. The man, in addition to being a specialist in his field, also had thirty years of practical experience behind him. Before his arrival, I worked in collaboration with the Director of the Fifth Department to find seven exceptional graduates who were talented and interested in graphology. I met them (a woman and six men) and found them to be very suitable for training. I informed them that they were to be graphologists and that up until their retirement they would have to work in this field and could not change their jobs. The students were all under thirty and they accepted my conditions.

On the first day of his arrival in Tehran, I met the Israeli teacher and introduced his students to him. The necessary preparations had been made before his arrival. If he needed anything which could not be found in Iran he was asked to bring it with him and it would be paid for. He announced that the training would last nine months and I agreed. His wife was also allowed to join him and all the necessary facilities were provided for the couple. He also, according to the regulations, introduced the best students of his class to me. I established a graphology section in the Fifth Department and chose the most talented student as the head of this section. Another six people were employed as personnel of this section. The graphologists stayed in this job until the 1979 Islamic Revolution and proved to be exceptionally useful to the Fifth Department. I also allowed the police and the justice department to make extensive use of these seven experts, a move which surprised both organizations greatly.

During his nine months stay in Iran, I met and asked questions of the Israeli teacher quite often. I once asked him if a graphologist who was an expert in the Arabic language could also be an expert in Latin handwriting. He answered in the positive and said that a graphologist is a specialist in all languages even if he does not recognize the words of different languages, the reason being that graphology is based on the recognition of the style of writing and not on recognition of the words. He gave a positive answer to a second question I asked him which was could the psychological nature and the character of a writer be determined from his handwriting. He believed that at least 80% of a person's character could be understood from his/her handwriting because personal characteristics were reflected in writing and could not be avoided. He presented examples which showed the difference between the handwriting of males and females, between people of a nervous disposition and those of a tranquil nature, the style of writing of famous historical figures and how a change in their fortunes at various stages of their lives was also reflected by a change in their handwriting. When I asked him how it was possible that no training centres existed for such an important field of expertise, he claimed that this was not so and that two unofficial centres gave qualifications at the end of their courses. Later, two out of the seven experts were sent by SAVAK to France to complete their training.

INTERROGATION TRAINING

Interrogation was one of the fundamental tasks of SAVAK, and at the time when I began work at SAVAK, the methods employed by the interrogators were very basic. From the time of Airam and Mokhtari and even before them, interrogation did not exist in a scientific sense, whatever information was acquired from a suspect was extracted through torture. This method was used by the Military Governorate and during the early years of SAVAK's establishment; Colonel Zibai and Amjadi were considered to be expert interrogators!

I did not favour these methods because first of all the prisoner would in many cases lie under pressure to avoid further pain, this had happened many times in the past. Secondly, it was not possible to use torture against everybody, for example, a distinguished figure could not be beaten in order to extract information from him. Thirdly, although judiciary officials generally prosecuted on SAVAK's recommendations, confessions extracted through torture did not have validity and in some cases could create confrontations between judiciary officials and SAVAK. I have explained before that Seyavosh Behzadi, (the general prosecutor of the army) quarelled with Tajbakhsh and rejected his allegations against the accused, whose statements had been made under torture, and set him free. Therefore, I decided to introduce an updated scientific system of interrogation to SAVAK.

At first, I asked the responsible bodies a question: "Is interrogation a science or not?" Neither SAVAK nor the second department of the army (military intelligence) were able to answer. Again, to find a solution, I turned to MI-6 and CIA stations, but, as before, they were sorry but they could not help. Thus, I consulted Nimrodi. He agreed to help, and the best expert in interrogation was sent from Israel, and it was said that there were not many like him in the world.

Thirty talented students had already been chosen to undergo the training and everything had been prepared for the instructor's arrival, including arrangements for his stay in Iran. The training period had to last for only four months and therefore classes were held both in the morning and afternoon.

Upon his arrival, I personally received the instructor and introduced his students to him. He bagan teaching without any delay. He had brought a book with him on interrogation in the French language. I started translating the training manual into Persian. However, I asked the Israeli instructor to show up in my office every other day and while here he helped me overcome any problems I had in understanding the book. This book was translated completely and was placed at the disposal of interrogators, a number of copies were also stored in the library of the Training Department.

The senior member of the class described the teaching methods of the Israeli instructor as very skilful and updated. Since he was speaking in French, a SAVAK interpreter attended the classes to translate his lectures into Farsi, thus allowing the students to take notes. The students also took part in practical exercises in the class in order to better acquaint themselves with the updated interrogation methods being taught. Having finished the training, the students were called "expert interrogators" and, upon the recommendation of the Israeli teacher, could be promoted to the highest grade in SAVAK's charter and enjoy all the advantages of this grade in order to encourage them to stay in their job.

After the training ended, it was agreed that from that date onwards only "expert interrogators" would be allowed to interrogate people. Two top students of the Israeli's class were chosen to train the next class of would-be interrogators. According to Brigadier-General Kangarlu, Director of the Fourth Department who also looked after SAVAK's prisons, physical torture was not practised in jails for a time. He only reported two cases of torture to me and Moqaddam and I handed in our resignations to Nasiri in protest. Nasiri denied one case and said that in the second case the jailor had beaten the accused without having been ordered to do so. He promised that he would be punished for his action. Consequently, we withdrew our resignations.

This was a short period in the history of SAVAK when we attempted to introduce scientific methods of interrogation into the organization. Torture was common practice in SAVAK when it was under the control of Mostafa Amjadi and Teimur Bakhteyar and when I first joined the organization. Mohammad Reza did not object to this practice because it was serving the interests of his monarchy. After Moqaddam and I had left the organization, Nasiri turned once again to the brutal method of torture, to the extent that SAVAK was put on top of the black list of the international human rights organizations and still the Shah did not object.

In my opinion, there are three reasons why Nasiri once again resorted to torture, thus initiating a period more infamous than even that of Bakhteyar's and Colonel Zibai's. First of all, one could not expect anything better from such an uneducated person as Nasiri. Secondly, ambitious people such as Sabeti who were only after quick promotion did not want to waste their time thinking of other methods. According to the Israeli instructor, FBI ambition or other weaknesses also led American interrogators, who at the first stage of interrogation were usually ordinary policemen, to widely resort to torture. The third and more important reason was that scientific interrogation in the world's intelligence and security organizations has a limit, and wherever, because of a sensitive political situation, this method becomes somewhat ineffective, torture is resorted to in order to get speedy results or to create terror and fear. In normal circumstances, the aim of the interrogation is to extract information and so naturally the more scientific and thorough the methods the better! But in sensitive political situations where security is seen to be threatened, the interrogators' aim is not only at getting information, they also aim at breaking the suspect and creating panic in society. Later, I learned that this method of interrogation was common practice in Israel. From 1972-8, such practices were also common in Iran. Nasiri was given free rein on security matters and the experiment in "scientific interrogation" failed.

The Israeli instructor sometimes spoke of his private life when he came to see me in my office. He claimed that he had been an interrogator for thirty years. At first, he worked as an interrogator for the FBI and was a resident of the United States. He later emigrated to Israel and during the past thirty years he as had no other job than that of interrogator. He was very satisfied with his financial situation and stated that expertise was valued very highly in Israel and experts were treated in such a way that they did not even consider changing their jobs. He also disclosed that at that time his salary and the advantages of his job were greater than those of the head of the Israeli security organization. He claimed that the American intelligence sources recognized him as a seasoned interrogator and asked his help in some of their more difficult cases. At the end of the training period, I thanked him and gave him a gift in appreciation of his efforts.

Chapter 6
Internal Security During Pahlavis

PAHLAVI REGIME AND NATIONAL SECURITY DOCTRINE

Every state has a "National Security Doctrine" (NSD) which determines the basis of its foreign and domestic policies. No two countries have the same NSD, indeed they cannot have for various historical, political, economic, religious, ethnic and geographical factors, neighbouring states and relations with them, customs and culture, the internal situation etc. all affect the NSD of any country. So, it could be claimed that for the number of nation states which exist, an NSD also exists.

In fact, the durability or the fall of a government depends on its doctrine and its conformity with the above factors. If the NSD takes all these factors into account and gives a positive response to them, then the result would be a stable government; if not, the government would be unstable.

As a person who was well informed of the security affairs of Shah's regime, and who had served in key posts such as the Chief of SIB, Deputy Chief of SAVAK and later the inspector general of the realm (Head of the Imperial Investigation Organization) and was well acquainted with the security organizations and intelligence services of different countries especially Britain, in my mind the Pahlavi regime did not have an NSD which conformed with the influential factors in Iranian society at that time and this was the main reason for its collapse. An NSD either had no meaning during the Pahlavi regime or the dominant foreign powers imposed their plans on the regime to preserve their own interests and Reza Shah and his son, Mohammad Reza simply carried out these plans. These plans, especially the "White Revolution" totally changed the very basis of the Iranian society, destroyed customs which had formed over the centuries and which ensured the existence of a nation, and had many disastrous consequences.

A. The Reza Shah Era

Reza Shah had no problem with his foreign policy. The British, the most powerful international force at the time, nad brought him to power and supported his regime. The Soviet government which at that time was very weak backed Reza Shah's leadership and even later did not create any problems for his government. So, there was no foreign threat and the information provided by Iranian secret services and the British Embassy was enough to handle the security of the country.

Reza Shah's lack of a comprehensive understanding of the world affairs led him to support Germany's Hitler during the World War II. He shared many similar mental characteristics with Hitler and came to be branded as an undesirable element by the British and this brought about his collapse.

On internal security, Reza Shah resorted to the army, the only weapon he was familiar with. Despite Iran's relative small population, he had formed a 100,000 strong army. About 15,000 soldiers served in a Division, their number depended on the region they were deployed. However, the two central Divisions had about 20,000 to 25,000 personnel. The gendarmerie, with about 50,000 to 60,000 personnel, was under the command of the Chief of Staff of the Armed Forces. This military force, with the establishment of army units in large cities and the gendarmerie in the countryside, suppressed all opposition. The police, in addition to their usual responsibilities, were charged with discovering any individual opposition or opposition parties, a task which was later delegated to SAVAK.

Reza Shah had issued instructions requiring his ministers to ensure order in the government organizations, and directly supervised the appointment of governor generals. Thus, internal security was provided by the army, gendarmerie and police, all of which were under his command. Reza Shah accorded prime importance to military units and devoted much of the oil revenues from the AIOC (225 million pounds which later increased to 32 million pounds annually) to the military units. The two top military posts in the country were the Chief of Staff of the Armed Forces (gendarmerie was also included) and the Chief of Police. The post of prime minister was the top post in the non-military branches of his regime.

After dismissing Teimourtash, Reza Shah did not appoint another Court Minister. However, a Court chief was appointed but this post did not carry any special importance. The Court chief was more or less like someone who saw to the running of the house.

The fundamental threat to Reza Shah's leadership came from two groups namely the Shi'ite clergy and the tribal leaders.

Reza Shah did not also hesitate to get rid of the Shi'ite clergymen who before his rise to power had control over many phases of public life. The *ulama* were a big challenge to his government. So, he took steps to break down their power and prestige.

The British knew about the organization of the Shi'ites. I remember that once Shahpour J. probably in 1959 spoke of the power of the *ulama* and claimed that throughout the Iranian history, whenever Shi'ite clerics confronted the kings, the kings were always overcome. Upon Reza Shah's orders, respected clergymen were abused and except for a few whose names appeared on the police list, the rest were defrocked. I saw a case in the street where some of them had their turbans rolled around their necks and were pulled along the streets. This caused much public resentment toward Reza Shah.

In our district, Khaniabad, a Sheikh and a Seyed were our neighbours and both had been forbidden by the police from wearing their religious attire. This move on the part of the authorities caused the people to respect these two personalities even more. People queued up in front of their houses waiting to meet them and they still preached regularly to the people although covertly. Therefore, neither 20 years of Reza Shah's rule nor Mohammad Reza's 37-year leadership could destroy the people's beliefs in the clergymen who were the most powerful opposition force to the Pahlavi monarchy.

The tribal groups were the second strong force against the Pahlavis. Like his Turkish counterpart Ataturk, Reza Shah ruthlessly suppressed the opponents to his rule especially in Kurdestan and Fars Provinces. He displayed implacable hostility to tribal rebels which soon, with the blessings of Britain, brought every corner of the land under the control of the highly centralized government. Kurdish opposition leaders agreed to surrender on condition that Reza Shah swore on the Holy Quran not to continue his attacks. However, Reza Shah broke his promise and severely suppressed the tribes. In Fars Province too, Reza Shah used both carrot and stick to bring unrest under control.

Consequently, with the use of such policies at home and support from abroad, Reza Shah's NSD was formed but it did not conform with the realities of the Iranian society and only served the interests of his foreign backers, mainly Britain.

B. The Mohammad Reza Era

Mohammad Reza's reign of power could be divided into two periods, before and after the August 19,1953 coup. Before the coup, Mohammad Reza was unable to bring all corners of Iran under his tight control and therefore, could not implement any NSD.

In March 1951 Mossaddiq secured passage of a bill in the Majlis (Parliament) to nationalize the vast British petroleum interests in Iran. Mossaddiq's power grew rapidly, and by the end of April the Shah was forced to appoint Mossaddiq Premier. A two-year period of tension and conflict followed. In August 1953 the Shah tried to dismiss Mossaddiq but was himself forced to leave the country by Mossaddiq supporters. Several days later, supporters of the Shah with CIA and MI-6 help restored Mohammad Reza to power and gradually formed a NSD.

> "... for the next 25 years, the Shah of Iran stood fast as the United States' closest ally in the Third World, to a degree that would have shocked the independent and neutral Mossaddiq. The Shah literally placed his country at the disposal of U.S. military and intelligence organizations to be used as a cold-war weapon, a window and a door to the Soviet Union... One year after the coup, the Iranian government completed a contract with an international consortium of oil companies which left Iran as the owner of the oil industry in name only, for obvious public consumption, and the consortium as de facto owners. The sole ownership the British had enjoyed previously was reduced to 40%, another 40% now going to American oil firms, the remainder elsewhere. The British, however, received an extremely generous compensation for their former property"[1]

On some topics, the Shah was briefed by the British where I liaised and on some other topics the Americans, who had established a strong influence in the army and who set up SAVAK, gave their instructions.

The British were very interested in seeing a centralized national security system set up in Iran, and during my training in Britain, they underlined the establishment of a special bureau like that of the British Joint Intelligence Committee (JIC) to determine the country's NSD.

Mohammad Reza agreed to set up a "State Security Council" (SSC) at the SIB. I was also the Secretary of SSC but later lack of cooperation on the part of council members weakened the council and as stated earlier the Shah ordered the retirement of both Major-General Bakhteyar, Chief of SAVAK and Major-General Keya, Chief of Army's Intelligence.

Although the council was allowed to summon the Prime Minister or explain ambiguous matters, SSC for reasons explained earlier failed to sketch the policies on domestic security and foreign policy.

Later, with the help of Shahpour J., First and Second-Class Coordination Councils replaced the SSC but despite their activities no special branch was set up at the SIB and Mohammad Reza himself or the Americans or British dictated the domestic and foreign policies. The main topics were as follows:

1. Like his father, Mohammad Reza based his power on the army. He named himself the Commander-in-Chief of the Armed Forces. He returned the oil revenues to the West for the purchase of sophisticated and the most up-to-date weapons for the army and employed American advisors to train army personnel.
2. He paid much attention to the police and the gendarmerie and more for the latter since he considered it a wing of the army. The topmost rank in gendarmerie was a four-starred general while a major-general led the police.
3. Mohammad Reza also saw SAVAK as a very important organ and did not impose any financial restrictions on the organization. The Third Department of SAVAK was above other departments since it handled the internal security. The Second, Seventh, and Eighth Departments were more or less for the name sake only since the Americans and Britons fulfilled SAVAK's foreign information and anti-espionage activities. The Shah sought to secure his own safety and that

was the responsibility of the Third Department.

4. Except the Shah, no authority was allowed to interfere in the affairs of the army, police, gendarmerie and SAVAK, not even the Prime Minister.
5. These organizations were very watchful of each other, but the respective chiefs were advised not to interfere in each other's affairs.
6. The "Supreme Coordination Council" and the SIB stood at the top of the country's intelligence system. Mohammad Reza satisfied with the functioning of the SIB and time and again he expressed his satisfaction before ranking officials.
7. For Mohammad Reza, the cabinet, despite its important role, was mainly responsible for carrying out his wide-ranging urgent plans. The executive committee did not dare to object to his plans and they all took advantage of their position anyway and Mohammad Reza's plans worked in their favour too. Mohammad Reza was only looking for loyal civil servants and their speciality was in the second place.
8. He was not afraid of any opposition from the government organizations and believed that he was powerful enough to foil any opposition activity.
9. He did not predict any place for parties and in this he was no different from his father. During the Pahlavi dynasty, no real party existed in effect. Mohammad Reza did not tolerate a multi-party system. He had taken charge of the operation of the government. Manuchehr Eqbal, leader of the *Melliyun*, or Nationalist Party, was openly saying that he was the servant of the Shah. The *Mardom*, or People's Party, headed by Assadollah Alam, a long-time associate of the Shah and Iran Novin, or New Iran Party led by Hassan Ali Mansur, which replaced the Melliyun which had pledged to support the Shah's government or fulfilled the functions of loyal opposition, were free to criticize the internal policies of the government but not the conduct of foreign affairs. Then, the Shah dissolved the parties and set up his own party "Rastakhiz" that soon reached a dilemma. According to SAVAK, within a few months, about 20 million joined the party but it was dissolved within a day.
10. Like his father, Mohammad Reza was very frightened of the clergy, his fear became more obvious on the June 5, 1963

uprising. Of course, he employed some other policies to destroy the religion and the clergy but, contrary to Reza Shah, he did not appeal to violence. He did not have a precise understanding of the clergy and his judgement was based on his own vanity; moreover, SAVAK's reports were also poor.

11. Mohammad Reza made the utmost effort to stop student discontent and provide as many facilities for them as possible, but he often wondered why his efforts did not satisfy the students. SAVAK also failed to discover the roots of public discontent and, therefore, attributed their activities to the Soviets and the Tudeh Party.
12. Again like his father, Mohammad Reza punished the clans but observed moderations. He was very afraid of the Kurds and the Bakhteyari tribes but did not feel any threat from other tribes since they were few in number or their leaders were obedient to the government.
13. Implementation of the "Land Reform" programme at first satisfied farmers. There was a case where one landlord possessed over 400 villages, he employed some agents to look after his lands; he maltreated farmers and some lands became ruined because of carelessness. In some cases, a landlord possessed one or two villages and carefully administered his lands. Villages had common problems such as dredging the wells etc. which were solved by the landlords.. The "Land Reform" plans did not cause any harm to large landowners except only small landowners. Many exceptions were added to the original law and whoever was wealthy or had close relations with the top people in authority made use of these exceptions and kept his most fertile lands, while small land owners lost everything.

    Later, the government announced that it would leave all wasteland however large to those interested. This created contradiction in land ownership. The policy caused the aqueduels to dry up and the villages were ruined. Moreover, little facilities and shortages did not allow farmers who were deprived of any financial support to produce anything. The developments coincided with petro-dollar projects in large cities and the subsequent migration of villages to the sites of small industrial projects. This was all an American plan to keep Iran dependent on wheat imports from the U.S. It was Gratian Yatsovic, chief of the CIA station in Tehran that later became one of the world's biggest wheat dealers in the 70s.

An article in the Economist said that Americans had intervened in the oil-rich Nigeria which was on the verge of wheat self-sufficiency to keep the African nation dependent on U.S. imports. Americans helped the Nigerian currency to increase five-fold which led to a sharp decline in agricultural production since farmers were paid only one-fifth of the real price of their commodities. Low-income farmers who could not afford the costs of an ordinary life deserted their lands and migrated to large cities. This was a major reason that on December 31, 1983 the civilian government was deposed in an almost bloodless military coup led by Maj.-Gen. Muhammad Buhari.

There had remained no doubt that the Americans kept all their options open for the sale of their products abroad and Shah's "Land Reform" programme was one of these options. Though the plan was carried out under the pretext of satisfying the villagers and was the basis of Mohammad Reza's NSD, it served U.S. objectives.

14. Mohammad Reza's over-reaching giant plans provided a means for returning the oil revenues to Western companies. Of course a dramatic hike in the price of crude oil in 1973 was engineered by the then U.S. President Richard Nixon and implemented by Mohammad Reza. That was again aimed at serving Washington's short term ends. The U.S. companies had stored a lot of oil at home. They encouraged Shah's government to support an increase in the price of the crude oil. Subsequently, the prices increased four-fold. American companies sold their oil to European and Third World countries, thanks to Iran's Shah for supporting the policy. The dollars paid to Iran were also returned in the form of the sale of weapons and the giant projects. Anyhow, the main losers were the European states excluding Britain. London had been kept informed before the price hike.

    Shah's development projects caused a rush of villagers to Tehran and a sudden double increase in the population of the capital and the arrival of experts from foreign countries.

15. His campaign against overcharging and extortion and the wrong implementation of the initiatives caused torment for the shopkeepers and the dissatisfaction of traders.
16. In his foreign and especially regional policy he fully imitated the Americans and the British. This NSD turned Iran into an anti-Soviet U.S. base in the region and, contrary to the principles of good neighbourly relations, Iran allowed the U.S. to base its radars in northern Iran and take photographs 5,000 kilometers deep inside the Soviet territory.

What came to be called the "Nixon doctrine" advocated that the security of the Persian Gulf region should be arranged around a local power which would perform the function of a policeman in the area, with American backing and American arms but without direct American involvement. Iran was clearly the best qualified candidate to take on this role. It was beyond the human resources of Saudi Arabia; Iraq was still in a disturbed state. That left only Iran which had every qualification for the job. So, when the British government announced that it would withdraw all its military forces from the Persian Gulf by the end of 1971, the Shah stated that Iran was the state best fitted to exercise leadership in this region.

The military and the executive branch (cabinet, disciplinary forces, SAVAK) served these ends. The judiciary and legislative powers were the silent executive bodies of Mohammad Reza's plans. The legislative power approved any law and the judiciary followed the dictated instructions on important cases and was not allowed to make any decisions independently. Both the military and civilian branches were under the command of Mohammad Reza. That was the NSD of the Shah.

SUPREME COORDINATION COUNCIL AND PROVINCIAL ISSUES

Here, I would like to try to explain about some provincial issues which were touched upon in the "Supreme Coordination Council" (SCC) or which I was informed about through the SIB.

Isfahan

Isfahan for years had attracted the attention of the British mainly because of its central role connecting the north to southern Iran.

During the Qajar period, rulers in Isfahan were the most powerful and influential figures. During the reign of Reza Shah and Mohammad Reza, the British appointed Saremal-Dowleh as their agent to run their affairs in Isfahan. His son enjoyed his father's talent and for a time he was Mohammad Reza's aide-de-camp. The two did their best to persuade the Shah to select Isfahan as the capital and believed that because of its geographical proximity to northern borders, Tehran was vulnerable to any Soviet attack while Isfahan was 400 kilometers deep inside Iran and the Bakhteyari range of mountains gave the city a natural defence.

Another issue concerning Isfahan and which is worth speaking is the setting up of the "iron-melting factory" which became a matter of debate in the SCC. The factory attracted many Soviet engineers and technicians. The council delegated the Eighth Department of SAVAK to watch the Soviet nationals in Iran. Therefore, the SAVAK branch in Isfahan was allocated massive facilities.

Ilam

The only issue worth mentioning about Ilam could be the affair of Raufi. Raufi was a retired army colonel and an innovator who always called to see me in my office. He was a Kurd and held the posts of Governor in Marivan and Mehran and Governor General of Kurdestan and Lurestan respectively. Despite the fact that he had a very admirable character and he had met Mohammad Reza several times, he became jobless soon. I appealed to Mohammad Reza to help him, but my efforts failed. I assume Raufi himself never learned the reason for his dismissal. Perhaps a brief explanation would be fitting here. When he was Governor General of Lurestan, the U.S. ambassador and his wife wrote and asked him to allow them to tour Lurestan Province. Raufi, without securing permission from the responsible bodies, received them and took them to visit many places. After the trip, the ambassador wrote a letter thanking him for his hospitality and officially invited him to visit the U.S. He gave me all his documents to pass on to Mohammad Reza to study.

The last time I saw Raufi was when Shahpour Bakhteyar led the government. He came to my office once again to see me. He appeared smartly dressed and was armed. He said that he planned to go to Kudestan and I never saw him again. When he was Governor of Mehran, he constructed a park and a soil dam without permission from the higher authorities. The construction upset the Iraqis since the water of the Ganjancham River was stockpiled before the dam and deprived the Iraqis of the water. The Iraqis protested the move to the Foreign Ministry and that led to Raufi's dismissal.

Kermanshah

An important point about Kermanshah was the border between Iran and Iraq. Disputes occurred between the two countries over the border. The Iraqis protested that in two or three places the border demarcations had been pushed into Iraqi territory and that was in violation of the mutual agreement which existed between the two countries. The agreement, copies of which were filed in the Foreign Ministries of the two countries, was concluded under Britain's supervision when Iraq was a British colony. Certainly, it is quite possible that where there are no natural barriers such as mountains, rivers etc. the border demarcations may change. An Iranian delegation led by General Jahanbani was sent to the Western border region to settle any dispute with the neighbouring country; but the differences with Iraq were because of strained political relations and more important Iran's support of the Kurdish leader Barezani. The disputed region was about 10 kilometers wide and 100 kilometers long. Finally, in 1973 Iraqi troops occupied the disputed region and disarmed the Iranian border guards. The usual practice was in such cases that neither side ordered its army to intervene since it would begin a war and the problem was left to the border military units to settle. Anyhow, the dispute was settled under the Algiers Accord in 1975.

Here an important point to mention is Gholamali Oweisi who because of his personal hostility towards Abbass Qarabaqi tried to push the dispute into a war between the armies of the two sides. At the time, Oweisi was the commander of the Ground Force and Qarabaqi was his deputy. Qarabaqi was always trying to undermine Oweisi's military knowledge and their differences continued for a year. Oweisi did not object but planned his revenge. Finally, he took advantage of the strained relations with Iraq and created a command post in the western border and proposed Qarabaqi for the post. Mohammad Reza also approved his proposal on the understanding that he was helping Qarabaqi seize a command post. Immediately after Shah's approval, Qarabaqi invited me to his house and complained that Oweisi was becoming more hostile towards him. I told him that Oweisi had heard Qarabaqi's many criticisms of him and now he was taking his revenge. I advised Qarabaqi to thank the shah for allowing him his new post and to take it since there was no other option. He also said that Oweisi had given him a month in which to leave the house the government had given him and hand it over to his new deputy, General Seyushans. He asked me what he should do with his family and I said that it was better to take them with him to Kermanshah. He agreed and during his stay there, the Iraqis occupied the border checkpoints.

Oweisi told the Shah that the best solution was to strengthen the border guards and protect them with the artillery of the army, and Mohammad Reza agreed. Qarabaqi opposed the intervention of the army and believed that it was the task of the border guards to settle the dispute themselves and requested help from me. Oweisi inculcated his belief upon the Shah that Qarabaqi had enough forces and requesting help was meaningless, Mohammad Reza agreed with him. After a few weeks, Oweisi suggested that Qarabaqi be replaced with General Farrokhneya who, in the opinion of Oweisi, was a vigorous officer, Mohammad Reza again accepted the proposal.

Qarabaqi and his family returned to Tehran and he awaited a new post. Oweisi had achieved his ends. Any officer who had to wait to be given a new post was, according to the regulations, retired. Qarabaqi invited me every night for dinner in restaurants since his house had been given to another officer, and asked for help. I told him to plead in writing with Mohammad Reza in a month's time and describe his past record. I promised that I would write some words of approval for him. He did as I told him and I wrote a recommendation for him separately.

Mohammad Reza agreed to appoint him as Commander of Gendarmerie. He kept his post until the government of Sharif-Emami and since he had meetings with Mohammad Reza and finally he was promoted to the rank of a General. Farrokhneya, who succeeded Qarabaqi, also believed that it was the responsibility of the border guards to settle the dispute with the Iraqis. Oweisi who had not accepted Qarabaqi's view backed this idea and therefore the army did not intervene in the dispute.

Khorasan

During the formation of the SCC, no obvious Soviet movement was witnessed in Khorasan Province. The issues discussed about Khorasan in the council were as follows:

A. Taibad, a city in the eastern part of the province and close to the Afghan border, was a main road used for drug trafficking from Afghanistan. Opium and other drugs were placed into tankers and were distributed by the wide-ranging networks and were rarely discovered by gendarmerie. The imported opium was exchanged with gold.

B. Because of the massive rush of Afghans into Iran, gendarmerie could hardly control them. The Afghans were ready to work hard and accepted low wages therefore they were able to find jobs easily in Iran. Before the revolution, about 1.5 million Afghans were living in Iran. A number of them came for pilgrimage to Mashhad but did not return home and travelled to other Iranian cities in search of jobs. The main reason for the immigration of Afghans into Iran was unemployment in Afghanistan.

Khuzestan

The British and Americans paid particular attention to Khuzestan. The chief of MI-6 station in the British Embassy often urged Mohammad Reza to carry out development plans in the province in order to keep the people happy since the spirit of autonomy and independence was strong among native Arabs in the province. I also raised the issue in the SCC meetings but no one paid any attention to the matter. The major issues concerning Khuzestan Province discussed in the SCC meetings were as follows:

A. ***The smuggling of different kinds of goods from the southern littoral states to the country:*** The smugglers were well-organized and even the custom officials themselves and other authorities in the province were involved in the smuggling. High-ranking provincial officials were officially smuggling goods and it gradually became a usual practice. Wives of officials travelled to Kuwait often and brought back 20 or 30 suitcases full of goods. Customs also acted as middlemen. Since custom employees were allowed to sell smuggled goods, they sold their goods to the officials.

B. ***Illegal mass exodus of unemployed Iranians to Kuwait:*** The Kuwaiti government either deported the Iranian workers or allowed them to seek employment. Some networks existed in the province which took money from these workers and helped them to find jobs in Kuwait.

The main reason for the rush of Iranian workers to Kuwait was the high salary paid by the Kuwaiti government. An Iranian was able to afford living expense for a year in Iran by working for only three months in Kuwait. Trips to Kuwait sometimes claimed lives when worn-out small ships sank with about 50 to 100 people on board and passengers drowned in the sea.

C. ***The Tahrir Front of Khuzestan:*** SAVAK was very worried about the activities of the front. The Third Department of SAVAK published monthly or bi-monthly bulletins and a copy was also sent to the SIB. SAVAK believed that leaders of the front were backed by Iraq. The goal was to detach the Province of Khuzestan from Iran, and the methods included sabotage and propaganda. It had already named the province "Arabestan or Arabia". The group later became the Popular Front for the Liberation of Ahvaz. Many of the group's personalities lived in Baghdad, Basra and its suburbs, they penetrated into Khuzestan whenever there was a good opportunity and distributed papers and carried out other secret activities. SAVAK did not stay idle and penetrated into some networks and arrested a number of its members. Some tribal leaders in the province supported the front and some others were faithful to the central government. Their activities continued until the victory of the 1979 Islamic revolution.

Sistan-Baluchestan

I already explained about the role of Alam family in the Province of Sistan-Baluchestan and here I will limit myself to discussing issues about the province which were brought up in the SCC.

A. Nasiri once raised the issue of the trip of the Senator Khazineh Alam to Zahedan which led to the dismissal of the Chief of SAVAK bureau in Zahedan because of his heedlessness.

B. The gendarmerie repeatedly reported cases of robbery on the road between Zahedan and Chahbahar. The road was about 600 kilometers long and the lack of asphalt had made it difficult for gendarmerie to control the region. As Commander of Gendarmerie, Qarabaqi reported several times that the bandits had identified themselves as supporters of Alam. Nasiri and Azhari, Chief of Staff of the Armed Forces, lambasted Qarabaqi and denied the allegations as baseless but still Qarabaqi did not leave the subject alone but changed his approach saying that robbery and unrests were provoked from outside and the culprits were set free by the judicial bodies after arrest; thus, encouraging them to continue with the plundering and robbery. It was clear that Alam was behind the provocative acts and he was trying to keep his prestige and insist the responsible bodies that he could play a vital role in ensuring security in the region. When Oweisi was Commander of Gendarmerie, he attributed the turmoil to the people's poverty and not Alam, the council approved his judgement.

C. An issue raised in the council by General Kamal, Chief of Army's Intelligence, was the autonomy of Baluchestan. He maintained that the British had planned to create an independent Baluchestan state consisting of the Baluchestan Province of Iran and that of Pakistan. Azhari always recommended that the issue not be included in the proceedings and believed that it was only a matter of debate and said that he would not allow the British to partition the province as long as the army was there.

General Kamal took the plan very seriously but Azhari's approach defused his attempts. In fact, during Bhutto's leadership, unrest spread in the Pakistani Province of Baluchestan but Mohammad Reza fooled some Baluch leaders and prevented the unrest from spreading to Iran.

D. Another issue about the province was the semi-secret smuggling of drugs in Zahedan where government agents also took advantage of their position and did not or were not able to stop the smuggling.

E. The smuggling of opium and goods through the Saravan border point brought in by trucks was another point discussed at the meetings. The gendarmerie either discovered the contraband or allowed the smugglers to pass after receiving bribes.

F. The entrance of Pakistani Baluches and Afghans who were seeking jobs was a long-standing issue concerning the province.

G. The gendarmerie's complaints about poor facilities. Border checkpoints were far away from one another and in some cases the distance between the posts exceeded 150 kilometers. Moreover, the shortage of funds and poor conditions aggravated the situation for the personnel.

H. The illegal entry of immigrants into southern Iranian waters was another issue which was sometimes dealt with by SAVAK. Mostly, they were Pakistani Baluches who were travelling to the

United Arab Emirates in search of work.

I. There was little smuggling of weapons and goods through the southern waters.

J. The construction of a main road from Chahbahar to Zabol via Zahedan connecting it to Qandhar and Kabul, Afghanistan, was also discussed but later Bandar Abbass was preferred. A part of the road was constructed but the project was abandoned for political reasons.

Gorgan and Gonbad

The Soviets tried to take advantage of their geographical proximity and created networks to penetrate into the region and increase Soviet influence among the people. The Eighth Department of SAVAK, however, being aware of the Soviet's efforts, formed some groups, which on several occasions foiled their attempts to carry out their job. Soviet spies moved at night, reached the border and entered the Soviet Union after receiving special signals from the Soviet border guards. They passed on their information and returned the same night after briefings.

Gilan and Mazandaran

In view of SAVAK's strong presence in these two northern provinces, the Soviet plans mostly failed and the British intelligence service led by Mahutian formed special networks. The Americans and the British had an active intelligence role in these two provinces where America had established its listening posts.

Hormozgan

The Province of Hormozgan had been recently formed and occupied some parts of Baluchestan, Kerman and Fars provinces. The issues discussed concerning this province in SCC meetings were as follows:

A. Bandar Abbass was not able to facilitate the extensive volume of imports and exports and usually the council discussed the shortage of port installations. The police, SAVAK and gendarmerie passed on reports based on reports from local authorities. I dispatched a team from the SIB and the Imperial Investigation Organization to study closely the state of affairs in Bandar Abbass.

The results indicated that over 800 cargo ships were waiting to get their consignments off-loaded. The ships had to wait for six months and during the first eight months of the year, the government paid more than two billion dollars in damages to ship owners.

Certainly, one reason was the lack of enough facilities but more important was government's failure to coordinate its foreign trade. Sometimes, the goods arrived in time but the respective bodies which had ordered the goods were not prepared to receive the consignments. The council urged the SIB to inform Mohammad Reza of the situation. Therefore, a comprehensive report was prepared and passed on to the shah and he, as usual, wrote, "Give it to Prime Minister" (Hoveida). Hoveida also put it on his desk and told the chief of his office to inform His Majesty that his orders had been carried out and that was enough for Mohammad Reza.

B. Another important issue was lack of a road along the coast to connect the southern ports. Khatib, a wealthy and influential local leader was asked to finish the project and not the Ministry of Roads as was the usual practice. Unfortunately the work was badly done. He made a 20-30 kilometer third class road but every year rainfalls destroyed it.

DASHNAKTSUTYUN AND THE ARMENIAN ISSUE

Among the groups the Shah allowed to have semi-covert activities was the Armenian political faction "*Dashnaktsutyun*" and the "*Armenian Secret Army*".

According to SAVAK reports, the population of the Armenian community in Iran was about 70,000 most of them living in Tehran and Isfahan and the rest scattered in different Iranian cities. The Constitution allowed the Armenians to elect two representatives to the Majlis or Parliament. For years, Alexander Aqayan and later his son, Felix, who became a Senator with Shah's blessings represented southern Armenians in the Parliament. I used to meet Aqayan repeatedly since he was a close friend of the Shah. Saqinian was another representative of the Armenians in the Parliament and he was also the editor-in-chief of the Armenian newspaper, Alik. At the beginning of my term in SAVAK, I met Saqinian several times of his request. Later, he came to SIB to solve any problems he had with his newspaper.

Like any other community, the Armenians should be categorized into three groups, the wealthy, middle class and the poor. The lower class were mostly technical workers, the middle class owners of sandwich shops and the upper class were wealthy businessmen of whom Felix Aqayan was the richest.

Armenians mostly live in the Soviet Republic of Armenia and this is considered the home land of the Armenians. For the same reason, Iranian Armenians have great ethnic and religious ties to this part of the world. The religious centre of Armenians is in Yeravan, capital of the Armenian Republic, and the other is in Palestine (Beit-ol-Moqqaddas or Jerusalem).

Armenia is described by visitors as a beautiful place. It could be said that Armenians, unlike Jews before the creation of Israel, were not in suspension and could return home whenever the international climate required. For the same reason, there is a great cultural relationship between the Armenians living in Iran and those of the Armenian Republic in the Soviet Union. The Soviet Embassy was always crowded with Armenians waiting to get visas to travel to Armenia. Upon returning home, in their letters to friends and relatives in Armenia, the travellers always praised the situation in Iran and wrote against the Soviet rule and the situation in Armenia. Surprisingly, the letters reached their destination in Armenia. SAVAK believed that the Soviet authorities were well aware of the letters and that the writers of these letters were actually working for the Soviets since they travelled as experienced agents. The Eighth Department was warned that it must either ban the travel of Armenians or become powerful enough to impose strict secret control regulations.

It was not powerful enough to choose the second option. Therefore, the government warned that no Armenian would be allowed to return home if he travelled to Armenia. However, checking their return into Iran was a difficult task for SAVAK and some of them passed the border secretly. The travellers were mostly from the lower class. Rich families, on the other hand, although they had strong ties to Armenians never travelled to Armenia and mostly went to Israel, Europe and America.

When I became Deputy Chief of SAVAK, Saqinian time and again asked me to receive the Chief of "Armenian Secret Army". The request indicated that Alavikya had already established relations with him. I hesitated in meeting the man who most certainly enjoyed international fame. Finally, I agreed to meet him. Saqinian and he came to my office in Zahedi Street. He was a handsome, 30 -year old man with fair hair and blue eyes. He was very polite and clever and only once spoke harshly when he said that any one who attempted to persecute the Armenians would be killed. If the *Armenian Secret Army* needed a qualified leader, he was naturally the best choice.

I asked him to explain about his election to the post and he said that there existed a secret management which elected the chief. He explained that the chief once elected was not replaced until he died. Perhaps Saqinian was also in the management but he treated him with great deference and this itself showed the man's superior position.

Later, I wished to meet him again. This time I asked him about the activities of the Armenian Secret Army all over the world. He answered that the secret army did not exist in countries where the Armenian population was very small, but still they were backed by the secret army. The decisions, he explained, were made at an international level and an Armenian member of the secret army living in Turkey may be given the order to assassinate an opponent in the Philippines. Therefore, it could be concluded that there was a single Armenian secret army all over the world and the decisions were made by the management chiefs of the armies in different countries. He did not hide his deep enmity towards Turkey and believed that the major part of the Armenian territory was usurped by the Turkish government and held the Turksih leaders responsible for the massacre of millions of Armenians. It was believed that Turkey was the arch-enemy of the Armenians and, therefore, it was the main target of the secret army.

KURDESTAN AND THE KURDS

The Kurds are a fierce nomadic people dwelling in the western mountains of Iran, northern Iraq, south and southeastern Turkey, northeastern Syria, and parts of Armenia and Azerbaijan in the Soviet Union. The Kurds are from the Aryan race and have a population of 8 to 10 million people scattered in these countries. The Kurds constitute a small percentage of Iran's population. According to the official figures released in the early 70s, the Kurdish population in Turkey was estimated around 3,200,000, in Iran 2,000,000, in Iraq 1,500,000, in Syria and Lebanon 350,000 and in the Soviet Union 88,930.

Because of long range of mountains in the Kurdish regions of the above countries, excluding the Soviet Union, Kurds are able to easily pass the border and no strict border control could be enforced for them.

At the time of World War I, the Kurds called for an independent Kurdish state but British regional policy did not approve it and later, the West did not show any tendency to support the call. The main reason was that the establishment of a Kurdish state would have damaged the integrity of Turkey, with the largest Kurdish population. Turkey's Mustafa Kemal later surnamed Ataturk massacred Turkish Kurds and even banned the use of the term "Kurd" and gave them the title of "*mountain Turks*".

The Kurds were troublesome for Reza Shah and subsequently for his son. The real trouble came when the Kurds under Qazi Mohammad declared autonomy in Mahabad in 1946 with the help of the Soviet Red Army.

The longest and the most troublesome Kurdish unrest was in Iraq which also created a major security threat to Iran. At the time of autonomous Kudish government in Mahabad, Iran, it was said that Mulla Mustafa Barezani and his supporters who had formed the Kurdestan Democratic Party (KDP) had been defeated by Iraq's Nouri Saeed who was supported by Britain and had escaped to Mahabad. Following the fall of Qazi Mohammad government in Iran, Barezani escaped to the Soviet Union along with 500 horsemen through the Caucasus and the border guards failed to block their way because of their knowledge of the land. They married Soviet women and settled in the Soviet Union for more than a decade.

The Kurds welcomed the coup d'etat of 1958 which brought Abdul Karim Qassem to power in Iraq. The Qassem regime (1958-63) declared a general amnesty for the Kurds and Barezani and his compatriots returned to Iraq immediately. The Qassem government, however, did little or nothing to improve the social and economic conditions of the Kurds.

Barezani soon found Qassem instigating rival leaders against him, and in June 1961 a protracted war against Qassem broke out. Unable to defeat Barezani forces, the successor Ba'th government agreed that a democratic regime would be established and that the Kurds would enjoy autonomy but not independence. Negotiations between the Kurds and the Baghdad government led to no agreement. Until then, only the Soviets supported Kurdish autonomy, while Britain and the U.S. described it as a serious threat to their *protege* regimes in Turkey and Iran.

Although Barezani had himself been the recipient of Soviet aid, and had in fact lived in Moscow between 1945 and 1958, he was now appealing to the United States on the grounds that the Iraqi government had allied itself with the Soviets.

Nixon and Kissinger promised to assist the Kurds as a gesture to an ally (Iran) who felt threatened by a traditional enemy (Iraq). What the Americans were aiming at was not an outright victory by the Kurds over Baghdad, which would enable them to claim some form of independence—this would have been a grave embarrassment to Iran with its own Kurdish minority - but to supply enough aid to give the Kurds a considerable nuisance value. Thus, in line with the U.S. policy, Iran came in support of Barezani and strengthened the Kurd's position against the Iraqi regime.

At the time of my tenure of office in SAVAK, a man identified as Brigadier General Mansurpour one day came to my office and said that SAVAK had appointed him to keep in touch with Barezani and sometimes he did not appear for many days or weeks at SAVAK. I became informed of his links with the Kurds and allowed him to keep them up. Mansurpour, a Kurd himself, was well acquainted with Kurdish leaders especially the "Kurdish councils" in Europe and had a good understanding of the developments in the region. Personally, he was calm, clever and confident. He had friendly relations with Barezani and liaised between the Shah and the Kurds. He also administered a local headquarters in the region occupied by supporters of Barezani. After the 1975 Algiers Accord and the entry of Barezani into Iran, Mansurpour was still believed to have held meetings with him. He served in SAVAK with the rank of Brigadier General for years and since Mohammad Reza wished to promote him to a higher rank, he was transferred to the gendarmerie where he became a Major General. He often came to see me to discuss Kurdish affairs.

When Barezani was at war with the Iraqi regime, Mansurpour shuttled between Tehran and the Iraqi Kurdestan and conveyed messages to Mohammad Reza and Barezani. Mansurpour said that a deep, long, natural cave was the command headquarters of Barezani. A generator supplied the required electricity and Barezani's family also lived in the cave. He explained that Barezani had two headquarters, one for summer and one for winter.

Supporters of Barezani hid in caves 300-500 meters above the valleys in order to inflict more damages and casualties on the Iraqis in their attacks.

The Iraqi troops were mostly unfamiliar with the mountainous regions and, therefore, were not able to discover the Kurds. During the winter, the Kurds held full control over the region and the Iraqi army was unable to launch any attacks. Mansurpour provided weapons through the army to the Kurds. SAVAK bought a powerful transmitter from abroad and installed it in Iraqi Kurdestan for propagation purposes. Barezani's troops were *peshmergas* units equal to a brigade in a regular army. There were about 30,000 *peshmergas* and each unit consisted of between 3 to 5 thousand troops. The Iraqi army usually sent 4 to 5 Divisions to fight the *peshmergas* but they always sustained great losses. Again, in retaliation for the defeat, the Iraqi army bombed the Kurdish regions; thus, inflicting material damages and casualties on the people. Despite the bombardments, the people supplied food and other essential material to Barezani and backed his cause. Air raids were the only way the Iraqi army could fight the Kurds since ground offenses always failed, popular support for the Kurds also hampered the army's progress.

Fighting continued for some years and the Iraqi army had no hope of victory. Major General Mansurpour believed that the war of attrition would undermine the Iraqi army and eventually the Baghdad government would be persuaded to respect the will of the Kurds. Under such circumstances, the U.S. finally intervened. Saddam Hussein had now emerged as the strong man in Iraq with a great expansionist desire and a favourite pawn of Washington. Both the Shah and Saddam attended the OPEC conference in Algiers in March 1975, and through the good offices of Houari Boumedienne, the Algerian President, a meeting between the Shah and Saddam was arranged at which the Shah agreed to cut off all aid to the Iraqi Kurds. The Iraqi army took complete control of the Kurdish areas by the end of March.

According to the Algiers Accord, Iran received some concessions in Kermanshah and Iran's sovereignty was officially recognized and in return Iran agreed to stop supporting the Kurds. To me, the treaty was in favour of Iraq and was like paying $1,000 against $5 because it solved the most serious problem of Iraq that was the Kurdish rebellion. Why had the United States until 1975 encouraged

Mohammad Reza to back the Kurds and undermine the Iraqi government but then called for a cessation of the Kurdish rebellion and the stability of Iraq? The change of policy was because the U.S. found an expansionist Saddam Hussein a good troublemaker that could materialize its objectives in times of need, and it was necessary to ensure that the Iraqi army survived.[2]

Barezani had no option but to defect to Iran. The change of policy inflicted a heavy blow on KDP and indicated that for years he had been a puppet in the hands of the Americans. Under pressure, Barezani and his 90,000 followers sought refuge in Iran.

Barezani and other Kurdish leaders settled in Azimieh, a suburb of Karaj, and the rest were scattered in different provinces and were employed in factories. Hundreds of millions of dollars were allocated for the construction of Kurdish towns. One-third of the budget was used and two-thirds were squandered by government agents. The deplorable living conditions made some Kurds return to Iraq. Barezani got ill and was hospitalized in the United States for treatment. He later died of his illness.[3]

> "The Kurds," so the proverb goes, "have no friends except the mountains. However, if it is true that the Kurds have no friends, it is also true that they have been their own worst enemies. They have allowed themselves to be used as the cat's paws of competing regional states and of the world powers that in the twentieth century have sought to dominate the affairs of the Middle East.
>
> The Kurdish rebellion in Iran was crushed after the 1979 Islamic Revolution but the flashpoint of Kurdish rebellion continues to remain in Turkey and Iraq.
>
> In Turkey, the Kurdestan Workers Party (PKK) has, since 1984, been sprearheading a drive for establishment of an independent state for the 12-million Kurdish population in south-east Turkey. The Kurdish rebellion is Turkey's most immediate national problem where "Kurdestan" is a taboo as are the Kurdish national colours of red, yellow and green. The Kurds in south-east Turkey joke that the colours are so taboo that even traffic lights will be banned next.
>
> In Iraq, Kurds have suffered most. In 1988, in retaliation for Kurdish support for Iran in the 1980-8 Iran-Iraq war, Saddam ordered poison gas used on the town of Halaja, killing 5,000

Kurds. After the 1991 Persian Gulf war, the anti-Iraq alliance established the so-called "safe haven" in April 1991 in north of 36th parallel to persuade about two million Kurds who fled to Turkey and Iran that could safely return home.

Iraqi Kurds established their own government following general elections which resulted in an even split between the two main rivals, the Kurdestan Democratic Party (KDP) and the Patriotic Union of Kurdestan (PUK). The PUK and KDP each won 50 of the self-proclaimed Kurdish parliament's 105 seats in 1992 which was dismissed as illegal by the Baghdad government. The international community also did not recognize the self-proclaimed Kurdish administration.

After neither party won a decisive numbers in the 1992 elections, the two agreed to share government power equally with Irbil and the capital. Differences between PUK's Jalal Talebani and KDP's Masoud Barezani made the exercise of a central authority almost impossible. The administration was paralysed after clashes broke out in May 1994 over power-sharing and the distribution of tax revenue.

Saddam intervened in support of Barezani when clashes flared up anew in September 1996, with the aim of extending his rule over Iraq's Kurdish region. Barezani justified his alliance with Saddam on the grounds that Iran was supporting Talebani's PUK. Barezani was favouring negotiations with Baghdad for an autonomous Kurdish region within a federal Iraq but Talebani, while rejecting independence, distrusted Saddam's regime.

The anti-Iraq alliance comprised of mainly U.S., Britain and France failed to protect the Kurdish population, and the "safe haven" was filled instead with American intelligence agents. Kurdish displacement and sufferings do not seem to be ending.[4]

TRIBAL UNREST

From the beginning of the Shah's 25-year dictatorship until the victory of the 1979 Islamic Revolution, two events jeopardized Mohammad Reza's monarchy; they were tribal unrest in the south in 1961-2 and the massive famous June 5, 1963 uprising. First, I would like to comment on the unrest in the south known as the "Fars fuss".

"Within the general region of the Zagros range which runs to the south are the Shahseven, Kurds, Lurs, Bakhtiaris, Qashaqis, Mamassanis and Kuh Galuis ... (they) speak dialects which may be related to Old Persian or to other ancient Indo-Iranian languages...

These nomads and many lesser groups are the most picturesque element of the Iranian population, representing the best physical type with a bravery which has always furnished the stiff backbone of Iranian armies, and several ruling dynasties have sprung from tribal warriors. A tribe, called eel after the Turkish term, may number only a few hundred. In the case of the Qashqai, ... the tribe is divided into numerous smaller divisions or parts, with a division either a unit or itself sub-divided into ten, twenty or fifty smaller groups. Such sub-tribes or clan groups are variously known as tayifeh, tireh and dasteh. In several regions the tribal leader is known as the khan and the heads of the sub-tribes as kalantars...

According to season the tribes move from their garmsir, or winter quarters, to the sardsir, or summer quarters. These Persian terms are paralleled by the Turkish terms, qishlaq, and yeylaq. In the fall the tribes of the zagros range move down to the warm low plains along the Iraq frontier and towards the shores of the Persian Gulf to sow their cereal crops. In the spring, leaving behind some members of the tribe to reap the harvest, they migrate again into the highest mountain valleys where their flocks can find good grazing throughout the summer. The seasonal migrations may cover distances of more than two hundred miles and may take weeks. They follow an eel-rah, the tribal road, which winds its way alongside stretches of cultivated land, and sources of water for flocks...

Family life is pursued in the black tents which are made of a tough goat's-hair cloth woven by the women of the tribes. Their vertical side-walls and slightly sloping tops are supported by stout poles, and the tent can be quickly struck and packed in a small space for transportation from one site to another. The furnishings are extremely simple. The floor coverings are usually rugs woven by the women, or thick felt mats; the blankets are piled against one wall and along the other walls are placed the copper utensils, goat-skin containers for liquids, earthen ware jars, bags of grain, and occasionally a wooden chest for clothing."[5]

The nomadic tribes have been usually at odds with the Iranian rulers in one way or another. During the reign of Reza Shah efforts to establish the authority of the government throughout the country gave rise to a number of tribal revolts. The army responded ruthlessly and suppressed the unrest.

The Qashqai tribes resumed active anti-government activities in 1962. Naser Khan and Khosrow Khan Qashqai took measures against the central government and finally left Iran for abroad after a year or two with the US mediation. Khosrow went to live in Germany and the Shah ordered SAVAK to pay him 10,000 tumans per month to stop his anti-government activities. I presume, the amount was sincreased to 20,000 tumans later to keep him satisfied.

One of his brothers was living in Iran and I usually met him in the house of Jam. He and his wife were very polite. Since Qashqai was spending his leisure time in Jam's house during the latter's ambassadorial post to Spain, we gradually became friends. He complained about his financial shortages and in return, I repeatedly helped him financially after permission from Mohammad Reza, and he was grateful for my assistance.

As the tribes began to create serious trouble for the central government, the army attempted to disarm the tribesmen and launched offensive from 1961 onwards which led to widespread unrest in the south. The unrest coincided with the establishment of the SIB.

Malek, Commander of Gendarmerie, always commented in the council meetings on Shah's orders to disarm the tribes. To the Kurds, Fars tribes and Lurs a gun is like a wife which must be kept at home and safe. Guns are the dignity of the tribesmen. They hid their weapons in graves 2-3 meters deep and no one else knew where they were hidden. Despite strict orders to disarm the tribes, gendarmerie failed to do so and could only seize a worn-out rifle out of three or four hidden guns. In some cases, some tribe rebels in attempt to save their cache of guns would voluntarially give their old weapon to the gendarmerie and would in return receive a special card. This became a usual procedure and meant that the gendarmerie were unable to disarm them. The resaon behind the gathering of weapons by the tribesmen was because of their traditional way of life.

Anyhow, the strong measures taken by the gendarmerie led to the uprising of tribes in Fars. The Shah appointed General Aryana to suppress the rebels and strengthened his position by sending fresh troops to the region.

At the time, Alam persuaded the Shah to allow him to despatch 400 Baluches to Fars Province to help Aryana crush the rebellion. The issue was brought up in the council and after a lengthy debate it was decided not to allow any despatch of Baluch troops to the province. It was believed that such a decision would inflame the conflicts since the tribes would never accept defeat at the hands of the Baluches and the clashes would continue for years until all the Baluches were killed or forced out of the region.

The Shah approved the new decision but Alam was very annoyed with the council members. Anyhow, Aryana rushed to Fars to crush the rebellion as the commander of the southern forces. General Karim Vraharam (a Senator) was the Governor General of Fars Province and Masoud Hariri was the chief of SAVAK in the province. Vraharam, a native of Tabriz, for a time was an army commander in the western borders. He was a selfish, drunken, womanizing, and dishonest person.

Since he was a student at the Officer's College, Aryana always compared himself to Nepolean and dressed like him in public. All the officers and his friends knew what he was like. Aryana even followed a story told about Nepolean who is said to have fallen in love with the wife of a sergeant major after he conquered Egypt. He invited the man to France and the woman also sat beside him when he reviewed the guard of honour. Aryana, too, repeated this scene in Shiraz and reviewed the guard of honour with whichever prostitute he had spent the previous night with. He taught the woman to salute the guard of honour too. While in Shiraz, Aryana was always drunk. Reports reached my office indicating that he drank wine round-the-clock and vodka also was a supplement in between.

Vrahram, too, received women instead of local authorities in the governor general office and made appointments with them. Like his colleague he was a heavy drinker. The fate of the province lay in the hands of these two idiots. Their relations with the prostitutes in Shiraz and the suburbs had evil consequences. They competed with each other in picking up prostitutes. I felt that the situation was deteriorating and may lead to grave consequences. A comprehensive pictorial report about their relations with pay girls was prepared and passed onto Mohammad Reza. The Shah in response said, "It's also necessary to have fun in the war zone but remind them to observe moderation!"

Aryana issued orders while drunk. Upon his order, a Brigade entered a valley with no support. About 50 tribal rebels ambushed them and killed all of them. There were no survivors. Another brigade was also ambushed and only one-third escaped unhurt. Heavy casualties made me realize that the tactics employed against the rebels were weak. I recalled Major General Fatemi, a university professor who specialized on tribal warfare, and upon Shah's approval he was despatched to Shiraz to join Aryana as an expert on partisan warfare. His initiatives helped Aryana defeat the rebels and the war was brought to an end within six months. A large number of tribesmen were killed and the rest captured. On Shah's order, a number of tribal leaders were also executed.

After the war, Aryana arrived in Tehran as a conqueror and seized the post of the Chief of Staff of the Armed Forces with the rank of a General. After a period of time, he had Fatemi retired. Later, I invited him to work in the Imperial Investigation Organization and arranged for him to travel to France and Italy to study the possibility of constructing a sub-way in Iran.

Major-General Nazem also played an important role during the Fars fuss. I saw Nazem for the first time in the house of Jam. He was a colonel and a native of Azerbaijan. He was very frank and his rude behaviour and language did not concern him. He criticized the behaviour of high ranking army officials and mocked people like Qarabaqi and Mobser. He was single. His only sister was married to a deputy of Khatami who was an air force commander. He was tough even with his sister and bossed her about a lot.

During the rebellion in Fars, he was a strong brigade commander and killed many rebels. Khosrowdad supported Nazem with a parachute unit. Nazem abused many rebels and defeated them in many fronts. His morale frightened Aryana. He gradually became Brigadier General and later Major General. Because of his morale, the Shah did not allow him to be promoted to the rank of General.

Nazem was a close friend of Jam but constantly ordered him about. His manner of speaking was dictatorial. Jam not only did not object to his behaviour but also could not tolerate his absence. When Jam became the Chief of Staff, Nazem was the decision maker. He always gave advice to Jam while he himself needed ten advisors. Nazem showed me a great deal of respect and never dared speak out against me. In return, I also respected him. I usually saw him once or twice every week in private banquets. After his retirement, Nazem rented a large piece of land near Varamin, in the southern suburbs of Tehran. It belonged to General Batmanqelich. The farmland had 4-5 deep water wells and was strategic site. He administered the nearby village like a military base. Later, the land was returned to its owner. Of course, Nazem was quite able to refuse to return the land to Batmanqelich but he did so and only kept a small part of the land for rent. Then, he became involved in the building and road construction business and at parties he always boasted about his endeavours. He became rich and bought a large bungalow in Niavaran which was worth millions of Tumans even at that time. Sometimes, Jam, Dr. Omid and I went to his house. Only a Japanese or a Philipino servant lived there with him and no one else.

One thing which surprised me about Nazem was when he proposed a coup d'etat to oust the Shah in a banquet to Jam. The two sat away from the others and Nazem suggested that Jam organize a coup against Mohammad Reza's government. Nazem, then, would seize power. At the time, the Shah's government was powerful enough to silence any opposition or coup attempt and the proposal indicated that foreign hands were involved and would support the coup attempt. Jam who was the Chief of Staff of the Armed Forces became very frightened even by the proposal of a coup, let alone accepting it. However, Nazem did not fear anything and even in front of me referred to the Shah as "lad". I will explain about the situation of Nazem after the revolution in the coming chapters.

1963 UPRISING

One of the important issues of the famous June 5, 1963 uprising against the Shah's government was the absolute unfamiliarity of the Shah's intelligence apparatus with the popular rising opposition to the government. The Shah did not take the activities of the clergy seriously and considered Teimour Bakhteyar a more dangerous threat to his administration.

Ayatollah Ruhollah Khomeini had started writing against the government's policies since the 50s. In 1961-2 he was holding regular weekly meetings in Qom with other clerical leaders to discuss their attitude toward governmental policies. This was the period of the American "Point Four" programmes, as U.S. advisors pushed the Shah to make fiscal and social reforms that was believed would put the economy on a more solid capitalist foundation.

The Shah's programme included the total suppression of all opposition, the massive strengthening of the apparatus (army, police, and SAVAK), and the implementation of structural changes, like land reform, that would facilitate capitalist growth. The Shah's measures for reshaping the political, economic and social life of Iran which he called the "White Revolution" had become a model to test and analyze any opposition to the government. Any opposition to his dictatorship was considered opposition to the land reform act and was described as *feudal*. The use of the term was so general that even Alam, the then prime minister, attributed student protests to the feudal land lords or Teimur Bakhteyar. "Land Reform" became a phrase the Shah habitually used in his speeches. SAVAK, too, adopted this approach to the unrest and viewed everything around the land reform programme. The reports of the Third Department about the activities of the clergy claimed repeatedly that their opposition was directed against the land reform plan.

From autumn 1962 on, Ayatollah Khomeini's manifestoes propelled him into increasing confrontation with the Shah's government. He had began to preach against the Shah in Feizieh Seminary in Qom. The Shah ordered that the opposition be severely crushed. In March 1963, on the anniversary of the martyrdom of the sixth Shi'ite Imam, Jafar Sadeq, the seminary was attacked by paratroopers and SAVAK. A number of students were killed and Khomeini was arrested. Released after a short detention, he resumed his denunciations of the government and its policies. He lambasted the United States for supporting the Shah's repressive policies.

On June 3, he condemned Shah's acts which were in contradiction with the Constitution. The next day, on the anniversary of the martyrdom of Imam Hussein, he was arrested before dawn. When the news of his arrest was publicly announced in Tehran, processions of mourning for Imam Hussein turned into massive demonstrations. The protest rallies quickly spread to major cities. Despite heavy troop deployments on Friday June 7, the uprising continued. Troops opened fire and killed dozens of demonstrators.

The Third Department of SAVAK and the police were not aware of the massive June 5 demonstrations even the night before and no reports were sent to my office. Since the event was not pre-planned and was a popular uprising, no preparations were made to stop the uprising and, therefore, SAVAK was subjected to a sudden unrest which shocked the pillars of Mohammad Reza's power.

As usual, in the morning of June 5, 1963, I arrived at the central department of SAVAK at 7:30. Director of the Third Department, Brigadier General Mostafa Amjadi, was waiting for me in my office. He informed me that a large crowd of demonstrators had taken to the streets. I was astonished and asked for the number of demonstrators. He said that people were moving in 7 main groups each with 5 to 7 thousand. Smaller groups of about 500 were scattered in different parts of the city. When asked he said that Pakravan, Chief of SAVAK, had also been informed of the event and that he had telephoned Mohammad Reza about the uprising. The Shah ordered the then Major General Oweisi, a Division commander, to crush the demonstration and remain in direct touch with him for briefings. I asked him to explain why SAVAK was not already aware of the demonstrations since such a big event required secret preparations at least for a month. He explained that he had not received a single report about the event. There was nothing we could do about the demonstrations and I had to wait for later developments. Anyhow, I asked him to telephone me round the clock and inform me of any new developments. The reports frightened Mohammad Reza and he telephoned Oweisi every ten minutes to closely follow the affairs.

An American manual existed how to deal with demonstrations. There was no Farsi translation of the American manual since it was not studied at the university. In 1959-60, I received a copy of the manual and got the text translated by an experienced army translator. Then, after the approval of the army headquarters, the manual was printed in the army's printing house with a circulation of 1,000. Copies of the translated manual were sent to the Officer's College, War University, the ground, air and navy headquarters, the police, gendarmerie and SAVAK. Army headquarters issued a directive ordering that the book be taught in the training centres and other military departments. The title of the maunal was "How to Control Unrest". I studied the manual carefully several times but it was not taken seriously by the training centres.

During the June 5 uprising, the people's actions were exactly what the manual had predicted and Oweisi acted in complete contradiction to its recommendations. The manual stipulated that riot police should disperse the crowd but this did not happen on June 5. About seven or more groups of demonstrators marched in the streets and were divided into smaller groups. The main direction of the protestors was toward the former Sepah street. Within a short period of time, the demonstrators divided into 30 smaller groups and Oweisi unwisely despatched a number of troops in similar groups to scuffle with the demonstrators. He divided his Division into thirty units. Some of these did not have more than 10 soldiers. Each group of demonstrators with between 500-1000 people was quite able to disarm the units and return fire. Of course, this did not happen and only in a few cases did the demonstrators disarm the units and cause some casualties. The American manual strongly believed that demonstrators try to divide the military in order to defeat the riot police. The riot police should be aware of this and should avoid reducing his unit. Only in rare cases could a riot unit be reduced to a reinforced Company and less than this would constitute disarming the unit. It stipulated that there was no need to confront the demonstrators unit by unit but a motorized brigade should intervene to crush the protestors. Having dispersed a group, the brigade should rush to disperse other groups. In this case, the brigade would always be victorious since demonstrators are not able to disarm a brigade. Perhaps Oweisi had not studied this basic principle or through fear had lost his ability to command properly. I, with great astonishment, predicted grave consequences after the incident.

Anyhow, at noon, Oweisi telephoned me and said that there were no troops even to protect his office against any attack by demonstrators. I said that an officer who ignores the regulations and is always going after something else he should not expect a better result. I told him that his only option was to arm all the people in his Division including the cooks and the servants.

I advised him to commission an officer to arm the employees to defend him against any possible attacks. I also promised him that I would ask General Malek, Commander of Gendarmerie, by telephone to despatch a Company to protect him. I asked Oweisi to gather as many of his troops as possible. Oweisi then carried out my advice.

Hours of walking in the streets and lack of a calculated plan caused the demonstrators to make a big mistake and go to restaurants for a free lunch offered by restaurant owners; thus, allowing the troops time to gather again. Between 12 and 14 clock, the streets were empty. In this time Oweisi was able to gather together about 2,000 troops. He waited until the demonstrators had gathered again in the afternoon. At 16 or 17 hours, Oweisi attacked them with the help of a motorized brigade in the Sabzeh Meidan district and the area around the Bazaar and peppered the civilians with bullets. The people were gradually dispersed and martial law was imposed banning any gathering. In this way the June 5 uprising came to an end leaving us quite astonished. Had there existed a calculated plan and two factors had been taken into consideration it certainly would have led to Mohammad Reza's ouster.

A. If the demonstrators could have armed themselves with the capacity of a motorized brigade or any army motorized brigade joined them and 5,000 people marched towards Sa'adabad Palace, the Shah would have rushed to the airport by helicopter and would have escaped abroad before the people could reach his residence. His departure would have demoralized the Imperial Guard and they would have surrendered to the people. The 1953 coup d'etat and the revolutionary uprising in 1978 revealed that Mohammad Reza would have escaped if his rule was jeopardized. Only a lapse by the Imperial Guard troops in preventing the demonstrators from reaching the palace would have ended Mohammad Reza's dictatorship.

B. The two hour break in the demonstration allowed Oweisi to gather his troops again. Certainly if there had existed a calculated plan and the demonstration had continued without a break, the demonstrators could have disarmed the troops and ousted the Shah from power.

Until noon, Mohammad Reza, the Americans and the British were of the opinion that the massive demonstration was a well-organized plan to overthrow the regime and were very afraid of the consequences of the incident. At the time a clever American advisor was working in the Third Department of SAVAK. To me, even Colonel Yatsovic, chief of the CIA station at the U.S. Embassy was inferior to him. I had repeatedly recalled him and requested him to advise SAVAK on operational affairs and he extended close co-operation with me. In the morning of June 5, a SIB officer said that the American advisor had requested to stay in the SIB and had brought a translator and a radio with him. I allowed him to stay in SIB until five in the afternoon and having received my permission he passed on the information available in the SIB to the U.S. Embassy. The SIB officer said that the American advisor who was the cleverest American agent in Iran was very worried about the demonstration. The U.S. Embassy believed that the uprising was an orchestrated plan to overthrow the regime and therefore feared that SAVAK buildings may be stormed and there was no safety. At five, when the advisor was informed that the demonstration had been crushed, he left the SIB greatly pleased. The incident revealed the ignorance of the American and the British intelligence services who like SAVAK, were not aware of the rising opposition to the Shah's government.

The uprising had a pleasant ending for Mohammad Reza since there were no plans behind the demonstration. At eight in the evening, the Shah recalled Oweisi and I to discuss about the incident. He received us warmly and praised Oweisi for his success in ending the unrest. Of course Mohammad Reza did not know that Oweisi's wrongdoings had put his administration on the verge of total collapse. He was very dissatisfied with the function of SAVAK and believed that there were some conspiracies at work by supporters of Bakhteyar to keep SAVAK ignorant. Mohammad Reza asked the reasons behind SAVAK's failure to discover the uprising and I said that Chief of SAVAK, Pakravan, was responsible for the failure. Then he asked who was after him and I said Amjadi, Director of the Third Department. Shah ordered to dismiss Amjadi but did not order any other punishments. The next day, I appointed Naser Moqqaddam (a SIB officer) to succeed Amjadi. The appointment upset Pakravan but he did not object when he learned it was Shah's order.

Moqqaddam had to rectify the weaknesses of SAVAK and prepare a report within a few days about the reasons behind the incident. He started investigations within the model Mohammad Reza favoured. A picture of Bakhteyar was discovered who was in a Beirut beach with a man (perhaps Musavi). Moqqaddam claimed that Bakhteyar had paid two million tumans to the man to incite the uprising. Colonel Mowlavi also claimed that about 10,000 maces have been shipped to Tehran from Qom to fight police. The man whom Moqqaddam claimed to have received the money from

Bakhteyar was interrogated but nothing was achieved. Some allegations were also raised about Egypt's Abdul Naser helping incite the unrest. It was clear that the claims by Moqqaddam and Mowlavi was only to cover their own weaknesses and compensate SAVAK's unawareness with Mohammad Reza in a way that satisfied the Shah. It never became clear who received the money from Bakhteyar or Naser and who masterminded the demonstration or how and by whom the maces were shipped to Tehran and why no maces were seized from the demonstrators.

Anyhow, the file was closed and no documents were provided to prove Moqqaddam's claims. Of course, that was enough to satisfy the monarch. About 10 people were arrested and tried in a military court led by Major General Aminzadeh on charges of inciting the rebellion. Despite Pakravan's opposition to any capital punishment, two of the detainees were executed and the rest were put into prison.

At the time of the uprising, Assadollah Alam, a trusted agent of the U.S. and Britain, was Prime Minister. Nevertheless, Hassan Ali Mansur, son of Mansur-ol-Molk, was proposed to succeed Alam. Mansur was also a British puppet who was introduced to the Americans and therefore enjoyed the support of both powers. I was not aware of his nomination for the post. In early 1964 Mohammad Reza was on a month-long trip to Switzerland for ski where he usually held annual meetings with the Chief of MI-6 and Shahpour J. Mansur called on me and requested to inquire when his decree for the post of prime minister will be issued. I was not aware of his imminent appointment. He requested to send a telegraph to the Shah about the issue. The telegraph was returned with Shah's response saying he would issue the decree upon returning home. I informed Mansur of the message by telephone. Immediately, he rushed to SAVAK and asked the date of Mohammad Reza's departure from Switzerland. I said, twenty days later. He complained that it was too late. Again a telegraph was sent urging the Shah to hasten issuing the decree. Mohammad Reza, in response, said he may return earlier and there was nothing to hasten about. Mansur did not object but was angry about the delay.

Upon arrival, the Shah in a decree appointed Mansur Prime Minister. During his tenure of office Mansur carried out many pro-Western plans, one of them an agreement with Washington that granted full diplomatic immunity to all U.S. military personnel and their dependents stationed in Iran.

After more than two months in prison, Ayatollah Khomeini was released and again resumed his political protests. When he called for a boycott of the parliamentary elections of October 1963 he was arrested a third time and remained in prison for nearly eight months.

When he emerged from prison, he soon launched back into opposition activity and denounced what was known as the "Capitulation Agreement" between the Iranian government and the United States which in the words of Khomeini destroyed the dignity, integrity, and political independence of Iran.

The agreement included a provision that provided American military personnel stationed in Iran with full diplomatic immunity. The Shah had in fact accepted a policy that clearly represented an assault on Iranian national sovereignty. The law effectively exempted Americans serving in military advisory positions in Iran from Iranian law to a degree that those officials, together with their dependents, could no longer be held accountable in any Iranian court for any crimes that they may have committed in Iran.

The Shah's government quickly responded to Khomeini's speech. Already under government surveillance, the Ayatollah was picked up and sent to exile in Turkey on November 4, 1964.

There had remained no doubts for me that Washington was behind the exile of Ayatollah Khomeini to Turkey as it urged the Shah to appoint Mansur Prime Minister. To me, the Shah himself did not support Khomeini's exile and even was afraid of doing that.[6]

The night before Khomeini's exile, Mohammad Reza had a party in his Palace with about 200 guests. Mansur also attended the party. He walked with Mohammad Reza for about half an hour and I was watching them. It looked to me that Mansur was insisting on an issue which Mohammad Reza did not favour. By chance, I heard that the Shah was telling him why he was insisting on that. Mohammad Reza recalled me and asked me reluctantly with his usual gesture to see what Mansur was commenting about.

Mansur believed that Ayatollah Khomeini should be exiled to Turkey as soon as possible. Pakravan was also informed and he requested a chat with the Shah on phone. Mohammad Reza talked to Pakravan in a safe house and the decree was issued overnight.

Mowlavi, Tehran's chief of SAVAK, flew to Qom the same night and took Ayatollah Khomeini to Tehran and put him on a flight to Turkey the next morning. Mowlavi later was transferred to gendarmerie and died in a helicopter crash on his way from Abali, eastern Tehran to the capital. Mansur whose story is famous was assassinated 2-3 months later by Khomeini's supporters.

Anyhow, Ayatollah Khomeini's opposition to the policies of the Shah posed a threat to his administration. Moqqaddam, contrary to Amjadi, was trying to inform the Shah about the activities of the clergy. Besides daily reports from the Third Department and police which highlighted on anti-Shah activities of some clergy figures, the Third Department kept sending regular bulletins once every three months to SIB which covered the speeches of opposition clergy figures.

Important topics were also sent to the Shah for study. SAVAK estimated the number of clergies all over the country to about 350,000 and always mentioned their unsatisfactory financial situation whose salary did not exceed 300 to 500 rials per month. Mohammad Reza was of the opinion that he could undermine the influence of Khomeini if he could establish relations with some clergymen and help them financially. To achieve that, Mohammad Reza launched some efforts to exert his influence among the clergy. Moqqaddam sometimes met a clergyman in Qom called Ayatollah Ruhani. He welcomed Moqqaddam and commented on the affairs in the Qom theological school and gave proposals to ease tension between the clergy and the government. Moqqaddam believed that the meetings were more effective even than the measures taken by SAVAK bureau in Qom. Since 1971 onward, a clergyman came to SIB and introduced himself Ayatollah Milani. He said that many people were complaining to him and he planned to pass the complaints to SIB for investigation and response. I told the officer to closely investigate the complaints and write answers to the letters. Moreover, I asked the officer to verify if he was the same famous Ayatollah Milani of Mashhad. Later it became known that he was residing in Tehran and was different from that of Mashhad. Anyhow, he passed on the complaints to SIB and answers were also prepared accordingly. Farideh Diba, mother of Empress Farah, used to meet Ayatollah Khansari in Sarsabil district of Tehran once every week in Islamic hijab. Her meetings were not private and she publicly went to greet the Ayatollah on her and Farah's behalf.

Farideh also passed the complaints, 30-40 each week by telephone to SIB. She requested answers for all the questions. An officer was appointed to investigate the complaints and write answers and pass them on to Farideh after I signed the letters. The process continued for about 5-6 months before the revolution and Farideh was grateful of me for that.

Before the revolution, Farah travelled to Karbala and Najaf, two holy cities in Iraq. The film of her trip was screened from the TV. In her trip, she requested a meeting with Ayatollah Khoi but no answer was given to her plea. Farah went to Ayatollah's house in Islamic dress and it was said that she was not received warmly. Mohammad Reza made efforts to win the support of some top religious figures and rushed assistance including medicine and physician in case of their illness whose assistance was also not received warmly. The government had strong relations with Ayatollah Shariatmadari and the Shah had some private meetings with him. Around 1966-7 the Imperial Guard informed me that Shariatmadari had come to meet Mohammad Reza and the Shah had ordered that nobody should see him. He entered the Saadabad Palace in a car and held a meeting with the Shah. I presume he had two secret meetings with the Shah that year. The Court, Prime Minister's Office and SAVAK set up links with the theological centres, the costs of which exceeded millions of tumans annually and was paid from prime minister's secret budget. Nevertheless, there was no tranquillity in favour of the Shah in the theological centres and the main reason for that was Ayatollah Khomeini's opposition to his administration. Colonel Badiei, chief of SAVAK bureau in Qom who was a clever and informed man once said, "If only one man cooperated with me, I could maintain security easily in the city." I asked whom did he mean and he said, "Ayatollah Khomeini". I asked why did he not approach him and he said that the Ayatollah did not allow any links unless he became his and if he proved to be loyal the Ayatollah would receive him. He added that if he was able to meet such conditions then he would not be chief of SAVAK bureau in Qom.

The government felt it had broken the back of the resistance to the Shah's regime. The Shah felt free to move ahead on his in programme of modernization, westernization, and secularization without significant resistance. Although the 1963 uprising was crushed it was a rehearsal for the revolutionary uprising a decade and a half later.

June 3, 1963

THE AFTERNOON OF ASHURA

This speech, delivered at Feizieh Madrasa (Seminary) in Qom, is particularly notable for its fearless words of reproach addressed to the Shah.*

It is now the afternoon of Ashura. Sometimes when I recall the events of Ashura, a question occurs to me: If the Umayads and the regime of Yazid ibn Mawiya wished to make war against Hussein, why did they commit such savage and inhuman crimes against the defenseless women and innocent children? What was the offense of the women and children? What had Hussein's six month-old infant done? It seems to me that the Umayads had a far more basic aim: they were opposed to the very existence of the family of the Prophet. They did not wish the Bani Hashim to exist and their goal was to root out this "goodly tree".

A similar question occurs to me now. If the tyrannical regime of Iran simply wished to wage war on the maraji, to oppose the ulama, what business did it have tearing the Quran to shreds on the day it attacked Feizieh Madrasa? Indeed, what business did it have with the seminary or with its students, like the eighteen year-old Seyed who was killed? What had he done against the Shah, against the Government, against the tyrannical regime? We come to the conclusion that this regime also has a more basic aim: they are fundamentally opposed to Islam itself and the existence of the religious class. They do not wish this institution to exist; they do not wish any of us to exist, the great and the small alike.

Israel does not wish the Quran to exist in this country. Israel does not wish the ulama to exist in this country. Israel does not wish a single learned man to exist in this country. It was Israel that assaulted Feizieh Seminary by means of its sinister agents. It is still assaulting us, and assaulting you, the nation; it wishes to seize your economy, to destroy your trade and agriculture, to appropriate your wealth. Israel wishes to remove by means of its agents anything it regards as blocking its path. The Quran is blocking its path; it must be removed. The religious scholars are blocking its path; they must

* Khomeini va Junbesh; pp. 4-7.

be eliminated. Feizieh Seminary and other centres of knowledge and learning are blocking its path; they must be destroyed. The tullab might later come to block their path; they must be killed, pushed off the roof, have their heads and arms broken. In order for Israel to attain its objectives, the government of Iran has continually affronted us in accordance with goals and plans conceived in Israel.

Respected people of Qom! On the day that mendacious, that scandalous referendum took place - that referendum contrary to all the interests of the Iranian nation and conducted at bayonet-point you witnessed a gang of hooligans and ruffians prowling around Qom, on foot and riding in cars, going down the streets and thoroughfares of this centre of religious learning that stands next to the shrine of Fatima, the Immaculate One (peace be upon her)! They were shouting: "Your days of parasitism are at an end! Your days of eating pulao (rice) are over!"

Now, these students of the religious sciences who spend the best and most active part of their lives in these narrow cells, and whose monthly income is somewhere between 40 and 100 tumans - are they parasites? And those to whom one source of income alone brings hundreds of millions of tumans are not parasites? Are the ulama parasites - people like the late Hajj Sheikh Abd al Karim, whose sons had nothing to eat on the night that he died, or the late Borujerdi, who was 600,000 tumans in debt when de departed from this world? And those who have filled foreign banks with the wealth produced by the toil of our poverty-stricken people, who have erected towering palaces but still will not leave the people in peace, wishing to fill their own pockets and those of Israel with our resources - they are not parasites? Let the world judge, let the nation judge who the parasites are!

Let me give you some advice, Mr. Shah! Dear Mr. Shah, I advise you to desist in this policy and acts like this. I don't want the people to offer up thanks if your masters should decide one day that you must leave. I don't want you to become like your father.

Iranian nation! Those among you who are thirty or forty years of age or more will remember how three foreign countries attacked us during World War II. The Soviet Union, Britain, and America invaded Iran and occupied our country. The property of the people was exposed to danger and their honour was imperilled. But God knows, everyone was happy because the Pahlavi had gone!

Shah, I don't wish the same to happen to you; I don't want you to become like your father. Listen to my advice, listen to the ulama of Islam. They desire the welfare of the nation, the welfare of the country. Don't listen to Israel; Israel can't do anything for you. You miserable wretch, forty-five years of your life have passed; isn't it time for you to think and reflect a little, to ponder about where all this is leading you, to learn a lesson from the experience of your father? If what they say is true, that you are opposed to Islam and the religious scholars, your ideas are quite wrong. If they are dictating these things to you and then giving them to you to read, you should think about it a little. Why do you speak without thinking? Are the religious scholars really some form of impure animal? If they are impure animals, why do the people kiss their hands? Why do they regard the very water they drink as blessed? Are we really impure animals? I hope to God that you did not have in mind the ulama and the religious scholars when you said, "the reactionaries are like an impure animal," because if you did, it will be difficult for us to tolerate you much longer, and you will find yourself in a predicament. You won't be able to go on living; the nation will not allow you to continue this way. The religious scholars and Islam are Black Reaction! And you have carried out your White Revolution? Why do you try to deceive the people so? Why do you threaten the people so?

I was informed today that a number of preachers and speakers in Tehran were taken to the offices of SAVAK and were threatened with punishment if they speak on three subjects. They were not to say anything bad about the Shah, not to attack Israel, and not to say that Islam is endangered. Otherwise, they can say what they like! But all of our problems and all our differences with the government comprise exactly these three. If we overlook these three subjects, we have no dispute with the government. Even if we do not say that Islam is endangered, will that mean that Islam is not endangered? Or if we do not say, "The Shah is such-and-such," will that mean that he is not in fact such-and-such? And what is this lie, this link, between the Shah and Israel that makes SAVAK consider the Shah an Israeli? Does SAVAK consider the Shah a Jew?

Mr. Shah! Maybe those people want to present you as a Jew so that I will denounce you as an unbeliever and they can expel you from Iran and put an end to you! Don't you know that if one day, some uproar occurs and the tables are turned, none of those people around you will be your friends? They are friends of the dollar; they have no religion, no loyalty. They are hanging responsibility for everything around your miserable neck!

You know that vile individual - I'll mention his name at the appropriate time - who came to Feizieh Seminary and whistled to signal for the commandos to gather, then ordered them to attack, to assault, to plunder all the rooms in the seminary and destroy everything. When he is asked, "Why did you commit these crimes?" he replies, "The Shah told us to do it. It was his royal command that we destroy Feizieh Seminary and slaughter these people."

There is much to be said, far more than you can even imagine. Certain things are happening that endanger our country and our Islam. The things that are happening to this nation and those that are about to happen fill me with anxiety and sorrow. I feel anxiety and sorrow at the state of Iran, at the state of our ruined country, at the state of this cabinet, at the state of those running our government.

I pray to God Almighty that He remedy our affairs.[7]

October 27, 1964

THE GRANTING OF CAPITULATORY RIGHTS TO THE U.S.

Imam Khoemini delivered this speech in front of his residence in Qom. Together with the declaration he issued on the same subject, it was the immediate cause for his forced exile from Iran on November 4, 1964.*

I cannot express the sorrow I feel in my heart. My heart is constricted. Since the day I heard of the latest developments affecting Iran, I have barely slept; I am profoundly disturbed, and my heart is constricted. With sorrowful heart, I count the days until death shall come and deliver me.

Iran no longer has any festival to celebrate; they have turned our festival into mourning. They have turned it into mourning and lit up the city; they have turned it into mourning and are dancing together with joy. They have sold us, they have sold our independence; but still they light up the city and dance.

If I were in their place, I would forbid all these lights; I would give orders that black flags be raised over the bazaars and houses, that black awnings be hung! Our dignity has been trampled underfoot; the dignity of Iran has been destroyed. The dignity of the Iranian army has been trampled under foot!

A law has been put before the Majlis according to which we are to accede to the Vienna Convention, and a provision has been added to it that all American military advisors, together with their families, technical and administrative officials, and servants - in short, anyone in any way connected to them - are to enjoy legal immunity with respect to any crime they may commit in Iran.

If some American's servant, some American's cook, assassinates your marja in the middle of the bazaar, or runs over him, the Iranian police do not have the right to apprehend him! Iranian courts do not have the right to judge him! the dossier must be sent to America, so that our masters there can decide what is to be done!

First, the previous government approved these measures

---

* S.H.R., Barrasi va Tahlili az Nihzat-e Imam Khomeini (Najaf) n.d." pp. 716-26.

without telling anyone, and now the present government just recently introduced a bill in the Senate and settled the whole matter in a single session without breathing a word to anyone. A few days ago, the bill was taken to the lower house of the Majlis and there were discussions, with a few deputies voicing their opposition, but the billwas passed anyhow. They passed it without any shame, and the government shamelessly defended this scandalous measure. They have reduced the Iranian people to a level lower than that of an American dog. If someone runs over a dog belonging to an American, he will be prosecuted. Even if the Shah himself were to run over a dog belonging to an American, he would be prosecuted. But if an American cook runs over the Shah, the head of state, no one will have the right to interfere with him.

Why? Because they wanted a loan and America demanded this in return. A few days after this measure was approved, they requested a $ 200 million loan from America and America agreed to the request. It was stipulated that the sum of $ 200 million would be paid to the Iranian government over a period of five years, and that $ 300 million would be paid back to America over a period of ten years. So in return for this loan, America is to receive $ 100 million - or 800 million tumans - in interest. But in addition to this, Iran has sold itself to obtain these dollars. The government has sold our independence, reduced us to the level of a colony, and made the Muslim nation of Iran appear more backward than savages in the eyes of the world!

What are we to do in the face of this disaster? What are our religious scholars to do? To what country should they present their appeal?

Other people imagine that it is the Iranian nation that has abased itself in this way. They do not know that it is the Iranian government, the Iranian Majlis - the Majlis that has nothing to do with the people. What can a Majlis that is elected at bayonet-point have to do with the people? The Iranian nation did not elect these deputies. Many of the high-ranking ulama and maraji ordered a boycott of the elections, and the people obeyed them and did not vote. But then came the power of the bayonet, and these deputies were seated in the Majlis.

They have seen that the influence of the religious leaders prevents them from doing whatever they want, so now they wish to destroy that influence!

According to a history textbook printed this year and taught to our schoolchildren now, one containing all kinds of lies and inaccurate statements, "It has now become clear that it is to the benefit of the nation for the influence of the religious leaders to be rooted out."

They have come to understand well that:

If the religious leaders have influence, they will not permit this nation to be the slaves of Britain one day, and America the next.

If the religious leaders have influence, they will not permit Israel to take over the Iranian economy; they will not permit Israeli goods to be sold in Iran - in fact, to be sold duty-free!

If the religious leaders have influence, they will not permit the government to impose arbitrarily such a heavy loan on the Iranian nation.

If the religious leaders have influence, they will not permit such misuse to be made of the public treasury.

If the religious leaders have influence, they will not permit the Majlis to come to a miserable state like this; they will not permit the Majlis to be formed at bayonet-point, with the scandalous results that we see.

If the religious leades have influence, they will not permit girls and boys to wrestle together, as recently happened in Shiraz.

If the religious leaders have influence, they will not permit people's innocent daughters to be under young men at school; they will not permit women to teach at boys' schools and men to teach at girls' schools, with all the resulting corruption.

If the religious leaders have influence, they will strike this government in the face, they will strike this Majlis in the face and chase these deputies out of both its houses!

If the religious leaders have influence, they will not permit a handful of individuals to be imposed on the nation as deputies and participate in determining the destiny of the country.

If the religious leaders have influence, they will not permit some agent of America to carry out these scandalous deeds; they will throw him out of Iran.

So the influence of the religious leaders is harmful to the nation? No, it is harmful to you, harmful to you traitors, not to the nation! You know that as long as the religious leaders have influence, you cannot do everything you want to do, commit all the crimes you want, so you wish to destroy their influence. You thought you could cause dissension among the religious leaders with your intrigues, but you will be dead before your dream can come true. You will never be able to do it. The religious leaders are united.

I esteem all the religious leaders. Once again I kiss the hand of all the religious leaders. If I kissed the hands of the maraji in the past, today I kiss the hands of the tullab. I kiss the hands of the simple grocer.

Gentlemen, I warn you of danger!

Iranian army, I warn you of danger!

Iranian politicians, I warn you of danger!

Iranian merchants, I warn you of danger!

Ulama of Iran, maraji of Islam, I warn you of danger!

Scholars, students! Centres of religious learning! Najaf, Qom, Mashhad, Tehran, Shiraz! I warn you of danger!

The danger is coming to light now, but there are other things that are being kept hidden from us. In the Majlis they said, "keep these matters secret!" Evidently they are dreaming up further plans for us. What greater evil are they about to inflict upon us? Tell me, what could be worse than slavery? What could be worse than abasement? What else do they want to do? What are they planning?

What disasters this loan has brought down upon the head of the nation already! This impoverished nation must now pay $ 100 million in interest to America over the next ten years. And as if that were not enough, we have been sold for the sake of this loan!

What use to you are the American soldiers and military advisors? If this country is occupied by America, then what is all this noise you make about progress? If these advisors are to be your servants, then why do you treat them like something superior to masters? If they are servants, why not treat them as such? If they are your employees, then why not treat them as any other government treats its employees? If our country is now occupied by the U.S., then tell us outright and throw us out of this country!

What do they intend to do? What does this government have to say to us? What is this Majlis doing? This illegal, illicit Majlis; this Majlis that the maraji have had boycotted with their fatwas and decrees; this Majlis that makes empty noises about independence and revolution, that says: "We have undergone a White Revolution"!

I don't know where this White Revolution is that they are making so much fuss about. God knows that I am aware of (and my awareness causes me pain) the remote villages and provincial towns, not to mention our own backward city of Qom. I am aware of the hunger of our people and the disordered state of our agrarian economy. Why not try to do something for this country, for this population, instead of piling up debts and enslaving yourselves? Of course, taking the dollars means that someone has to become a slave; you take the dollars and use them, and we become slaves! If an American runs over me with his car, no one will have the right to say anything to him!

Those gentlemen who say we must hold our tongues and not utter a sound - do they still say the same thing on this occasion? Are we to keep silent again and not say a word? Are we to keep silent while they are selling us? Are we to keep silent while they sell our independence?

By God, whoever does not cry out in protest is a sinner! By God, whoever does not express his outrage commits a major sin!

Leaders of Islam, come to the aid of Islam!

Ulama of Najaf, come to the aid of Islam!

Ularna of Qom, come of the aid of Islam! Islam is destroyed!

Muslim peoples! Leaders of the Muslim peoples! Presidents and kings of the Muslim peoples! Come to our aid! Shah of Iran, save yourself!

Are we to be trampled under foot by the boots of America simply because we are a weak nation and have no dollars? America is worse than Britain; Britain is worse than America. The Soviet Union is worse than both of them. They are all worse and more unclean than each other! But today it is America that we are concerned with.

Let the American President know that in the eyes of the Iranian people, he is the most repulsive member of the human race today because of the injustice he has imposed on our Muslim nation. Today the Quran has become his enemy, the Iranian nation has become his enemy. Let the American government know that its name has been ruined and disgraced in Iran.

Those wretched deputies in the Majlis begged the government to ask "our friends" the Americans not to make such impositions on us, not to insist that we sell ourselves, not to turn Iran into a colony. But did anyone listen?

There is one article in the Vienna Convention they did not mention at all - Article 32. I don't know what article that is; in fact, the chairman of the Majlis himself doesn't know. The deputies also don't know what the article is; nonetheless, they went ahead and approved and signed the bill. They passed it, even though some people said, "We don't know what is in Article 32." Maybe those who objected did not sign the bill. They are not quite so bad as the others, those who certainly did sign. They are a herd of illiterates.

One after another, our statesmen and leading politicians have been set aside. Our patriotic statesmen are given nothing to do. The army should know that it will also be treated the same way: its leaders will be set aside, one by one. What self-respect will remain for the army when an American errand boy or cook has priority. If I were a deputy in the Majlis, I would resign. I would not agree to be disgraced.

American cooks, mechanics, technical and administrative officials, together with their families, are to enjoy legal immunity, but the ulama of Islam, the preachers and servants of Islam, are to live banished or imprisoned. The partisans of Islam are to live in Bandar Abbass or in prison, because they are religious leaders or supporters of the religious leaders.

The government clearly documents its crimes by putting out a history textbook that says, "It is to the benefit of the nation to root out the influence of the religious leaders." This means that it is for the benefit of the nation that the Messenger of God should play no role in its affairs. For the religious leaders of themselves have nothing; whatever they have, they have from the Messenger of God. So the government wants the Messenger of God to play no role in our affairs, so that Israel can do whatever it likes, and America likewise.

All of our troubles today are caused by America and Israel. Israel itself derives from America; these deputies and ministers that have been imposed upon us derive from America - they are all agents of America, for if they were not, they would rise up in protest.

I am now thoroughly agitated, and my memory is not working so well. I cannot remember precisely when, but in one of the earlier Majlises, where Seyed Hassan Modarris was a deputy, the government of Russia gave Iran an ultimatum - I can't remember its exact content - to the effect that "Unless you accept our demand, we will advance on Tehran by way of Qazvin and occupy it!" The government of the day put pressure on the Majlis to accept the Russian demand.

According to an American historian, a religious leader with stick in hand (the late Modarris) came up to the tribune and said: "Now that we are to be destroyed, why should we sign the warrant for our own destruction?" The Majlis took courage from his act of opposition, rejected the ultimatum, and Russia was unable to do anything!

That is the conduct of a true religious leader; a thin, emaciated man, a mere heap of bones, rejects the ultimatum and demand of a powerful state like Russia. If there were a single religious leader in the Majlis today, he would not permit these things to happen. It is for this reason that they wish to destroy the influence of the religious leaders, in order to attain their aims and desires!

There is so much to be said, there are so many instances of corruption in this country, that I am unable in my state at the moment to present to you even what I know. It is your duty, however, to communicate these matters to your colleagues. The ulama must enlighten the people, and they in turn must raise their voices in protest to the Majlis and the government and say, "Why did you do this? Why have you sold us? We did not elect you to be our representatives, and even if we had done so, you would forfeit your posts now on account of this act of treachery."

This is high treason! O God, they have committed treason against this country. O God, this government has committed treason against the Quran. All the members of both houses who gave their agreement to this affair are traitors. Those old men in the Senate are triators, and all those in the lower house who voted in favour of this affair are traitors. They are not our representatives. The whole world must know that they are not the representatives of Iran. Or, suppose they are; now I dismiss them. They are dismissed from their posts and all the bills they have passed up until now are invalid.

According to the very text of the law, according to Article 2 of the Supplementary Constitutional Law, no law is valid unless the mujtahids exercise a supervisory role in the Majlis. From the beginning of the constitutional period down to the present, has any mujtahid ever exercised supervision? If there were five mujtahids in this Majlis, or even one single religious leader of lesser rank, they would get a punch in the face; he would not allow this bill to be enacted, he would make the Majlis collapse.

As for those deputies who apparently opposed this affair, I wish to ask them in protest: If you were genuinely opposed, why did you not stand to do something? Why did you not rise up and seize that wretch by the collar? Does "opposition" mean simply to sit there and say, "We are not in agreement," and then continue your flattery as usual? You must create an uproar, right there in the Majlis. You must not permit there to be such a Majlis. Is it enough to say simply, "I am opposed," when the bill passes nevertheless?

We do not regard as law what they claim to have passed. We do not regard this Majlis as a Majlis. We do not regard this government as a government. They are traitors, guilty of high treason!

O God, remedy the affairs of the Muslims! O God, bestow dignity on this sacred religion of Islam! O God, destroy those individuals who are traitors to this land, who are traitors to Islam, who are traitors to the Quran.

And peace be upon you, and also God's mercy.[8]

Fig. 19: Ayatollah Khomeini's speech on the occasion of "Ashura" on June 4, 1963 where he denounced Shah's economic and political program known as the "White Revolution". He also condemned the attack a few weeks earlier by Shah's agents of the Feizieh Madrassa in Qom. His speech led to his immediate arrest

Fig. 20: After Ayatollah Khomeini denounced an agreement between Iran and the United States known as the "Capitulation Agreement" which gave American military personnel diplomatic immunity, he was sent to exile

Fig. 21: Revolution gains momentum

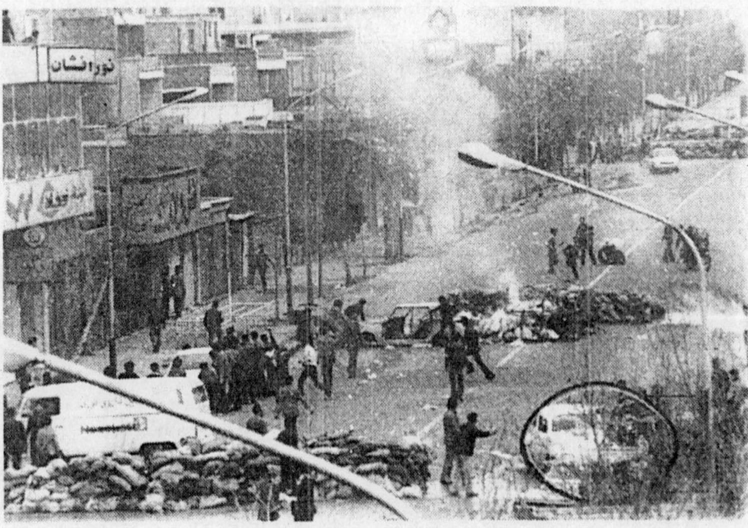

Fig. 22: Revolution is in the making

Fig. 23: A scene of people's demonstration during "Ashura" in 1978. A call for the establishment of an Islamic government

Fig. 24: The Shah turns to Shahpour Bakhteyar as his last hope to survive his regime. But to no avail. Bakhteyar is receiving a vote of confidence from the Parliament just to be ousted a month later

Fig. 25: A car pulls a statue of Mohammad Reza Shah in a Tehran street as joyous mobs celebrate the imminent downfall of his regime

Fig. 26: A confused and exhausted man. On his departure from Tehran on January 16, 1979, he wept like a woman for the imminent loss of his monarchy

Fig. 27: A historic moment. Shah's tearful flight to exile

Fig. 28: End of the Pahlavi dynasty: 11 February, 1979, people pull down Mohammad Reza's statue in Tehran

Fig. 29: Imam Khomeini returns to Iran aboard a charted Air France 747 after 14 years of exile

Fig. 30: A headline welcomes the return of Imam Khomeini to Iran

Fig. 31: Imam Khomeini's first address to the nation after his return to Iran in Behesht-e-Zahra cemetry in southern Tehran in February 1979. "I will choose the government with the support of the people", he said.

Fig. 32: Newspaper headlines during those fateful days

Fig. 33: Bazargan is sworn in as Iran's first post-revolution head of government in 1979. He described his government as a "blade without a handle". He resigned to protest the seizure of U.S. Embassy in Tehran a few months later

Fig. 34: (Seated from left to right) Ebrahim Yazdi, foreign minister of the Provisional Government, Akbar Hashemi Rafsanjani, a top member of the Revolutionary Council, Founder of the Islamic Republic of Iran, Imam Khomeini, and Mehdi Bazargan head of the Provisional Government (the person on the right is not identified

Fig. 35: Leader of the Freedom Movement of Iran (FMI), Mehdi Bazargan, as an MP in post-revolution Parliament. Next to him is Yadollah Sahabi (both with glasses), another top member of the FMI

Chapter 7

Pahlavi Regime, Superpowers and Middle East

PAHLAVI REGIME, SUPERPOWERS AND MIDDLE EAST

In this chapter, I would try to explain Iran's stance in the strategic policies of the Western powers especially the United States and Britain and Iran's stance towards them. In my comments, both reality and theory are mixed and most cases might be accurate. The source of my analysis; that is the information I obtained during 19 years of my tenure of office at SIB, could be categorized as follows:

1. A top secret U.S. monthly bulletin was sent directly to the Shah and he put it in a box after studying and sent it to me for my study. I read the contents of the bulletin and then destroyed it. The bulletin was between 20 to 40 pages and commented on the international developments.
2. SAVAK sent important articles published in the world press about Iran to SIB and I studied all of them.
3. I also studied the monthly bulletins of SAVAK's 7th Department and the army's intelligence.
4. I received the news reels broadcast on the world radios about Iran and were summorized for study.
5. I received side information from foreign intelligence agents in meetings, banquets, etc.
6. I also got information during the meetings of the FGCC and SGCC.
7. I received side information from my military friends stationed in CENTO Headquarters.

SUPERPOWERS AND IRAN

The World War II changed many things and created a new political and economic atmosphere there. Although before the war Britain was a strong colonial power and there was no sunset in its possessions, it lost its might and image during the war and London gradually lost its pre-war international role and preferred to compromise with the newly emerged power, the United States and maintain an influential but limited role in the international community. Post-war Europe was divided into Eastern and Western spheres of interests of the two superpowers. Western Europe, the one time cradle of civilization and industry, had no option but to appeal to the undamaged powerful U.S. for loans and financial assistance to repair its damaged economy. The U.S. emerged as the strongest economic power in the world and actively entered the international markets. Gradually it compromised with the seasoned British politicians and London provided Washington with first hand information which paved the way for America's supremacy.

There were some reasons to believe that Washington was seeking a rival in the post-war era. For that end, it helped Moscow to emerge as a superpower. Therefore, the world was divided into Western and Eastern blocs. Why? Because the existence of the Soviet Union as a Communist superpower could guarantee Washington's influence and its supremacy in Western Europe and other parts of the world.

The United States in fact saved the Soviet Union from an imminent defeat in the hands of Germans during the war. The cold winter had not effectively worked against Hitler's army to give up its expansionism and the powerful Germany was able to tolerate the freezing weather and get rid of the Soviet Union in spring.

Was it not the Soviet Union which was forced to sign the Bert Litofesk peace treaty with Germany when it was on the verge of a certain defeat?

During World War II, Germany's power was ten-fold compared to that of the First World War and if the United States did not intervene the Soviet Union would have been forced to make more concessions and sign a more humiliating treaty.

America's military assistance to the Soviet Union was shipped in two ways:

— Modern military brass were shipped through Iran which

was called the "Bridge of Victory" to the Soviet Red Army.

— They were shipped through Italy, Americans deceived Germans and in attempt to disperse the German and Italian armies during the war, they opened a new front in Italy and France. Dunkerque front in northern France involved all of the German troops in western Europe and; thus, caused Germany to pull a great number of troops out of the Soviet Union and reinforce its western fronts to avoid any military disaster. Certainly, if no new front was opened, Germany was quite able to increase the number of its troops by threefold in the Soviet Union.

As the Allies closed in on Germany, Britain's Winston Churchill, Russia's Josef Stalin and America's Franklin Roosevelt met in the little-known Black Sea resort of Yalta from February 4 to 10, 1945 to carve out a new map of post-war Europe. Already it was clear that Britain was the junior partner at Yalta and France was not simply invited. The conference decided that Europe be split into two ideologically hostile blocs maintained by the United States and the Soviet Union.

Conquered Germany was to be divided and demilitarilized. The Baltic republics of Litvania, Latnia and Estonia and a part of Romania were annexed to the Soviet Union and Poland, Bulgaria, Hungary, Czechoslovakia, Romania and East Germany became its satellites. In the last days of the war, Roosevelt's sudden support of Stalin saved Moscow from a total defeat. Thereafter, Stalin's far-reaching dreams caused him to mistakenly believe the U.S.-Britain rivalry. But why Stalin's calculations did not come true? Because of two main reasons: First the United States was trying to take the advantage of the situation created after the war and seize all British colonies. Second, Washington was intent on to create a bi-polar system with the powerful U.S. on one side and the Soviet Union with an ailing economy and weakened political system on the other side. Undoubtedly, American policy makers had learned that establishing bi-polar system would meet their interests and would allow them to extend their supremacy all over the world especially in Western Europe.

In post-war period, the United States kept playing games with the Soviets. There were no markets abroad for Soviet industrial products. Lack of markets for Soviet goods could have led to the collapse of Soviet industries but America's assistance again saved the Soviets from a serious economic recession and allowed Moscow to impose its ideology on the importing countries as well. However, the U.S. had put some restrictions on the activities of the Soviets and did not allow Moscow to go beyond its limits. Any prudent Soviet action was seriously repelled by the U.S. and hostilities between the two superpowers led to the cold war.

Two main objectives were on the top of the list of America's world strategy after the war. They were keeping the Soviet Union as a rival power and; second, undermining Soviet ambitions and keeping the options open for America's influence all over the world. Now the question is what was the extent of America's influence?

Doctrine of U.S. presidents did not allow any outbreak of war on the U.S. soil. During both wars, penetration of allies into America could not be ruled out and a Japanese attack on the U.S. western ports was quite possible. Therefore, after the war, the United States set up a defense system on its soil. Western Europe was the front defense barrier in the east. Some islands in the Pacific Ocean, under U.S. possession, Taiwan, the Philippines, etc. were the defense barriers on the west. The two regions were considered America's defense space and the sphere of its influence where the Soviets had no right to exert influence in that region. The region would be sacrificed in case of any new war to save America. The U.S. troops would also be dispatched to the region to fight the enemy and avoid any war on the U.S. soil. West Germany and Japan were considered 'dangerous nations' and therefore, military restrictions were imposed on them and the two countries were forced to follow America's dictated economic policies. The U.S. kept the two countries away from any Communist penetration and deployed atomic and modern conventional weapons on their soil. Central and south America was the third region of U.S. influence.

After the war, on the basis of Monroe Doctrine, the U.S. declared the continent of America the sphere of its influence and cut the hands of European countries from the continent with the motto of "continent of America belongs to Americans".

> "By the Monroe Doctrine the United States had long ago declared its opposition to the extension of European colonies in the western hemisphere, but the British, French, and Dutch colonies

in existence did not fall within the scope of the doctrine."[1]

The U.S. failed only in case of Cuba where Communists under Fidel Castro took power. To guarantee U.S. interests, military dictatorships were brought to power in southern and central American countries which severely suppressed any opposition. Supressive measures led to people's resentment of the U.S. government. Of course, the reasons behind the establishment of dictatorial regimes should be sought in the culture and traditions of the Latin American countries. Otherwise, repeated pro-U.S. coups could not be justified.

The next sphere of the U.S. influence was the black African continent mainly because of its rich mineral resources and its defense capabilities in case of a marine clash. However, the Middle East was accorded a top priority in the U.S. world strategy and American policy makers did not allow any Soviet penetrations in Pakistan, Iran and the oil-rich Persian Gulf Arab states. Iran was allowed to play a vital role in the region.

It could be stated that Moscow's 'limited role' in Eastern Europe was recognized and the U.S. extended its hegemony in the strategic and rich regions. However, the Soviet expansionist desires certainly did not approve American-dictated world divisions. Anyhow, the Soviet Union became the second superpower after the war and gradually its ideological, political and economic ambitions urged Moscow to fight the U.S. influence all over the world. The first instance of such campaign was the Soviet occupation of Iran' northern Azerbaijan Province and its provocations in northern Greece.

During and after the war, the Soviet Union made utmost efforts to bring Greece under its umbrella. To achieve its ends, the Soviets tried to spread Communism in the mountainous northern Greece which borders Bulgaria and Yugoslavia and offered extensive military assistance to that part of Greece. At the time, the Communist population in Greece did not exceed three million. Britain which until then had dominated the country acknowledged its failure and paved the way for Americans to intervene. It was said at the time that President Truman had made a deal with Stalin in which the U.S. would allow Moscow to increase its influence in Greece on the condition that the Soviet troops pull out of Iran's Azerbaijan.

After the Soviet pullout, the U.S. put Moscow under pressure and Stalin was forced to cut military assistance to Communists in northern Greece. Therefore, the United States brought Greece under control. The remaining Communists were also exterminated after the establishment of military governments in Greece. At the time, a monarchical regime was ruling in Greece and Konstantin was the Shah but the real power was in the hands of his generals. When Americans became assured that there was no Communist threat, they removed the monarchy and declared a Republican regime there.

The situation in Greece was similar to that of Iran. The Soviets also failed in Iran and were forced to pull out of Azerbaijan. On the other hand, Americans gradually increased their influence in Iran and destroyed any sign of Soviet influence after the August 19, 1953 coup. If the words of MI-6 station chief in Iran comes true, at the time Americans intended to install a military dictatorship led by Teimur Bakhteyar but the British convinced the Americans that no officer was able to play the role of Mohammad Reza in the army or the society. Zahedi came to power with the blessings of Washington after the coup. Assadollah Alam who enjoyed the support of the British convinced the Americans to remove Zahedi from the post of premiership and recognize Mohammad Reza's absolute administration. Though Americans accepted the plan, they, however, did not forget to establish a dictatorial regime in Iran. Being new to the game, the Americans lacked the subtlety with which the more experienced British manipulated Iranian politics and politicians.

> "In the nineteenth century Persia was the diplomatic battle ground on which the empires of Britain and Tsarist Russia competed for supremacy. After World War II the same battleground has seen new antagonists, the United States replacing Britain and the Soviets the Tsars. Now that the Gulf is the area which produces 60 per cent of the world's most essential commodity, oil, and owns 70 per cent of the world's proved oil reserves, not to mention the fact that this is the area which generates half the cash which flows each year into the world markets, the stakes are obviously immeasurably higher than they were in the nineteenth century.

Suitably enough the Tehran embassies which symbolize this confrontation are no ordinary diplomatic outposts... The Soviet Embassy is a complex of buildings enclosed behind a high wall. Here are several palaces, several smaller houses and bungalows as well as apartment blocks, a hospital and a power station... Naturally, the Embassy compound is extremely well protected. Supplementing the high wall, there was an electric fence. Everybody inside the compound is a Russian national, from the ambassador down to the cooks. In normal times the staff of the Embassy amounted to between 120 and 140, with about thirty-six guards.

The American Embassy... is no less impressive for being strictly contemporary. It covers an area of sixty acres in the centre of the city, triangular in shape and includes about thirty buildings of one sort or another, a large central office, the ambassador's residence, the headquarters of the military mission, the information centre, the commercial department, the houses of the service attaches and so on.

Here then were these two superpowers ranged against each other, with sharply conflicting interests and aims in the area... The Americans used to have virtually everything they wanted... and so they wished at all costs to preserve the status quo. The Russians, on the other hand, had been excluded from the area, economically and strategically. Yet it was an area on their borders and where this influence had once been considerable. It was therefore in their interests to see the status quo upset - not violently upset, perhaps, because the Russians are not keen to see violent revolutions on their doorstep - but altered gradually in their favour. So in Iran it was the Russians who looked for change; the Americans who resisted it.... So it was that the American Embassy in Tehran became the nerve centre for the control of the whole area. When Iran began to play the role of policeman in the Gulf region, it was the American Embassy which became the police station."[2]

For the Americans, Iran with a 2200-kilometre joint border with the Soviet Union including the Caspian Sea, was an important security belt to check the spread of Communism and minimize the influence of Moscow in the region. So, Iran could be used as a stronghold against any Soviet penetration and its efforts to reach the warm waters of the Persian Gulf as desired since the days of Peter the Great. That was why the Shah was happily allowed to play the role of the policeman in the region. On the other hand, Iran was the gateway for U.S., Western Europe and Japan to import their required oil from this part of the world and keep their factories working. The daily crude exports through the Strait of Hormuz topped some 27 million barrels, and the United States was determined to grip its hold over the strait. American companies, however, persuaded their British allies to leave everything for them and therefore they took a considerable share in Iran's oil through their consortium and shared the revenues with their European allies.

So, establishment of a pro-Soviet government in Tehran would jeopardize the interests of the West and would pose a great danger to the Western economy.

IRAN AND CENTO TREATY

The establishment of the North Atlantic Treaty Organization (NATO) was one of the most important measures taken by the United States to extend its dominance all over the world. The U.S.-led NATO was a military-political organization set up to counter the Soviet Union and its allies. Besides Western Europe, it stretched to southern Europe and included Greece and Turkey.

The organization's make-up allowed it to check the activities of the Soviet naval force in the Mediterranean Sea. The Soviet naval force had to pass through the Dardanelle and Bosphorus Straits and Turkey could block their way whenever it wished to do so. Turkey's geographical position was of strategic importance to NATO. The Mediterranean Sea was a locked waterway for the Soviets since most of the strategic ports were under NATO control. In case of a war, NATO was quite able to launch a coup and oust pro-Soviet governments in Libya and Syria and install puppet governments instead. NATO's superior role helped the organization to acquire a prestigious position in the world. Perhaps its topmost sensitive role was to materialize the doctrine of the U.S. which aimed at creating a bi-polar system in the world.

The military-political Central Treaty Organization (CENTO) was set up after the World War II. CENTO replaced the Baghdad Pact Organization (formed in 1955) after the withdrawal of Iraq in March

1959. The alliance was comprised Iran, Pakistan, Turkey, Britain and an Associate Member, the United States.

As a small branch of NATO, the alliance aimed to provide mutual security and defence for member countries against Communist aggression and subversion and seeked the peaceful economic development of the region through cooperative efforts.

The establishment of CENTO prompted Soviet attacks describing CENTO in the world political circles as an anti-Soviet alliance. Of course, I have to make it clear that CENTO did not pose any serious threat to the Soviets because Britain and the United States, the two main members of the treaty, were not able to dispatch troops to the region and Turkey too had devoted many of its troops to NATO and, therefore, three members of the alliance could not extend any real backing. They could only provide show of power or verbal support or put Moscow under diplomatic pressure if it invaded any of the CENTO member states.

On March 5, 1959, Iran and the United States signed a bilateral agreement that provided for American aid in case of aggression against Iran. This agreement again was bitterly attacked by the Soviet Union and caused a deterioration in the relations between Tehran and Moscow.

In CENTO, all the expenses were jointly paid for by member states. It was distinguished mainly by two sections namely Military and Economic Committees and all the five member states had delegates in both committees. The Iranian military attache was proposed by the Joint Staff of the Armed Forces and the eco-political representative was proposed by the Ministry of Foreign Affairs. Both had to receive approval from the Shah. SIB did not pass any reports about CENTO to the Shah but the respective departments were in direct touch with the Shah and informed him of the latest developments.

However, from time to time, SAVAK sent bulletins about CENTO activities which were summarized and were then sent on to Mohammad Reza to study. The bulletins were not sent to me regularly and, therefore, I do not remember much about them. To the best of my memory, Hoshang Batmanqelich was Iran's political envoy to CENTO. He was a friend of Ardashir Zahgedi and later served as Iran's ambassador to Turkey. He may have gone to the U.S. from Turkey after the revolution to join his two daughters who were studying there. Military representatives of the CENTO member states were appointed on a two-year term. Most of the members of Iran's military delegation to the alliance were my friends.

SOVIET UNION

I briefly explained about Communism and the history of the relations between the Shah's regime and the Soviet Union. Here, I would like to comment on some issues which I have not touched upon so far.

One has to ask whether in the U.S. regional strategy, the Western troops were expected to launch offensives against the Soviet Union through Iran's soil in case of a new world war and CENTO was to act as a bystander? Certainly the answer is negative. The Soviet Union was a big country with many mineral resources. Its massive economic, industrial and military installations were concentrated on Russian soil as were 220 million out of its 300-million population. Therefore, any western invasion of the Soviet Union through Iran would have led to the defeat of the U.S. and its allies and little damages could have been inflicted on the Soviet military might. Any U.S. attack from the eastern and northern borders of the Soviet Union would have had the same result.

For these reasons, the United States focused its hypothetical plans on the western borders. On the other hand, Moscow had, in advance, reinforced its positions on the western fronts and had deployed advanced weapons in the eastern European countries. Therefore, it could be said that Iran's oil resources, its strategic importance in the Persian Gulf as well as its geographical proximity to the Soviet Union were the main reasons for its vital role in the U.S. regional strategy but it could not be used to attack the Soviet Union. However, Iran was close enough to be used as a base from where the Americans could conduct espionage activities in attempts to weaken the Soviet Union.

What did article 6 of the 1921Accord between Iran and the Soviet Union mean? Was Moscow entitled, according to the agreement, to occupy Iran whenever it wished so? The accord stipulated that the Soviets were allowed to deploy troops on Iranian soil (border line) only if domestic turmoil in Iran affected the Soviet border cities and caused disturbances there. The 1921 accord was signed at a time when both the Soviet and Iranian governments had been weakened.

Did expansion of economic and political ties between Iran and Moscow contradict Iran's dependency on the U.S.? It is an intricate question. The Soviets were well aware of Iran's anti-Communist role and were not satisfied with the Shah. Moscow, however, was aware that the Americans had deployed radars in northern Iran. Moreover, the Shah's regime was an ally of the United States and a member of CENTO. The Soviets respected the sphere of influence of their rivals and had learned that expansionism in some regions of the world would cost them too much. Therefore, Moscow did its utmost during the conferences held between the allies to exert influence in its own political circles. If that was not the case, the Soviets could have taken tougher actions against Iran and could have provoked domestic political tension in Iran through their agents namely the Tudeh Party.

Since Moscow had learned that the U.S. would not allow occupation of Iran by Soviet forces or Iran's annexation to the Communist bloc, it always gave up its aims when it was put under pressure. Certainly, installing a Communist government in Iran was an ideal situation for the Soviets but America's influence had hampered the materialization of their objectives and, therefore, they preferred to come to terms with the Shah's regime.

Stalin established cordial relations with the Shah and was the only head of a superpower who personally called on Mohammad Reza at his palace. The Shah always remained in Stalin's favour. Stalin invited Princess Ashraf to Moscow twice and on each trip he offered her valuable leather overcoat as a gift. Later, Tehran-Moscow relations worsened and at the time of Breznev, again cordial relations were restored. The two head of states shuttled between the two capitals several times. The four-star General Shafaqat who had accompanied the Shah on one of his trips to Moscow as his aide-de-camp said that the Soviets received the Shah warmly and showed him many of their economic installations especially the dam-building industries and took him by train to Siberia for an amusement visit.

As the Shah's regime was consolidated at home, gradually Iran's relations with the Soviet Union and the Eastern European countries were promoted within a framework authorized by the Americans. Of course, there were some limitations to the economic co-operation between Iran and the Eastern Bloc countries while geographical proximity and easy transportation encouraged improved trade links between Iran and its giant northern neighbour. I had been told that in the past about 80 per cent of Iran's exports were shipped to the Soviet Union and the Soviets were the best purchasers of Iran's cotton and dry fruits. On the contrary, European states never showed any tendency or willingness to import the unsatisfactory packed Iranian dry fruits.

On large-scale contracts, several trade transactions were concluded between Iran and the Eastern European states including the sale to Iran of Romanian tractors despite the fact that they were not in much demand in the world markets. A contract was also concluded with Bulgaria on the purchase of foodstuffs from that country which continued until the 1979 Islamic revolution. The establishment of the Iran Smelting Factory in the suburbs of Isfahan was first proposed to the Germans but they refused and believed it was too early for Iran to have such a plant and, therefore, the Soviets picked up the giant project. All agreements with the Soviet Union, including the sale of gas, were first approved by the Americans or were concluded upon their recommendations.

The construction of store-pits (silos) was another giant agreement concluded with the Soviets. Of course, Italian and other Western European countries also won contracts to construct some silos in Iran. The then Prime Minister Amirabbass Hoveida objected to their proposed cost while the Soviets proposed less expenses and were ready to accomplish the project quicker. The issue was discussed in a meeting presided over by Hoveida and attended by Investigation experts. The experts confirmed that the proposal of costs made by the European companies was higher than those proposed by the Soviets. After consultations the European partners accepted price similar to that of the Soviet Union's on the condition that they set up more silos instead of reclaiming the expenses.

"On 1st January 1992, the Soviet Union was formally disbanded and replaced by a Commonwealth of Independent States composed of 11 former Soviet republics. Michail Gorbachev, the last Soviet leader who introduced his Prestroika and Glasnost (economic libralization and political openness) was described as a man who killed Communism in wanting to save it.

Imam Khomeini who had predicted the death of Communism

sent his envoys to Moscow in January 1989 inviting Gorbachev to "seriously look into Islam."

The unprecedented message, Imam's only message to a foreign leader, said, "... from now, Communism should be looked for in the museums of political history.... The first step that will certainly bring you success is your reconsideration of your predecessors' policies to obliterate God and religion which has, no doubt, dealt the severest blow to people in the Soviet Union. There is no other option to have a right approach to world issues other than this one ... The main problem your country is facing today is not the issue of ownership, economy and freedom, but rather disbelief in God, the same problem that has brought or will eventually bring the West to a stalemate and tediousness."

Imam Khomeini's message had its tradition in the historical message of Holy Prophet Muhammad (PBUH) who sent emissaries inviting the Byzantine and Persian kings - the two great powers of the day - to accept Islam."[3]

AFGHANISTAN

"The boundaries of Afghanistan were established in the late 19th century, mainly as a result of the rivalry between Britain and Russia. In the 20th century Afghanistan became a pawn in a struggle of political ideologies and a search for commercial influence. Part of the struggle was the invasion of Afghanistan by the Soviet Union in 1979."[4]

Britain made every effort in Iran and Afghanistan to stop Soviet influence from spreading into the Indian peninsula as long as greater India (including today's India, Pakistan, Bangladesh, and Sri Lanka) was its colony.

The British were determined to hamper any Soviet access to the present Pakistan through Afghanistan or Iran and did not even avoid military confrontation to block Moscow's expansionism. After the Partition of India in 1947, Afghanistan lost its strategic role and London was less interested in the land-locked country.

After World War II, the Soviets tried to increase their influence in the region and along with the U.S. and Western European countries, Moscow made investments and enhanced trade activities there. The Soviets approached the then Afghan leader Mohammad

Zaher Shah and set up development projects in that country and constructed a main road connecting northern Afghanistan to the south; thus, paving the way for easy access to the warm waters of the Indian Ocean.

By that time Prime Minister Mohammad Davud Khan took a stronger line on Pashtunistan, and, to the surprise of many, turned to the Soviet Union for economic and military assistance. The Soviets ultimately became Afghanistan's major aid-and-trade partner. They began to train the Afghan army with their own methods and Moscow became the dominant power in Afghanistan.

It was clear that the Americans had given the go-ahead to the Soviets to exert their influence in the land-iocked country in order to save Iran from any Soviet threat. The U.S. had little to do in Afghanistan while Iran was an oil-rich strategic country in the Persian Gulf region and the U.S. could not ignore it.

When the Soviets became assured that there would be no Western intervention in Afghanistan, they decided to depose Zaher Shah who was on good terms with both the Soviets and the Western powers. Moscow intended to extend its influence all over Afghanistan and, therefore, ousted Zaher Shah from power in a virtually bloodless coup in 1973 when he was on a state visit to Italy. The coup was led by Mohammad Davud Khan, a brother-in-law and cousin of Zaher Shah. Davud Khan was a pro-Soviet agent who had helped Moscow increase its influence in Afghanistan during his premiership. There were no immediate reports available in Tehran about the transfer of power in Kabul to a pro-Soviet regime. The Kabul-based foreign embassies had informed SAVAK's agent in the Iranian Embassy that the United States had turned down a request by France, Germany and Italy to invest in southern Afghanistan.

> "During Davud Khan's second tenure as prime minister, he attempted to introduce socio-economic reforms, to write a new constitution, and to effect a gradual movement away from the socialist ideals his regime initially espoused. Afghanistan broadened and intensified its relations with other Muslim countries trying to move away from its dependency on the Soviet Union and the United States. In addition, Davud Khan and Zulfiqar Ali Bhutto, the Prime Minister of Pakistan, reached tentative agreement on a solution to the Pashtunistan problem...

The two major leftist organizations, the People's (Khalq) and Banner parties, then reunited against Davud Khan after a 10-year separation. There followed a series of political assassinations, massive anti-government demonstrations and arrest of major leftist leaders. Before his arrest Hafizullah Amin, a U.S.-educated leader of the People's Party contacted party members in the armed forces and devised a makeshift but successful coup. Davud Khan and most of his family were killed, and the Democratic Republic of Afghanistan was born on April 27, 1987.

Nur Mohammad Taraki was elected President of the Revolutionary Council and Prime Minister of the country and the Secretary-General of the combined People's Democratic Party of Afghanistan (PDPA). Babrak Karmal, a Banner leader, and Hafizullah Amin were elected deputy prime ministers. The leaders of the new government insisted they were not controlled by the Soviet Union and proclaimed their policies to be based on Afghan nationalism, Islamic principles, socio-economic justice, nonalignment in foreign affairs, and respect for all agreements and treaties signed by previous Afghan governments.

Unity between the People's and Banner factions rapidly faded as the People's Party emerged dominant... Hafizullah Amin became Prime Minister in March 28, 1979 although Taraki retained his posts...

Taraki was killed in a confrontation between Taraki and Amin supporters on September 14, 1979. Amin then tried to broaden his internal base of support and to again interest Pakistan and the United States in Afghan security. Despite his efforts on the night of December 24, 1979, the Soviets began their invasion of Afghanistan, and Amin and many of his followers were killed on December 27."[5]

Iran enjoyed cordial relations with Afghanistan during Zaher Shah but the Hirmand River always was a potential source of dispute between the two countries. the river originates from Afghanistan and moves into Iran's Sistan-Baluchestan Province. The river's water is a major source for irrigation in the province. According to an agreement signed between the two neighbours, both Iran and Afghanistan shared the water equally but disputes erupted after the Afghans built a dam that deprived Iran of its equal share. Kabul argued that Iran received more than its share in the winter and spring seasons when the river's uncontrolled water was massively running into Iran and that Iran could store water on its side too. The two countries sat at the negotiating table and the dispute was quickly resolved.

Iran later signed a contract with Japanese firms to construct artificial lakes on the border with Afghanistan to pump water for irrigation in summer.

Another problem with Afghanistan was the opium trade. Shipments of opium from Afghanistan to Iran intensified after Iran, upon U.S. recommendations, banned the cultivation of poppy in Iran with the aim of helping the neighbouring Turkey's economy. After the ban, it was shipments of opium pouring into Iran from Afghanistan and Turkey and it was gold that was given in return.

With the Shah's government in Iran ousted, the Soviet Union invaded Afghanistan in December 1979 to extend its direct control over the land-locked country.

> "With Afghanistan under Soviet occupation, the Afghans launched a jihad, or holy war, to free their country from foreign domination. The Afghan Mujahideen factions joined forces for 13 years to expel the Soviets in 1989 and topple its Communist successor regime in 1992.
>
> Having conquered the capital, Kabul, a council of Mujahiddeen factions elected the leader of Islamic Salvation National Front, Sibghatullah Mojaddedi as President of the Islamic State of Afghanistan. The Jameyat-e-Islami Leader Burhanuddin Rabbani was soon to succeed Mojaddedi. Contrary to expectations for a return to peace in the country, factional fightings erupted, each group vying for power. Ever since, Afghan factional leaders have been unable to agree on which of them should run the country. It was a brutal power struggle based on centuries-old religious, ethnic and tribal rivalries, and intensified by foreign intervention that brought total destruction to Afghanistan with tens of thousands dead and millions more in refugee camps.
>
> Shifting alliances among the warring factions left little hope for a reconciliation or a durable peace. Rabbani who had promised to step down in early 1995 refused to do so since the

situation was not ripe for a power transfer or establishment of an interim government.

The Taliban, who sprang into prominence when they captured the southern city of Kandahar in November 1994, captured Kabul in September 1996, and imposed a harsh Islamic law. Iranian Leader Ayatollah Seyed Ali Khamenei denounced the brand of Islam practiced by the Taliban. "The world does not accept what the Taliban are doing in the name of Islam. What they (Taliban) are doing is not Islamic", he said.

The Taliban closed school girls, banned women from work, ordered men to grow beard, suppressed all their opponents especially Shi'ites. The Taliban proved their anti-Shi'ite thinking they killed Abdul Ali Mazari, leader of the Shi'ite Hezb-e-Wahdat in March 1995 after they had arrested him in southwestern Afghanistan.

The militia's capture of Kabul was highly interpreted as having been designed by the United States, financed by Saudi Arabia, and logistically supported by Pakistan. The American did not, however, conceal their happiness to see in Taliban a force to help Washington contain Iran's regional influence.

With about two-thirds of Afghanistan under Taliban control, forces loyal to Rabbani under the command of Ahmad Shah Masood formed an alliance with the former communist General Abdul Rashid Dostum's National Islamic Movement, and Karim Khalili's Shi'ite Hezb-e-Wahdat-e-Islami to fight back Taliban from the one-third under their control in northern Afghanistan."[6]

PAKISTAN

"The Islamic Republic of Pakistan was brought into being at the time of the Partition of British India in 1947 in order to create a separate homeland for India's Muslims in response to the demands of Muslim nationalists.

From independence in 1947 until 1971, Pakistan (both de facto and in law) consisted of two regions - West Pakistan in the Indus River Basin, and East Pakistan, located more than 1,000 miles (1,600 kilometers) away in the Ganges River Delta. In response to grave internal political problems, however, an independent state of Bangladesh was proclaimed in East Pakistan in 1971."[7]

The Muslim League, the movement among Muslim population of the India-Pakistan subcontinent that culminated in the creation of Pakistan stemmed from the historical fact that during the British domination of India, Muslims were prevented from acquiring real power. Mohammad Ali Jinnah, leader of the *Muslim League*, eager to bring British rule to an end, was at length driven to the conclusion that the only way to preserve Indian Muslims from complete subordination to the Hindus was to establish a separate Muslim state.

The existence of many ethnic communities in Pakistan has always caused political and ethnic violence and has created trouble for the central government. Pashtuns and Baluches were outstanding among the various ethnic groups. Pashtuns mostly live in the snow-covered mountainous areas and, therefore, are tough and brave. They hold themselves superior to other ethnic groups. Baluchs who mostly live in southwestern Pakistan bordering Iran have strong independent desires and created much trouble for the Bhutto government.

After the creation of Pakistan in 1947, the southern port city of Karachi, the largest and most populous city, was chosen the capital. The moist atmosphere prevented heavy work and made workers lazy. People were suffering from acute poverty. Many people slept on the pavements and had little or nothing to eat. A few years later, the government announced Islamabad as the new capital city which at that time looked like a village. Gradually, the government provided all the facilities necessary for a capital including an airport, the transfer of governmental buildings, etc. to Islamabad. A city situated in northern Pakistan, it enjoyed pleasant weather and was surrounded by mountains which provided a natural shelter to the capital.

Pakistan is a poor country. The existing economic installations and facilities were erected when it was a British colony. The British influence can be witnessed in the railway, roads, army, universities etc. and still it lingers on in Pakistan.

As happened in Iran, after the termination of World War II, the United States entered Pakistan's political and economic scene and Washington's financial assistance to that country helped the White House to win the support of many Pakistani politicians. Gradually pro-U.S. politicians and military figures seized the key posts. There was no definite rule about the establishment of political parties in Pakistan and any politician could set up a party in some cases, some of them formed coalition parties but they quickly disintegrated because of rivalries.

Zolfiqar Ali Bhutto's People's Party of Pakistan (PPP) was a well-organized political party in Pakistan. However, political power lay in the hands of the army which had about 300,000 personnel. The army suffered from a shortage of military equipment and for long was dependent on Iran's gratuitous aid. Later, the Americans also promised gratuitous aid to Pakistan. Currency income also came from Pakistan military experts and technicians who were employed in Arab states to help strengthen their armies.

The United States expected the Pakistan army to first protect Washington's regional interests especially to block any Soviet penetration to the south following Moscow's domination over Afghanistan and, secondly; to interfere in political affairs especially when ethnic and political differences threatened the country.

When President Iskandar Mirza in a presidential proclamation in October 1958 abolished the political parties, abrogated the Constitution and placed the country under martial law, General Mohammad Ayub Khan, Minister of National Defense, was the chief martial law administrator.

> "General Ayub Khan became Prime Minister, and three lieutenant generals were named to the Cabinet... The eight civilian members included businessmen and lawyers, one being a young newcomer, Zulfiqar Ali Bhutto. That same evening the new military ministers called on the President, with contingents of armed soldiers, and informed him that he was to resign. After a short interval, Mirza was exiled to London. A proclamation issued by Ayub Khan announced his assumption of the presidency.
>
> Martial law lasted 44 months. During that time, a number of army officers took over vital civil service posts. There were considerable imbalance between East and West; during the 1950s East Pakistan was becoming poorer in per capita terms every year, whereas the West was achieving positive growth.
>
> In December 1971 India successfully invaded East Pakistan. The establishment of a Bangladesh government with Mujib as Prime Minister followed in January 1972. Accepting responsibility for the defeat and break up of Pakistan, President

> Yahya Khan resigned on December 20, 1971 and Bhutto became the undisputed leader of former West Pakistan."[8]

Bhutto carried out reforms upon America's recommendations and became increasingly autocratic, jailing opponents and employing militant methods against the restive Pashtuns and Baluchs.

In 1977 Elections were held. The campaign was marked by violence, the results were a sweeping victory for Bhutto's PPP. Mounting protest soon brought chaos to Karachi and other major cities especially in Baluchestan.

Mohammad Reza who feared the turmoil may spread into Iran's Baluchestan officially invited Bozenju, the Governor General of Pakistan's Baluchestan, to Iran and promised him financial aid in a bid to avoid the spread of the unrest into Iran. Bozenju accepted the Shah's offer and cooperated with Iran.

As the unrest spread in the country, Bhutto was compelled to call out the army and proclaim martial law. To avoid total chaos, the chief of staff of the army, General Mohammad Zia ul-Haq, took over as chief administrator of martial law.

Bhutto was executed on April 4, 1979 on charges of killing a political opponent. I do not know the accurate reason behind Bhutto's downfall because his powerful party enjoyed popularity. The accusation levelled against him by Zia ul-Haq was not convincing and perhaps some other reasons were behind Bhutto's execution. I guess Bhutto perhaps had disclosed some secret documents to the Soviets and received bribes in return and was punished for committing that treason though there were no documents to prove my supposition. A similar incident led to the execution of Adnan Menderes in Turkey. It could be concluded that the military was the most powerful in the Pakistani leadership and the United States could take advantage of its influence among military officers and achieve its objectives.

> "The invasion of Afghanistan by the Soviet Union in December 1979 became central to Pakistan's internal and foreign affairs. Zia embarked upon a military buildup supported by the United States and by other Islamic countries and opposed by India."[9]

The Shah and his twin sister Princess Ashraf had established close relations with Bhutto since he was appointed foreign minister.

Bhutto was very ambitious and made every effort to take the seat of presidency. The Shah also extended assistance to him to help him achieve his objectives.

Since the intelligence services of the two countries had high-level links and exchanged information, there was no need for any specific secret activity by SAVAK in Pakistan. Moreover, no restrictions were imposed on SAVAK's agents and the two country's membership in CENTO alliance had facilitated military and economic cooperation between the two neighbours.

The heads of the two states, shuttled between the two capitals and I presume Zia ul-Haq made over ten state visits to Iran and received huge financial and military assistance from the Shah. Responsible officials said that a number of aircraft along with spare parts and tanks were among the donations the Shah extended to Pakistan.

Iran's donations to Pakistan were given on the advice of the U.S. and Britain which believed Iran, an oil-rich nation, had to assist its friends in CENTO.

TURKEY

The Republic of Turkey was mapped out after the disintegration of the Sick Man of Europe, the Ottoman Empire after the World War I. The dissolution of the empire coincided with the Bolshevik revolution in Russia. Britain which was the only superpower in the world at the time, focused all of its attention on three countries in the Middle East in order to deny the Soviets access to the Mediterranean Sea and its Asian protected regimes namely Iran, Poland and Turkey.

In Iran, Britain helped Reza Khan to seize power and created the Pahlavi dynasty, in Poland Marshal Jozef Pilsudski was installed as president and in Turkey Mustafa Kemal later surnamed Ataturk was brought to power. Ataturk was an army Brigadier General when he came to power. He had gained fame during a war with Greece and army officers were very obedient to him.

Kemal saw the solution of Turkey's problems in a process of Westernization. To do this it was necessary to change the very basis of society in Turkey, and to suppress, ruthlessly if need be, the opposition. Between 1922 and 1938, the year of his death, Kemal carried through a series of far-reaching reforms to Europeanize the Turkish society. He harassed the clerics, banned the Islmaic veil or hijab for women, forced people to wear European clothes, reformed the Turkish language, replaced the Arabic with Latin script and did whatever was necessary to make Turkey resemble a European country.

The same happened in Iran. Like his Iranian counterpart, Ataturk too suppressed the tribes including the Kurds, and slaughtered thousands of people. He banned the use of the term "Kurd" and attributed the name of "mountain Turks" to them. Ataturk whose policies led to hostilities between Turks and Armenians, unleashed suppressive measures against the Armenians living in Turkey.

He was a military man but not a politician and, therefore, his role ended after he had suppressed the opposition. Ismet Inonu was his close associate who, during the war with Greece, was Ataturk's chief of staff and it seemed that the British had installed Inonu, a smart politician who ran many of Ataturk's affairs, as his aide. The British believed that Ataturk could make political blunders without Inonu and, therefore, would go astray. Inonu was appointed prime minister several times and finally succeeded Ataturk after his death in November 1938. He remained in the topmost executive post for years and died at the age of 90.

Members of the Iranian delegation to CENTO quoted their Turkish counterparts as saying that Ataturk stayed away from politics in the last years of his public life and preferred to stay at his palace and keep womanizing and drinking wine. He used to be drunk before he went to bed. Many pretty girls waited at his palace and Ataturk took each of them to bed every night. That was the way Ataturk lived in the last years of his life. Inonu met all his needs and made every effort to keep Ataturk's private life secret.

During World War II, Hitler wanted Turkey to join Germany and, therefore, appointed his most seasoned politician Von Papen as ambassador to Turkey. The fall of France, the hostile attitude of the Soviet Government, and the extension of German power over most of Europe, led the Turkish government to the conclusion that nothing would be gained by provoking an almost certain German conquest. While continuing to recognize the Alliance and despite German efforts, Turkey remained neutral. When German expansion in the Balkans had brought the German armies within 100 miles of Istanbul, the Turks further protected themselves by signing a friendship and trade agreement with Germany in which, however, they stipulated that Turkey would maintain her treaty obligations to Britain.

The Western powers increased pressure on Turkey to enter the war. While stopping short of actual belligerency, the Turks, especially after 1942, entered into closer economic and military relations with the West and aided the Allied cause in a number of ways. In August 1944 they broke off diplomatic relations with Germany to prove their friendship to Britain.

Turkey acceded to full membership of NATO in early 1952. Fidelity to NATO and CENTO remained the basis of Turkey's foreign policy through the next ten years. By the beginning of 1960, Turkey decided that such a policy need not be incompatible with less frigid relations towards Russia, and a visit in April to Moscow by Prime Minister Adnan Menderes was announced for July. Before it could take place the Menderes regime was overthrown. The Americans could not simply tolerate any Turkish strong inclination towards Moscow.

Turkey enjoyed a strategic geographical position and its control of the Dardanelles and Bosphorus Straits added to its geo-political importance and thus was vital for Western interests. Moreover, since Turkey bordered the Soviet Union, it was accorded prime military and intelligence sensitivity and since it could serve the interests of the West, the United States extended the Turkish Government a great amount of economic assistance. Turkey's membership in NATO foiled any Soviet attempt to make use of hundreds of small and big islands in the Mediterranean Sea and it allowed the West, especially the U.S. to set up military bases and powerful radars on Turkish soil for espionage activities.

Its strategic importance encouraged its NATO allies to strengthen Turkey's 500,000 strong army. Since Turkey was a poor country, only U.S. gratuitous aid could feed its army. Though the salary of Turkish military personnel was one-third of their Iranian counterparts, they were satisfied since they had additional incomes because of the special characteristics of the Turkish army.

The army is the most powerful political party in Turkey. A rule approved by the Turkish ruling clique, which was perhaps inserted in the Constitution at the time of Ataturk, allowed the army to warn the Government and the Parliament to take decisions in case of any foreign threat and if they failed to thwart the threat, the army was entitled to take over in a bloodless coup. Thus, coups do not occur in Turkey as they may do in other countries but the army's takeover goes through as an almost legal procedure. The procedure, recommended by the U.S., was adopted to guarantee the government's stability and to protect against any Communist penetration. Therefore, no weaknesses could be witnessed in the central government and the West was assured of Turkey's stability. The army, after taking over when the government seems threatened will return to power to the parties after the crisis settles down. It could be concluded that there is no real party democracy in Turkey and the army has the last say.

A takeover by the army happened in 1960 when Menderes, the competent Turkish premier, was in power. That clearly proved that the Turkish armed forces have constituted the determining factor in the politics of the Turkish republic. The U.S., having been informed that Menderes had established secret links with the Soviets, used the army to remove him from power and executed both Menderes and his foreign minister who was involved in the affair. When the situation returned to normal, the army gave power back to the civilian government.

In 1974, Bulent Ecevit, leader of the Republican Party, had formed an uneasy coalition government. Ecevit's coalition government was unable to curb inflation, unemployment, and political violence, all of which increased rapidly and led to the imposition of martial law in 13 provinces. He was forced to resign and Suleiman Demirel formed a minority government in November 1979.

By 1980 the military, which had watched the growing violence and the government ineffectiveness with alarm, again intervened. They precipitated a bloodless coup in September 1980. General Kenan Evren was named the head of state who quickly dissolved the Assembly, political parties, suspended the Constitution, and imposed martial law.

> "After three years of military rule, civilian government returned to power in 1983 with Motherland Party's Turgust Ozal as Prime Minister. Ozal, a reform-minded economist who introduced sweeping market reforms in Turkey, was elected President in 1989. He died of a heart failure in April 1993 and Prime Minister Suleiman Demirel's centre-right True Path Party took over as President.

In June 28, 1996, the pro-Islamic Welfare Party leader Necmittin Erbakan was elected Prime Minister, bringing Islamists to power in Turkey for the first time since it became a secular republic in 1923. Erbakan formed a government in coalition with Tansu Ciller's True Path Party, and won a vote of confidence from Parliament on July 8. The military was clearly displeased with Erbakan but this time there was no military intervention.

Since the first day he came to power, Erbakan's government started implementing a new foreign policy which called for boosting ties with Islamic countries. The Islamist premier made his first foreign trip to Tehran in August 1996 that provoked a strong U.S. criticism. Erbakan signed a $ 20 billion natural gas accord with Iran and promised that bilateral trade would double from $1 billion to over $ 2 billion.

On Erbakan's proposal, a cooperation organization dubbed as D-8, patterned on the G-7 gathering of seven most industrialized nations was announced in January 1997. D-8 groups included Turkey, Iran, Bangladesh, Egpyt, Pakistan, Nigeria, Malaysia and Indonesia, all Muslim countries."[10]

ISRAEL

The Shah's government recognized Israel as a *de facto* government and that was enough for Israel to unofficially open its embassy in Tehran. Iran's good relations with Israel led to transfer of a number of Iran's extraterritorial bases monitoring the Arab countries to Israel and the Israeli intelligence agency launched extensive activities in Iran.

Israel considered Iran to be its only ally in the region and, therefore, helped SAVAK train its members. Iran's Islamic culture and the Shah's fear of the Arabs did not allow him to officially recognize Israel and the U.S. and Britain also did not recommend that he did so since Iran was the best means of liaison between Israel and the Arabs.

Israel, a money-making country for the U.S., is America's main base in the Middle East. Israel's existence compels the rich Arab governments to return their oil revenues to the West through arms purchases and the U.S. also generously allows Western European countries to sell their arms to the Arabs. Israel was also beneficial to the Soviet Union since it also took a share of the arms sales to the Arabs.

Although Israel is the only Jewish state in the world, it is in fact the centre of the Jewish power, it does not enjoy the capacity to host all Jews scattered all over the world. Jewish minorities throughout the world are very influential especially in the U.S. politics and, therefore, Israel cannot be described as a country under U.S. domination but it is the U.S. which is administered by influential Jews.

According to the 8th Department of SAVAK, the Jewish population in Iran was estimated at 70,000. Before the creation of Israel in 1948, Jewish minorities in Iran were calm people and were not politically active. They focused all their attention on economic affairs. Jews in Iran, like other minorities, have deep feelings of comradeship. There are poor and rich families among them but few are without jobs. Jews in Iran do not marry non-Jews and for the same reason they have kept their ethnic origin. Contrary to the Bahais and Christians who try to urge Muslims to convert to Bahaism or Christianity, no such activities were observed by Iranian Jews and in fact they could be described as an ethnic minority, rather than a religious minority.

After the creation of Israel in 1948 and especially following the military victory of Israel in the 1973 Middle East war, Iranian Jews became proud of their fellow Jews but in order not to provoke the sentiments of the Iranian people they hid their happiness. Israel never encouraged Jews living in Iran to emigrate to Israel. The reason was that Jews living in Israel were all educated, rich people who had emigrated there from America or Europe but Jews living in Iran were mostly poor and were not educated to as high a level and, therefore, they did not interest Israel.

Only a few Iranian Jews asked permission to emigrate but Israel set two conditions for their entry; they had to be rich in order to invest money in Israel or they had to be young in order to serve in the army. A number of them who satisfied the conditions emigrated to Israel but returned to Iran after a year or two. It was believed that some of the immigrants had received intelligence training during their stay in Israel and that they retuned to Iran to protect Israeli interests there.

Israel covers a small area which does not exceed 30,000 square kilometers if one calculates the Gaza Strip, West Bank and the suburb of Jordan river and the Golan Heights which were occupied in the 1973 Middle East war, and this also restricted the immigration of Iranian Jews into Israel. About three million Jews and one million Palestinians live in Israel while economically they suffer because they do not have fertile lands and sufficient water for irrigation. Therefore, it could be said that there is a population explosion in Israel and the government prefers to make good use of Jews in different countries instead of inviting them to live in Israel.

The Israeli Embassy in Tehran was active in a diversified area of activities and in addition to its intelligence operations it prepared social meetings, organized activities aimed at strengthening the morale of the Jews and collected donations to be sent to Israel. SAVAK agents also attended the monthly meetings. The Embassy sometimes held banquets and invited foreign ambassadors, Jewish personalities and even Iranian officials including those in the 8th Department of SAVAK.

Moreover, the Israeli Embassy from time to time invited Iranian officials to pay visits to Israel which were aimed at informing Iran of the agricultural and industrial developments in Israel. In 1961, the Israeli agriculture ministry invited an Iranian delegation to visit Israeli irrigation facilities. The Iranian delegation took up the invitation. A SIB officer also accompanied the delegation. Upon arrival home, the officer prepared a comprehensive report on his trip and sent it to me to study. The report indicated that Israel had made surprising progress in the field of agriculture and irrigation. The Iranian delegation had first visited the conjunction where the Jordan river makes the border between Israel and Jordan. At the site, a large concrete tunnel had been constructed where the Israeli share streamed through. The water was carried by pipes from the north of the country to the south. Smaller pipes branched out to take a supply of water to the cities and farmlands but measures were taken to prevent the water being wasted. This was very interesting for me because in Iran millions of square meters of water are wasted every year. The Iranian delegation was taken to the last pipeline station in the Naqib Desert. The Israelis had also gained considerable success in desalinating the water of the Mediterranean Sea.

Once, an Israeli irrigation expert arrived in Iran and visited some provinces. He said that Iran could in no way be counted as being among those countries which suffered from a shortage of water. He claimed that if Israel had a few rivers such as the ones which streamed through Kurdestan province, it would be able to make Israel a flourishing country. He believed that the water of the rivers and springs in Iran were wasted and even if they were used for irrigation at least 50 per cent of the water would be lost through evaporation. He rejected the Kurty system of Irrigation and said that the application of the system wasted the water.

"The Israeli Embassy was handed over to the Palestine Liberation Organization after the 1979 Islamic Revolution and it became the PLO Embassy. However, after PLO members were found to be speaking about pan-Arab nationalism and socialism in gatherings of Iranian Arab-speaking citizens in the southwestern part of the country, the Islamic government authorities ordered that all PLO members other than a skeleton staff at the Tehran Embassy be expelled from Iran." [11]

"The Camp David Accord signed between Egypt and Israel in 1979 broke the unity of Arab frontier governments and instead discord was spread amongst them and further weakened the stance of the Arabs. Although Arab states imposed boycott on Egypt as punishment, the accord had broken the back of Arab unity.

In 1991, the U.S.-sponsored so-called Middle East peace process was launched in Madrid, Spain, with the participation of Syria, Lebanon, Jordan, Israel and representatives of Palestinians. The declared objective was to reach a just and comprehensive peace in the Middle East.

However, in September 1993, Israeli Prime Minister Yitzhak Rabin and Palestine Liberation Organization (PLO) Chairman Yasser Arafat signed a limited autonomy accord in Washington. The agreement, which had sceretly been negotiated between Israel and PLO in August 1993 in Oslo, Norway, would grant self-rule for Gaza and the West Bank town of Jericho as a first step toward full Palestinian autonomy in the territories Israel occupied during the 1967 war.

Under the agreement, Israel will recognize the PLO, at the same time, the PLO will recognize Israel, and change tracts of its charter that call for destruction of Israel and declare all of Israel to be occupied Palestinian territory.

The agreement also stipulates that Israel will control the Jordan River bridges near Jericho which link the West Bank to Jordan, there will be no corridor linking Jericho, which is in the West Bank, and Gaza, which lies on the Mediterranean Sea, Israel will retain control over foreign relations and security matters, no Jewish settlements in the occupied territories will be force to dismantle and Israel will maintain responsibility for the settlers' security and the Palestinian Authority will not have powers and responsibilities in the sphere of foreign relations and will have no right to form an army or publish banknotes.

Moreover, Arafat dropped demands that the permanent status negotiations include the total application of Resolution 242 adopted in 1967 by the U.N. Security Council that calls for Israeli withdrawal from the territories it occupied in the 1967 war, recognition of all states in the area and a just settlement of the refugee problem.

Arafat claimed that the deal was the first step toward the establishment of an independent Palestinian state with East Jerusalem (Beit-ul-Moqaddas) as its capital. Israel, however, insisted that an undivided Jerusalem will remain its eternal capital.

Ten Palestinian groups denounced the agreement as a "sell out" of Palestine with the Islamic Resistance Movement (HAMAS) saying, "the Land of Palestine will never be a product to sell off and so Hamas will never be a party to any agreement in this game".

Iran also denounced Arafat for signing the deal with Israel and described it "the most grievous page" in the history of the Islamic Jihad in Palestine.

Syria and Jordan expressed "surprise" and were irritated that they were not consulted in advance about the deal. The agreement was also contrary to the negotiating rules established at the start of the peace process in Madrid that the goal was a global peace in the Middle East, which ruled out separate agreements with Israel. President Hafez al-Assad whose government neither opposed nor approved the agreement said the deal "has left everything in the hands of Israel".

In November 1995, Israeli Prime Minister and Labour Party

leader Yitzhak Rabin was gunned down in Tel Aviv by Yigal Amir, a 25-year old Jewish fanatic opposed to the PLO-Israel deal. Foreign Minister Shimon Peres took over but his Labour Party waş defeated in the May 1996 elections and the more extremist Likud Party leader Banjamin Netanyahu was elected Prime Minister.

Netanyahu rejected the principle of land-for-peace, which had been the basis of negotiations between Israel and Arab countries, pledged to develop Jewish settlements in the so-called Palestinian territories, outrightly rejected the creation of a Palestinian state, and rejected any negotiations to return the Golan Heights to Syria in exchange for peace. The U.S.-sponsored so-called peace process that was initially declared to pursue a" just and comprehensive peace" has been neither just nor comprehensive. The peace process is in shambles and the deadlock, more or less, lingers on."[12]

IRAQ

Iraq was among the Arab provinces of the Ottoman Empire which was created after the disintegration of the Sick Man of Europe in the aftermath of World War I. During the war, the land of today's modern Iraq was occupied by the British. Iraq's geo-political importance and its huge oil reserves encouraged the British to secure a foothold in Iraq. They brought Faisal, the son of Hussein Sharif Mecca, to power in Iraq and his brother Abdullah in Jordan. King Abdullah was the grandfather of King Hussein now ruling Jordan. The decision was part of London's plan to dominate the region and, therefore, they allowed the Hashimite Family to administer a part of the Hijaz and brought the Saudi Family, a rival faction in another part of the Hijaz, to power. Appointing two rival families as heads of two states was the British policy of "Divide and Rule".

Britain, since the creation of Iraq, was the key broker of power politics in the country and after the World War II it continued to exercise influence in Iraq until the Baghdad Treaty was concluded in 1955 which allowed Iraq to play a central role in the region.

At the time, King Faisal II was ruling Iraq but his Prime Minister General Nouri Saeed, a British puppet, masterminded all the affairs. I saw King Faisal several times in Shah's palace in Tehran. He was very young and polite. His nephew Abdullah managed all the court affairs. Abdullah was ten years older than Faisal himself and had established close links with the British.

Saeed was known as a powerful dictator of Iraq. He was very committed and clever. All Iraqi government officials obeyed his orders. He pretended to love the king but he did not.

Given Britain's interference in Iraq's internal affairs and Arab nationalism spreading by Egypt's Naser, anti-British sentiments grew in Iraq and the Soviets were also encouraging it. King Faisal II, together with the Crown Prince and Saeed lost their lives in the course of a coup de'tat on July 14, 1958, by units of the Iraqi Army. The coup de'tat was successfully carried out after a border dispute occurred with Syria. A Brigade led by Qassem was despatched along with Aref to the border region. As the Brigade moved out of the capital, Baghdad, instead of moving towards the border region, Qassem attacked the presidential palace and Aref the radio broadcasting station. King Faisal II and the Crown Prince Qaem Abdullah and all the royal family members were disarmed and executed. Prime Minister Saeed who had managed to escape and hide in a cave was arrested and killed. The dead bodies were pulled through the streets to show them to the people. Power was placed in the hands of a council of sovereignty exercising presidential authority and of a cabinet led by Brigadier Abdul Karim Qasem with the rank of Prime Minister. The coup in Iraq caused anxiety in the neighbouring countries including Iran and led to a strain in the relations between Iran and Iraq.

The coup was described as a pro-Soviet development in the region. The change of power in Iraq led to the expansion of Communist activities in Iraq which was regarded as very detrimental to U.S. and British interests in the region. Therefore, the United States and Britain strengthened the regimes of Iran and Jordan and simultaneously made efforts to infiltrate into the army and pave the way for the young Saddam Hussein's promotion in the later years.

A struggle for power developed between the two main architects of the July coup detat Brigadier (later General) Qassem, Prime Minister, and Colonel (later Field Marshal) Abdul Salam Mohammad Aref, the Deputy Prime Minister and Minister of Interior. Qassem's decision to transfer 95 per cent of the Iraqi oil company to the government prompted severe U.S. criticism of

Qassem's government. Subsequently, Qassem announced the withdrawal of Iraq from the Baghdad Pact on March 24, 1959.

Earlier the Communist elements in Iraq had been refused representation in the government. The coup facilitated their infiltration into the armed forces of Iraq and into the civil service. Then, Qassem began measures which would limit Communist influence inside the government and the administration of the country and later disarmed them when fightings occurred in 1959 in Iraq's Kurdestan.

In March 1961, a considerable section of the Kurdish population in northern Iraq rose in rebellion under Mustafa Barezani, leader of the Democratic Party of Kurdestan - a party established in 1958 after the return of Barezani from exile. The refusal of the central regime at Baghdad to grant the reiterated Kurdish demands for an autonomous status had contributed to bring about the insurrection.

Barezani in March 1961 proclaimed an independent Kurdish state. The Kurds consolidated their hold over much of northern Iraq during the course of 1962. The government tried to suppress the Kurds but fighting continued with no solution in sight but later subsided.

A military coup on February 8, 1963 overthrew the regime of Qassem who was captured and killed. Colonel Aref who had established connections with the Americans was raised to the office of President. Although the coup was orchestrated with the full support of CIA, the Americans did not acknowledge their involvement in the coup. Of course in 1975 it was divulged in the Senate that the CIA had hatched some coup plans to assassinate Qassem.

On April 1966 Aref was killed in a helicopter crash. His brother Major General Abdul Rahman Aref succeeded him as president.

The bloodless coup de'tat of July 17, 1968 brought down Aref and General Ahmaed Hassan Al-Bakr, a former prime minister, took over. Al-Bakr forced Aref to go into exile in Britain. The deportation of Aref to Britain strengthened the idea that he was a British agent. At the time, Saddam Hussein was the Secretary of the Revolutionary Council and Vice-President. The appointment of Al-Bakr to the post of presidency indicated that the Iraqi army did not support Saddam's leadership. Gradually Saddam's power was strengthened and soon it became clear that he was running all the affairs in the country. I have no doubt that helping Saddam, a favourite agent for America, to emerge as a dictator was planned long in advance. When Al-Bakr was president, Saddam suddenly appeared with the uniform of a four-star General, the highest military rank in the Iraqi army, and inaugurated the War University. Saddam was a civilian and his uniform angered some officers who left the ceremony in protest.

> "Relations deteriorated with Iran in the early months of 1974, when frontier fighting broke out, and it was after the appointment of a UN mediator in March that normal relations on the frontier were restored, and they deteriorated again in August. Further border clashes took place in December 1974.
>
> At the OPEC meeting at Algiers in March 1975, Saddam and the Shah signed an agreement which "completely eliminated the conflict between the two brotherly countries". The Arvand River was defined according to the Thalweg Line, which runs down the middle of the deepest shipping channel. Both countries also agreed to end "infiltrations of a subversive character", and the Kurdish rebellion collapsed. Barezani felt that he could not continue his struggle without Iran's aid and fled to Tehran."[13]

Now it should be asked why the United States encouraged termination of the Kurdish rebellion in Iraq and urged the Shah to sign the 1975 Accord with Iraq? Why did the conclusion of the treaty coincide with the increase of Saddam's power? Why and upon the advice of which party did Mohammad Reza agree to sign the important treaty with Saddam instead of President Al-Bakr? The answer to all these questions is clear. As long as Saddam, America's favourite agent, did not enjoy strong power, the Shah supported Kurds against the Baghdad government. Kurds were considered a serious threat and had won the support of one third of the army. During the conflicts, heavy losses and casualties were inflicted on the Iraqi army. In 1975 the U.S. decided to put an end to the Kurdish rebellion and, therefore, the famous 1975 Accord was signed between the Shah and Saddam with the mediation of the then Algerian President Houari Boumedienne.

The accord benefitted Saddam most and met America's interests, otherwise why did Al-Bakr himself not sign the accord. The 1975 Algiers accord compelled Iran to recall 90,000 pro-Barezani Kurds which led to the cessation of border conflicts and improved

Saddam's image before the Iraqi army. Therefore, Saddam was portrayed as a hero who put an end, although temporarily, to the Kurdish rebellion. The accord left no doubt that Saddam was a favourite American agent. Members of the Iranian delegation in Algiers told me that Saddam was flattering the Shah before and after the meeting and was begging the Shah to allow him to kiss his hand.

Saddam's pro-U.S. role was further revealed when the idea of an Iraq-Syria alliance was put forward. It was believed that Al-Bakr backed the idea and therefore the Syrian President Hafez Al-Assad flew to Baghdad. It was clear that unity between Iraq and Syria would serve the interests of the Soviets and both the U.S. and Britain opposed the idea.

The chief of MI-6 station at the British Embassy in Tehran explicitly told me that the British government backed an independent Iraq and opposed any alliance between Iraq and Syria. Saddam, upon the advice of Washington, disrupted the plan and politely saw off Assad with empty hands at the airport. Later, Saddam put Al-Bakr under house arrest under the pretext of him being physically weak and murdered pro-Syrian Bath Party members and declared himself president in 1978. The rapid developments left no doubt that Western intelligence services were behind the affairs in Iraq. I have already explained about Israel's extra-territorial bases and its activities in Iraq. After Qassem's coup in 1958, Israel paid particular attention to Iraq and engineered long term plans to achieve its objectives.

From 1975 onwards, Saddam who had successfully dealt with a Kurdish uprising, began to exterminate Communist party members. The Communists in Iraq were not powerful and sought reconciliation with the government. Whenever the central government put them under pressure they appealed to Barezani or turned to the government when the pressure was relaxed and, therefore, failed to win the support of the people. The government also began to reinforce the army. The army's intelligence reported that although Iran acted as a policeman in the region with high military spending, Iraq allocated more of its budget to strengthening its army than Iran. In 1978 Iraq possessed eight Divisions and two or three independent Brigades and 75,000 military personnel, nearly more than half of that of Iran's.

Upon the advice of the U.S., Iraq, during these years, played the role of a hardline Arab state against Israel and pretended to sacrifice itself for the Arab cause in order to be identified as a popular country. At the same time, Iraq adopted a policy of intimidation in the Persian Gulf region. Reports from the 7th Department of Savak indicated that Iraq was acting very imprudently in the Arab littoral states and had despatched forces to create fear and turmoil there.

In 1978, the tiny Arab states feared the power of Iraq while Iraqis treated Iranians in the Arab states with great respect. Iraq repeatedly lay claim to the Kuwaiti Bubayan island but it was rejected by Kuwait and other Arab states. Iraq after a few years failed in its attempt to annex the island which is close to Basra, Iraq's only outlet to the Persian Gulf, to its territory and subsequently requested Kuwait to allow her to rent the island. Again, Kuwait turned down Iraq's demand but the dispute caused animosity between the two neighbours. If the annexation had come about, Iraq's marine facilities would have been increased and more ships could have anchored at its ports.

> "In the days of Nuri Said and the Hashemites, all Iraq's ambition were directed westwards, towards Syria, and towards realization of the dream of a single Fertile Crescent state which should unite the rival Umayyad and Abbasid capitals of Damascus and Baghdad. But after the revolution in Iran and Egypt's signing of a peace treaty with Israel in 1979, the centre of gravity had moved away from Mediterranean to the (Persian) Gulf, away from the Suez Canal to the Straits of Hormuz, and it was southwards and not westwards that the leaders of Iraq were directing their attention.
>
> Saddam who was now desperate for supremacy in the Middle East felt that he had a leading role to play in the Arab world and realized or better to say was made to realize by the Americans that perhaps the Persian Gulf rather than the Mediterranean was the area in which that role was to be played...
>
> The agreement signed in Algiers in 1975 between Saddam Hussein and the Shah was supposed to settle all outstanding problems between the two countries. It did, in fact, resolve what had become Iraq's most urgent problem, the war in Kurdestan. When the revolution took place in Iran, Saddam felt it was the time for him to play his expected role."[14]

So, by 1978 Iraq under Saddam Hussein was able to fill the

vacuum left by Mohammad Reza's downfall and play the role of the policeman in the region for several purposes. First, it could block the infiltration of the Soviet Union into the Arab states. Second, Iraq could maintain its reputation as a leading Arab nation against Israel and, therefore, ensure the West's control over Arab nationalism and finally prevent the spread of the Islamic revolution in the regional countries by provoking Arab sentiments. These objectives encouraged Saddam to play his role as the policeman.

> "As early as September 1979, Israeli intelligence reports from Baghdad had warned that Iraq was preparing for a full-scale invasion of Iran. Baghdad's aim was to annex the oil-rich Province of Khuzestan, which runs along the Persian Gulf to Iraq. And Baghdad had reason to be confident - it saw the Iranian military in a state of disintegration. Most of the generals and admirals had either escaped Iran or been executed...
>
> On September 2, 1980, the Iraqis attacked southern Iran in the first big border clash, the precursor to the all-out offensive that began on September 22. Saddam Hussein had decided that he should establish his control over Arvand River (Shatt Al-Arab), the confluence of the Tigris and Euphrates rivers in Iraq and the Karun river of Iran, and then go on to take over the oil fields in Khuzestan. Iraqi troops poured into Iran, but the Iraqi army was not as good as we had feared. Their airforce was also ineffective in its attempts to destroy Iranian air force bases. The Iraqis quickly became bogged down by a surprisingly good defensive campaign launched by the Iranian military and volunteers."[15]

Saddam was of the opinion that either Iran will suffer an internal collapse, or the newly established Islamic government will be defeated and that he would detach Khuzestan from Iran before there could be any Iranian resistance. Iraq launched a full-scale invasion of Iran with Saudi Arabia's financial assistance estimated at $90 billion dollars deposited in American and European banks.

In my opinion Iraq's invasion of Iran brought the following benefits to the U.S.:

— The check of the spread of the Islamic Revolution in Iraq and other regional countries.

— The suppression of the Shiite uprising in Iraq.
— The strengthening of Israel's position and its recognition by Arab states.
— The sale of expensive weapons to the rich Arab states.
— It caused some Arab countries especially Saudi Arabia, Kuwait, UAE etc. to be further dependent on the United States.
— It created solidarity and ethnic unity between Arabs against Iran and the Shiite movement in the region, and, therefore, weakened the anti-Israel Arab solidarity.
— Egypt was re-admitted to the Arab League after its expulsion for signing the 1979 Camp David peace treaty with Israel.

Iraq had about 300 to 350 fighters less than Iran and had about 1,800 armoured vehicles. Iran had 2,400. The only superiority the Iraqi army had against Iran was its combat preparedness which it had gained during the conflicts with its own Kurdish population. The Iranian army's unpreparedness could be witnessed during riots in Fars Province. Moreover, Iraq possessed a paramilitary army comprising three units that could be employed to protect the cities. As a matter of fact, Iraq possessed the most powerful army among the Arab states.

"Saddam Hussein who was hoping to capture Tehran in a matter of days gradually lost all the territory it had occupied in the early months of his occupation of Iranian territory. After eight years of a devastating war, Iran and Iraq agreed to a UN-brokered ceasefire in August 1988 but are yet to sign a formal peace treaty.

On the basis of Paragraph 6 of the United Nations Security Council Resolution 598, the then U.N. Secretary General Javier Perez de Cuellar, in a report to the council in December 1991, declared Iraq the initiator of the war with Iran.

Having failed in his war with Iran, Saddam Hussein turned his gun toward a tiny but wealthy neighbour that had financed Baghdad's military machine during its aggression against Iran. On August 2, 1990, Iraqi troops invaded Kuwait, and Saddam Hussein annexed it to his territory as Iraq's 19th province.

In February 1991, a U.S.-led multinational force evicted Iraq from Kuwait by force, and the United Nations imposed crippling sanctions on the country, further adding to the suffering of the Iraqi people."

"If Saddam Hussein did not exist, we would have to invent him. He is the linchpin of American policy in the Mideast. Without him, Washington would be stumbling in the desert sands... Since the United States needs to maintain a long-term policy as the region's balancer, it needs allies abroad and public support at home. The existence of Saddam Hussein immeasurably help both tasks. If not for Saddam, would the Saudi royal family, terrified of being seen as an American protectorate (which in a sense it is), allow American troops on their soil? Would Kuwait house more than 300,000 pieces of American combat hardware, kept in readiness should the need arise? ... With enemies like him, who needs friends? ... But imagine the situation without Saddam Hussein. Had the United States "finished the job, "gone to Baghdad and deposed Saddam Hussein, it would first have had the unenviable task of governing - or being responsible for - Iraq, with its Kurdish rebellion in the North and its Shi'ite rebellion in the South. Saddam is able to manage this because he is a rapacious dictator who runs a police state... He is an evil man who runs an evil regime, with particularly tragic consequences for the Iraqi people. But a post-Saddam world would have its own thorny problems. His successors would be no angels. The immidiate beneficiary would be Iran. And most important, without Saddam Hussein to worry about, anti-Americanism would grow in Arab streets - and also in Arab palaces... With all its problems, a Middle East with a defanged but still threatening Saddam helps secure American interests."[16]

OMAN

The Sultanate of Oman occupies the southeastern coast of the Arabian peninsula. By 1971, Britain was due to pull out its forces from the Persian Gulf and decided to officially delegate the responsibility of providing security to the region to Iran's Shah. The decision was put into effect in the same year and Iran, receiving America and Britain's prior permission, took over control of the islands of Abu Musa, the Greater and Lesser Tunbs and was, therefore, allowed enough bases to provide security to the region.

During the period, the Shah was very proud of himself and the sudden hike in oil prices which brought huge oil revenues for Iran doubled Shah's ambitions.

For some years there had been a smouldering Marxist-oriented rebellion in the Dhofar region of Oman bordering South Yemen since 1967 by the Popular Front for the Liberation of Oman (PFLO). In 1972 the new young Sultan of Oman, Qabus ibn Said, who had come to power in July 1970 as a result of a British-inspired coup which ousted his father, began an offensive against the rebels. Qabus, who had been trained in Britain at the Royal Military Academy, had brought additional British personnel and equipment into Oman's armed forces to help put down the rebellion. Britain which was pulling out from the region left only a symbolic force and delegated its responsibility for crushing the Dhofar rebels to Mohammad Reza.

Dhofar, a fertile region in southern Oman bordering the then Marxist South Yemen, is separated from the rest of Oman by several hundred miles of open desert. Three coterminous mountain ranges from a crescent in Dhofar around a long, narrow, coastal plain on which is located the provincial capital of Salalah.

In 1973 Iranian troops with the capacity of three Brigades entered the conflict on the side of the Sultan. The Shah was glad that the world should see that the policeman was on the job. The Iranian forces attacked the rebels with artillery, mortar fire and by air attacks while the rebels possessed only light weapons. By December 1975 the plain around Salalah had been freed from the threat of attack, the mountains were cleared of rebel activity, and the rebellion was crushed after an all-out offensive against the insurgents.

In a propaganda move to show that the region was secure, Oman invited Prince Abdul Reza for hunting in the Dhofar region. Soon after the elimination of the rebels, Sultan Qabus invited the Shah to officially visit Oman. Before the Shah's visit, Khatami, commander of the counter-intelligence of the Royal Guard who was also a SIB officer travelled to Oman to make preparations for Mohammad Reza's visit. There was a marvelous red-carpet welcome accorded to the Shah in Muscat. During the visit Mohammad Reza and Qabus visited the Dhofar region, the birth place of the Sultan, as two conquerors.

No reports were sent to the SIB on the army's operations in Oman and the chief of staff of the army personally informed the Shah of the developments in the Dhufar region. The operations were not classified and the files may be available in the army headquarters.

Fig. 36: Two Americans taken hostage after their Embassy was stormed by Islamic militants on November 4, 1980. They were held for 444 days. The crisis brought down the Carter administration

Fig. 37: Two militants inside the U.S. Embassy compound carry garbage in a U.S. flag

Fig. 38: U.S. Embassy officials destroyed some, not all, of the sensitive communication equipment and documents. Students who seized the Embassy in November 1980 put the shred of papers together. The documents were later published confirming Washington's efforts to prevent the victory of the revolution, identifying CIA agents in Iran, etc.

Fig. 39: Draped in a red, white and green flag of Iran with monarchial symbols, Shah's coffin lies in state in the Abdin palace, Cairo in August 1980. "I am fed up with living artificially. I don't want to live like Tito," the 60-year-old Shah had said shortly before his death from complications of lymphatic cancer two days earlier

Chapter 8

Revolution and Fall of Dynasty

A REVIEW OF THE REVOLUTION

In 1978, Iran appeared to be stable and the Shah seemed to be firmly in control. The Shah was assured of the West's support especially that of America and Britain. The Soviets had also recognized his stay in power and had established cordial relations with his government.

After the 19 August 1953 coup until 1978, Mohammad Reza was the undisputable ruler of Iran and the American policy was designed to back his dictatorial regime.

As stated in the previous chapters, the British believed that Iran's geo-political position strongly required a monarchical system of government. It was believed that Iran with a 2,200-kilometre joint border with the Soviet Union and a long history required a monarchical regime in order to guarantee the government's stability against any Communist penetration. A Republican regime could provide an opportunity for a leftist candidate to win the polls with Soviet assistance and put the country at the disposal of the Soviet Union. Even if this did not happen, the West would have had to fund presidential elections in Iran while the existence of a monarchical regime eliminated any external threat or effort to destabilize the government. That was why the Americans supported Mohammad Reza's reinstatement on 19 August; otherwise, they would have installed a military dictator like Teimur Bakhteyar to rule the country as they did in South America and South East Asian countries. It was on the basis of this British analysis that after the Second World War monarchical regimes were set up in Iraq, Jordan and Saudi Arabia.

Mohammad Reza was confident that his monarchical rule would continue for a long time. In 1970 in a letter to Empress Farah, the regent and Jam, chief of staff of the army, wrote that the armed forces after him should be supervised by Farah. At the time, the Crown Prince Reza had not reached the legal age to take charge. All military and civilian high-ranking government officials were ordered to show up at Shah's Palace regularly and explain their responsibilities to Reza and Farah. Reza was very reluctant to listen but Farah was very keen to know everything from top to bottom. The main reason behind such briefings was to help Farah and Reza prepare themselves for future leadership.

The Jam affair occurred and the Shah ousted him from his post and also annulled his order about Farah's future supervision of the armed forces. Why? Because Mohammad Reza was very skeptical about his successor and had pinned many hopes on his monarchical rule. Later, Crown Prince Reza was sent to the United States to undergo flight training at the U.S. air base in Texas. The Crown Prince was accompanied by Brigadier General Khatami on his trip. Upon arrival home, Khatami disclosed that in addition to flight training American professors were invited to teach him politics. Richard Helms, who had just completed his mission to Iran as ambassador, was among the instructors invited to teach Reza.

The Shah was satisfied with the internal situation, so were his major allies the United States and Britain. Only two years before the revolution, a writer in a book written in English surprisingly predicted the downfall of the Shah. In 1979, no one including myself took the prediction seriously.

In 1977, the responsible bodies did not feel that a revolution was imminent until nation-wide demonstrations spread and domestic turmoil broke out. Western governments and even the Soviet Union and China strongly believed that the Shah was stable and his government was described the "island of stability". I am quite sure that the British and American Embassy staff members whom I had talked to had not even the inkling that the Shah's regime was on the verge of collapse and a revolution was soon to happen.[1]

The election of Jimmy Carter as President of the United States in November 1976 came as a blow to the Shah. During the U.S. presidential campaign, the Shah extended his political and financial assistance to the Republicans. The Shah, in his many years of dealing with U.S. presidents, had always had more success with

Republicans than with Democrats, so he could not welcome the shifts in parties.

The personal and official ties that Richard Nixon and Henry Kissinger had woven with the Shah were unique. However, it was evident that the U.S. under Carter had no visible strategic alternative to a close relationship with Iran. Consequently, the Carter Administration devoted considerable efforts during its first year to reassure the Shah that there was no intent to alter the basic nature of the relationship.

The use of torture and political persecution had become commonplace during the 70s. The feared SAVAK was given full powers to identify and intimidate political opponents of the Shah. The critical reporting of organizations such as Amnesty International drew public attention in the U.S. to Shah's repressive policies against the opposition. The Shah who was very sensitive to the growing tide of uncomplimentary reporting in the U.S. media responded positively to Carter's calls for reforms to the level that criticisms by the world public opinion against the Shah and America's policy in the Middle East diminished. The Shah was not ready to jeopardize Iran's relations with its biggest foreign supporter.

The Shah's decision to introduce limited reforms must also be interpreted as a measure intended to preserve the half century of Pahlavi rule into future. The reforms did not bear any fruits. Mohammad Reza seeing Prime Minister Hoveida was not favoured by the Americans forced him to resign and introduced Jamshid Amuzegar as his successor announcing that he wanted to give the people more liberty. With his implicit agreement, moderate opponents formed the "human rights society". The British also confirmed Carter's reform plans for Iran and shared with him the view that it was time to create some variety in the "island of stability". The introduction of the reforms, however, led to a reconciliation between the Shah and Carter.

Public discontent and massive protests were on the rise but were largely ignored by the government. No responsible body was willing to seriously deal with the situation. It was 1953 uprising that was resurfacing in 1977 but this time it was more powerful. There were extreme corruption in higher circles, prices were skyrocketing, inflation roared along at an annual rate of 40 to 50 per cent, and food production had come to a halt as a result of

Shah's White Revolution. The Shah had distributed land to the peasants to keep them happy but he had destroyed their life support systems. Shah's attention was on the military, not food production. Industrialization consisted mainly assembly plants for foreign-made parts. And Iran, once self-sufficient in food, became one of the world's largest food importers. By 1978 most supplies were being imported. Non-profiting and expensive projects allowed a few to make huge embezzlements and caused inflation in the country. The economic policies of the Shah attracted villagers to cities in search for jobs. Ceremonial charges including the 2500-year celebrations, Shiraz art ceremonies and pointless invitations extended to foreign heads of state as well as the purchase of expensive weapons returned the oil revenues to the British and American companies and the Shah did not bother to trouble himself about the charges.

In 1973, the price of crude oil hiked four-fold. As the nation's wealth increased, the Shah grew more convinced of his own infallibility and as his image of himself grew, he stopped consulting even his closest advisors. When I told him the realities, my words fell on deaf ears.[2]

Another reality Mohammad Reza failed to understand was the increasing influence of the clergy. After the 5 June 1963, Moqaddam, the then Chief of SAVAK, stepped up efforts to keep the government informed of the situation in the theological schools and though the Shah was aware of Ayatollah Khomeini's influence and his opposition to the government, he was convinced that the links already set up with the so-called influential ulema and the bribespaid to them would help SAVAK win their support.

SAVAK attributed any opposition to the Communists and certain political dissidents, whereas in reality Iranians always seek refuge from suppression in mosques and holy shrines and appeal to the clergy for support. Therefore, the people sided with those clerics who defended their rights against the ruling despots and not those who came to terms with them. You may be surprised to learn that I had similar sentiments though I was not oppressed throughout my life. Anyhow, in my childhood, when I lived with my family in Khaniabad, south Tehran, I learned that people respected the clergy. In our neighbourhood Seyed Mahmoud, a local cleric, was the most respected man. When Reza Shah's agents defrocked Seyed, he became more popular. Whenever I learned that a clergyman had met Mohammad Reza, willingly or unwillingly, I hated him. I was not happy in my heart with those who received Shah's representatives and I did not hold such clerics in esteem. The Shah also did not respect them because he was aware that they were grovelling to him and were very shallow minded.

SAVAK estimated the total population of clergymen in Iran to be about 350,000. Badei, Chief of SAVAK Bureau in Qom, believed that Ayatollah Khomeini enjoyed the greatest influence in the holy city. There was no need for the clergy to make preparations for their establishment since they were scattered all over the country and showed up in remote villages where perhaps some people did not know the Shah. Shahpour J. had earlier acknowledged that in Iran no government had been able to survive without enjoying the support of the clergymen. But Mohammad Reza felt strong enough to deal with the public discontent and the growing influence of the celrgymen. He held the strongest army in the Middle East and SAVAK had the government and Upper and Lower Houses (Parliaments) under watch and had many lackeys in the country. The United States and Britain were also convinced that Iran's strong army was able to secure the government's stability.[3]

The revolution broke out and everyone was taken by surprise. How did the revolution happen? I am sure no former government official was able to answer this question because the occurrence of the revolution was not tangible. Some officials, including myself felt that a new phenomenon had come into existence but had not emerged overtly.

I received at least 10,000 reports on nationwide demonstrations and clashes in the streets, all of which were passed on to the Shah. Comprehensive reports reached me but I only skimmed through without paying too much attention.

Revolutions have always happened within a few days with swift and heavy clashes while the revolution in Iran took place gradually. In Iran people did not appeal to violence and a policy of attrition was adopted until it finally led to victory. No revolution has a similar record and usually those who mastermind revolutions consider that to prolong one would cause its failure, while the Iranian revolution happened within nine months.

RESIGNATION OF HOVEIDA AND AMUZEGAR'S PREMIERSHIP

Amir Abbass Hoveida served the Shah as Prime Minister for nearly 13 years and as Court Minister for one year more. While in power, Prime Minister Hoveida once called me to his office to discuss financial embezzlements. He said the Shah had told him that financial misappropriations had increased in governmental departments.

"Did you not expect such things to occur?" I inquired.

"Certainly not", he answered.

"So, why did you not carry out the plan prepared by the SIB on key posts with Shah's recommendations?" I asked.

He agreed he had made mistakes and promised to consult the Shah in future. I also explained to him that a prime condition for assuming a key post was honesty and that a corrupt minister was equivalent to a corrupt ministry.

"You have labelled the case of ministers who embezzled millions of tumans as dead records but persecuted clerks who appropriated small sums of money," I said to him.

Our conversation took place at a time when U.S. presidential elections were underway. The telephone rang and our conversation was interrupted. Hoveida talked on the telephone briefly and then turned to me and said sadly that Jimmy Carter had won the elections.

"We have to pack up our bags and leave," he whispered.

Hoveida was disappointed because both the Shah and he had fallen victims to the misreadings of Ardashir Zahedi, Iran's Ambassador to Washington.

Zahedi and Alam had encouraged the Shah and Hoveida to help fund the U.S. presidential elections. The Shah gave large sums of petro-dollars to Zahedi to propagate for the Republican candidate Richard Nixon. However, Zahedi shared the money with Alam and spent it on travelling and enjoying himself. By accident, Nixon defeated his Democrat rival in the elections and the Shah thought his initiatives had helped Nixon win the elections! The Shah's supposition that billions of dollars spent by U.S. firms in the presidential elections did not affect the results and his 40-50 million dollars of assistance affected the outcome of the polls showed Mohammad Reza's vanity and not Zahedi or Alam's cleverness.

Anyhow, Shah's contribution to the elections further improved his relations with Nixon. Later, the Watergate scandal broke out and Nixon stepped down and Gerald Ford succeeded him.

In the next term, Alam and Zahedi again encouraged the Shah and Hoveida to throw their backing to the Republican candidate Gerald Ford and again millions of dollars were allocated for propagating for the Republican nominee. This time, the Democratic candidate Jimmy Carter won the elections. Carter's victory angered both the Shah and Hoveida.

The Shah and Hoveida's intervention in U.S. elections dissatisfied the Democrats. Mohammad Reza in a bid to appease Carter dismissed Hoveida and introduced Jamshid Amuzegar as prime minister and promised to allow political liberty at home. Amuzegar for long had been seeking the post of premiership and in fact he deserved the post.

When Carter took office, American secret bulletins which I had been receiving for years stopped coming to me. The American press were not writing in Shah's favour. The Carter administration accused Iran of abusing human rights and put the Iranian government under pressure. A delegation arrived in Iran to visit the prisons. An informed source in SAVAK told me that a few of the 3,000 political prisoners who could create trouble were temporarily taken to other prisons. The walls were painted and preparations were made for the visit. Both Richard Helms, Washington's ambassador to Iran and George Ball, Carter's representative, accompanied the delegation. It was believed that Helms had given a pro-Shah report and Ball prepared a report confirming the allegations about the violation of human rights in Iran and Carter reportedly sided with Ball.

Human rights delegations made a number of other visits to Iran but criticisms ceased after Amuzegar took office as prime minister. The change of post satisfied Washington and Hoveida received the post of Court Minister.

Amuzegar, who enjoyed the support of Democrats, felt he enjoyed a strong position and when criticisms on human rights stopped, the U.S. and Britain resumed supporting the Shah as before. Amuzegar who was appointed a few weeks after the victory of Carter in U.S. elections remained in office for more than a year. The relations between Tehran and Washington became very friendly. Iran's purchases from the U.S. exceeded 40 billion dollars.

Iran signed two contracts with France and four with Germany to set up nuclear plants.

Amuzegar felt his position secure and did not worry about his future just as Americans and Britons who were not aware of Shah's destabilized situation did not worry either. He felt no threats from the clergy and therefore after he assumed office he cut the budget allocated for establishing relations with the clergymen. He said, "I do not pay for nothing."

Relations with the Carter administration improved and the Shah was officially invited to visit the U.S. in November 1977 in order to remove all misunderstandings. In the week before his arrival, tens of thousands of demonstrators opposed to Shah's government poured into the U.S. capital. Wearing masks to prevent identification by SAVAK, they gathered and chanted anti-Shah slogans in the streets surrounding the White House. Zahedi proposed to invite some 10,000 pro-Shah students to Washington during Shah's stay in the U.S. He again deceived the Shah and received a lot of money to pay for hotels, food and facilities for the students. Zahedi only invited some 500 students some of whom did not dare to go out of their hotels for fear of being beaten by opposition students.[4]

During the welcome ceremony, Carter stood by the Shah before the demonstrators and shook hands with him to show that he would back the Shah's government despite the protest.

About six weeks later, President Carter and his wife returned Shah's visit and arrived in Tehran on New Year's Eve and New Year's Day.[5] When the domestic situation in Iran got tense, the Shah made efforts to get Carter involved in Iran's domestic unrest hoping his mediation would put an end to the turmoil. Now, one has to ask, "was Carter able to save the Shah?" No. When the people did not support the Shah, what could the Carter administration do?

The situation in the capital was extraordinarily hectic. The government-controlled *Ettela'at* newspaper, on January 7, 1978 published an article ridiculing Ayatollah Khomeini (soon known as Imam Khomeini). This event came two months after the mysterious death by SAVAK of Ayatollah's elder son, Mostafa. It also coincided with the religious fervour associated with the end of the holy month of Moharram and also happened to be about one week after Carter's visit to Tehran.[6]

Two days after the article appeared, a demonstration was organized in Qom. The police opened fire, killing a number of people. The revolution had begun.

In Shi'ite Islam, a religious ceremony is traditionally held forty days after a death. The shootings in Qom set off a series of demonstrations at forty-day intervals throughout much of 1978, eventually culminating in Shah's departure.

The fortieth day after the Qom shootings was February 18. On that occasion violence broke out in Tabriz, the capital of the northwest Province of East Azerbaijan. Forty days later there were again demonstrations and violence in cities throughout Iran.

Amuzegar reluctantly left office and Sharif-Emami was brought in the hope that he may save the regime.

CONTACT WITH THE CLERGY

The first option exercised by the Shah's regime to confront the clergy was to set up a bureau at the Court to deal with the mullahs. Court Minister Hoveida was in charge of the bureau and he devoted all his activities to establishing relations with certain figures at theological schools.

It was winter of 1977 and Hoveida was living in Teimur Bakhteyar's well-decorated house, next to Sa'adabad Palace. Bakhteyar once invited me to his royal-style beautiful house for a lunch. I was ushered to the second floor. Hoveida greeted me and said he was waiting for Amuzegar. Within minutes, Prime Minister Amuzegar showed up with a smile. Hoveida said that he would talk about an important issue after lunch and, therefore, we chatted on miscellaneous affairs. After lunch Hoveida touched upon the main topic for discussion and said that the Shah had ordered that influential clergymen be recognized officially and be supported against Khomeini in an attempt to undermine the unity of the clerics.

Hoveida first asked me if I had any proposals. I reminded him that he himself had relations with Ayatollah Shariatmadari and he accepted this and then asked Amuzegar for comments. Amuzegar said without hesitation that only one top clergyman had to be contacted and he would discuss all the matters with other clergymen. "I personally respect Ayatollah Khoi", said Amuzegar. Hoveida agreed and asked Amuzegar to contact Khoi and added that he would not approach Shariatmadari unless no improvement was achieved. Amuzegar agreed to get in touch with Ayatollah Khoi who was residing in Najaf, Iraq. A few weeks later, Islamineya disclosed that Hoveida had still kept up links with Shariatmadari meaning that Amuzegar had failed to win Khoi's support. Hoveida established relations with some other clergymen and merchants and spent money in attempts to undermine the activities of the cerlgymen. Sometimes letters reached me complaining that some were paid more than others. Deputy Court Minister Behbahanian who was in charge of financial affairs time and again travelled to Qom with a suitcase full of money to meet Shariatmadari. Hedayat Islamineya was another member at the court who was active at the bureau.

Islamineya for some time was in charge of Tehran Chamber of Commerce. He was a good friend of Nasiri who introduced Islamineya to me. Later, differences between the two erupted and they cut relations. Islamineya sought friendship with Sheikh Bahai who for sometime was the chief of Chamber of Commerce. Islamineya, a native of the northern Mazandaran Province, possessed a beautiful villa in Varyan, in suburbs of Karaj next to a lake. He used to spend holidays there sailing on the lake in his own boat. I, along with other friends, often joined him at his villa.

He had established cordial relations with some clergymen in Qom and had friends in Tehran bazaar. On holidays, Islamineya talked about his plans and his meetings with Hoveida. He acknowledged that they had discussed the domestic situation and that Hoveida had briefed him on how to behave with the clergymen. Then Islamineya went to Qom and conveyed Hoveida's message to Shariatmadari which mostly centered on how to ease the tension.

Shariatmadari always gave the same answer saying that he hoped the situation would return to normal and that nothing would threaten the Shah if he gave more powers to the government and did not interfere in trivial matters. The meetings, twice a week, were aimed at improving the Shah's morale. Islamineya disclosed that Shariatmadari was making efforts to win the support of other clergymen urging them to join him. The meetings continued until the victory of the revolution. He, however, kept up his links with those merchants who promised to urge others to help keep order in the bazaar.

SHARIF-EMAMI, CHIEF OF FREEMASONS

After the protest rally in the last weeks of Amuzegar's premiership, the situation became tense but still the regime's imminent fall could not be predicted. American and British representatives shuttled between Tehran and their capitals expressing support for the Shah's government.

Only in March within a six-day period, Frederic Mally the then British Defense Secretary, U.S. Republican presidential nominee Ronald Reagan and leader of the British Conservative Party Margaret Thatcher visited Tehran. Despite the West's strong diplomatic support for the Shah, more people poured into the streets to voice their dissatisfaction with the government. Gradually, the people openly called for the fall of the regime. The Shah was adviced to take serious measures in order to satisfy the public and he felt that one of the answers was to dispose of Amuzegar and allow Jafar Sharif-Emami to take over as premier.

Sharif-Emami took over in July with a policy of "national reconciliation". He had been Prime Minister briefly in the early 1960s. He was expected to have become more experienced and professional over the years. He was still confident, calm and strong both physically and mentally. Sharif-Emami, born in a religious family, was chief of Freemasons in Iran.

He introduced some plans aimed at pacifying the people. He promised freedom of political participation to opposition parties, abandoned the imperial calendar (which calculated years from the time of Cyrus the Great) in favour of the Islamic calendar (which began with the holy Prophet Mohammad's flight from Mecca in 622 A.D.) forgetting that he had previously praised the change of calendar into the imperial, closed gambling casinos and some other gregarious symbols of westernization but his programme failed to gain support or credibility.[7]

The new Prime Minister himself was viewed as a loyal courtier and was generally believed to have shared in the corrupt practices of the past. His political manoeuvres were regarded by the opposition as a cynical appeasement effort and by his supporters as an admission of weakness and vulnerability.

JALEH SQUARE MASSACRE

The opposition had begun a direct challenge to the new government of Sharif-Emami on September 4 and 5 with two very large demonstrations in Tehran celebrating the end of Ramadan. The government refused permission for these marches but did not interfere. The opposition leaders pressed for outright confrontation with the government and called a general strike. The government responded by imposing martial law in Tehran and 11 more cities. The new rules were announced in the evening of September 7 and did not receive much publicity until early the following morning.[8]

On Thursday September 7, there were reports confirming that the people were preparing to take part in a massive demonstration in Jaleh Sqaure, south Tehran, the following morning. September 8 was Friday, a holiday in Iran. As usual, I was with Islamineya at his villa in the suburbs of Karaj. I was informed of the bloody confrontation by telephone. My secretary at SIB told me that thousands of people had begun to congregate in Jaleh Sqaure for a rally from the early morning. Troops at the site ordered the crowds to disperse. When they refused, soldiers opened fire on the crowd. The gunfire by the troops went on and on, and scattered firefights continued throughout Tehran for the remainder of the day. For each demonstrator the troops shot down another sprung up to fill the gap. The confrontation meant that Sharif-Emami's "national reconciliation" plan had totally failed.

All previous clashes between the government and the opposition paled into insignificance in comparison with this bloody event which went down in the history as the "Black Friday".

Both the U.S. and Britain backed the decision and again encouraged the Shah to resist the opposition.. At the end of the day, the Shah, after a survey of the city by helicopter, said that his capital looked like a wasteland.

I believed that such measures would aggravate the situation. Employment of the army to quell the uprising could not be justified. How was it possible to convince the clergy and the bazaar merchants not to support Ayatollah Khomeini. A few hours later, I telephoned my office and asked my secretary to invite all members of the First-Grade Co-ordination Council to attend a meeting at nine the next morning in order to discuss the situation. Oweisi who was not a member of the council but was Tehran's Military Commander was also invited to the meeting.

The next morning, the council went into deliberations. I told the meeting that the nation-wide demonstrations were religiously-motivated and soldiers would not easily open fire on their brethren. I also explained that army's intervention would gradually weaken the army's status and that soldiers would eventually start to join the people. I urged that the police should be the ones to intervene and that the army should be used only as a backup. I rejected proposals which called for an "iron fist" policy in order to suppress the people.

Both the Shah and Sharif-Emami believed that all the crisis stemmed from government's financial embezzlements and if these were promptly seen to, public discontent would settle down. Only at that time did Mohammad Reza review thousands of records which had been previously put aside. It was clear that the American and British ambassadors had advised him to do this and the Shah was convinced that the initiative would solve the problems. I carried out his order but it did not stop the momentum of the revolution.

As long as marshal law was enforced, street clashes continued to take place. I suggested that marshal law be lifted. Oweisi, Commander of Ground Force, was responsible for supervising the marshal law and the evening curfew. Oweisi, who always had a holy Qoran in his pocket, swore on it that he would back my proposal. He regretted the September 8 killings. He blamed the shootings on Badrei, Commander of the Imperial Guard because, he said, Badrei had ordered the soldiers to open fire on the crowd. Oweisi said his orders had been for the army not to open fire on the demonstrators. Reports confirmed that Badrei had convinced the Shah that the dispatch of army troops to Jaleh Square was essential and with Shah's approval, troops were dispatched and the catastrophic incident occurred. Except Oweisi, other members of the council did not support my view. Marshal law remained in force and Oweisi changed his approach. He telephoned the clergy in every city and asked their views about the commander in charge of the marshal law in their cities and if they complained he fired the respective commander. He sacked two commanders in Mashhad until a third one satisfied the clergymen whom he was in touch with in the province.

The Shah was convinced that if the army was deployed in the streets, protest rallies would stop while I was sure that army troops would gradually join the people if they stayed any longer in the streets. If military units were deployed in streets at certain hours and then returned to their barracks, certainly the situation would have been different. The main problem was that the demonstrations were religiously-motivated and since people of all walks of life were involved, there were no solutions and the army could not stop them.

Top military leaders did not represent the army, the real army was made up of soldiers and officers who were reluctant to fire on the demonstrators.

Until strikes began, Iran was the second largest oil exporter in the world, after Saudi Arabia, supplying some five million barrels per day to the international oil markets, excluding 500,000 to 800,000 barrels per day consumed within Iran. By early November, strikes and political turmoil in the oil fields had reduced Iran's exports to less than a million barrels per day, effectively withdrawing up to four million barrels a day from the international markets just as the heavy winter demand was beginning. The situation had become critical.

Sharif-Emami in a meeting with U.S. ambassador Sullivan and British ambassador Parsons had said that the Shah was incapable of making any decision and he himself concluded that the crisis was developing and that a military government was required.

AYATOLLAH KHOMEINI EXILED TO PARIS

By September it had become unmistakably clear that Ayatollah Khomeini, from his residence in exile in nearby Iraq, was not only inspiring opposition to the Shah's regime but was in fact orchestrating the rebellion (confrontation). The steady stream of Iranian pilgrims to the holy city of Najaf came back armed with cassettes of the Ayatollah's latest sermons attacking the Shah, along with new instructions that were quickly translated into action through the network of mosques.

The Shah's government found this intolerable and prevailed on the Iraqis to clamp down. The secular Iraqi leaders probably required little persuasion, since they had to fear the effects of a militant uprising of their own Shi'i inhabitants, who comprised more than half of the Iraqi population. On September 23, Iraqi forces surrounded the Ayatollah's house, severely limiting access to him.

During the first week of October, Khomeini yielded to the pressure and attempted to leave Iraq. At first he attempted to go to Kuwait. I learned of this when I received an urgent telephone call from Richard Cottam, who informed me that Khomeini and his party had cleared the border post in Iraq but were refused entrance into Kuwait. Iraq then refused to permit them to cross back, and the entire party was trapped in the no man's land between the two border posts...

Eventually Khomeini and his party were permitted to return to Baghdad, where they took a plane to Paris on October 6. The French government permitted them to enter, reportedly after consulting with Iran. (He settled in the small house of Neauphle-le-Chateau, twenty miles west of Paris). French officials subsequently insisted that Iranian officials seemed entirely unperturbed by the Ayatollah's arrival in Paris and made no effort to intervene. In fact, the Iranians (Shah's government) seemed to have calculated that the Ayatollah's great distance from Iran, without access to the steady flow of religious pilgrims, would make it much more difficult for him to influence events. That proved to be a colossal - and ultimately fatal - error...

The immediate effect of Khomeini's flight to Paris was a new outburst of demonstrations in Iran. As October wore on and the forty-day mourning date of the Jaleh deaths approached, conditions deteriorated throughout the country...[9]

After the September 8 massacre it was evident that the martial law had failed and that the Shah adopted new policies in confronting the people. Court Minister Hoveida was removed from his post on September 9 and arrested on October 29. The Rastakhiz Party was dissolved on September 24. The riot police did not have enough riot control material to cope with the situation and quell the uprisings. Soon the required materials including rubber bullets and tear gas were imported from Britain. The United States used its good relations with Iraq's Saddam Hussein to request the expulsion of Khomeini from Iraq. The Shah thought that Khomeini's exile to Paris would make it easier for him to control his activities and that the street rallies would come to an end. That proved to be a fatal mistake.[10]

Contrary to Shah's expectations, many Iranians travelled to France to meet Ayatollah Khomeini, now better known as the Imam. They returned home with his message for the Iranian people in which he openly invited them to topple the Shah's government. New demonstrations occurred almost daily, with reports of new civilian deaths, and strikes began to hurt key industries, notably the vital oil industry, where production dropped to about one-tenth its normal level. As the time passed the government became more destabilized. Sabeti and Atapour who came to meet me talked about Khomeini's activities in Paris and said that some experienced SAVAK agents were watching him. To me, (Imam) Khomeini had no covert activities and his comments and his meetings with others were quite open and were published in many papers around the world.[11]

THE ROLE OF GENERAL QARABAQI

General Abbass Qarabaqi was Interior Minister in Sharif-Emami's cabinet. Before that he was Commander of Gendarmerie. He quit the ministerial portfolio when Bakhteyar took office and succeeded Azhari as the chief of the joint staff of the army. Simultaneously, he was a member of the Regency Council.

Ever since he assumed his ministerial post, he was regularly in touch with Ambassadors Sullivan and Parsons. He also called on me almost daily for consultations. What the two ambassadors told Qarabaqi showed the attitude of the two powers towards the impending revolution.

Qarabaqi told me that he informed them of the latest developments and even took notes before his meetings with the ambassadors so as not to forget anything. He answered a variety of questions on cabinet meetings, government decisions and views expressed about different matters. They also discussed how to reinforce the government and encourage the Shah to resist, even urging him to resort to an "iron fist" policy if necessary to suppress the demonstrators.

A proposal to arm pro-Shah tribesmen was put forward during Shairf-Ememi's government. The proposal was aimed at crushing the demonstrations and put an end to the domestic turmoil.

One day, Qarabaqi, Interior Minister at the time, accompanied by Mohaqqeqi, Commander of Gendarmerie, came to my SIB office. Mohaqqeqi who had just succeeded Qarabaqi said some tribesmen were willing to receive arms and support the government. He insisted that the plan would be translated into action soon. I asked Qarabaqi for comments and he confirmed the idea. I told Mohaqqeqi that the prime responsibility of gendarmerie was to disarm tribesmen and that his proposal was in sharp contradiction with his responsibility. I urged him to forget the idea and seek other solutions and he agreed.

Contrary to his promise, the plan to arm the tribesmen was partly carried out and in some parts of the country, the ruffians hired by gendarmerie, police and SAVAK attacked demonstrators but to no avail.

AZHARI'S MILITARY GOVERNMENT

The failure of Sharif-Emami's "national reconciliation" plan was certain. Public protests were rapidly increasing and Ayatollah Khomeini, from his place of exile in France, was insisting that the monarchy must go.

> Brzezinski assured the Shah of the unshakable support of the U.S. government for whatever decisions he took with regard to the formation or composition of a new government. He told the Shah that concessions to the opposition would only make the situation more explosive.[12]

On November 6 the Shah announced the new military government in a nation-wide address and General Gholamreza Azhari succeeded Sharif-Emami. It was only one month before Moharram. Although Azhari, as Chief of Staff of the Armed Forces, was an obvious choice to head the government, he was personally a mild man who had no stomach for politics. He was not among the generals who had been pressing the Shah to crack down, and he went out of his way from his first day in office to let it be known that he had accepted his new post with the greatest reluctance and wanted nothing so much as to be rid of it again. If the Shah was primarily concerned about avoiding a possible military takeover or the emergence of a military rival to himself, Azhari was the perfect choice. That was why the Shah favoured Azhari to lead the military government at the time of growing protests in the country.

I have known Azhari since I started studying at the War University. At the time, he was a colonel and led the teaching department.. He was very polite and calm. All the manuals taught at the U.S. War Army College had been translated into Persian and were taught at our university. Azhari had a perfect command of both written and spoken English and his knowledge of English helped him establish close relations with American advisors. For sometime, he was commander of an army Division in western Iran before being appointed Chief of Staff of the Armed Forces.

Of the eleven cabinet ministers appointed by Azhari, only six were military, and even this number was whittled down in the following weeks. The military cabinet ministers, for the most part, had no experience in their respective areas of responsibility. In short, the hotly debated change to a military government was, in practice, more cosmetic than real.

The Shah's assumption that Azhari would not commit any treason against him was enough to appoint him as premier. If Mohammad Reza himself was a resolute, strong-minded person Azhari was a good choice for Prime Minister, but the problem was that neither of them could make decisions. Azhari could have acquired the vote of confidence from both Houses within a day claiming that it had to be hurried because of the state of emergency in the country, but it took him a week to receive approval. Azhari was submissive in acquiring the vote of confidence and appealed to both Houses for vote from the position of weakness while he could have acted confidently and assertively in the Houses.[13]

UNREST REACHES CLIMAX IN MOHARRAM

"With Moharram to begin on December 1, both Washington and Tehran began buttoning down the hatches for what was expected to be the climatic confrontation between the military government and the people.

Ayatollah Khomeini refused any deal with the Shah considering the talks a trick aimed at aborting the revolution. On the eve of Moharram, Khomeini underlined his uncompromising position by issuing a proclamation that called on the people of Iran to "unite, arise and sacrifice your blood".

He called for disobedience of the government's order banning demonstrations. The month of Moharram, he stated, would be the month when "blood will triumph over the sword, the month of the strength of right, the month the oppressors will be judged and the satanic government will be abolished."

The beginning of Moharram was marked by widespread public disobedience of the military government's order prohibiting demonstrations. Enormous crowds flocked to the mosques for religious observance, spilling over into the streets and ignoring the early-evening curfew. At night, the citizens of Tehran climbed to their roofs at night and chanted revolutionary slogans.

The authorities recognized that it would be impossible to sustain the ban against demonstrations during the high holy days of Tasua and Ashura (literally, the Ninth and Tenth of Moharram), commemorating the martyrdom of Imam Hussein at Karbala in the Seventh century at the hands of the False Caliphe, Yazid. Imam Hussein's martyrdom is marked annually by mass processions of men rhythmically striking themselves with fists and chains in sorrow and exultation...

No one, including the Shah and the Americans, could be sure that the monarchy would survive the coming demonstrations. The media also reported that President Carter had relatively lost his hopes to keep the Shah in power.

The marches of Tasua and Ashura were massive, as expected but relatively free of violence. Everybody regarded the marches as a street referendum against the monarchy. All the banners and slogans named Khomeini as the only leader. Concurrently, there were signs of a breakdown of discipline within the military. After a survey of the capital by helicopter that day, the Shah told Azhari "what is the use of remaining in this country under such circumstances". The weakness of Azhari's military government caused the army to disobey orders and commanders adopted a policy of procrastination"[14]

"With the approach of Moharram, we are about to begin the month of epic heroes and self-sacrifice - the month in which blood triumphed over the sword, the month in which truth condemned falshood for all eternity and branded the mark of disgrace upon the forehead of all oppressors and satanic governments; the month that has taught successive generations throughout history the path of victory over the bayonet; the month that proves the superpowers may be defeated by the word of truth; the month in which the leader of the Muslims taught us how to struggle against all the tyrants of history, showed us how the clenched fists of those who seek freedom, desire independence, and proclaim the truth may triumph over tanks, machine guns, and armies of Satan, how the word of truth may obliterate falsehood.

The leader of the Muslims taught us that if a tyrant rules despotically over the Muslims in any age, we must rise up against him and denounce him, however unequal our forces may be, and that if we see the very existence of Islam in danger, we must sacrifice ourselves and be prepared to shed our blood.

Now the regime of the Shah is ruling tyrannically over our oppressed people today. He continues to rule in defiance of the law and the wishes of the people, who have risen up against him throughout Iran, and he threatens the higher interests of the Muslims and the dictates of Islam with imminent destruction for the sake of his own satanic rule and his parasitic masters. It is the duty of the entire nation that has now risen in revolt to pursue and broaden its struggle against the Shah with all its strength and to bring down his harmful, disastrous regime.

The military government is usurpatory and contrary to both the law of the land and the Sharia. It is the duty of everyone to oppose it, to refrain from aiding it in any way, to refuse to pay taxes or render any other assistance to this oppressive regime of transgressors, and it is the duty of all oil company officials and workers to prevent the export of oil, this vital resource...

Now, with the month of Moharram here like a divine sword in the hands of the soldiers of Islam, our great religious leaders and respected preachers, and all the followers of the Lord of the Martyrs (peace and blessings be upon him), they must make the maximum use of it. Trusting in the power of God, they must tear out the remaining roots of this tree of oppression and treachery, for the month of Moharram is the month in which the forces of Yazid and the stratagems of Satan are defeated.

Let assemblies for the commemoration of the Lord of the Oppressed... be organized as magnificently and as frequently as possible. Let the bloodstained banners of 'Ashura' be raised wherever possible, as a sign of the coming day when the oppressed shall avenge himself on his oppressor.

Respected preachers, dear speakers! Attend even more than before to your duty of exposing the crimes of the regime, so that you may hold your heads high in the presence of God Almighty...

The history of Iran is witnessing today the most sensitive days that Islam and our dear Muslims have experienced. Today, great nation, you have come to a fork in the road: one way leads to eternal dignity and splendour, and the other (God forbid), to perpetual humiliation and degradation.

There is no excuse for any class of people in the nation to remain inactive today; silence and apathy mean suicide, or even aid to the tyrannical regime. To abandon the straightforward path of the nation and Islam would be treason to Islam and the nation. The traitors who imagine that they can defeat this Islamic movement and save the Shah by keeping silent, or in some cases even moving to support his tyrannical regime, are mistaken. For now it is too late, and the Shah is on his way out; no one can save the Shah by selling himself. Even if he were to be saved, he would not remain loyal to those who saved him, as we can all see.

I extend a hand of affection and devotion to the noble people of Iran, who, with power they derive from Islam, have given a heavy punch in the face to the Shah and his supporters...

The echo of the great Iranian Revolution is reverberating throughout the Islamic world as well as other countries, and it is a source of pride to them, too. Noble nation, you have alerted the noble young people of other Islamic nations, and we may hope that your powerful hand will raise up the proud banner of Islam in all regions."[15]

SHAH TURNS TO BAKHTEYAR

During a cabinet meeting, Azhari suffered an heart attack and fainted before ministers. He was immediately hospitalized and his doctor banned any meetings with him. To me, Azhari's heart attack was politically-motivated and since he was not able to stop the progress of the revolution, he resorted to having a "heart attack" as an excuse to justify his failure. I was told that Azhari was in good health in private but he pretended to be ill in public. The Shah accepted Azhari's resignation.

Then Ali Amini was invited to lead the government and in response he said that although it was too late he would agree to act as Shah's advisor. The Shah welcomed his role and Amini stayed late in the Shah's Palace everyday to discuss the daily events. Chief of SAVAK Naser Moqqaddam who was known as a power broker in domestic political affairs was ordered to invite leader of the National Front Karim Sanjabi for the post of premiership. Sanjabi requested the Shah to temporarily leave the country for a holiday before he could resume the post. The Shah refused.

This time Moqqaddam was delegated to ask Bazargan to meet the Shah to discuss the premiership, but he refused it. Then it was Dr. Siddiqi's turn. The Shah was not sure Siddiqi would succeed in forming a government and anticipated that marshal law would have to be imposed and the military take things in hand again. Although Siddiqi at first accepted the proposal, Shah's efforts to form a civilian government again suffered a setback when he withdrew the day after.

Finally, the Shah called in Bakhteyar and offered him the charge. He accepted the post but on condition that the Shah leaves the country temporarily for a period of two months and the Shah accepted.

During Azhari's era, American and British officials were in touch with the Shah and voiced their support for him. Azhari as usual, was in constant touch with Brezenski and promised to support the government if the Shah fought against the uprising. Zahedi was attempting to seize the post of premier and always recommended Mohammad Reza not to leave the country and remain strong as long as Washington was backing his government. During this period, Brigadier General Khatami, commander of the counter-intelligence of the Imperial Guard with 17 years of service in the SIB came to me for briefings. Khatami said that Carter telephoned the Shah every day and promised to support his government and even encouraged him to resort to violence. Carter's telephone calls and his public support did not influence the Shah since he was witnessing that the situation was getting worse day by day and therefore, he turned down Zahedi's request for the post. The bitter reality for the Shah was that he was unable to stop the momentum of the developments and the future looked very dim. Finally he was convinced that it would be better to leave Iran; he accepted Bakhteyar's proposal and left the country.

An important event during Azhari's government was a deadly attack on an Imperial Guard officer in Lavisan by two unidentified soldiers. They had entered the canteen and had threatened all officers and ordered them to put their "hands up". They fired some bullets in the air and then entered Badrei's office. Having seen that his office was empty, they fled but one of them was killed and the other escaped uninjured. At the time of the incident, Badrei was in Shah's Palace. Badrei requested permission to return to his office and investigate the incident. The Shah asked him to order his deputy to carry out the investigation. The incident for sure demoralized the Shah.

The Shah had lost whatever resoluteness he ever had and could no longer make decisions. I remember that once when the Third Department of SAVAK in a report addressed to the SIB disclosed that Ayatollah Khomeini had set up a "revolutionary council". The Shah was unable to decide what to do about it and noted "order SAVAK to leave them alone".

SHAH'S LAST DAYS IN IRAN

The Shah was not sure that General Azhari had the physical stamina to act after his heart attack and he wondered whether Iranian troops would be willing to execute a harsh policy. When Azhari's military government fell, Shah's all hopes collapsed. Negotiations with Siddiqi, a leader of the National Front, did not succeed in forming an effective government and the Shah was only letting precious days slip away at a time when there was no time left.

In late December and early January, it was evident that the Shah was planning to leave the country in an act tantamount to abdication. Bakhteyar had stipulated that the Shah should go abroad for a short leave if he wanted him to accept the post of Prime Minister. Khatami, commander of the Imperial Guard's counter-intelligence used to meet me regularly and said that the Shah's family were moving abroad and only the Shah and his Empress Farah were to remain in Iran.

One day he disclosed that Prince Gholamreza and his wife planned to leave the country but the Shah ordered Gholamreza to remain and two days later he allowed his wife to be put on a foreign flight out. She took jewels and many other valuable possessions with her. Two days after Bakhteyar took office as Prime Minister, the Shah officially declared in a press conference on January 1 that he would leave the country to be hospitalized abroad. On January 3, he appointed Qarabaqi Chief of Staff of the Armed Forces. Oweisi resigned as the Military Commander of Tehran.

JAM, NAZEM AND BAKHTEYAR

On New Year's Day, 1979, Shahpour Bakhteyar addressed the nation. He outlined an ambitious reform programme that he said would lead to a truly 'social democratic' society. He reminded the people of his service in the cabinet of Mohammad Mossadiq nearly thirty years earlier, and he managed to complete his twelve-minute speech without once mentioning the Shah.

Two questions were much on the mind of political leaders in Tehran and Washington. First, would Bakhteyar be able to attract credible group of ministers? Second, when and under what circumstances would the Shah actually leave the country?...

The appointment of Minister of War was widely regarded as the key to a viable new government, and Bakhteyar had let it be known that his choice for this position was retired General Fereidyun Jam. Jam, who was living in exile in London, had resigned as chief of staff many years earlier after a dispute with the Shah over use of the army to put down domestic dissent. He was unique among Iranian military leaders as a man who was highly respected by the professional military but who had dissociated himself from the Shah's policies of repression. His acceptance of the military portfolio would constitute a powerful vote of confidence for Bakhteyar.

The Shah dashed these hopes. General Jam, he told Sullivan, had declined the position. This was very bad news indeed, for it would be interpreted as a signal that Jam did not believe the Bakhteyar government would succeed.[16]

As soon as Bakhteyar was sworn in as Prime Minister, he made it clear that he had in mind to appoint General Fereidyun Jam, a former husband of Shah's elder sister, Princess Shams, as Minister of War. Bakhteyar needed him very much to give a military show of strength. His decision to introduce Jam as War Minister was a wise choice and perhaps one of the two Embassies had recommended that he give Jam the post because Bakhteyar himself had little knowledge of the situation. The Shah approved Jam's nomination for the post when the latter arrived in Tehran from exile.

Ever since he married Shams, Jam had been a good friend of mine but I did not see him again after the revolution. I met Jam at Major General Nazem's house where he remained during his stay in Tehran. When I arrived there about twenty of Jam's friends were also there. Jam took me straight away into a private room. He told me that he had not yet made up his mind about the proposed post and asked me for my opinion.

I said, "Bakhteyar's government is not stable and I do not think you will come to terms with him."

At this time, Qarabaqi and Mobser entered the room and Jam decided to include them in the conversation. Nazem also joined us. Qarabaqi pledged to support him if he accepted the post. Nazem intervened and addressed Qarabaqi in stern manner, "you cannot even speak for yourself let alone others, you are talking nonsense." He also rebuked Mobser who had also expressed loyalty to Jam.

Nazem and I believed that Bakhteyar was not able to resist the strong waves of the revolution and recommended Jam not to accept the proposal or give in to Shah's pleas.

Nazem told Jam, "I have time and again told you that the polite way to refuse the post is that you let me meet the Shah and inform him that you (Jam) would accept the post only if Ayatollah Khomeini does not raise objection to your nomination"

"No, it is not a good idea", Jam said. Then Nazem urged him to turn down the request under the pretext of family problems and leave the country. Jam welcomed the offer and the day after he informed the Shah of his decision and left Iran on January 8.

Jam's refusal to accept the post dashed Bakhteyar's hopes. This was disappointing for Bakhteyar because it would be interpreted as a signal that the Bakhteyar government would not succeed.

Jam telephoned me to say goodbye before his plane took off and I did not see him again. Later, my son, Shahrokh, met him twice in London when he was stopping over there on his way to the U.S. Jam once said to him, "I am very happy that your father has been given a post in the Islamic government". Shahrokh said he did not think this was so as I was always at home. "It's not necessary for you to know this. Your father is a clever man. He knows how to keep a job without you finding out about it", he told him.

Nazem's insistence that Jam avoid accepting the post reinforced my suspicion that Nazem was planning a coup to oust Bakhteyar and take power. But what could he do with the masses who only wanted Ayatollah Khomeini as their leader. Perhaps Nazem had anticipated that Bakhteyar would fail and that the future government would belong to the clerics. He thought the clerical government would give post to an officer who had a dispute with the Shah years earlier. Anyway, Nazem who had been forced to retire by the Shah's government was happy to see the monarchy go.

In the first months after the victory of the revolution, my brother Nasratollah told me that Nazem had been given a post in the revolutionary courts. I said that if this is so it is very good for me. I had his brother's telephone number but by accident when I rang Nazem himself answered. He immediately recognized my voice and confirmed that he had been offered a post.

He said, "I was invited to join the new revolutionary courts and when I went there I saw seven bearded clergymen with turbans. I did not accept the offer because it was not possible for me to work with them".

Later, before my arrest, I heard that Nazem had escaped from Iran through Kurdestan. When I was in detention, my interrogators said that Nazem was involved in anti-Iran propaganda in Turkey.

Anyhow, Bakhteyar failed to win Jam's support and appointed General Jafar Shafaqat War Minister. Shafaqat lacked adequate military knowledge and was not clever. It was also reported that he had embezzled money but no investigations were made into his wrongdoings. To the best of my knowledge, Shafaqat after the revolution secretly escaped to the U.S. and then settled in France.

GUADELOUPE CONFERENCE

In the early days of January, the Shah had made it clear that he intended to make a statement that he would leave the country for a rest. He made his decision public after viewing demonstrations from his helicopter in Tehran. The Shah, despite the West's all-out support for his regime, was confused and unable to deal with the situation, so too were his backers.

The National Front of Bakhteyar was a last-ditch attempt by Washington to prevent the victory of the revolution and save the monarchy. At this juncture, leaders of the United States, Britain, France and Germany held a conference in the Caribbean island of Guadeloupe on January 4, 1979 to discuss the crisis in Iran.

Parviz Sabeti, Director of SAVAK's Third Department, informed me of the decisions made during the conference. Sabeti, after consultations with the Head of CIA's Tehran station, said that at the conference President Carter had told his European counterparts that the Shah was irreparably wounded and was not able to stay in power any longer. The three other heads of states, British Prime Minister James Callaghan, West German Chancellor Helmut Schmidt, and French President Valery Giscard d'Estaing, at first argued otherwise but they succumbed to Carter's argument after he gave them an American analysis of the situation in Iran.

The prospect of the Shah's departure had been raised a month before the conference. Carter was in constant touch with the Shah and made every effort to keep him in power. Mohammad Reza was broken and was not prepared to hold onto his rule and there was nothing the Carter administration could do for him.

GENERAL HUYSER'S MISSION

General Robert Huyser, deputy commander of the Supreme Allied Command in Europe, had arrived in Tehran unannounced on January 4, at approximately the same time that President Carter and leaders of Britain, France and Germany were arriving on the Caribbean island of Guadeloupe for their planned summit meeting to discuss the situation in Iran.

Neither the Shah nor I were aware of Huyser's arrival. I heard later that Badrei had informed Mohammad Reza a few days after Huyser's arrival. The Shah complained to Ambassador Sullivan for failing to inform him of Huyser's trip and the day after on 11th January both Sullivan and Huyser met the Shah. As soon as they went to the meeting, Huyser, without apologizing, asked Mohammad Reza when he would leave the country. The Shah answered angrily, "that is a personal matter; I will leave whenever I wish to." Sullivan intervened and in an attempt to justify Huyser's failure to inform the Shah of his arrival said, "heavy work prevented him from seeing you. He only asked to make sure you are in good health."

What was Huyser's mission in Tehran? I did not have any information and surprisingly, he did not telephone me and I did not see him at all. Qarabaqi was in constant touch with Huyser during the latter's stay in Tehran. Huyser, it was said, had arrived in Iran to remove some instruments from F-14 fighters and dismantle radars based in northern cities which monitored activities inside the Soviet territory.[17]

> "Huyser had arrived in Iran to maintain contact with Iranian military leaders as a show of continuing U.S. support. Huyser had worked closely with the Iranian military over a period of years and was personally acquainted with many of the top generals... He was to convey to the top military leaders that the United States regarded it as vital that the Iranian people have a strong and stable government friendly to the United States. Huyser was to urge military leaders to remain in Iran and to offer assurances that the United States would stick with them. The military-supply relationship would be maintained, and U.S. support personnel would remain as needed. Special concern was expressed about the security of sensitive military equipment...Just before Huyser arrived, the Americans had privately reported that the Iranian military was about to carry out a coup. Several such reports were received during the first days of January after news began to circulate about the Shah's impending departure."[18]

The Moscow based daily "Pravda" on January 29 wrote, "the American officer plans to launch a quite coup with the help of officers who were still loyal to the Shah in order to prevent the victory of the revolution. That means Huyser, like Iranian military leaders, is involved in the killing of thousands of demonstrators in the streets of Tehran and other Iranian cities."

> "Ambassador Sullivan and General Huyser spent two hours with the Shah on January 11. The Shah expressed deep concern about the suffering of the Iranian people and urged the United States to approach Khomeini to stop the potential bloodshed and to give the Bakhteyar government a chance. The Shah reviewed the list of names for the Regency Council that was about to be formed... Huyser who had originally anticipated remaining in

Iran only a few days, was ordered to remain and pursue his contacts with the military leadership. The overriding U.S. objective was the preservation of the military and the possibility of a military government was again not excluded. Huyser had spent endless hours in talks with the military leaders, and was not convinced that the military was prepared to throw full support behind Bakhteyar when the Shah departed. Having failed in his mission, Huyser left Iran on February 3."[19]

SHAH FLEES ABROAD

At 12:30 p.m. on 16 January 1979, four helicopters left off from the grounds of Tehran's Niavaran Palace, one of them carrying the Shah and his wife. Shahpour Bakhteyar, appointed Prime Minister two days ago, was in the Parliament to obtain a vote of confidence. The Shah waited until Bakhteyar received the vote of confidence.[20]

When the Shah and his Empress stepped from their helicopter at Mehrabad Airport, it was the end. I was sure he would never return.

> "How long will you be away Sir?", a guard had asked.
>
> "It depends on the state of my health", he had replied wistfully as the Empress, her chestnut hair pushed up under a fur hat, linked her arm through his. His body was riddled with cancer. He was a broken man.
>
> Shops, banks and offices were closed as mobs roamed, chanting "Death ... death to the Shah". Many of Shah's friends had simply deserted him. The rich families he knew had already traded in million of rials for dollars, Francs and Deutschmarks and fled to relatives in the west...
>
> The Shah, a small parcel of Iranian soil tucked in his pocket, took the controls of the aircraft and flew off into the sunless sky. The Shah's rule was over.[21]

The plane was ready to take off. Bakhteyar, speaker of the two Houses, Badrei and Rabie, together with the Chief of Staff of the Armed Forces General Qarabaqi, had arrived at the airport to see the Shah off.

As their Imperial Majesties walked toward their silver and blue Boeing 707, the street mobs shouted with joy and smashed the statues erected in his honour. Bakhteyar asked the Shah where he should send daily reports and he replied, "I do not need reports, do what you deem necessary yourself!" The Shah gave a similar answer to Qarabaqi when he asked what his role in the army would be and how much power he could exercise in that role. The Shah told him, "You are in charge of the army and police and you are allowed to make logical decisions on your own. I know the situation is very difficult, even so, you have friends such as Fardust and you can consult with him."

I was sincerely happy that he escaped the wrath of the people and that he could have a pleasant life in Europe or America if he was clever enough to make wise decisions.

The Shah had been persuaded by some of his advisors to remain as close as possible to Iran in case of a sudden turn of events. It was recalled that in the course of Operation Ajax in 1953 the Shah had fled the country briefly, only to be recalled in triumph a few days later. Perhaps he still anticipated a similar reversal in 1979. Therefore, he first stopped in Egypt but gradually he lost all hope of keeping his dynasty and so went further away from Iran.

> In Egypt, the Shah seemed to be convinced of the considerations that the Iranian armed forces could manage to overwhelm an unarmed street crowd led by nothing but rhetorical exhortations from the mullahs. Contrary to his original plans he chose to stay as a guest of the Egyptian government for an indefinite period of time. We learned from our observers in Egypt that he felt there would soon be a military confrontation with the revolution and that the armed forces would prevail. He seemed convinced that, in such an event, he would be recalled to Tehran as he had been in 1953 and would be able to resume the throne as in that earlier experience. This seemed to me to be the most unrealistic sort of thinking on the part of all concerned. Therefore, in due course I sent a message to Washington suggesting that these wishful thoughts were pure moonshine and that we should instead be preparing ourselves for the fact that the revolution was going to succeed and that we needed to accommodate ourselves to it in the most effective way in order to protect U.S. national interests.
>
> In response to this message, I received the most unpleasant cable from Washington ... As an apparent prophylaxis against

my seditious views, Washington made clear in direct communications to Prime Minister Bakhteyar that he enjoyed the full support and confidence of the United States government.[22]

BAKHTEYAR'S 37-DAY GOVERNMENT

The news of Shah's departure was greeted by widespread popular celebrations. The military was close to a state of shock. There was talk about a possible coup, mostly spread by the Americans since they argued that the credible threat of a coup would buy time for Bakhteyar to consolidate his position.

I met Bakhteyar only once after the Shah left Iran. I did not know him before that but I had been told that the National Front was a pro-West political party which Bakhteyar was a member. I went to his office and had to wait a while before I could see him. As I entered the room, he came to me for greetings. After exchange of pleasantries, we went to talks.

"What are you doing now?" he asked.

"I am in charge of two organizations namely the Imperial Investigation Organization and SIB. I am doing my job as before but now without the Shah," I replied.

At this moment, Bakhteyar's secretary interrupted us to tell Bakhteyar that Ambassador Sullivan was waiting to meet him in the waiting hall. Bakhteyar hastily saw me to the door and said, "Hopefully we will meet again." As I was leaving his office I saw Manuchehr Aryana, Bakhteyar's Labour Minister who, before receiving the post, was a regular visitor to my office and showed me great respect, but that day he treated me in a very arrogant manner.

Bakhteyar helplessly was struggling to maintain his loose government. His prime objective was to prevent the fall of the dynasty. The United States and Britain continued their unconditional support of Bakhteyar who was clearly seen as the last-ditch attempt to preserve the monarchy and encouraged him to resist the public protest.[23]

Bakhteyar had no popular base and even the National Front withdrew its support for him after he assumed power. Bakhteyar had little to do against a nation which wanted him and the monarchical regime removed to be replaced by an Islamic government. Bakhteyar's leverages in confronting the people were many in name but few in practice.

Cabinet Ministers: Bakhteyar assumed the post of Prime Minister without holding a key job prior to his appointment. Did his abilities help him to become premier? No! He became prime minister because nobody else was willing to accept the post. Now we have to ask what did this person who had come from nothing to reach such a high position think about his circumstances? One moment he presumed he was a useless man and the next he saw in himself a Shah. One minute a word from Komeini could strike fear into his heart and the next he would tell Khomeini that it was not wise for him to return home. Bakhteyar's bahaviour reflected his contradictory feelings.

He either saw himself as one against the whole nation or when the American and British ambassadors voiced their support for his government he felt that he was in a position of strength. Sometimes he planned to escape abroad and at others he wished to transform the monarchical regime into a Republican one and become president. To me, his only advantage was that he did not show his weaknesses and exaggerated his abilities. This was what was apparent during his 37-day rule. Sabeti said that Bakhteyar smoked opium and drank a lot and that while he was prime minister during the day at 10 a.m. and 5 p.m. he would satisfy this habit. It was obvious that after indulging he was a stronger man and could hide his weaknesses.

I did not know the cabinet ministers except Shafaqat and Aryana who was labour minister and a close friend of Bakhteyar. He used to join me at "Iran Javan" club every night and he invited me and his other friends to his house every fortnight. However, while he was a minister, he did not ring me even once.

Government Departments: It was clear that Bakhteyar had to mobilize all government departments if he wanted to confront the nation. Government departments, except a few officials, simply ignored Bakhteyar's orders and obeyed Khomeini's instructions.

Parliament: During Bakhteyar's era, MPs left Iran or because of fear joined the people. Some of those who were hesitant came to me for consultation.

Army: The army personnel gradually joined the people and Badrei said that on the 11th February, only 700 army personnel remained loyal to Bakhteyar's government. Therefore, no political faction, officer or Bakhteyar could carry out a coup.

Security Forces: General Mohaqqeqi was the Commander of Gendarmerie, who had been appointed on the advice of Qarabaqi. General Jafari who was the representative of the head of the City Police was uncertain and came to me for consultation. The status of security forces was very similar to that of the army and Bakhteyar could not rely on them.

SAVAK: General Naser Moqqaddam was the Chief of SAVAK during Bakhteyar's era and was very loyal to the Shah but he did not enjoy enough control over the secret organization and Sabeti who was deeply influential in SAVAK was trying to materialize his own ambitious dreams.

It was said that a meeting was held at Bakhteyar's office every day from 6 to 8 in the evening and was attended by the top army military brass and security officials. The meetings devoted a long time on trying to find ways to stop Khomeini from coming to Iran. The conversations were recorded on tape. Bakhteyar did not invite me to their discussions but some of the participants informed me of the decisions made at the meeting. Discussions at the meeting once even considered the possibility of blowing up the plane carrying Ayatollah Khomeini to Iran.

The participants were at odds on some topics. Bakhteyar and Qarabaqi sought the support of American and British ambassadors hoping to stabilize their position while Moqqaddam, Badrei and Mohaqqeqi were still loyal to the Shah and preferred his return to the country but Jafari was indifferent. The meeting was the only place where Bakhteyar could bluff his authority, because the mere participation of the officials was a sign of loyalty to Bakhteyar. He would reiterate the promises of support made by the two embassies and he would express his hope that the Shah would return home, in an attempt to encourage the participants to resist the protests.

Though Bakhteyar remained in office for 37 days, he embezzled more money than his predecessors. Sabeti told me that SAVAK agents had learned that Bakhteyar had embezzled about 60 million tumans from government's secret budget; 10 million of which was paid to Aryana. But this was little compared to the treason he committed when he cancelled orders for military equipment from the U.S. and Britain.

Certainly, one of the reasons behind Huyser's mission to Tehran was to cancel these military purchases since a military official was required to accept the cancellation. Iran had approximately $11 billion worth of military equipment on order from the United States, to be manufactured and delivered over a period of years. Most of the amount had already been paid in advance. I think Shafaqat, War Minister, and Qarabaqi committed the treason since they were involved in the affair and certainly Bakhteyar may have received a portion after he escaped abroad.

QARABAQI'S DREAMS

Qarabaqi who like me was one of the selected friends of Mohammad Reza since childhood remained a close friend of both the Shah and I up to the fall of the Shah's government in 1979. His good handwriting won Mohammad Reza's favour in 1936 while we were studying at Officer's Collage. He became Crown Prince's personal secretary. Qarabaqi and his wife always attended formal parties held at the Court and receptions at foreign diplomatic missions. The couple were pride of a souvenir photo with the former U.S. Ambassador to Iran and a former CIA Chief Richard Helms. They had decorated the picture in the guest room of their well-furnished house showing it to whoever went to meet them.

Qarabaqi had told me that since he became Intèrior Minister during Sharif-Emami's cabinet and later Chief of Staff of the Armed Forces during the Azhari government, he had almost daily separate meetings with U.S. and British envoys. During the meetings, he informed the ambassadors of the domestic situation and received their advice.

During the Bakhteyar government, Qarabaqi who was also a member of the "Regency Council", called on me every day but did not say a word about Bakhteyar. Since I knew Qarabaqi well, I realized that his refusal to say anything about Bakhteyar's abilities was a sign of respect to him. To me his show of respect was either because he enjoyed financial advantages, or Bakhteyar had promised him the highest post after him, or perhaps both. The reason behind Qarabaqi's silence was that Bakhteyar had recommended that he not seek my support for his government; otherwise, he probably would have informed me of Bakhteyar's plans and asked my advice about the policies.

During these 37 days, Qarabaqi saw himself as being a very important person. I learned of his thought when he called on me one day. He arrived in my office in military uniform with his medals on his coat and a marshal's stick in his hand. We had been friends for 42 years and I knew well that the louder he coughed the more proud he was of himself, and that day he coughed very loudly!. Anyhow, Qarabaqi sat with me for a while but did not discuss anything of any importance and then he left. I realized that something must have happened. I immediately telephoned Sabeti in SAVAK and he told me that the day before, Bakhteyar had addressed the "Regency Council" and stated that the best way to foil the revolution was to establish a republican government and had proposed that Qarabaqi be appointed vice-president after he assumed power as president. Sabeti went on to tell me how upset Badrei had become at his proposal and how he swore at Bakhteyar and nearly had a fight with him. Others at the meeting, however, had no objection to the proposal.

Anyhow, although Bakhteyar had no effective control over the army, the United States still pursued a policy designed to strengthen Bakhteyar's position as the only remaining means of avoiding a total monarchical collapse in Tehran. In his statements in Paris, (Imam) Khomeini called on the people to cooperate with the army which had almost surrendered to the people in restoring calm and proclaimed, "the Shah will definitely lose the army and with it his last hope."

> "The final days of January were almost totally preoccupied with rumours of Khomeini's imminent return to Iran and speculation about what might happen. Bakhteyar made a show of closing the airports, and he let it be known that he had his own plans for dealing with the event. One of those plans was to divert Khomeini's aircraft to the remote Kish Island in the Persian Gulf, where he would be detained with his key aides while the huge phalanx of journalists would be returned to Paris. Some of the generals had their own ideas about what would happen after that, one version of which involved eliminating as many as 50,000 Khomeini supporters in a single massive counterstrike. The events afterward made it clear that Bakhteyar was not in a position to carry out his plans...
>
> Bakhteyar had sent a message through an emissary proposing a meeting with Khomeini in Paris to discuss a solution to the crisis. Khomeini had refused to meet the emissary, although he

> had accepted the written message. According to Yazdi, Khomeini informed Bakhteyar that he would meet him only if he submitted his resignation. If Bakhteyar did resign, Khomeini would be prepared to appoint him immediately as a member of the provisional government. Over the following two days there was great uncertainty about whether or not Bakhteyar would in fact travel to Paris, but in the end he was unwilling to accept Khomeini's terms and the dialogue broke off.."[24]

As soon as I learned that Bakhteyar had proposed to meet Ayatollah Khomeini in Paris and that Khomeini had conditioned that he would be ready to meet Bakhteyar provided he announced his resignation, I intended to help form a compromise between Bakhteyar's handicapped government who had only the backing of a group of generals and the U.S. and British ambassadors and the revolutionary leaders who enjoyed the support of the nation so as to avoid a confrontation. Therefore, I recalled the influential General Farbod for that purpose. An employee of the Imperial Investigation Organization, Farbod had studied military affairs at U.S. academies. He was a symphathizer of the National Front and a right man in dealing with Bakhteyar.

I asked him to convery my verbal message to the premier and tell him that his resignation as a condition to meet Imam was the best option available to him and therefore he should not hesitate to do that. Farbod conveyed my message to him and Bakhteyar presumed that one of the two ambassadors had made the recommendation and, therefore, asked Farbod to make it clear which ambassador was behind the proposal. I asked Farbod to meet Bakhteyar again and inform him that it was not a message from one of the ambassadors but my own recommendation and Bekhteyar in response said he would have nothing to do with my recommendation. He refused to resign.

In the morning of January 29, Bakhteyar told a press conference that he no longer intended to fly to Paris and that the airports would be opened to permit Ayatollah Khomeini to return home.

Bakhteyar went into hiding after February 11, the day which marked the victory of the revolution.

BAKHTEYAR GOVERNMENT AND I

My statements prompted rumours about me and some accused me of betraying the Shah. What was the truth? The truth was I had predicted the fall of the regime from the time that Azhari took office as premier and I realized that nothing could pacify the wrath of the nation. The situation became worse and gradually the prospect of the Shah's short-term leave was raised. I knew Mohammad Reza very well and I was certain that he would not return after his departure. People were running out of patience and the army, Shah's strong base, was weakened. High-ranking officials were confused; the army could not be relied upon and the "Imperial Guard" was not powerful enough to defuse the situation. After the Lavisan incident, the guard also lost its credibility.

Gradually, I publicly declared my views about the stability of the Shah's government. The first man I spoke to was Jamshid Alam, a Senator and a friend of Mohammad Reza. He was a member of the "Iran Javan" club and every night he showed up there for games with his friends but he always came to see me in my room at the club before leaving.

Everynight he asked me about the growing tide of political crisis in the country. About two months before the revolution he asked me again what I thought of the Shah's position. I answered that I felt he would leave the country. He was a very impolite person and he arrogantly said, "you are talking non-sense." "Behave yourself," I answered He became afraid and stopped talking that way. The next time he came he said, "the Shah says that he is very stable." Certainly, he had told the Shah what I had said but Mohammad Reza showed no reaction. "Now, what is your assessment?", he added. "I still think the same and I do not like to talk about this matter any more," I said.

Anyhow, I carried out my responsibilities carefully both before and after the Shah's departure. SAVAK kept sending reports for the SIB and we passed the information to the Shah's palace. I showed up at Investigations in the morning and SIB in the afternoon. After Shah's departure, I had to make decisions myself and, therefore, I expressed my views explicitly. I found no reason to lie and console others. At work, at the club, etc. whoever asked me about the developments in the country I explicitly said that neither Mohammad Reza nor his family would ever return home.

Many came to me for consultations and it pleased me that they listened to me. I was not ever worried about myself; I do not know why but I never gave a thought to what may happen to me! I was exhausted and I welcomed a change and I could at last predict that I would be made to retire. I presumed that my houses and farm lands in northern Iran were enough to meet my future needs and I enjoyed thinking so.

I did not hold myself accountable or guilty for the Pahlavi regime and I was interested in (Imam) Khomeini and the people and dissatisfied with the corrupt government. Therefore, I urged those close to me, my children and sisters, to stay in Iran and promised that nothing would happen to them. The only exception was my wife, Tala, I told her to leave the country because she really annoyed me at home.

When the Shah left Iran my position was still the same. I was in charge of the Imperial Investigation Organization and I held myself responsible before any legal government which came to power. At the time, the organization possessed at least ten buildings, each with 100 rooms which were all rented. The furniture and everything else in them were luxurious and were procured during my 7-year stay there. We had an annual budget of 100 million tumans and 1,500 personnel including branches in provincial capitals. The budget devoted to the Imperial Investigation Organization was much higher than that of some ministries. Without me, disorder and confusion would have spread in Investigations and much of the furniture would have been lost. I was fond of my job and that was why I did not allow any laxity in the department's tasks. I did not find any particular reason to abandon my job and escape abroad. Though I had problems getting to my office because of the demonstrations I did not stop working.

As the Head of SIB during Bakhteyar's government, I kept sending daily reports to Aqili Ardalan, the then Court Minister and a member of the "Imperial Guard". I was not obliged to pass reports to Ardalan but I just wanted to keep the bureau going. I did not carry out Ardalan's orders. He believed that the Shah would return home and he would keep his post as court minister.

During the period, I kept ceremonial links with the Court and I never passed reports to Bakhteyar since SIB was not under the control of the premier. Surprisingly, Bakhteyar did not ask for information despite his many weaknesses. Perhaps he had heard my comments and since he knew I would not obey his orders, he sufficed himself with consulting Qarabaqi.

My presence in SIB and the Imperial Investigation Organization until February 11 helped keep the integrity of the two. My certainty at the time of political turmoil and state confusion surprised many officials and enhanced my credibility before them. They presumed that my tranquillity was because I had knowledge of the situation which others did not have and, therefore, they carried out my recommendations seriously. The old generation had not witnessed a revolution and did not know what would happen. We had only witnessed cabinet reshuffles. Oweisi escaped quickly because he feared he would be punished for his activities. Many who escaped abroad, deposited money in foreign banks but I had not deposited a single rial in foreign banks so as not to have any motivation to go abroad.

I received ten parliamentary deputies on January 28, a day after Gholamhussein Daneshi, an MP, narrowly escaped assassination. Boroumand, a deputy from the Tehran constituency, was their chief. A woman deputy, a retired Major General and Amir Ashayeri, a deputy from Kurdestan, were among the delegation. I do not remember the rest. Boroumand said that Parliamentary Speaker Javad Saeed had asked them to consult me about the domestic upheavals. That showed that even the Parliament did not recognize Bakhteyar's leadership. I explicitly stated that the only option available for MPs was to deliver their resignation to Ayatollah Khomeini. In the afternoon, Boroumand informed me by telephone that Saeed had accepted my recommendation and had mailed a message to Khomeini in Paris to inform him of the resignations.

A few days after Shah's departure, the public became well aware of my stance. During this period, I met Qarabaqi regularly and he, too, was aware of my stance. That was why people such as Badrei, Rabie, Khosrowdad and Neshat, who were very optimistic about the Shah's return, were not willing to meet me. General Mobser, who was very critical of the Shah, met me twice and said that some decisions had to be made for the future.

"My stance is quite clear. If you have any particular plans, you'd better see your close friend Qarabaqi," I said.

The next time he said that he had conferred with Qarabaqi and had given him some advice. Until then, I was not aware of Mobser's close relations with Qaranei. When Qaranei was Director of

SAVAK's Second Department, Mobser was his deputy. Mobser explained that they had been friends for years and said that Qaranei was willing to meet me. I replied, "I know him well and I have helped him frequently with his problems." Mobser said that they would come to meet me together but that never happened. Later, my brother Nosratollah said that Mobser went to Britain after he was released from prison.

Another man I met was General Fazlollah Jafari who had been an SIB officer for years. He replaced Samadeyanpour as Chief of Police after the latter escaped to Britain. He consulted me about his situation and I said, "I am aware that you attend Bakhteyar-led meetings but I think you should ask for an early retirement and leave Iran with your family altogether." He agreed and retired the same day. General Mehdi Rahimi succeeded Jafari. To my surprise, Jafari did not leave Iran and he was arrested after the February 11 at his house. Perhaps, Jafari presumed that early retirement was enough for him to be forgiven.

General Naser Moqqaddam, Chief of SAVAK, met me only once during the 37-day Bakhteyar government. He used to meet me because he was employed by the army's second department upon my recommendation. Our only meeting during Bakhteyar's era took place two weeks after Shah's departure. To make sure I was right in my judgement I asked what he would do if the Shah did not return. He replied, "I am committed to my oath. I have no plan to change my mind though I respect you too much." I learned that, like Qarabaqi, Moqqaddam had been deceived by Bakhteyar and, therefore, I did not want to go into details. He had come only to show his respect to me. I met several other officials with the aim of trying to convince them to join the revolution.

IMAM KHOMEINI RETURNS IN TRIUMPH

Ayatollah Ruhollah Khomeini (now known as the Imam) successfully arrived in Iran aboard a chartered Air France 747 on February 1 after 15 years living in exile. The army stood back and security was handled by the revolutionary forces. The Imam was greeted by joyous mobs in the millions, and during his visit to the martyr's cemetery in southern Tehran his car was nearly swamped by the crowds trying to catch a glimpse of him. The joyous people welcomed their leader with the popular slogan of that time:

With the Devil ousted, the Angel is coming[25]

I well remember the day Imam Khomeini returned to Iran. The television in the reception area was turned on a few hours before Imam's arrival in Iran and a technician was on alert to see to any problems which may occur. The TV suddenly went off a few minutes after the film of Imam's arrival began being screened. I telephoned Sabeti to find out the reason behind it and he said, "it is claimed that some technical problems have occurred but Bakhteyar ordered it to sabotage Imam's arrival." Later in the night the TV showed the ceremony four times. As usual I was at "Iran Javan" club; Pirshafiei, director of the club, called everybody including the cook to rush to the TV hall, which had the capacity of 200 people, and watch the programme.

"Ambassador Sullivan asked Washington what role he should play in terms of contacts with the various parties. He was informed that U.S. policy continued to support for constitutional processes and close consultation with the Bakhteyar government. If Bakhteyar asked him (Sullivan) to meet with Khomeini, he should do so. If Khomeini asked to see him, he should consult with Bakhteyar. He was ordered to have no dealings with the Revolutionary Council that would give the appearance of recognizing it either as a party or as a government... This guidance was received in Tehran on February 2. The following day John Stempel, the political officer of the Embassy, met with a member of Bazargan's Liberation Movement. This man told Stemple that their members had met with Bakhteyar for two hours the previous evening and had secured Bakhteyar's agreement to two alternative compromise proposals. The first was for Bakhteyar to remain as Prime Minister and to organize an immediate referendum in which the people would choose between the monarchy or an Islamic republic. The second was for Bakhteyar to resign as prime minister but to remain in a caretaker status while a referendum was conducted.

Reportedly, these proposals were then presented to Khomeini... who rejected both compromises. Bakhteyar had to

> go, since he had received his mandate from the Shah. The Regency Council was illegal. The only course of action was to name a temporary Islamic government to supervise the referendum."[26]

On February 5, the provisional government headed by Mehdi Bazargan was formed to organize the referendum and run the State. The referendum was held on April 1, 1979. An absolute majority of the voters cast their votes in favour of establishing an Islamic Republic. Immediately as the results of the referendum became known and the Islamic Republic of Iran was formally proclaimed, Imam Khomeini made a public speech on the same day.

> "I offer my sincere congratulations to the great people of Iran, who were despised and oppressed by arrogant kings throughout the history of the monarchy. God Almighty has granted us His favour and destroyed the regime of arrogance by His powerful hand, which has shown itself as the power of the oppressed. He has made our great people into leaders and exemplars for all the world's oppressed, and He has granted them their just heritage by the establishment of this Islamic Republic.
>
> On this blessed day, the day the Islamic community assumes leadership, the day of the victory and triumph of our people, I declare the Islamic Republic of Iran.
>
> I declare to the whole world that never has the history of Iran witnessed such a referendum, where the whole country rushed to the polls with ardour, enthusiasm, and love in order to cast their affirmative votes and bury the tyrannical regime forever in the garbage heap of history. I value highly this unparalleled solidarity by virtue of which the entire population - with the exception of a handful of adventurers and godless individuals - responded to the heavenly call of "Hold firm to the rope of God, all together" (Quran, 3:103) and cast a virtually unanimous vote in favour of the Islamic Republic, thus demonstrating its political and social maturity to both the East and the West.
>
> Blessed for you be the day on which, after the martyrdom of your upright young people, the sorrow of their grieving mothers and fathers, and the suffering of the whole nation, you have overthrown your ghoulish enemy, the pharaoh of the age. By casting a decisive vote in favour of the Islamic Republic, you

have established a government of divine justice, a government in which all segments of the population shall enjoy equal consideration, the light of divine justice shall shine uniformly on all, and the divine mercy of the Quran and the Sunna shall embrace all, like life-giving rain. Blessed for you be this government that know no difference of race, whether between black and white, or between Turk, Persian, Kurd, and Baluch. All are brothers and equal; nobility lies only in the fear of God, and superiority may be attained only by acquiring virtues and performing good deeds. Blessed for you be the day on which all segments of the population have attained their legitimate rights; in the implementation of justice, there will be no difference between women and men, or between the religious minorities and the Muslims. Tyranny has been buried, and all forms of transgression will be buried along with it.

The country has been delivered from the clutches of domestic and foreign enemies, from the thieves and plunderers, and you, courageous people, are now the guardians of the Islamic Republic. It is you who must preserve this divine legacy with strength and determination and must not permit the remnants of the putrid regime of the Shah who now lie in wait, or the supporters of the international thieves and oil-bandits, to penetrate your serried ranks. You must now assume control of your own destiny and not give the opportunists any occasion to assert themselves. Relying on the divine power that is manifested in communal solidarity, take the next steps by sending virtuous, trustworthy representatives to the Constituent Assembly, so that they may revise the Constitution of the Islamic Republic. Just as you voted with ardour and enthusiasm for the Islamic Republic, vote too for your representatives, so that the malevolent will have no excuse to object.

This day of Farvardin 12 (April 1) the first day of God's government, is to be one of our foremost religious and national festivals; the people must celebrate this day and keep its remembrance alive, for it is the day on which the battlements of the twenty-five hundred-year old fortress of tyrannical government crumbled, a satanic power departed forever, and the government of the oppressed - which is the government of God - was established in its place.

Beloved people! Cherish and protect the rights you have

attained through the blood of your young people and help to enact Islamic justice under the banner of Islam and the flag of the Quran. I stand ready to serve you and Islam with all the strength at my disposal during these last days of my life, and I expect the nation to devote itself similarly to guarding Islam and the Islamic Republic.

I ask the government that, fearing neither East nor West and cultivating an independent outlook and will, it should purge all remnants of the tyrannical regime, which left deep traces upon all the affairs of our country. It should transform our educational and judicial systems, as well as all the ministers and government offices that are now run on Western lines or in slavish imitation of Western models, and make them compatible to Islam, thus demonstrating to the world true social justice and true cultural, economic, and political independence.

I ask God Almighty that He grant dignity and independence to our country and the nation of Islam."[27]

FALL OF THE DYNASTY

Although I received Moqqaddam only once during Bakhteyar's month-long government, I maintained relations with SAVAK until the last days of the Pahlavi dynasty.

Parviz Sabeti, a top-ranking SAVAK official used to come to my office at SIB once a week and he would speak about the public uprisings and the protest demonstrations throughout the country. Then he asked me for my views on the issue. Gradually he became convinced that the Ayatolah Khomeini would arrive home soon and nothing could be done to foil his arrival to Iran.

He said SAVAK maintained a strong presence in Paris and was aware of the Ayatollah's meetings and statements but he did not explain more when I said that Khomeini's statements were carried by foreign newspapers anyway. Anyhow, he came to my office to say farewell ten days before the victory of the revolution and said that his American counterpart had promised him a post with the CIA. Sabeti appeared satisfied with the promise of his new career and said that Atapour was still in Iran if I needed to consult with anyone. I telephoned Atapour every night and he expressed willingness to meet me and discuss the chaotic situation in the country. Atapour, contrary to Sabeti, was sure that the dynasty was on the verge of total collapse. He was very critical of the corruption in governmental departments as well as the state of affairs in SAVAK and said that disorder and confusion had spread since I left the organization. His long stay in SAVAK and his sensitive post had given him a vivid picture of the situation in the country. The next time I spoke to him he said he planned to go to Israel since the Israeli intelligence agency, Mossad had promised him a post. Atapour left Iran a few days before February 11 and informed me of his departure by telephone.

I did not make any changes in my leisure time and every night I went to the "Iran Javan" club and on holidays I used to stay at the Height Hotel since the winter season did not allow me to go to the suburbs of Karaj.

The deterioration of the political crisis in the country convinced many officials to flee abroad and remain safe from trials. Sabeti like many others left Tehran for Paris twenty days before the victory of the revolution. I no longer saw Khabiri and Naseri at the club. Aryana, Bakhteyar's labour minister disappeared. I sent Tala, my wife, to the United States. Only Dr. Omid, Sheibani, Shahrokh, Tavakoli and Minu Eram were among the distinguished people I knew who remained in Iran and they stopped attending the club regularly. I had lunch with Dr. Omid on Fridays at the Height Hotel and we stayed there together throughout the afternoon to keep each other company.

I started having contacts with Bazargan after Mohammad Ali Afrashteh told me that the new premier wanted to talk to me. Afrashteh was a distant relative of Bazargan. The son of Bazargan's brother who I was told had acted as the chief of Bazargan's private office after the revolution had married the daughter of Abbass Afrashteh, Mohammad Ali's cousin and the couple lived in the house of Bazargan's brother.

On February 10, Qarabaqi telephoned me and said, "I am in Lavisan and two respected personalities Messrs Bazargan and Sahabi are with me". His tone made it clear that the two were listening. He added, "following street clashes in the capital, Messrs Bazargan and Sahahbi have asked me to form a commission tomorrow morning at army headquarters of high-ranking military officials and declare that the army no longer supports Bakhteyar's government. I would now like to have your comments on this".

I welcomed the proposal and recommended that they should

go ahead with it. After a few seconds, Qarabaqi said, "Both men thank you. The commission will be formed tomorrow".

I then telephoned Afrashteh to get directions for the address for my proposed meeting with Bazargan but he told me that the meeting had been cancelled. I realized that the subject of the proposed meeting was to be that which Qarabaqi had just raised with me, i.e. forming the commission, and as it had now been discussed and a decision reached, there was no need for the meeting.

On the morning of February 11, I went to the Imperial Investigation Organization as usual. At about ten o'clock, Qarabaqi telephoned me and said the commission had been formed at army headquarters and that I was requested to join them. I immediately rushed there. About 100 armed troops were guarding the building. I entered the conference hall and all the participants stood up as a sign of respect. About 30 top-ranking military officials were present, in uniform, and a lack of chairs meant that a few had to stand. Qarabaqi acted as president and to his right were Shafaqat, myself, Badrei, Rabie and Habibollahi; General Hatam and others sat on his left. Qarabaqi turned to me and siad, "This commission was formed this morning, and the discussion centres around whether the army should support Bakhteyar or not. Everyone here has different ideas, some agree, some disagree, and the commission had not yet been able to reach a decision. Therefore, the commission members requested that you come here to give us your views".

I asked Badrei, who was sitting next to me, "How many troops are available?" "There were 700 this morning but by now the number may have decreased", he answered. Then I asked, "Do you have a plan?" "No, what plan?" Badrei replied, and added, "it would be a great achievement if we could guard our barracks." It was obvious that he was very worried, but he managed to contain himself. General Rabie, who was next to Badrei, was listening very carefully to what I was saying. (I thought that if the Americans wanted to carry out a coup he would be their number one man).

Then, addressing the gathering, I said that according to the law the army was responsible only to protect the territorial integrity of the country against foreign invasion and was not expected to take sides with the tremendous political tides. Then I asked all those who agreed with me to raise their hands. All raised their hands, Rabie did so only when I looked at him. (Of course, I was not right in what I said because the law did allow use of the army to crush domestic rebellions and declare marshal law).

Then, I asked General Hatam to write a statement and read it out before the participants and let all make their comments and then sign it. I asked that the statement be immediately passed to the radio station to be broadcast. The statement was prepared and read out before the audience and all agreed to sign it except Shafaqat since he was the war minister in Bakhteyar's cabinet.

I placed my signature first and then the members signed one by one. During the meeting, Qarabaqi left his seat twice to make a telephone call to Bakhteyar from another room. The first time he returned said, "If we sign this statement, Bakhteyar will leave the country."

"We are not asking Bakhteyar to leave; we are only deciding what the army should do and what not," I answered.

Qarabaqi left the conference hall and came again in a hurry and said, "Bakhteyar has left!"

At this interval (when Qarabaqi went to call Bakhteyar) Hatam made use of the opportunity and said, "General Qarabaqi has not received me even once for months as his deputy but has given audience to General Huyser every day and right now Huyser is at the headquarters!"

General Tabatabi came to me and asked, "What will happen to us if His Majesty returns home?" I replied, "Tell him I was the one who masterminded the statement!" At this time, Aminafshar told me that about 2000 demonstrators were approaching the headquarters. I immediately left the conference hall and Qarabaqi followed me and said, "you'd better meet Huyser and his entourage who are here." "It is better to postpone the meeting since demonstrators are coming," I answered.

All soldiers had left their guns and deserted the compound. I sat in the car and my driver, Dusti, drove to SIB before the demonstrators could reach the headquarters.

I was in my office at SIB. At four in the afternoon, demonstrators were marching in Sepah and Pasteur streets heading towards the Prime Ministers's office. They were shooting in the air and some of them climbed over the wall of the SIB building. A man who said he was the bureau's cleaner took me to the western entrance of the building. On leaving my office, I ordered the soldiers to join the people and embrace them and they did so immediately. The demonstrators soon forced open the main iron gate at the entrance to the building and a few of them entered the grounds, but it was obvious that their target was the Prime Minister's office. The cleaner took me out of the western gate and a few SIB employees also followed me. On the way, I ordered about 20 officers who were standing in the corridor to leave the building and follow me into the side-street and walk towards the north of the city. Two soldiers (they cleaned SIB rooms) and my driver, Dusti who had deserted his vehicle because of the demonstrations, accompanied me. After a while, suddenly a man called my name. He was Namju, a weight-lifting champion. He told us to get in his car and he drove us to the house of my friend Dr. Omid.

As soon as I entered Dr. Omid's house, I telephoned my sister, Turan, and gave her my whereabouts. I do not remember well but I think I had a call the same evening. Omid picked up the phone and said Prime Minister Bazargan wants you. It became clear that Afrashteh, my sister's husband, had told Bazargan where I was staying and had given him the number. I talked to Bazargan on the telephone and he said that he would ring again. A few minutes later, Qarabai telephoned and said that Bazargan had given my numbers to him. He refused to disclose his number and said that his landlord had warned him that he would be asked to leave if his whereabouts was disclosed.

The army had totally withdrawn to barracks in favour of the revolution and there was no reliable information about Bakhteyar's whereabouts. About four o'clock in the afternoon of February 12, the telephone rang again. As usual, Omid picked up the phone and told me that Bazargan wished to talk to me. I took the receiver and after exchange of pleasantries Bazargan asked, "Do you know Qaranei?"

"Of course", I replied.

Qaranei took the receiver and said, "You must come to my house right now." I got his address and number and Dusti immediately took me there. I knocked at the door and introduced myself. The door was opened and I went in. Qaranei's wife directed me to a room upstairs. I sat down and waited about half an hour until Qaranei came in his uniform. He greeted me and sat beside me and said, "There are two jobs you should carry out; first, telephone Badrei, Khosrowdad and Rabei and urge them to stop being childish." He added, "they plan to launch a coup tomorrow with the support of the Lavizan unit."

"Certainly, I will do my best, how stupid they are!", I said.

Then Qaranei added, "Second, you must introduce four men for the posts of commander of the ground, air and naval forces as well as SAVAK.

"Did Bazargan himself recommend that you ask me to do that?", I asked.

"I'll ask", he said. He went into another room to telephone and after a few minutes came back and said, "the Prime Minister said they should be introduced immediately."

I introduced General Hushang Hatam as Commander of Ground Force, General Azar Barzin for the Air Force, Rear Admiral Ahmad Madani for the Navy and General Moqqaddam for SAVAK. Qaranei declared that the four men should assume their posts without any hesitation.

To meet his first demand, I left Qaranei's house and returned to my residence that was Omid's house. The sun was setting. First, I telephoned Badrei; his wife took up the phone and said that she was not aware of Badrei's whereabouts. I said it was vital for him to talk to me and I left a message along with my number for him. Then, I telephoned Khosrowdad. His servant gave me a similar answer. There was nobody at Rabie's house. I waited for two hours but I did not receive a single phone call. I telephoned Qaranei and told him that I could not contact them and he said, "O.K. they are in Lavizan. I'll do it myself." He added that Moqqaddam had refused to accept the top post of SAVAK and urged me to persuade him to accept the post. I got Moqqaddam's number and urged him to accept the offer. He immediately accepted.[28]

It was in the evening of February 13 when Bazargan telephoned me again and invited me to meet him at the Prime Minister's Office at 8 in the morning. He said that he had also invited Colonel Memar Sadeqi. The next morning, Dusti dropped me off near the Prime Minister's Office. The street was blocked. A youngman, in the uniform of the auxiliary forces who recognized me, ordered the guards to allow me in. He was an air force Major. He accompanied me to Prime Minister's Office which was situated next to Pasteur street. Colonel Sadeqi, an employee of SIB was also there. Air force cadets were guarding the building. I informed the officer in charge that I had been summoned. After nearly an hour, he came back and said, "A few hours before, an armed group in a vehicle fired at the building and the Prime Minister left his office for Imam

Khomeini's residence." Bazargan did not telephone me again.

I stayed for about five days at Omid's house. The situation was getting worse and former officials such as Badrei, Rabei, Khosrowdad, Amini Afshar, Nasiri etc. were executed one by one. It was clear that Bazargan and Qaranei were in full control of the situation and I feared that I too would be arrested and killed. Then, I learned that Moqqaddam who was put forward for the post of chief of SAVAK had been arrested. Omid was very worried and constantly talked to his friends on telephone or stood behind windows looking out.

One morning the telephone rang and as usual Omid answered. Then he said, "I have just spoken to someone who introduced himself a member of the Central Committee and he said we should go to his address since our residence is under watch. The address was near to the Swiss Embassy. I tried to pacify Omid and said that I would go by myself. Dusti took me to Afrashteh's house and we stayed there until evening. From then I changed the places of my hiding in order to escape arrest.

Finally, with the help of Afrashteh I talked to Bazargan on telephone and I read out what I had already written to acquit myself of any wrongdoings.

Bazargan asked me to send my plea to him. I wrote out a neat copy again and gave it to the son of Bazargan's brother who was the chief of his private office. In my plea, I explained about my stance and activities in the final months prior to the victory of the revolution. I made it clear that I was not involved in financial embezzlements and the corruption which existed during Mohammad Reza's reign and requested to be forgiven. Bazargan in reply urged me to stay indoors at an unknown address. When I was writing the plea, Nosratollah requested that his name be included but I refused and asked him to write a separate plea. He refused and gave himself over to a revolutionary court. He was imprisoned for a while and then released.

It was on the eve of the new year that I went to my sister's house, Iran, at Amirabad and stayed there for two years. I wrote a second plea to Bazargan and requested financial support since the newly established Foundation for the Needy and Disabled had seized all my belongings. I also asked him to help me to leave the country under those circumstances. After a short period of time, Bazargan's government collapsed and I did not receive any answer. I met

Bazargan's brother at Afrashteh's house and he promised me financial support but it never materialized. Since then, I had no relations with Bazargan and he was not in a position to extend any assistance to me.

BAZARGAN GOVERNMENT FALLS

The Provisional Government headed by Mehdi Bazargan* was formed on February 5, 1979. Bazargan, leader of Iran Freedom Movement, repeatedly admitted that he was no revolutionary and the government put together was strongly tinged with conservatism. His ministers belonged to his own class of liberal-minded technocrats.

Bazargan's predominantly Western-educated cabinet members headlessly revealed their eagerness to have good relations with the United States and Bazargan quickly announced that Iran would soon resume normal oil shipments to all its customers. However, Bazargan whose policies ran contrary to the principles of the Islamic Revolution laid down by Imam Khomeini could not exercise wide powers and described his government as "a knife without a blade".[29]

On Sunday November 4, 1979 the students known as "Followers of the Imam's Line" seized the U.S. Embassy and took 53 of the staff hostage. That happened some two weeks after the Carter administration admitted the deposed Shah to the United States. The confrontation had risen to a new level. It was the "second revolution" as described by Khomeini.[30]

Although Ambassador Sullivan had ordered reference files boxed and shipped back to Washington, still some files were available in the embassy. When the attack finally came it was not possible to shred and burn all of these files in the short time available.

The students who took the embassy pieced together shredded documents, but most of the remaining embassy files were taken intact. Copies of the documents were subsequently published in a series of volumes including messages, letters and memos dating back as far as the early 50s.

*** Bazargan died of a heart stroke in Zurich, Switzerland on January 20, 1995 on his way from Iran to the United States for treatment.**

The students who took the embassy were convinced that the United States had secretly managed political events in Iran for years, that it had directed the Shah's campaign against the revolution and that it was engaged in efforts to destablize Iran and undermine the newly established Islamic government through contacts with dissidents and other political elements.

At the time of the attack, Bazargan and his Foreign Minister Ibrahim Yazdi who had privately met Brzezinski in Algiers were on their way to Tehran. Upon arrival, both Bazargan and Yazdi submitted their resignation in protest and it was accepted by the Imam and government operations were turned over to the Revolutionary Council.[31]

DEPOSED SHAH DIES

"Originally, the Shah was supposed to fly from Iran directly to the United States. However, he decided to stop in Egypt and his visit continued there for a week. Then, he flew to Morocco as the guest of King Hassan. In the meantime, Khomeini returned to Tehran, the Bakhteyar regime collapsed and, on February 14, the U.S. Embassy was attacked by armed militants.

Had the Shah come to the United States in January 1979 as expected, his presence would have been regarded as entirely normal... But as the political situation deteriorated and the United States monoeuvred to retain some measure of political contact with Iran, the Shah's indecision and procrastination gradually transformed what would have been a routine event into a political issue... It seems likely that the Shah, during these first initial weeks, continued to hope that events would turn in his favour, as they had in 1953, and if he was to be called back to Iran, it would obviously be preferable to return from an Islamic country rather than the United States. Traumatized by events and lacking any plans for the future, the Shah finally made his decision to seek asylum in the United States...

By the first week in March, both the Shah and his hosts were becoming anxious. King Hassan of Morocco was politely letting the Shah's entourage know that his continued presence in the country was becoming a political liability. The Shah, in turn, had contacted a series of other governments without success. The Moroccans, in an effort to accelerate a process that was becoming an embarrassment to them, engaged a U.S. public relations firm to make the necessary legal and practical arrangements for the Shah to move to the United States.

Summarising these contacts on March 6, David Aaron informed President Carter that if the Shah came to the United States, it was entirely possible that a guerrilla group could retaliate against the remaining Americans, possibly taking one or more Americans hostage and refusing to release them until the Shah was extradited. President Carter approved a plan to seek other countries of possible asylum for the Shah...

The Bahamas proved an unhappy choice. The villa where the Shah was housed was visible from the public beach and provided no security. Moreover, the cost of the villa and associated quarters for his retinue proved to be prohibitive, even for a man of the Shah's wealth. He remained there for more than two months, unhappy and exposed to the curious gaze of any tourist who could afford entrance to the exclusive Paradise Island Resort...

The Shah had moved on June 10 from Bahamas to Cuernavaca, a resort town southwest of Mexico City, but throughout the summer of 1979 the issue of his possible entrance into the United States continued to be discussed, largely as a political problem.

According to the medical history that eventually became known, the Shah had discovered a lump above his abdomen while on a skiing trip to Switzerland in 1974. He contacted two French doctors, Dr. Jean Bernard and Dr. Georges Flandrin, who discovered that the Shah had an enlarged spleen. They diagnosed the Shah's malady as lymphoma - a cancer or the lymph system that resembles leukemia... by the time the Shah arrived in Bahamas, his condition had begun to deteriorate markedly. The lymph nodes in his neck had become swollen and painful, and Dr. Flandrin, who was called to the Bahamas diagnosed a second form of cancer known as Richter's syndrome, which is usually fatal...

Because of serious political implications it could entail, the Shah had taken extreme measures to keep his illness secret. By September 1979, the Shah was suffering from a variety of complications that could no longer be cancealed and that required medical treatment. He had sharp stomach pains, fever, chills and nausea. His physical appearance worsened almost by the day.

The Shah was admitted into the United States on October 22. He arrived in New York from Mexico City by a chartered jet. His trip to the United States almost coincided with the seizure of the U.S. Embassy in Tehran by students. American leaders desperately looked for another place for Shah's residence hoping that could ease the situation. Panama was an inevitable choice since General Omar Torrijos, the strong man of Panamanian politics had already indicated readiness to offer him asylum.

On December 16, the Shah left Texas for Panama City. He took up residence in the home of Gabriel Lewis, Panama's former ambassador to the U.S. on the Pacific island of Cantadora... On December 18, President Aristides Royo of Panama told the U.S. Ambassador that his government had been contacted by Iran requesting the Shah's extradition... Royo said that Panama would not extradite the Shah, but he was intrigued by the possibility that Panama could assist in devising a face-saving plan that might result in the hostages' release...Panama was forced to find a solution following daily student demonstrations protesting the Shah's stay in their country... Gradually Mohammad Reza let it be known that he wanted to move to another country. At the same time, his physical condition was deteriorating. His spleen was badly swollen and had to be removed.

There were no other countries available; only Sadat of Egypt could receive him. On March 23, 1980 the Shah left Panama for Egypt. After months of painful lymphatic, he died of cancer in the morning of July 27, 1980 in a military hospital in the Egyptian capital. The final blow came when his pancreas began to hemorrhage. After he had lost over 4 pints of blood, the Shah fell into a coma. His doctors tried unsuccessfully to revive him with electric shock treatment; then they removed his tubes and life-support systems.

He was buried in the Al-Rifaie Mosque which contains the tombs of King Farouq, the last king of Egypt and his father King Foad. The Shah's own father, Reza Shah, had been entombed at the same mosque for several years after his death in exile in 1944.

The Shah's death was greeted in Iran with a radio announcement that "Mohammad Reza Pahlavi, the bloodsucker of the century has died at last". The afternoon newspapers of Tehran rushed out special editions bearing the huge headline: Shah mord (the Shah is dead). With the headlines were pictures of the former Shah with staring eyes."[32]

MY LIFE AFTER THE REVOLUTION

I was in hiding for five years before I was arrested by the revolutionary intelligence agents. My recommendations to Bakhteyar to offer his resignation and my invitation of ten Parliamentary deputies to resign as well as my role in the February 11 meeting of army leaders prompted rumours about me with some former officials accusing me of betraying the Shah.

As I said, I went into hiding after the February 11. I was afraid of being arrested and killed but Bazargan's telephone call to me and the later developments pacified me.

On the fifth day of my stay, Omid politely let me know that he no longer wanted me to stay in his house citing security reasons. Then, I sought refuge in the house of Turan, my sister. Her husband, Mohammad Ali Afrashteh, appeared worried. A short while later, Afrashteh, after answering a telephone call claimed that some people were coming for a discussion with me. Afrashteh was uncomfortable with my stay in his house; therefore, I escaped to Qaranei's house. The next day, I went to see Afrashteh to verify his claim and I found that no one had come for a discussion. It was obvious that both Omid and Afrashteh had lied.

Some time later, I stayed for about two weeks in the house of a relative of my brother, Nosratollah. There, I read an Ettela'at newspaper report about the execution of former high-ranking officials. The report caused me concern about my safety; therefore, I wrote a plea to Bazargan.

Staying indoors was embarrassing for me and I had to remain there until my older sister, Iran, invited me to her house in Amirabad. It was during this period that I learned that I had been accused of co-operating with an Islamic organization. A radio station run by Bakhteyar began circulating rumours about me alleging that I had been employed by the new regime's intelligence services and that made me happy. I also became happy when I learned that Mohammad Reza in an interview with a U.S. television network, apparently accused me of committing treason against him

I did not care if the deposed Shah and others spoke for or against me since I only wanted to be remembered.

Before his death in Egypt, Mohammad Reza told a British reporter that he had not been convinced that I had betrayed him. The Shah insisted that it is rumoured that I had betrayed him. The Shah in one of his books described Qarabaqi a traitor but made no mention of me perhaps deliberately in order to avoid accusing me of committing treason against him.

Azadeh Shafiq, a reporter, had attributed the murder in Paris of Ashraf's son to me and I was happy that I was portrayed as a mysterious man who had cheated the French police and escaped.

According to my son, Shahrokh, the U.S. press attributed the assassination in America of Ali Akbar Tabatabai, the Press Attache of the Iranian Embassy in Washington and an agent of Ardeshir Zahei to me.

Later, I started coming out of hiding and I went walking in Laleh part to pass my time. I became acquainted with a merchant there and gradually I introduced myself to him. In order to continue our friendship, I told him that the new regime had forgiven me.

Bakhteyar radio's comments about me convinced my brother's wife to allow me to stay in their house otherwise she was not willing even to prepare lunch for me.

I had no motivation to escape abroad. My family lived in Iran, my possessions were in Iran and I had no deposits abroad. Although I encouraged some people to leave Iran, I did not want to go abroad myself. I liked to see myself more intelligent than others.

You may think that since I was a seasoned politician I must have been making a plan during Bakhteyar's government for my future which I am not willing to reveal. No, this is not true. I liked to work irrespective of rank, position etc. I had been convinced that nothing could be done to save the Shah but some people such as Badrei were of the opinion that a coup could save the Shah's regime from total collapse.

FARDUST DIES

The wave of executions in the first months of the revolution gradually settled down and Fardust remained safe under the protection of the "Provisional Government". Fardust in his memoirs has made it clear that if the remnants of the former regime were not exterminated, even General Moqqaddam would have remained in his post as the Chief of SAVAK and individuals such as Nasiri and Hoveida would have retired and spent the rest of their days peacefully.

Fardust neither during the Provisional Government nor after its collapse played a role in the formation of the newly-established post-Shah intelligence services. The Iranian Islamic Government gradually learned that in addition to the self-established popular organizations such as the "Islamic Republic Guards Corps"(IRGC) and "Komiteh" which were formed by the Iranian youth, intelligence and security services were also required. The intelligence branch of IRGC was a new security set-up which played a historical and effective role in protecting the achievements of the revolution.

During these years, Western governments and opponents of the Islamic Government who had escaped abroad continued circulating rumours about Fardust. Besides Bakhteyar who made the allegations because of his disagreements with Fardust during his 37-day government, the outlawed Communist Tudeh Party also played an important role in spreading fabricated information about Fardust.

In 1983, the intelligence branch of IRGC was investigating the secret and complicated relations between the Tudeh Party and the Soviet KGB and GRU. The Tudeh Party appealed to new tricks and tried to introduce itself as the target of the Western intelligence services led by Fardust as the head of "SAVAMA".[33]

Before the establishment of the Ministry of Intelligence, IRGC's intelligence branch, Revolutionary Courts, Komiteh's intelligence branch and the Investigation and Intelligence Unit of the Presidential Bureau looked after security affairs. The appearance of a number of intelligence branches, an inevitable phenomenon after the revolution, was a fundamental shortcoming and a centralized intelligence system was required in the country.

Although these popular intelligence branches established by the people foiled the plots of the opposition groups and those of foreign countries, weaknesses gradually became evident and, therefore, the Ministry of Intelligence was set up. The new intelligence services were aware that Fardust was in Iran but the rumours about him led them to believe that he was working for one of them.

Anyhow, the new intelligence branches were merged and the

issue of Fardust was immediately put on the agenda. Efforts were launched aimed at discovering why Fardust did not escape abroad? Why he went into hiding in Tehran? Did Fardust remain in Iran to help materialize the complicated objectives of the Western intelligence agencies?... the Intelligence Ministry studied Fardust's case carefully and learned that Fardust himself helped spread the rumours about him and finally he was arrested in 1983 in his father's house in Vesal Shirazi street.

The investigations carried out by experts at the Intelligence Ministry and information arising from the interrogations of Fardust made it clear that Fardust was a propaganda psychological phenomenon rather than a political or intelligence puzzle because he allowed the West to launch a propaganda campaign against the revolution and helped spread rumours about himself.

Hussein Fardust was a symbol who wasted his life serving the former regime. He was from a poor family who accidentally found his way to the Court. In his childhood and youth, he was humiliated by the corrupt wealthy men at the Court and this made him become a quite obedient person. His quite personality won the favour of the Shah and Mohammad Reza felt safe appointing Fardust as the head of the security and intelligence organ of his regime.

An inferiority complex also caused Fardust to avoid showing up at banquets and he did not seek fame for himself. His personal characteristics and his position which empowered him to see to the affairs of people at the Court and government officials, and the Shah's reliance on him gradually portrayed Fardust as a "mysterious" agent in governmental circles and caused others to respect and at the same time fear him. Since he did not get himself involved in power struggles or financial embezzlements, nobody looked at Fardust as a "rival" and since he was in charge of sensitive organizations, many were afraid of him.

Developments in the early days after the revolution were in favour of Fardust and his past experience put him in good position for making a future for himself but the strong waves of the revolution shook the liberal government and Fardust sought solitude and started a mentally distressing life in hiding. During this time, he felt that he had lost all he had and became depressed. Moreover, his relatives did not like to jeopardize their life by giving shelter to him.

After his arrest, experts at the Intelligence Ministry discovered that Fardust had valuable memories of the Pahlavi era; therefore, they asked him to write them down. This he did. His memories are his written statements during his interrogations and interviews, a part of which was aired on the Iranian television.

Unfortunately, Fardust died of a heart attack on May 17, 1987 before being able to put all his memoirs on paper especially those of events in the 40s.[34]

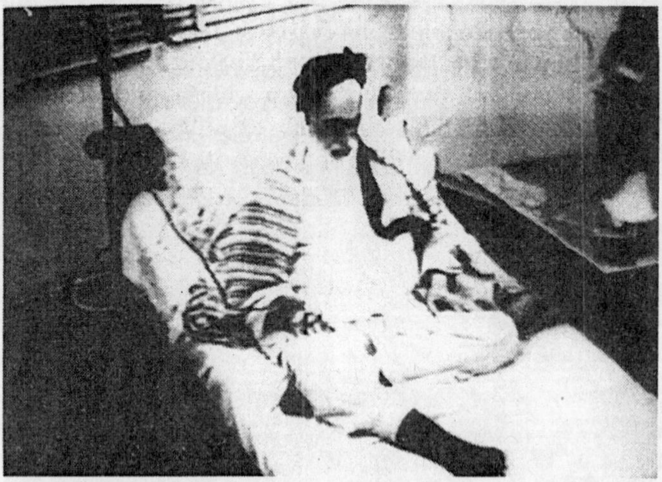

Fig. 40: The last days of the life of a man who shook the world and destroyed a regime which was considered to be the pillar of Western diplomacy in the Persian Gulf region. In May 1989, the Imam fell ill. He is praying Allah at the hospital bed a day before his operation

Fig. 41: A view of the shrine of the Founder of the Islamic Republic of Iran Imam Khomeini in Behesht-e-Zahra cemetry—the resting place of hundreds of thousands of martyrs—southern Tehran

Fig. 42: People mourn the demise of their leader. A newspaper headline says farewell to the Imam

Fig. 43: Another historic moment. Imam Khomeini passed away on June 3, 1989, a decade after he toppled the pro-West Shah's regime. Millions of Iranians flocked to pay their last respect to their guide. His coffin is lying in state

References

Chapter 1

FROM MY ENTRY INTO COURT TO FALL OF REZA SHAH

1. "Until I was given the title of Crown Prince, I had lived with my mother and my brothers and sisters. After the coronation, however, I was separated from them, and my father directed that I should receive what he termed 'a manly education'... My father also engaged a French governess to take charge of my life at home. To her I owe the advantage of being able to speak and read French as if it were my own language; and beyond this, she opened my mind to the spirit of Western culture. I shall always remain indebted to Mme Arfa, as my governess was called. She died in Paris in 1959."

   Above from *Mission for My Country: His Imperial Majesty Mohammad Reza Shah Pahlavi*, Hutchinson and Co. (Publishers) Ltd., 1961-8; p. 52.
2. Cheraqalikhan Savad Kuhi was Reza Shah's uncle and his aide. For a while, he was Governor of the northern Mazandaran Province and then was appointed Deputy Court Minister. He died in 1930 in Berlin, Germany and was buried in south Tehran. *Above collected by the compiler of Fardust's Memoirs, the Institute for Political Studies and Research, published as footnotes in the Persian text of the book.*
3. A special Kremlin honour guard was accompanying us. Reza Shah did not leave the port until the ship disappeared in the sea. The Russian government on the occasion of Crown Prince's arrival in Russia declared amnesty to all Iranian prisoners. *Above collected by the compiler of Fardust's Memoirs, the Institute for Political Studies and Research, published as footnotes in the Persian text of the book.*
4. Bahador's only daughter, Neino, was married to Flix Aqayan, an Armenian aristocrat. Later, Princess Ashraf, Reza Shah's younger daughter, fell in love with Bahador's son but they never married. *Above collected by the compiler of Fardust's Memoirs, the Institute for Political Studies and Research, published as footnotes in the Persian text of the book.*

5. Le Rosey boarding school was situated near a town called Rolle, between Lausanne and Geneva. It was a famous private school and for years, Belgium students were studying there. One had to apply in advance for registration and pass an entrance exam. When we were registered, Henry Karnak's son was owner of the school and his American wife had internationalized the school. *Above collected by the compiler of Fardust's Memoirs, the Institute for Political Studies and Research, published as footnotes in the Persian text of the book.*
6. "Since my father was so determined to Westernize Iran, no one was surprised when he decided to send me to school in the West. He wanted the heir to his throne to become more familiar with Western civilization.... I had graduated from the elementary military school in Tehran in May of 1931; so, after a summer's vacation, it was time for me to leave for Switzerland in September. My father had determined to send with me Dr. Moadab Nafisi, who was to be both my guardian and my personal physician. Mostashar, my professor of Persian, was also to go with me and continue his teaching.

   In addition, my father thought it would be wise for my brother Ali Reza and a couple of friends from the military school to accompany me. I suggested *Hussein Fardust*, my good companion as one and for the other I proposed Mehrpour Teymourtach, a son of my father's Minister of the Imperial Court. My father approved these nominations. Later, however, my father had a serious disagreement with his Minister of Court, and to my regret Mehrpour had to return home."

   Above from *Mission for My Country*: *His Imperial Majesty Mohammad Reza Shah Pahlavi*; Hutchinson and Co. (Publishers) Ltd., 1961-8; pp. 59-60.
7. Ali Amini was a famous Freemason and had become a British favourite. He served as Prime Minister during the reign of Mohammad Reza. Reza Shah used to talk to the Crown Prince two hours a day except holidays after we returned from Switzerland. He shared his views with his son on domestic problems and foreign policy matters to test Mohammad Reza's abilities and prepare him for new political assignments. Reza Shah usually studied history books every night before going to bed to improve his understanding of the international developments. *Above collected by the compiler of Fardust's Memoirs, the Institute for Political Studies and Research, published as footnotes in the Persian text of the book.*
8. Of course, Reza Shah did not hate the Proun for being a spy only since I was left in no doubt that there were many British agents in the Court. His concern was because Proun was a gay and he was spreading homosexuality in his Imperial Court. *Above collected by*

the compiler of Fardust's Memoirs, the Institute for Political Studies and Research, published as footnotes in the Persian text of the book.

9. "...following my return from Europe, and towards the end of my studies at the Military College, Reza Shah decided to provide for me a suitable bride. In doing so I think he had a double motive: he wanted to find a princess of good descent to marry his son; and at the same time he sought, through a marriage link with another royal family, to cement relations with a nearby state... My father officially inquired whether Princess Fawzia of Egypt would be available as a wife for his son. Negotiations rapidly progressed, and the first thing I knew I was betrothed. That was in 1938."

   Above from *Mission for My Country: His Imperial Majesty Mohammad Reza Shah Pahlavi*, Hutchinson and Co. (Publishers) Ltd., 1961-8; p. 218.

10. "My father's daily routine was simple indeed. Usually he arose at 5 a.m. After hurrying through his washing and shaving, he sat down for breakfast and began to read the news of the day and any reports that had been sent him up to that hour. Exactly at 7:30 he would go to his office, where he received those who had business with him, starting with his chief secretary. Conferences with ministers and other officials continued until 11:30, when he lunched.

    About 2 p.m. he started his afternoon work, which consisted chiefly of inspecting the army and new civil projects and institutions. The Council of Ministers, as our Cabinet is called, often held afternoon meetings in his presence. Then from 6 to 8 p.m., after all his other work, he would study the reports he had received during the day. Exactly at 8 p.m. he took his supper, and he retired at 10 p.m. However, he used to say that even in bed his plans were revolving and forming in his mind; thus he was never entirely idle.

    As this work schedule suggests, my father's outstanding characteristic was his observance of order and care in everything he did."

    Above from *Mission for My Country: His Imperial Majesty Mohammad Reza Shah Pahlavi*, Hutchinson and Co. (Publishers) Ltd., 1961-8; p. 46.

11. With the departure of Reza Shah from Iran, Moluk expelled Esmat from the Palace and became the undisputable power in the Court. Esmat in the last days of Pahlavi dynasty used to come to "Iran Javan Club" to spend his time with Fardust in northern Tehran. *Above collected by the compiler of Fardust's Memoirs, the Institute for Political Studies and Research, published as footnotes in the Persian text of the book.*

12. Fazlollah Zahedi was a British puppet who handed over Sheikh Khazal to Reza Shah in Tehran while the Sheikh was able to resist

against Reza Shah for long. Zahedi held no key post during Reza Shah's rule and usually spent his time with women until he became ambassador to Europe. His son, Ardashir who was a favourite of the Americans was appointed ambassador to Washington. *Above collected by the compiler of Fardust's Memoirs, the Institute for Political Studies and Research, published as footnotes in the Persian text of the book.*

13. "The British clearly recognized that Reza Khan could serve their interests very well. He could provide the order and stability their commercial interests needed, particularly in oil production, and he could control difficult tribal groups whom the British otherwise would have had to subsidize."

    Above from *Shi'ism and Social Protest*, edited by Juan R.I. Cole and Nikki R. Keddie, Yale University Press,1986; p. 67.

14. "For a time it appeared that a way out might offer itself if Iran could be turned into a republic - an idea which son supported as a result of the example of Kemal Ataturk, and which Reza Khan encouraged. He also had himself named Commander-in-Chief of the armed forces (in place of the Shah), in preparation for the proclamation of a republic, probably before the Iranian New Year in 1924. But as the possibility became more real, opposition to the idea became more vocal and more organized. Then the example of Turkey backfired: the Turkish parliament abolished the caliphate and disestablished the Muslim clergy. The implicit threat to the power and privileges of the mullas should a republic be proclaimed in Iran was obvious... On 31 October 1925, the Majlis deposed Ahmad Shah... When they did so on 6 December 1925 a new period in the history of the nation was formally opened..."

    For details please see *Twentieth Century Iran*, Hossein Amirsadeghi and R.W. Ferrier, William Heinemann Ltd., 1977; pp. 26-7.

15. "In the Cossacks, the young man rose rapidly through the Persian ranks, and by the time the Communist revolution took place in Russia, he was known as Reza Khan and was the senior Persian serving under the Russian officer cadre. Consequently, when the revolution occurred and the Cossack officers left, Reza Khan succeeded to the command of the Cossack Brigade.

    The British, sensing the opportunity that was presented to them by the collapse of the Russian presence in Persia, moved rapidly to try to establish their total hegemony over the country. General Ironside, who was the senior British officer serving in Persia, suggested to Reza Khan that he bring the Cossack Brigade down from the north to the outskirts of Tehran and place pressure on the Qajar Shah to accept a British protectorate.

Reza Khan did bring his brigade to the gates of Tehran and did put pressure upon the Qajar dynasty. But his goals were not those of the British. He wished to force the Qajar Shah to abdicate, and to create a republic.

In this ambition he was following the course of Kemal Ataturk, who, in next-door Turkey, had moved in the wake of the collapse of the Ottoman empire to establish a republic in Ankara and to set out on a course that would modernize, westernize, and secularize that ancient Islamic empire. This was the role that Reza Khan also saw for himself.

Over the period of the next few years in which he manoeuvred with respect to the British and to the Qajar dynasty, Reza Khan eventually placed himself in a situation in which he was able to overthrow the Qajars and to assume a position of power for himself. By this time, however, largely at the urging of the senior members of the Shi'a clergy, Reza Khan had abandoned his idea of establishing a republic. The Shi'a clergy, who were enormously influential in the country, preferred to retain a monarchy."

Please see *Mission to Iran*, William H. Sullivan; W.W. Norton and Company, 1981; pp. 47-8.

16. Please see *Twentieth Century Iran*, Hossein Amirsadeghi and R.W. Ferrier; William Heinemann Ltd., 1977; pp. 23-4.

17. "Mohammad Taqi Erani ... had studied in Germany before Hitler came to power and had many contacts with German Communists. When he came back to Iran he felt that the situation there was very much like that of the Weimar Republic and required the same drastic remedies. (He was arrested with 52 of his companions after the government launched a campaign to hunt down the Communists.) Erani died in prison in the late 1930s, but in 1941 some of his disciples founded a Communist Party called the Tudeh (Masses). Because of its close association with Moscow, the Tudeh Party was always suspect, particularly at this period when, ironically enough, it took up a position opposed to the nationalization of oil, because what Moscow wanted was new concessions, not the nationalization of old ones."

Above from *The Return of the Ayatollah: The Iranian Revolution from Mossaddiq to Khomeini*, Mohammad Heikal; Andre Deutsch Limited, 1981; p. 57.

18. For details please see *Twentieth Century Iran*, Hossein Amirsadeghi and R.W. Ferrier; William Heinemann Ltd., 1977; pp. 47-8.

19. "In the 1930s Reza Shah carried out many policies that should have distanced him from the British. He forced a renegotiation of the oil agreement, but one of only modest proportions. His real declaration of independence came with his policy toward Hitler's Germany.

Commercially and politically the shift toward Germany was important. Because of the seriousness of the threat Hitler posed, the British could not accept this degree of independence from Reza Shah. In 1941 an Anglo-Soviet invasion of Iran took place, and Reza Shah was exiled to South Africa."

Above from *Shi'ism and Social Protest*, edited by Juan R.I. Cole and Nikki R. Keddie, Yale University Press,1986; p. 68.

20. Please see *Mission for My Country: His Imperial Majesty Mohammad Reza Shah Pahlavi*; Hutchinson and Co. (Publishers) Ltd., 1961-8; pp. 69-70.
21. The quotations have been extracted from former British Prime Minister Winston Churchill's statement from his history of the Second World War. For further details please see *Mission for My Country: His Imperial Majesty Mohammad Reza Shah Pahlavi*; Hutchinson and Co. (Publishers) Ltd., 1961-8; pp. 71-2.
22. Please see *The Return of the Ayatollah: The Iranian Revolution from Mossaddiq to Khomeini*, Mohamed Heikal; Andre Deutsch Limited; 1981; p. 35.
23. "Several times I urged him to write his memoirs. But he insisted that this he would never do, because he did not want to risk the chance that he might in advertently say something that, even indirectly, could bring some harm to his country".

For details please see *Mission for My Country: His Imperial Majesty Mohammad Reza Shah Pahlavi;* Hutchnison and Co. (Publishers) Ltd., 1961-8; p. 46.

Chapter 2

EARLY YEARS OF MOHAMMAD REZA'S REIGN

1. Above from *All Fall Down: America's Tragic Encounter with Iran;* Gary Sick, Random House, New York, 1985; pp. 8-9.
2. Please see *Twentieth Century Iran*, Hossein Amirsadeghi and R.W. Ferrier; William Heinemann Ltd., 1977; p. 53.
3. For further details please see *1946-1952 Years of Trial and Hope*, Memoirs by Harry S. Truman; Volume II; The New American Library, 1965; pp. 115-7.
4. Please see *Twentieth Century Iran*, Hossein Amirsadeghi and R.W. Ferrier; William Heinemann Ltd., 1977; p. 53, p. 48 and p. 56.
5. Sir Reader Bulard was born in suburbs of London in 1885. In 1906 he was employed in the Foreign Office and was Baghdad's Military Governor during the Iraqi revolution of 1920. When he was Britain's consul in Arabia, Saudi family were installed by the British government to run the country. Bulard was appointed

Plenipotentiary Minister to Iran in 1939. The Shah disliked his arrogant behaviour but London was heedless on this. His memories were published in 1961 in London. *Above collected by the compiler of Fardust's Memoirs, the Institute for Political Studies and Research, published as footnotes in the Persian text of the book.*

6. "In the treaty the two Allies stated that the presence of their troops on our soil did not constitute a military occupation, although I must add that all Persians continued to call it so. The Allies promised to respect our territorial integrity, sovereignty, and political independence, and to withdraw their forces within six months after the end of the war with the Axis. They also pledged themselves to ease Iran's economic difficulties arising from the war, and we in turn assured them of transit, communications, and other facilities needed to move supplies to Russia."

   For details please see *Mission for My Country: His Majesty Mohammad Reza Shah Pahlavi*; Hutchinson and Co. (Publishers) Ltd., 1961-8; pp. 75-76.

7. Davoud Monshizadeh was expelled from Iran in early 1960s because of his support of Teimour Bakhteyar. He resided in Germany and published a newspaper called *Sowgand*. Then, he started studying in Sweden. *Above collected by the author of the book, the Institute for Political Studies and Research.*

8. For details please see *Twentieth Century Iran*, Hossein Amirsadeghi and R.W. Ferrier; William Heinemann Ltd., 1977; pp. 82-9.

9. For details please see *Twentieth Century Iran*, Hossein Amirsadeghi and R.W. Ferrier; William Heinemann Ltd., 1977; pp. 62-4.

10. General Bradly (1893-1981) was the commander of U.S. forces during World War II. He commanded America's biggest military contingent with an estimated 1,300,000 personnel in Europe. He was appointed chief of the joint staff in 1948 and then the chief of NATO's military committee. He was working for the "Bulova Watch" company after retirement. *Above collected by the author of the book, the Institute for Political Studies and Research.*

11. Please see *The Return of the Ayatollah: The Iranian Revolution from Mossaddiq to Khomeini*, Mohammad Heikal; Andre Deutsch Limited, 1981; p. 55.

12. "... in February of 1949, I was attending the annual commemoration of the founding of the University of Tehran. In military uniform, I was just about to enter the Faculty of Law building, where the ceremony was to be held, when suddenly shots rang out, and bullets came in my direction. Fantastic though it may seem, three of them passed through my military cap without touching my head. But the gunman's fourth shot penetrated my right cheekbone and came out under my nose.

My would-be assassin—who had been posing as a photographer—was within six feet of me. He was now aiming his revolver at my heart. Both he and I were sufficiently apart from the crowd for me to know he had a good clear field of fire. At such point-blank range, how could he miss?

I can still remember my reactions at that instant. I thought, 'what should I do? Shall I jump on him? But if I approach him, I shall become a better target. Shall I run away? Then I shall be a perfect target to be shot in the back.

So I suddenly started shadow-dancing or feinting. He fired again, wounding me in the shoulder. His last shot stuck in the gun. I had the queer and not unpleasant sensation of knowing that I was still alive.

The man then threw down his gun and tried to escape, and in their fury at this assassination attempt, some of my young officers unfortunately killed him. He must have been a curious character. We discovered that he had been friendly with various arch-conservative religious fanatics, yet in his flat we found literature of the Tudeh or Communist party. His mistress was the daughter of a gardener at the British Embassy in Tehran.

I was bleeding like a young bull whose throat had been slit. I recall that I wanted to proceed with the ceremony, but those in my entourage overruled me and took me to the hospital. My blood-stained uniform was placed on display at the Iranian Officers' Club in Tehran, where it may still be seen."

Above from *Mission for My Country: His Imperial Majesty Mohammad Reza Shah Pahlavi*, Hutchinson and Co. (Publishers) Ltd., 1961-8; p. 57.

13. Please see *The Return of the Ayatollah: The Iranian Revolution from Mossaddiq to Khomeini, Mohamed Heikal*; Mohamed Heikal; Andre Deutsch Limited, 1981; p. 56.
14. Please see *Twentieth Century Iran*, Hossein Amirsadeghi and R.W. Ferrier; William Heinemann Ltd., 1977; pp. 74-5, pp. 73-5 and pp. 58-9.
15. Please see *Twentieth Century Iran*, Hossein Amirsadeghi and R.W. Ferrier; William Heinemann Ltd, 1977; p. 74.
16. Please see *Twentieth Century Iran*, Hossein Amirsadeghi and R.W. Ferrier; William Heinemann Ltd., 1977; p. 78.
17. This was incorrect. It was the Shah himself who sent his family abroad to guarantee their safety. The rest of his family remained in Iran. *Above collected by the compiler of Fardust's Memoirs, the Institute for Political Studies and Research, published as footnotes in the Persian text of the book.*

18. "On August 19,1953, Mossaddiq was overthrown by a coup that received direction, financing, and logistic support from the CIA in high-level collaboration with the British MI-6."

Above from *Shi'ism and Social Protest*, edited by Juan R.I. Cole and Nikki R. Keddie, Yale University Press, 1986; p. 74.

19. Above from *All Fall Down: America's Tragic Encounter with Iran*; Gary Sick, Random House, New York, 1985; p. 6.
20. Please see *The Isiamic Success: The Untold Story of the Islamic Revolution of Iran*, by Omid Souresrafil, Fast Books, 1996; p. 3.
21. Please see *The Fascinating Truth About the "CIA"*, Brian Freemantle, Futura Publications, London, 1984; p. 168.
22. Please see *The Life and Times of Ayatollah Khomeini* written by Mir Ali Asghar Montazam, Anglo-European Publishing Limited, London; p. 130.
23. Please see *The Return of the Ayatollah: The Iranian Revolution from Mossaddiq to Khomeini*, Mohammad Heikal; Andre Deutsch Limited, 1981; p. 66.
24. Please see *The Pride and the Fall: Iran 1974-1979*, Sir Anthony Parsons, Butler and Tanner Ltd., London, 1984; p. 5.
25. Above from *All Fall Down: America's Tragic Encounter with Iran*; Gary Sick, Random House, New York, 1985; p. 7.

Chapter 3

THE SHAH AND THE ROYAL COURT

1. The existing documents prove Fardust's correct understanding that the British intelligence had a hand in having Mohammad Reza divorced Fawzia.

In 1978, it was revealed that the June 1952 coup which toppled Farouq was masterminded by the U.S. Central Intelligence Agency (CIA) and MI-6. Both agencies believed that Farouq's corruption had paved the way for the rising influence of "Communism" in Egypt and therefore decided to facilitate the advent to power of the anti-Communist Jamal Abdul Naser to replace Farouq. Naser launched a brutal crackdown against Communists and Muslim activists. He murdered Seyed Gutb and five other top members of Ekhvan al-Moslemin and jailed some 3,000 of their supporters. Naser's suppression coincided with the arrest in Iran in 1954 of Ayatollah Kashani and the hanging of "Fadaeyan-e-Islam" group members.

Naser's role was similar to that of Saddam Hussein of Iraq during the 1990 Persian Gulf crisis. Although the British and Americans helped Naser to seize power, Andrew Telly, an expert on CIA affairs, believes that they failed to anticipate the trouble Naser could create for them later. *Above collected by the compiler of Fardust's Memoirs, the Institute for Political Studies and Research, published as footnotes in the Persian text of the book.*

2. The Shah gives another account for his separation with Fawzia.

"For reasons still obscure to medical science, Queen Fawzia bore only one child; thus unfortunately no male heir issued from our marriage. Under the Persian Constitution the crown must pass by direct line of descent to a male heir. This rules out not only my daughter but also my three sisters. The Constitution further stipulates that no one descended from the previous Qajar dynasty is eligible to become king. Since two of my father's wives were of Qajar blood, my half-brothers who are their sons are ineligible. In fact I had only one brother not related to the Qajar line, and to my sorrow he was to die in an aeroplane crash in 1954. With these limitations it is no wonder that my advisors felt it important for my wife to bear a son. It is true that the Constitution might have been amended, but the climate of opinion seemed opposed to tampering with the provisions relating to the royal succession.

Besides, I was young and, quite apart from the constitutional factor, I wanted more children. When Queen Fawzia went to Egypt on an extended stay, we decided on a divorce."

Please see *Mission for My Country: His Imperial Majesty Mohammad Reza Shah Pahlavi*, Hutchinson and Co. (Publishers) Ltd., London, 1961-1968; pp. 219-20.

3. Rasputin was a Russian priest during Czars era. He had a great influence over the ruling clique and controlled all segments of the government. Though he enjoyed no identified official post, he was the real ruler of Russia. *Above collected by the compiler of Fardust's Memoirs, the Institute for Political Studies and Research, published as footnotes in the Persian text of the book.*

4. "One day my daughter, Princess Shahnaz, her eyes even brighter than usual, told me that she and her husband had become acquainted with a young lady who, they thought, was qualified for the responsibilities of a queen. My son-in-law had for some time been interesting himself in the problems of our students abroad, and it seems that he had met the young lady in question when she came to his office to discuss the continuation of her studies in France. Her name, said my daughter, was Miss Farah Diba, and she was twenty-one years old.

Naturally I wanted to know something of the young lady's family background, her upbringing, her education, and her personality. On her father's side her people came from a famous old family of Tabriz in our Province of (East) Azerbaijan, and her ancestors on her mother's side were of a respectable religious family from our Caspian Province of Gilan. In Persian the name 'Diba' literally means silk.

Miss Diba's paternal grandfather had attended military school in Czarist Russia and had served as an officer in our army in Qajar times. Her father had some education in Russia and then went to France, where he studied law and received the Bachelor of Law degree. Then, deciding to prepare for a military career, he completed the officers' training course at St. Cyr.

After his return to Iran, Miss Diba's father was commissioned in our army, which assigned him to legal duties in Tehran. Here he met his future wife, whose parents had moved with her to the capital.

Queen Farah was born in 1938. She was the only child; but living in the same house with her was another only child, the son born to her uncle and his wife; and the two youngsters grew up much as a brother and sister. The little girl had great affection for her father, and much sadness came to her upon his death from cancer when she was only ten years old. Her distraught mother succeeded for a time in concealing the father's death from their daughter by telling her that he had gone to Paris for medial treatment; but the girl's grief knew no bounds when she realized that the family were wearing mourning costumes and the servants told her the truth...

In 1959 Farah returned to Tehran for her summer vacation. It was then that my son-in-law and my daughter met her. They invited her for dinner, and she and Princess Shahnaz soon found that they had many mutual friends and common interests.

Farah was asked to come again, and my daughter arranged that I should be present. Actually I had met Farah a few months earlier at a Paris reception for our Persian students; the reception was crowded and I must admit that I didn't remember her! I cannot object when she makes fun of me for this! But it was at my son-in-law's house that I had my first good discussion with her...

Farah wanted to buy her trousseau in Paris and to avoid elaborate protocol we decided that she would go in a private capacity and that we would defer announcing our engagement until after her return. Some of her relatives accompanied her on her journey.

Two days after Farah arrived back in Tehran, we announced our engagement. About three weeks later, on 21 December, 1959, we were married according to the solemn Muslim ritual. In accordance with Persian wedding tradition, during the ceremony Farah twice remained silent when she was asked if she would become my wife; only when the question was put a third time did she consent. We were joined in wedlock on the afternoon of the 21st, and that same evening my Queen and I presided at a large banquet and reception in the Oriental splendour of the old Golestan Palace. Affairs of state delayed our honeymoon for a few days, but then we had a long-awaited time together on the Caspian."

Above from *Mission for My Country: His Imperial Majesty Mohammad Reza Shah Pahlavi*, Hutchinson and Co. (Publishers) Ltd., London, 1961-1968; pp. 224-27.

5. Please see *The Return of the Ayatollah: The Iranian Revolution from Mossadiq to Khomeini*, Mohammad Heikal; Andre Deutsch Limited, 1981; pp. 93-5. The paragraph in parenthesis from *All Fall Down: America's Tragic Encounter with Iran*; Gary Sick, Random House, New York, 1985; p. 12.
6. Please see *Islam and Revolution: Writings and Declarations of Imam Khomeini*; translated and annotated by Hamid Algar, Mizan Press; Berkeley; 1981; pp. 200-208.
7. Please see *International Herald Tribune* (Paris), 13 and 14 May, 1973.
8. Please see *The Return of the Ayatollah: The Iranian Revolution from Mossadiq to Khomeini*, Mohammad Heikal; Andre Deutsch Limited, 1981; p. 33.
9. Ahmad Shafiq was son of Shafiq Pasha, chief of Egyptian King's office. Shafiq Pasha was sent to exile in Europe after Foad replaced the king. Ashraf's decision to marry Shafiq annoyed King Farooq who saw the marriage detrimental to the special relationship between the two monarchical families. Mohammad Reza ignored Farooq's anger and accepted Ashraf's request to allow her marry Shafiq. The fruits of their marriage was a boy and a girl. The boy whom they decided to call Shahriyar later became a navy officer and was assassinated in Paris after the 1979 Islamic revolution. Ashraf's daughter, Azadeh was crazy-sex like her mother. Above collected by the compiler of Fardust's memoirs, the Institute for Political Studies and Research, published as footnotes in the Persian text of the book.
10. For details please see *Twentieth Century Iran*, Hossein Amirsadeghi and R.W. Ferrier, William Heinemann Ltd., 1977; p. 102.
11. Above from *All Fall Down: America's Tragic Encounter with Iran;* Gary Sick, Random House, New York, 1985; p. 47.
12. For details please see *The Shah and I*, Memoirs of Assadollah Alam.
13. Above from *All Fall Down: America's Tragic Encounter with Iran;* Gary Sick, Random House, New York, 1985; p. 11.
14. Please see *Mission to Iran*, William H. Sullivan; W.W. Norton and Company, 1981; pp. 65-6.
15. Please see *Iran Religion, Politics and Society*, Nikki R. Keddie, Frank Cass and Company Limited, London, 1980; p. 146.
16. Please see *The Pride and the Fall: Iran 1974-1979*, Sir Anthony Parsons, Butler and Tanner Ltd., London, 1984; p. 67.

17. Please see *The Economist*, August 26, 1978.
18. Please see *Iran: Religion, Politics and Society*, Nikki R. Keddie, Frank Cass and Company Limited, London, 1980; pp. 220-1 and pp. 230-1.
19. Above from *The Pride and the Fall: Iran 1974-1979*, Sir Anthony Parsons, Butlers and Tanner Ltd., 1984; pp. 6-7.

Chapter 4

PAHLAVI DYNASTY, WEST'S ESPIONAGE BASTION

1. Please see *The Return of the Ayatollah*, Mohamed Heikal; Andre Deutsch Limited, 1981-1983; p. 16.
2. Please see *The Return of the Ayatollah*, Mohamed Heikal; Andre Deutsch Limited, 1981-1983; pp. 15-6.
3. "One other significant military official whom I very seldom met and with whom I cannot recall ever having had a social conversation was General Fardust, the inspector general of the realm. He, like Qarabaqi, had been one of that select group chosen to be classmates and companions of the Crown Prince, and he was now reputed to be closer to the Shah than any other officer; the monarch used him as his *"eyes and ears"*. By making him inspector general, the Shah fashioned an instrument of loyalty in whom he had complete confidence and who could act discreetly to check information he received from other officials. General Fardust constantly made unpublicized trips throughout the country, investigating not only military matters but also civilian government activities. He was particularly respected and feared among the bureaucracy, because his reports could result in the rapid termination of a career or even in a criminal action that brought corrupt officials into disrepute.

   Please see *Mission to Iran*, William H. Sullivan, W.W. Norton and Company, 1981; pp. 76-7.
4. Please see *Mission for My Country: His Imperial Majesty Mohammad Reza Shah Pahlavi*, Hutchinson and Co. (Publishers) Ltd., London; 1961-1968; pp. 176-7.
5. For details please see *Documents from the U.S. Espionage Den: America—Supporter of Usurpers of the Qods*, The Centre for Publication of the U.S. Espionage Den's Documents, p. 283.
6. For details please see *Documents from the U.S. Espionage Den: America—Supporter of Usurpers of the Qods*, The Centre for Publication of the U.S. Espionage Den's Documents; p. 273.
7. "Israel's principal intelligence and security authority is the *Va'adat Rashet Hasherutim* (the Committee of the Heads of Services), generally known as Va'adat. It coordinates the operations and

activities of its members. *Mossad Letafkidim Meyouchadim* (the Secret Intelligence Service) or Mossad, its common name, has the primary responsibility for foreign operations and is subordinate to the Prime Minister. *Sherut Bitachon Klali* (counterespionage and Internal Security), popularly known as Shin Beth, is responsible for security and is directly subordinate to the Prime Minister. *Agaf Modiin* (Military Intelligence) has the main responsibility for strategic military intelligence and communications intelligence and is under the command of the Chief of Staff of the Israeli Defense Forces. The Ministry of Foreign Affairs provides support in research and political planning to the Israel intelligence community."

For details please see *Documents from the U.S. Espionage Den: America—Supporter of Usurpers of the Qods*, The Centre for Publication of the U.S. Espionage Den's Documents, p. 265, p. 267 and p. 276.

8. "Yaccov Nimrodi (was) one of the richest men in Israel. An Iraqi Jew and a former Israeli military attache to Iran, he had established the first official government-run arms channel between Israel and Iran in the early 1960s. In 1967, after the Middle East war, he came back to Tel Aviv and made presentations to the chief of the General Staff of the Israel Defense Forces (IDF). He wanted to be military governor of the West Bank, which had just been captured, ... when the IDF general staff said they were not ready to appoint him, he told them that if he did not get the job he was going to leave the army and become a millionaire ...

   He surprised all. As soon as his resignation from the military went into effect, he returned to Tehran. Because of the friendship he developed with the Shah, Nimrodi, reached an agreement that any arms coming to Iran from Israel would have to be brokered by him—with a built-in commission."

   Above from *Profits of War: Inside the Secret US-Israeli Arms Network*, Ari Ben-Menashe, Sheridan Square Press, New York 1992; p. 168.

9. Above from *Bahaism, its Origin and its Role*: The Islamic Revolution Culture Publication, The Hague, the Netherlands; pp. 3-6.

Chapter 5

SECRET AGENCIES DURING PAHLAVIS

1. Please see *Mission to Iran*, William H. Sullivan; W.W. Norton and Company, 1981, pp. 94-6 and p. 99.
2. Please see *Profits of War: Inside the Secret US-Israeli Arms Network*, Ari Ben-Menashe, Sheridan Square Press, New York 1992; p. 27.
3. *Kermit Roosevelt*, a crucial CIA figure during the 1953 coup in Iran, in his book *Countercoup* writes that Iran and Israel had excellent

though informal relations. These relations, he says, became closer in later years when certain Israeli friends discreetly joined the CIA in helping to organize and give guidance to a new Iranian security service. The Israeli action was entirely 'under the table', essentially a clandestine operation - but it was of great assistance to the Iranians.

Kermit Roosevelt, *Countercoup: The Struggle for Control of Iran*, McGraw-Hill Book Company, New York, 1979.

Chapter 6

INTERNAL SECURITY DURING PAHLAVIS

1. Please see *The CIA: The Forgotten History*, William Blum, Zed Books Ltd., London 1986; p. 74.
2. Ibrahim Yunesi, translator of the book, *Edmondz, Kurds, Turks and Arabs* says, "Sadat of Egypt was mediating between the Shah and Saddam. In late February 1975, Barezani dispatched a delegation to Egypt to see what were the alleged secret negotiations in Baghdad between the representatives of Iran and Iraq. Sadat received the Kurdish delegation and ensured them that there were no talks being held at all. He betrayed them." *Above collected by the compiler of Fardust's memoirs, the Institute for Political Studies and Research, published as footnotes in the Persian text of the book.*
3. Molla Mustafa Barezani died a slow death from cancer in the United States from 1976 to 1979. Molla Mustafa's son, Masoud, who had joined the KDP in 1963, was elected to succeed his father as KDP leader. Masoud Barezani and his KDP welcomed the victory of the 1979 Islamic Revolution in Iran and in his interviews with domestic and foreign papers attacked the Pahlavi regime and the United States for their treason against the Kurds. *Above collected by the compiler of Fardust's Memoirs, the Institute for Political Studies and Research, published as footnotes in the Persian text of the book.*
4. Compiled from international wire services published in international newspapers.
5. Please see *Iran: Past and Present*, Donald N. Wilber, Princeton University Press, New Jersey, Eighth Edition, 1976; pp. 163-5.
6. On the same day SAVAK issued a statement: "Since, according to reliable information and sufficient evidence, Mr. Khomeini's attitude and provocations have been considered contrary to the interests of the State, and to the security, independence, and territorial integrity of the State, he has been exiled from Iran effective November 4, 1964".

7. Please see *Islam and Revolution: Writings and Declarations of Imam Khomeini*; translated and annotated by Hamid Algar, Mizan Press; Berkeley; 1981; pp. 177-80.
8. Please see *Islam and Revolution: Writings and Declarations of Imam Khomeini*; translated and annotated by Hamid Algar, Mizan Press; Berkeley; 1981; pp. 181-8.

Chapter 7

PAHLAVI REGIME, SUPERPOWERS AND MIDDLE EAST

1. Please see *The United States in World Affairs 1948-1949*; Harper and Brothers, New York, 1949; p. 360.
2. *The Return of the Ayatollah: The Iranian Revolution from Mossaddiq to Khomeini*, Mohamed Heikal; Andre Deutsch Limited, 1981, pp. 14-6.
3. Compiled from international wire services published in International Newspapers.
4. *The New Encyclopedia Britanica*, Volume 13, 15th Edition; p. 28.
5. *The New Encyclopedia Britanica*, Volume 13, 15th Edition; p. 38.
6. Compiled from international wire services published in international Newspapers.
7. *The New Encyclopedia Britanica*, Volume 25, 15th Edition; p. 79.
8. *The New Encyclopedia Britanica*, Volume 25, 15th Edition; p. 390.
9. *The New Encyclopedia Britanica*, Volume 25, 15th Edition; p. 391.
10. Compiled from international wire services published in International Newspapers.
11. Please see *Profits of War: Inside the Secret US-Israeli Arms Network*, Ari Ben-Menashe, Sheridan Square Press, New York 1992; p. 47.
12. Compiled from international wire services published in International Newspapers.
13. *The New Encyclopedia Britanica*, Volume 25, 15th Edition.
14. Please see *The Return of the Ayatollah: The Iranian Revolution from Mossadiq to Khomeini*, Mohamed Heikal, Andre Deutsch Limited, 1981-1983, pp. 202-5.
15. Ari Ben-Menashe, *Profits of War: Inside the Secret US-Israeli Arms Network*, Sheridan Square Press, New York, 1992, pp. 47-8.
16. The first part has been compiled from international wire services published in International Newspapers. For the second part please see *Newsweek*, September 16, 1996, p. 17.

Chapter 8

REVOLUTION AND FALL OF DYNASTY

1. "A comprehensive review of the intelligence problem was also initiated in November 1978 by the Select Committee on Intelligence of the House of Representatives, resulting in a public report in January 1979. This study concluded that intelligence collection and analysis were weak and that the confidence of policy makers in the Shah, which intelligence reporting did not challenge, further skewed the U.S. reading of the situation in Tehran and contributed to the warning failure.

The CIA, it noted, had produced two separate analytical pieces about Iran over the previous year that entirely failed to prepare Washington decision makers for the problem they encountered in late 1978. In August 1977 a 60-page study entitled "Iran in the 1980s" was based on the assumption that "the Shah will be an active participant in Iranian life well into the 1980s" and that "there will be no radical change in Iranian political behaviour in the near future."

The other, a 23-page study entitled "Iran after the Shah" was published in August 1978. Despite its provocative title, this study was limited to an examination of the conventional power structure of the Iranian elite—the royal family, senior political figures and the military—as possible participants in what was to be a smooth transition of power at some future date. The study was prefaced with the judgement, just one month before the Jaleh Square incident, that "Iran is not in a revolutionary or even a 'prerevolutionary' situation."

Above from *All Fall Down: America's Tragic Encounter with Iran*; Gary Sick, Random House, New York, 1985, p. 92.

2. "Over dinner at the palace one night, the wife of one of the Shah's nephews said, "Did you hear about the trouble at the bazaar over food prices?" The Shah pretended not to hear and someone next to her intoned sharply, "No bad news at the dinner table please".

At last SAVAK watered down its reports to please him... "No one dared to tell the truth to the Shah". Having cut himself off from his country, he had no way of knowing the extent of the growing opposition. The Americans might have notified him. But ambassador William Sullivan barred his diplomats from going into the field to talk to the mullahs and peasants. The CIA, which might have put out its own network, instead relied mainly on SAVAK for information; SAVAK reported that everything was under control. Even in June 1978, when there was rioting in Tehran, the Shah still had no inkling of the bloody revolution to come. In July he went off on his annual vacation to the Caspian Sea."

Above from *Newsweek*, August 4, 1980, p. 12.

3. Underestimation of people's support of the clerics and overestimation of Shah's power was evident in the Western press. An article in *The Economist* of August 26, 1978 wrote, "The Shah, impatient with those who oppose him, declares that his "white" revolution to create a land-reformed, prosperous, disciplined and equitable society is opposed by a "black-red" conspiracy of reactionaries and Marxists. No doubt the multifaceted opposition clings to certain common planks. But Iran's "reactionaries" are probably strong enough to dispense with internal left-wing support—although there are rumours that Russia is backing the religious leaders with Swiss bank accounts. Iran's local reds have neither guns nor manpower behind them. The blacks (mullahs) have no guns either—all evidence suggests that Iran's army is loyal to the Shah and will keep the peacock throne safe beneath him - but manpower they do have."
4. "Both sides used bull horns to outshout each other, and the noise level around the White House was so excruciating and incessant that some employees became physically ill.

   During the welcoming ceremony at the White House, the war of words between the opposing camps escalated to physical combat with staves and clubs. Police were forced to use tear gas to quell a battle on the nearby Ellipse, and whiffs of acrid gas wafted over the crowd assembled on the White House lawn."

   Above from *All Fall Down: America's Tragic Encounter with Iran*; Gary Sick, Random House, New York, 1985, p. 28.
5. "During the ride in from the airport, between miles of soldiers standing almost shoulder to shoulder, Carter and the Shah reached a verbal understanding concerning the nuclear non-proliferation agreement that was to accompany the sale of U.S. nuclear power plants to Iran. The two heads of state also discussed President Carter's request for a consolidated list of Iran's anticipated military needs over the next five years. Carter hoped that the development of such a list would enable both countries to address the strategic underpinnings of Iran's security planning while introducing a measure of order and predictability into the arms sales relationship. Both of these initiatives were thwarted and lost in the violence of 1978.... President Carter used the occasion as an opportunity to reassure the Shah once again that the relationship would remain sound... President Carter's opening reference to Iran as "an island of stability" was consciously intended to flatter and reassure the Shah, but the words he used also unconsciously reflected the

prevailing image of Iran as it had come to be accepted by successive administrations in Washington over the previous decade... comments in no sense suggested that the Shah was in serious danger of being overthrown. On the contrary, the briefing materials reflected the unspoken but unanimous view of virtually all observers at the time that the Shah was Iran and Iran was the Shah. President Carter did not invent that view. Neither did he question it. His willingness—and the willingness of those around him—to accept it at face value was to leave him singularly unprepared as the facade of Iranian "stability" crumbled with astonishing speed over the following twelve months... less than a month after these words were spoken, serious riots broke out in the religious city of Qom. Within a year, the Shah was preparing to leave Iran for exile."

Above from *All Fall Down: America's Tragic Encounter with Iran;* Gary Sick, Random House, New York, 1985, pp. 29-31.

6. "By the autumn of 1977 Khomeini's verbal assaults on the army had redoubled. He had already called on the soldiers to desert; now he urged them to take their arms with them. 'Leave in small numbers' were his instructions; 'singly, or in twos and threes. You are the soldiers of God. Take your weapons with you, for they are God's weapons.'

Counter-attack by the Shah's forces took many forms. Mention should be made here of one rather unpleasant incident because it demonstrated SAVAK's use of what I call censorship by commission as well as by omission. In Nove .nber 1977 Farhad Massoudi, the editor of the leading Tehran daily, *Et'tela'*at, had delivered to him an article attacking Khomeini. It was a particularly vicious personal attack, accusing the Ayatollah of corruption ... and so on. Massoudi knew of the authorities' habit of sending to the newspapers ready-made articles for publication, always neatly tailored to the style of each paper and its writers, but he was so shocked when he read this particular article that he got in touch with the Minister of Information and lodged a complaint. "If we print this," he said, "there is bound to be an attack on our office tomorrow." The minister confessed that he had not read the offending article; he had, he said, simply received the sealed envelope direct from the Palace, marked for onward transmission to Et'tela'at. But he promised to get in touch with the Palace. This he did, only to be told that publication was absolutely essential. When Massoudi protested about the inevitable reaction this would provoke, he was told, "Never mind, I'll tell the Minister of Interior to send you some protection." The expected attack duly took place, and all the windows in the front of the office were smashed by the indignant crowd. Later Massoudi learned that the article had been prepared in Information Department of SAVAK."

Please see *The Return of the Ayatollah: The Iranian Revolution from Mossadiq to Khomeini*, Mohammad Heikal, Andre Deutsch Limited, 1981, pp. 144-5.

7. "Khomeini was demanding the overthrow of the Shah, Shariatmadari and the other ayatollahs of Qom and Mashhad were preaching the restoration of the 1906 constitution and the limitation of the Shah's powers; the Tehran mullahs were divided. But no one was prepared to call for clam and moderation for fear of being outflanked by the implacable and uncompromising Khomeini. The troubles got worse. On August 12th martial law was proclaimed in Isfahan and the Shah began to take palliative measures. He announced the total freeing of the press and speech and that new elections would take place in 1979. No one listened. The Shiraz Festival was, sensibly, cancelled. Then, on August 20th, there was a catastrophic fire in a cinema in Abadan in which 400 people died. The government blamed it on terrorists; the opposition accused the government of direct responsibility. The mass of the people believed the opposition. This was the straw which broke the Amouzegar government. On August 27th, Amouzegar, detested by the mullahs as an unsympathetic and anti-Islamic technocrat, resigned. The Shah replaced him with Senator Ja'afar Sharif-Emami, a man of impeccable religious credentials, the President of the Senate, but tainted by having been the head of the controversial Pahlavi Foundation. This amounted to an effort by the Shah to demonstrate a clean break with the technocratic past - whatever else he may have been, Sharif-Emami was no technocrat - and to show the people that he understood their wish to return to a more traditional, Islamic path.

It was a turning point, but not in the way the Shah intended. Sharif-Emami is believed to have made it a condition of his acceptance of the Prime Ministry that he should have a free hand and be seen to be genuinely in charge with the support of parliament; the Shah himself should take a back seat. The Shah's monopoly of power had been breached.

Sharif-Emami started by following the pattern of conciliation of the traditional forces which the Shah had begun a few weeks earlier. The Shah's beloved Pahlavi calendar, another preposterous affront to the religious susceptibilities of his people, was cancelled. (It had been inaugurated in 1976. The traditional Iranian year was solar as opposed to the Islamic lunar year, but in common with the Islamic calendar the dating began from the date of the Prophet Mohammad's flight (Hijra) from Mecca to Medina. However, on the fiftieth anniversary of the Pahlavi dynasty in 1976, the Shah decided that dating should begin from the accession of Cyrus the Great, about

1,000 years earlier. At the time this pointless piece of imperial arrogance excited the fury of the mullahs, the derision of the intelligentsia and the resentment of the masses.) All casinos were closed, also in deference to the religious temper of the main opposition movement; ironically Sharif-Emami, as Prime Minister, was closing the same casinos which, as head of the Pahlavi Foundation, he had only recently been instrumental in opening."

Above from *The Pride and the Fall: Iran 1974-1979*, Sir Anthony Parsons, Butlers and Tanner Ltd., 1984; pp. 68-9.

8. Please see *All Fall Down: America's Tragic Encounter with Iran*, Gary Sick, Random House, New York, 1985, p. 50.
9. Please see *All Fall Down: America's Tragic Encounter with Iran*, Gary Sick, Random House, New York, 1985, p. 57-8.
10. "Sharif-Emami, who had been instrumental in the effort to reach a rapprochement with Iraq, knew that the Iraqis were tiring of the agitation emanating from the Ayatollah. They were concerned not only with the friction that this agitation was producing with Iran, but also with the difficulties it was causing with their own Shi'a Islam population, which constituted nearly 60 per cent of the country's inhabitants. Therefore, Sharif-Emami reasoned, he would prevail upon the Iraqis to expel the Ayatollah from Najaf, where he was able to smuggle his tape-recorded sermons back to Iranian territory. Sharif-Emami's thesis was that the Ayatollah, expelled from Iraq, would have to head westward, probably toward Europe, and that this would put him out of touch with most of the religious dissidents in Iran. He told Ambassador Parsons and me that once the Ayatollah got to Paris he would fade from public view and probably never be heard from again."

    Please see *Mission to Iran*, William H. Sullivan, W.W. Norton and Company, 1981, p 166.
11. "Khomeini knew well the effect the circulation of his *i'ilamiyahs (declarations)* was having in the country. The response to them was obvious, and he could be sure of the allegiance of the people. The problem was not how to sway opinion but how to overcome the forces of repression at the disposal of the Shah. He was not particularly worried by SAVAK—it might have 50,000 agents, but what could 50,000 do against thirty-five million? Long before he left Najaf, Khomeini had come to the conclusion that the real problem was the army.

    The Shah's army numbers 700,000, and somehow it had to be neutralized. Underground groups like the Mujahiddin Khalq and the Fedayin Khalq talked of armed resistance, and so too some members of Khomeini's staff. Ibrahim Yazdi was later to describe to me the atmosphere at Neauphle-le-Chateau in those days. He explained how he and those like him who had been educated in the West used to work in the ways they had been taught, preparing position papers which they would present at the Ayatollah's daily *Majlis* for his approval. Many of these papers dealt with the necessity for armed struggle, and their authors would try to back up their written arguments with spoken appeals. Khomeini would let them have their say, but would then intervene: "No, you cannot confront the army. Arms cannot be fought with arms. The only way to fight the army is to disarm it." He explained that somehow the chains which bound members of the armed forces to the Shah - their oath of loyalty, their habits of obedience - had to be broken."

Please see, *The Return of the Ayatollah: The Iranian Revolution from Mossadiq to Khomeini*, Mohamed Heikal, Andre Deutsch Limited, 1981, p. 143.

12. Above from *All Fall Down: America's Tragic Encounter with Iran*, Gary Sick, Random House, New York, 1985, p. 72.

13. "It was clear to me that Sharif-Emami's days were numbered and that the Shah had little recourse but to install a military government. In anticipation of this I sent a message to Washington late in October, giving my assessment of the situation and suggesting that a military government was imminent. I felt certain that the Shah, before taking this step, would like to have our views on such an action. I wished to anticipate such a request and therefore asked that Washington give me its instructions in advance so that I would know how to answer the question when it was put to me by the Shah.

Much to my surprise I received a rapid and clear answer within forty-eight hours. I was told the United States government felt that the political survival of the Shah was of the greatest importance to us and that the Shah should take whatever measures he felt necessary to preserve his position. If this involved the installation of a military government, then the United States would accept the Shah's judgement in this matter and give him its full support. Clearly this instruction was written on the assumption that a military government would apply the full force of martial law and that the political opposition would be crushed by the use of military force."

Please see *Mission to Iran*, William H. Sullivan, W.W. Norton and Company, 1981, pp. 170-1.

14. "I tried to make an objective assessment of the situation and determine the proper course of action that the United States government should pursue in order to protect our national interests in Iran. Shortly after General Azhari had taken office as Prime Minister, I reached the conclusion that this military government, in effect, represented the Shah's last chance for survival. If it failed to restore law and order and if it did not succeed in resuming the

industrial production in the country, the success of the revolution, I felt, was inevitable and we should face the consequences of that fact."

Please see *Mission to Iran*, William H. Sullivan, W.W. Norton and Company, 1981, p. 201.

15. Ayatollah Khomeini issued this declaration from Neauphle-le-Chateau one week before the beginning of Moharram, the month in which the Iranian people, emulating Imam Hussein (whose martyrdom took place on the tenth day of the month) advanced their confrontation with the Shah's regime to a point of no return. Please see *Islam and Revolution: Writings and Declarations of Imam Khomeini*; translated and annotated by Hamid Algar, Mizan Press, Berkeley, 1981, pp. 242-5.
16. Please see *All Fall Down: America's Tragic Encounter with Iran*, Gary Sick, Random House, New York, 1985, p. 130.
17. "Because Sullivan seemed unable to provide us with adequate reports from the military, which was a crucial source of information and advice, Secretary Brown and I concluded that we needed a strong and competent American representative in Tehran to keep me informed about the military's needs. One of his responsibilities would be to strengthen the resolve of the military leaders and encourage them to remain in Iran in order to maintain stability even if the Shah should decide to leave. I ordered General Robert Huyser, Deputy Commander of U.S. Forces in Europe, to carry out this assignment in Iran."

Please see *Keeping Faith*, Jimmy Carter (Memoirs of a President), Collins, London, 1982, p. 443.

18. Please see *All Fall Down: America's Tragic Encounter with Iran*, Gary Sick, Random House, New York, 1985, pp. 131-2.

"I was surprised on the evening of January 2, to receive a call on secure telephone from the supreme commander of the Allied forces in Europe, General Alexander Haig. Haig told me he had received information from Washington that his deputy Dutch Huyser, was being asked to undertake a mission to Tehran to help stabilize the Iranian armed forces. As Haig understood it, the reports that we had been sending in regarding the unrest in the armed forces and their concern about the departure of the Shah had caused Washington to propose that Huyser come to Tehran to help the military make the transition in loyalty from the Shah, in a situation in which they would be responsible to the government of Prime Minister Designate Shahpour Bakhteyar... Huyser arrived in Tehran, clad in civilian clothes, having flown in the cockpit of a 747 cargo plane transporting supplies to our military mission... Huyser showed me the brief instructions he had received concerning his mission, which he said he had read several times en route. Although they were vaguely worded, they indicated that his task was to meet with the senior officers of the Iranian military command in order to assure them of the continuity of American logistical support and to urge them to maintain the integrity of their forces in the difficult period that would accompany the departure of the Shah and the investiture of the Bakhteyar government. It was further indicated that one of his tasks would be to assist the military in the difficult psychological task of abandoning their oath to the Shah and transferring their loyalties to the civilian authority of the Prime Minister, to whom they would be subordinate."

Please see *Mission to Iran*, William H. Sullivan, W.W. Norton and Company, 1981, pp. 227-9.

19. Please see *All Fall Down: America's Tragic Encounter with Iran*, Gary Sick, Random House, New York, 1985, p. 139.
20. "The Shah did not leave Tehran until 16 January, alter than had been expected and than Bakhteyar had wished. The delay was partly due to the Shah's desire to take with him into exile some, at least, of the Crown Jewels. In particular he wanted the crowns used at his coronation for himself, the Empress and the Crown Prince. All these were now in the safes of the Central Bank (Bank Melli), but the employees of the Bank, like so many others, were on strike. The Shah ordered a detachment of the Royal Guards, known as "the Immortals" (the same title assumed by the bodyguard of the Achaemenian kings), to force the Bank officials to open the safes. On six successive days this detachment went in its armoured cars to the Bank, defying the demonstrators, and six times it had to come back empty-handed. The royal treasure was kept in safes twenty meters underground, and the officials who knew the combinations had disappeared; so in the end all the elaborate safety precautions the Shah had installed defeated his own purposes, and he had to leave without the crowns. The jewels, reported to be insured for between \$250 and \$500 billion, stayed in the Bank."

Above from *The Return of the Ayatollah: The Iranian Revolution from Mossadiq to Khomeini*, Mohamed Heikal, Andre Deutsch Limited, 1981, p. 172.

21. Please see *Profits of War: Inside the Secret US-Israeli Arms Network*, Ari Ben-Menashe, Sheridan Square Press, New York 1992, pp. 44-5.
22. Please see *Mission to Iran*, William H. Sullivan, W.W. Norton and Company, 1981, pp. 240-1.
23. "The 'Revolutionary Council' was already at work in Iran preparing the way for a transitional government that would organize elections for a constituent assembly. Ebrahim Yazdi, Khomeini's representative in the U.S. had given a lengthy description of the

principles and objectives of the future Islamic government. On the economic side, apart from restoring stability to Iran, the primary concern would be the revitalization of agriculture... Iran would sell oil to whoever would purchase it at a fair price, though Israel and the racist South Africa would be excluded.

In foreign affairs, Yazdi outlined a policy of strict non-alignment... They would not seek stability through a military buildup. He stressed the deep popular resentment and hatred towards the United States for its unconditional support of the Shah since 1953, but he felt that future relations were possible if America stopped interferring in Iran's internal affairs. He said Iran had "no better memories" of the Russians than of the Americans. They would seek friendly relations with the Soviet Union, but that process would be complicated by Soviet atheism and anti-religious policies.... there is no doubt that these and other statements by Yazdi accurately reflected the thinking of those around Khomeini. Their position was based on two fundamental assumptions: the Shah's policies had "destroyed" Iran; and the origin of those policies could be traced to external interference, particularly the United States. Consequently, it was implied, if Iran could rid itself of the Shah and of external meddling, the nation could heal itself under a popular government based on Islamic principles."

Please see *All Fall Down: America's Tragic Encounter with Iran*, Gary Sick, Random House, New York, 1985, p. 144.

24. Please see *All Fall Down: America's Tragic Encounter with Iran*, Gary Sick, Random House, New York, 1985, pp. 146-7.
25. Local Newspapers of Iran, February 1979.
26. Please see *All Fall Down: America's Tragic Encounter with Iran*, Gary Sick, Random House, New York, 1985, p. 150.
27. This declaration was issued in Qom, south Tehran, on the occasion of the formal proclamation of the Islamic Republic of Iran. Please see *Islam and Revolution: Writings and Declarations of Imam Khomeini*, translated and annotated by Hamid Algar, Mizan Press, Berkeley, 1981; pp. 265-7.
28. In the early days after the victory of the revolution, Bazargan's liberal-minded transitional government attempted to reorganize SAVAK and the then government officials confirmed that decision in their interviews. Bazargan was planning to appoint *Moqqaddam* and *Fardust* as top intelligence leaders but with the establishment of the Revolutionary Courts, he failed to materialize his intention and two different schools of thought came out; one was found in the revolutionary institutions and the other was the conciliatory policies of the transitional government. *Saddeq Khalkhali*, a cleric, in an interview with the *Kayhan* newspaper said that Bazargan opposed

Moqqaddam's arrest and he had a dispute with him at the late Imam's residence and called for Moqqaddam's release. *Above collected by the compiler of Fardust's Memoirs, the Institute for Political Studies and Research, published as footnotes in the Persian text of the book.*

29. "I received instructions advising me that the United States government had decided to continue diplomatic relations with Iran despite the change in the governments and that I was authorized to send a formal diplomatic note to the new foreign minister advising him of that fact... This I did."

 Please see *Mission to Iran*, William H. Sullivan, W.W. Norton and Company, 1981, p. 257.

30. "In the weeks before the attack on the Embassy, we had received assurances from Yazdi and Prime Minister Bazargan that the Embassy would be protected."

 Please see *All Fall Down: America's Tragic Encounter with Iran*, Gary Sick, Random House, New York, 1985, p. 176.

31. "While I was taking another telephone call at my desk, a murderous barrage of automatic-weapon fire opened up on the Embassy from all sides. Fifty and thirty caliber machine guns had been surreptitiously mounted on the roofs of all the high-rise buildings surrounding the twenty-three acre compound, and on a given signal at 10:30 A.M. they simultaneously opened fire. Window panes shattered, lead flew everywhere, and we had no recourse but to dive for the deck and slither across the floor to the safest spot we could find...

 The attack on the residence continued for over an hour, thus affording us additional time to seek a reaction force from the Iranian authorities. During this period the machine-gun fire continued and we were unable to move significantly within the chancery building, however, we did manage to scuttle out into the main corridor, and eventually I sent most of the people on the second floor into the communications vault... we were allowed to leave the room one by one and were taken down into the courtyard below, where once again we were welcomed by Yazdi... I walked down and out of the building, the bayonet man holding one of my arms and the AK rifleman holding the other. The press was there in great numbers and photographed my exit in such a manner that the man with the bayonet, who was actually my savior, appeared to be one of the guerrillas."

 Please see *Mission to Iran*, William H. Sullivan, W.W. Norton and Company, 1981, p. 258 and pp. 261-2.

32. Please see *All Fall Down: America's Tragic Encounter with Iran*, Gary Sick, Random House, New York, 1985, pp. 176-8, 180-4 and 242-4.

33. SAVAMA (the Persian acronym for the Iranian National Security and Intelligence Organization) was used by the rightist and leftist opposition groups to identify the new intelligence apparatus of the Islamic government and persuade the public that the newly-established organ was exactly the same as SAVAK.

The suspicious policies of the "*transitional government*" which not only tried to deceive the public and keep Iran under the influence of the West but also planned to reorganize SAVAK again justified the use of that term.

Shortly after the transitional government was formed, government spokesman Abbas Amir Entezam in an interview with the Persian daily "Kayhan" said, "SAVAK has sophisticated equipment worth billions of dollars and we are determined to check the activities of foreign nationals and spies... a group has been formed to purge the organization. It has to be stressed that the decisive stance of the *Revolutionary Courts* and the people's resentment of SAVAK did not allow the liberals and policy makers of the "transitional government" to materialize their objectives. If the liberal government remained longer in power, the achievements of the revolution would have been sacrificed by the nationalist officials and the old system including SAVAK would have been reorganized and preserved.

When the intelligence services of the Islamic Republic were turned into a ministry, it was to be known by Westerners as "VEVAK", a coined Persian acronym for the State Ministry for Security and Information". *Above collected by the compiler of Fardust's Memoirs, the Institute for Political Studies and Research, published as footnotes in the Persian text of the book.*

34. This section has been *collected by the compiler of Fardust's Memoirs, the Institute for Political Studies and Research.*